KNOTT'S

HANDBOOK FOR VEGETABLE GROWERS

FOURTH EDITION

KNOTT'S

HANDBOOK FOR VEGETABLE GROWERS

FOURTH EDITION

DONALD N. MAYNARD

University of Florida
Bradenton, Florida

GEORGE J. HOCHMUTH

University of Florida
Gainesville, Florida

JOHN WILEY & SONS, INC.

New York / Chichester / Weinheim / Brisbane / Singapore / Toronto

This text is printed on acid-free paper.

Library of Congress Cataloging in Publication Data:

Maynard, Donald N., 1932–
Knott's handbook for vegetable growers.—4th ed. / Donald N. Maynard, George J. Hochmuth.
p. cm.
ISBN 0-471-13151-2 (alk. paper)
1. Truck farming—Handbooks, manuals, etc. 2. Vegetables—Handbooks, manuals, etc. 3. Vegetable gardening—Handbooks, manuals, etc. I. Hochmuth, George J. (George Joseph) II. Knott, James Edward, 1897–1977 Handbook of vegetable growers. III. title.
SB321.M392 1997
635—dc20 96-33492

Printed in the United States of America

10 9 8 7 6 5 4 3 2 1

CONTENTS

PREFACE

Fourth edition

The pace of change in our personal and business lives continues to accelerate at an ever increasing rate. Accordingly, it is necessary to periodically update information in a long-running reference such as *Handbook for Vegetable Growers.* Our goal in this revision is to provide up-to-date information on vegetable crops for growers, students, extension personnel, crop consultants, and all those concerned with commercial production and marketing of vegetables.

To assist in fulfilling this aim, new technical information has been included on water management with drip irrigation, fertigation scheduling, petiole sap testing, plant tissue testing, worker protection standards, seed priming, seed germination tests, windbreaks, and weed management.

We are grateful to our colleagues who have provided materials, reviewed portions of the manuscript, and who have encouraged us in this revision. We especially acknowledge the assistance of Wallace Chason, Florida Department of Agriculture; G. A. Clark, Kansas State University; T. K. Hartz, University of California; A. A. Kader, University of California; S. J. Kays, University of Georgia; S. J. Locascio, University of Florida; C. A. McClurg, University of Maryland; M. D. Orzolck, Pennsylvania State University; S. A. Sargent, University of Florida; W. M. Stall,

University of Florida; C. D. Stanley, University of Florida; P. J. Stoffella, University of Florida; C. S. Vavrina, University of Florida; and L. A. Weston, University of Kentucky.

The authors are grateful for the splendid assistance of the editors at Wiley, Philip Manor and Millie Torres.

We hope that *Handbook for Vegetable Growers* will continue to be a timely and useful reference for those with interest in vegetable crops as envisaged by Dr. J. E. Knott when the *Handbook* was first published in 1956 and in the 1980 and 1988 revisions, for which the late Dr. O. A. Lorenz provided the inspiration and leadership.

D. N. MAYNARD
G. J. HOCHMUTH

PART 1

VEGETABLES AND THE VEGETABLE INDUSTRY

BOTANICAL NAMES OF VEGETABLES

NAMES OF VEGETABLES IN NINE LANGUAGES

VEGETABLE PRODUCTION STATISTICS

CONSUMPTION OF VEGETABLES

NUTRITIONAL COMPOSITION OF VEGETABLES

SELECTION OF VEGETABLE VARIETIES

BOTANICAL NAMES, COMMON NAMES, AND EDIBLE PLANT PARTS OF VEGETABLES

Botanical Name	Common Name	Edible Plant Part
Division Sphendophyta		
Equisetaceae	HORSETAIL FAMILY	
Equisetum arvense L.		Young strobili
Division Pterophyta	FERN GROUP	
Dennstaedtiaceae		
Pteridium aquilinum (L.) Kuhn.	Bracken fern	Immature frond
Osmundaceae		
Osmunda cinnamomea L.	Cinnamon fern	Immature frond
Osmunda japonica Th.	Japanese flowering fern	Immature frond
Parkeriaceae		
Ceratopteris thalictroides (L.) Brongn.	Water fern	Young leaf
Polypodiaceae		
Diplazium esculentum (Retz.) Swartz.	Vegetable fern	Young leaf
Division Anthophyta		
Class Monocotyledons		
Alismataceae	WATER PLANTAIN FAMILY	
Sagittaria sagittifolia L.	Arrowhead	Corm
Sagittaria trifolia L. (Sieb.) Ohwi	Chinese arrowhead	Corm
Alliaceae	ONION FAMILY	
Allium ampeloprasum L. Ampeloprasum group	Great headed garlic	Bulb and leaf
Allium ampeloprasum L. Kurrat group	Kurrat	Pseudostem and bulb
Allium ampeloprasum L. Porrum group	Leek	Pseudostem and leaf
Allium cepa L. Aggregatum group	Shallot	Pseudostem and leaf
Allium cepa L. Cepa group	Onion	Bulb

Allium cepa L. Proliferum group	Tree onion	Aerial bulb
Allium chinense G. Don.	Rakkyo	Bulb
Allium fistulosum L.	Japanese bunching onion	Pseudostem and leaf
Allium grayi Regel	Japanese garlic	Leaf
Allium sativum L.	Garlic	Bulb and leaf
Allium schoenoprasum L.	Chive	Leaf
Allium scorodoprasum L.	Sand leek	Leaf and bulb
Allium tuberosum Rottler ex Sprengel	Chinese chive	Leaf, immature flower
Allium victorialis L. var. *platyphyllum*, Hult.	Longroot onion	Bulb, leaf
Allium × *wakegi* Araki	Turfed stone leek	Leaf
Araceae	ARUM FAMILY	
Alocasia macrorrhiza (L.) Schott	Giant taro	Corm, immature leaf, petiole
Amorphophallus paeoniifolius (Dennst.) Nicolson	Elephant yam	Corm
Colocasia esculenta (L.) Schott	Taro	Corm, immature leaf
Cyrtosperma chamissonis (Schott) Merr.	Giant swamp taro	Corm
Cyrtosperma merkusii (Hassk.) Schott.	Gallan	Corm
Xanthosoma brasiliense (Desf.) Engler	Tannier spinach	Immature leaf
Xanthosoma sagittifolium (L.) Schott	Tannia	Corm and young leaf
Cannaceae	CANNA FAMILY	
Canna indica L.	Indian canna	Rhizome
Cyperaceae	SEDGE FAMILY	
Cyperus esculentus L.	Rushnut	Tuber
Eleocharis dulcis (Burm.f.) Trin. ex Henschel	Water chestnut	Corm
Eleocharis kuroguwai Ohwi	Wild water chestnut	Corm
Dioscoreaceae	YAM FAMILY	
Dioscorea alata L.	White yam	Tuber
Dioscorea batatas Decue.	Chinese yam	Tuber
Dioscorea bulbifera L.	Potato yam	Tuber

BOTANICAL NAMES, COMMON NAMES, AND EDIBLE PLANT PARTS OF VEGETABLES—Continued

Botanical Name	Common Name	Edible Plant Part
Dioscorea cayenensis Lam.	Yellow yam	Tuber
Dioscorea dumetorum (Kunth) Pax.	Bitter yam	Tuber
Dioscorea esculenta (Lour.) Burk.	Lesser yam	Tuber
Dioscorea rotundata Poir.	White Guinea yam	Tuber
Dioscorea trifida L. f.	Indian yam	Tuber
Iridaceae	IRIS FAMILY	
Tigridia pavonia Ker.-Gawl.	Common tiger lily	Bulb
Liliaceae	LILY FAMILY	
Asparagus acutifolius L.	Wild asparagus	Shoot
Asparagus officinalis L.	Asparagus	Shoot
Hemerocallis spp.	Day lily	Flower
Leopoldia comosa (L.) Parl.	Tuffed hyacinth	Bulb
Lilium spp.	Lily	Bulb
Limnocharitaceae	FLOWERING RUSH FAMILY	
Limnocharis flava (L.) Buchenau	Yellow velvetleaf	Young leaf, petiole and floral shoot
Marantaceae	ARROWROOT FAMILY	
Calathea allouia (Aubl.) Lindl.	Sweet corn root	Tuber
Maranta arundinacea L.	West Indian arrowroot	Rhizome
Musaceae	BANANA FAMILY	
Musa × *paradisiaca* L. var. paradisiaca	Plaintain	Fruit, flower bud
Poaceae	GRASS FAMILY	
Bambusa spp.	Bamboo shoots	Young shoot
Dendrocalamus latiflorus Munro	Bamboo shoots	Young shoot

Pennisetum purpureum Schum.	Elephant grass	Young spear
Phyllostachys spp.	Bamboo shoots	Young shoot
Saccharum edule Hassk.	Sugarcane inflorescence	Immature inflorescence
Setaria palmifolia (Koen.) Stapf.	Palm grass	Young plant
Zea mays L. subsp. mays	Sweet corn	Immature kernels and immature cob with kernel
Zizania latifolia (Griseb.) Turcz. ex Stapf.	Water bamboo	Swollen shoot/stem
Pontederiaceae	PICKERELWEED FAMILY	
Monochoria hastata (L.) Solms.	Hastate-leaved pondweed	Young leaf
Monochoria vaginalis (Brum.) Kunth	Oval-leaved pondweed	Young leaf
Taccaceae	TACCA FAMILY	
Tacca leontopetaloides (L.) Kuntze	East Indian arrowroot	Rhizome
Zingiberaceae	GINGER FAMILY	
Alpinia galanga (L.) Sw.	Greater Galangal	Floral sprout and flower; tender shoot
Curcuma longa L.	Turmeric	Rhizome
Curcuma mangga Valeton & Van Zijp	Temu mangga (Jpn)	Rhizome, young shoot
Curcuma zedoaria Roscoe	Long zedoary	Rhizome
Zingiber mioga (Thunb.) Roscoe	Japanese wild ginger	Rhizome, tender shoot, leaf, flower
Zingiber officinale Roscoe	Ginger	Rhizome and tender shoot
Division Anthophyta		
Class Diocotyledons		
Acanthaceae	ACANTHUS FAMILY	
Justicia insularis T. And.	Tettu	Young shoot, leaf, root
Rungia klossii S. Moore	Rungia	Leaf
Aizoaceae	CARPETWEED FAMILY	
Mesembryanthemum crystallinum L.	Ice plant	Leaf
Tetragonia tetragoniodes (Pall.) O. Kuntze	New Zealand spinach	Tender shoot and leaf

BOTANICAL NAMES, COMMON NAMES, AND EDIBLE PLANT PARTS OF VEGETABLES—Continued

Botanical Name	Common Name	Edible Plant Part
Amaranthaceae	AMARANTH FAMILY	
Alternanthera philoxeroides (Martius) Griseb.	Alligator weed	Young top
Alternanthera sessilis (L.) R. Br.	Sessile alternanthera	Young top
Amaranthus spp.	Amaranthus	Tender shoot, leaf, sprouted seed
Celosia spp.	Cockscomb	Leaf and tender shoot
Aponogetonaceae	APONOGETON FAMILY	
Aponogeton distachyus L. f.	Water onion	Tender shoot, flower spike
Apiaceae	CARROT FAMILY	
Angelica archangelica L.	Angelica	Tender shoot and leaf
Angelica keiskei (Miq.) Koidz.	Japanese angelica	Tender shoot and leaf
Anthriscus cerefolium (L.) Hoffm.	Chervil	Leaf
Apium graveolens L. var. *dulce* (Mill.) Pers.	Celery	Petiole, leaf
Apium graveolens L. var. *rapaceum* (Mill.) Gaud.	Celeriac	Root, leaf
Arracacia xanthorrhiza Bancroft	Arracacha	Root
Centella asiatica (L.) Urban	Asiatic pennywort	Leaf and stolon
Chaerophyllum bulbosum L.	Tuberose chervil	Root
Coriandrum sativum L.	Coriander	Leaf and seed
Cryptotaenia japonica Hassk.	Japanese hornwort	Leaf
Daucus carota L. subsp. *sativus* (Hoffm.) Arcang.	Carrot	Root and leaf
Foeniculum vulgare var. *azoricum* (Miller) Thell.	Fennel	Leaf
Foeniculum vulgare var. *dulce* Fiori	Florence fennel	Leaf base
Glehnia littoralis F. Schm.	Coastal glehnia	Leaf, stem, root

Hydrocotyle sibthorpioides Lam.	Hydrocotyle	Young shoot and leaf
Myrrhis odorata (L.) Scop.	Garden myrrh	Leaf, root and seed
Oenanthe javanica (Blume) DC. subsp. *javanica*	Oriental celery	Leaf and tender shoot
Pastinaca sativa L.	Parsnip	Root and leaf
Petroselinum crispum (Mill.) Nym. var. *crispum*	Parsley	Leaf
Petroselinum crispum (Mill.) Nym. *tuberosum*	Turnip-rooted parsley	Root and leaf
Petroselinum crispum (Mill.) Nym. var. *neapolitanum*	Italian parsley	Leaf
Sium sisarum L.	Skirret	Root
Araliaceae	ARALIA FAMILY	
Aralia cordata Thunb.	Spikenard	Tender shoot
Aralia elata Seeman	Japanese angelica	Young leaf
Asteraceae	SUNFLOWER FAMILY	
Arctium lappa L.	Edible burdock	Root, petiole
Artemisia dracunculus L. var. *sativa* L.	French tarragon	Leaf
Artemisia indica Willd. var. *maximowiczii* (Nakai) Hara	Mugwort	Leaf
Aster scaber Thunb.	Aster	Leaf
Bidens pilosa L.	Bur marigold	Young shoot and leaf
Chrysanthemum spp.	Edible chrysanthemum	Leaf and tender shoot
Cichorium endivia L.	Endive	Leaf
Cichorium intybus L.	Chicory	Leaf
Cirsium dipsacolepis (Maxim.) Matsum.	Gobouazami	Root
Cosmos caudatus Kunth	Cosmos	Leaf and young shoot
Crassocephalum biafrae (Oliv. et Hiern) S. Moore	Sierra Leone bologni	Young shoot
Crassocephalum crepidiodes (Benth.) S. Moore	Hawksbeard velvetplant	Young shoot and leaf
Cynara cardunculus L.	Cardoon	Petiole
Cynara scolymus L.	Globe artichoke	Immature flower bud
Emilia sonchifolia (L.) DC.	Emilia	Young shoot and leaf
Enydra fluctuans Lour.	Buffalo spinach	Young shoot and leaf

BOTANICAL NAMES, COMMON NAMES, AND EDIBLE PLANT PARTS OF VEGETABLES—Continued

Botanical Name	Common Name	Edible Plant Part
Farfugium japonicum (L.) Kitamura	Japanese farfugium	Petiole
Fedia cornucopiae DC.	Horn of plenty	Leaf
Galinsoga parviflora Cav.	Galinsoga	Young shoot
Gynura bicolor DC.	Gynura	Young leaf
Helianthus tuberosus L.	Jerusalem artichoke	Tuber
Kalimeris yomena Kitam.	Chi-erk-ch'ang	Leaf, young plant
Lactuca indica L.	Indian lettuce	Leaf
Lactuca sativa L. var. *asparagina* Bailey	Asparagus lettuce	Stem
Lactuca sativa L. var. *capitata* L.	Head lettuce	Leaf
Lactuca sativa L. var. *longifolia* Lam.	Romaine lettuce	Leaf
Launaea taraxacifolia (Willd.) Amin ex C. Jeffrey	Wild lettuce	Leaf
Petasites japonicus (Sieb. & Zucc.) Maxim.	Butterbur	Petiole
Polymnia sonchifolia Poepp. & Endl.	Yacon strawberry	Root
Scolymus hispanicus L.	Golden thistle	Root and leaf
Scolymus maculatus L.	Spotted garden thistle	Leaf
Scorzonera hispanica L.	Black salsify	Root and leaf
Sonchus oleraceus L.	Milk thistle	Leaf
Spilanthes acmella (L.) Murr.	Brazil cress	Young leaf
Spilanthes ciliata HBK	Guasca	Young leaf
Spilanthes iabadicensus A.H. Moore	Getang	Young leaf and flower shoot
Spilanthes paniculata Wall ex DC.	Getang	Young leaf and flower shoot
Struchium sparganophora (L.) O. Ktze.	Bitter leaf	Young shoot

Taraxacum officinale Wiggers	Dandelion	Leaf, root
Tragopogon porrifolius L.	Salsify	Root and young leaf
Tragopogon pratensis L.	Goatsbeard	Young root and shoot
Vernonia amygdalina Delile.	Bitter leaf	Young shoot
Basellaceae	BASELLA FAMILY	
Basella alba L.	Indian spinach	Leaf and young shoot
Ullucus tuberosus Lozano	Ulluco	Tuber
Boraginaceae	BORAGE FAMILY	
Borago officinalis L.	Borage	Petiole
Symphytum officinale L.	Common comfrey	Leaf and tender shoot
Symphytum × *uplandicum* Nyman	Russian comfrey	Young leaf and shoot
Brassicaceae	MUSTARD FAMILY	
Armoracia rusticana Gaertn., Mey., Scherb.	Horseradish	Root, leaf, sprouted seed
Barbarea verna (Mill.) Aschers	Upland cress	Leaf
Brassica carinata A. Braun	Abyssinian mustard	Leaf
Brassica juncea (L.) Czernj. & Coss. var. *capitata* Hort.	Capitata mustard	Leaf
Brassica juncea (L.) Czernj. & Coss. var. *crassicaulus*	Bamboo shoot mustard	Stem
Brassica juncea (L.) Czernj. & Coss. var. *crispifolia* Bailey	Curled mustard	Leaf
Brassica juncea (L.) Czernj. & Coss. var. *foliosa* Bailey	Small leaf mustard	Leaf
Brassica juncea (L.) Czernj. & Coss. var. *gemmifera* Lee & Lin	Gemmiferous mustard	Stem and axillary bud
Brassica juncea (L.) Czernj. & Coss. var. *involuta* Yang & Chen	Involute mustard	Leaf
Brassica juncea (L.) Czernj. & Coss. var. *latipa* Li	Wide petiole mustard	Leaf

BOTANICAL NAMES, COMMON NAMES, AND EDIBLE PLANT PARTS OF VEGETABLES—Continued

Botanical Name	Common Name	Edible Plant Part
Brassica juncea (L.) Czernj. & Coss. var. *leucanthus* Chen & Yang	White flowered mustard	Leaf
Brassica juncea (L.) Czernj. & Coss. var. *linearifolia*	Line mustard	Leaf
Brassica juncea (L.) Czernj. & Coss. var. *longepetiolata* Yang & Chen	Long petiole mustard	Leaf
Brassica juncea (L.) Czernj. & Coss. var. *megarrhiza* Tsen & Lee	Tuberous-rooted mustard	Root
Brassica juncea (L.) Czernj. & Coss. var. *multiceps* Tsen & Lee	Tillered mustard	Leaf
Brassica juncea (L.) Czernj. & Coss. var. *multisecta* Bailey	Flower-like leaf mustard	Leaf
Brassica juncea (L.) Czernj. & Coss. var. *rugosa* Bailey	Brown mustard	Leaf
Brassica juncea (L.) Czernj. & Coss. var. *strumata* Tsen & Lee	Strumous mustard	Stem
Brassica juncea (L.) Czernj. & Coss. var. *tumida* Tsen & Lee	Swollen stem mustard	Stem and leaf
Brassica juncea (L.) Czernj. & Coss. var. *utilis* Li	Pendunceled mustard	Young flower stalk
Brassica napus L. var. *napobrassica* (L.) Reichb.	Rutabaga	Root and leaf
Brassica napus L. var. *napus*	Vegetable rape	Leaf and young flower stalk
Brassica napus L. var. *pabularia* (DC.) Reichb.	Siberian kale	Leaf
Brassica nigra Koch.	Black mustard	Leaf
Brassica oleracea L. var. *acephala* DC.	Kale, collards	Leaf

Brassica oleracea L. var. *alboglabra* Bailey	Chinese kale	Young flower stalk and leaf
Brassica oleracea L. var. *botrytis* L.	Cauliflower	Immature floral stalk
Brassica oleracea L. var. *capitata* L.	White cabbage	Leaf
Brassica oleracea L. var. *costata* DC.	Portuguese cabbage	Leaf and inflorescence
Brassica oleracea L. var. *gemmifera* Zenk.	Brussels sprouts	Axillary bud
Brassica oleracea L. var. *gongylodes* L.	Kohlrabi	Enlarged stem
Brassica oleracea L. var. *italica* Plenck.	Broccoli	Immature flower stalk
Brassica oleracea L. var. *medullosa* Thell. Marrow	Marrow stem kale	Leaf
Brassica oleracea L. var. *ramosa* Alef.	Thousand-headed kale	Leaf
Brassica oleracea L. var. *sabauda* L.	Savoy cabbage	Leaf
Brassica perviridis Bailey	Spinach	Leaf
Brassica rapa L. var. *chinensis* (Rupr.) Olsson	Pak-choi	Leaf
Brassica rapa L. var. *narinosa* (Bailey) Olsson	Broad beaked mustard	Leaf
Brassica rapa L. var. *parachinensis* (Bailey) Tsen & Lee	Mock pak-choi	Leaf
Brassica rapa L. var. *pekinensis* (Lour.) Olsson	Chinese cabbage	Leaf
Brassica rapa L. var. (DC.) Metzg. *rapa*	Turnip	Enlarged root
Brassica rapa L. var. (DC.) Metzg. *utilis*	Turnip green	Leaf
Brassica rapa L. var. (DC.) Metzg. *septiceps*	Turnip broccoli	Infloresence
Bunias orientalis L.	Hill mustard	Leaf
Capsella bursa-pastoris (L.) Medikus	Shepherd's purse	Young leaf
Cardamine pratensis L.	Cuckoo flower	Leaf
Crambe maritima L.	Sea kale	Petiole and young leaf
Crambe tatarica Jacq.	Tartar bread-plant	Petiole and young leaf, root
Diplotaxis muralis (L.) DC.	Wallrocket	Leaf
Eruca sativa Miller	Rocket salad	Leaf
Lepidium meyenni Walp.	Maca	Root

BOTANICAL NAMES, COMMON NAMES, AND EDIBLE PLANT PARTS OF VEGETABLES—Continued

Botanical Name	Common Name	Edible Plant Part
Lepidium sativum L.	Garden cress	Leaf
Nasturtium officinale R. Br.	Watercress	Leaf
Raphanus sativus L. Caudatus group	Rat tail radish	Immature seed pod
Raphanus sativus L. Radicula group	Radish	Root
Raphanus sativus L. Daikon group	Daikon	Root
Sinapis alba L.	White mustard	Leaf and young flower stalk
Wasabia japonica (Miq.) Matsum.	Wasabi	Rhizome, young shoot
Cabombaceae	WATER LILY FAMILY	
Brasenia schreberi Gmelin	Watershield	Young leaf
Cactaceae	CACTUS FAMILY	
Opuntia ficus-indica (L.) Mill.	Prickly pear	Pad, fruit
Campanulaceae	BELLFLOWER FAMILY	
Campanula rapunculus L.	Rampion	Root and first leaf
Capparaceae	CAPER FAMILY	
Capparis spinosa L.	Capper bush	Flower bud
Cleome gynandra L.	Cat's whiskers	Leaf, young shoot, fruit
Platycodon grandiflorum A. DC.	Chinese bellflower	Leaf
Chenopodiaceae	GOOSEFOOT FAMILY	
Atriplex hortensis L.	Orache	Leaf
Beta vulgaris L. Cicla group	Chard	Leaf
Beta vulgaris L. Crassa group	Gardenbeet	Root and leaf
Chenopodium bonus-henricus L.	Good King Henry	Leaf
Chenopodium quinoa Willd.	Quinoa	Leaf

Kochia scoparia (L.) Schrader	Mock cypress	Tender shoot
Salsola komarovii Iljin.	Komarov Russian thistle	Leaf and young shoot
Salsola soda L.	Salsola	Leaf and young shoot
Spinacia oleracea L.	Spinach	Leaf
Suaeda asparagoides Mak.	Common seepweed	Young stem, leaf, plant
Convolvulaceae	BINDWEED FAMILY	
Convolvulus japonicus Thunb.	Rose glorybind	Root
Ipomoea aquatica Forssk.	Water spinach	Tender shoot and leaf
Ipomoea batatas (L.) Lam.	Sweet potato	Root and leaf
Crassulaceae	ORPINE FAMILY	
Sedum sarmentosum Burge	Sedum	Leaf
Cucurbitaceae	GOURD FAMILY	
Benincasa hispida (Thunb.) Cogn.	Wax gourd	Immature/mature fruit
Citrullus lanatus (Thunb.) Matsum and Nakai	Watermelon	Ripe fruit and seed
Citrullus lanatus var. *citroides* (Bailey) Mansf	Citron	Fruit
Coccinia grandis (L.) Voigt	Ivy gourd	Fruit, tender shoot, leaf
Cucumeropsis mannii Naudin	White-seeded melon	Fruit and seed
Cucumis anguria L.	West Indian gherkin	Immature fruit
Cucumis melo L. Cantaloupensis group	Cantaloupe	Fruit
Cucumis melo L. Chito group	Mango	Fruit
Cucumis melo L. Conomon group	Oriental pickling melon	Young fruit
Cucumis melo L. Flexuosus group	Japanese cucumber	Immature fruit
Cucumis melo L. Inodorus group	Honeydew melon	Fruit
Cucumis melo L. Reticulatus group	Muskmelon, Persian melon	Ripe fruit
Cucumis metuliferus E. Meyer ex Naudin	African horned cucumber	Fruit
Cucumis sativus L.	Cucumber	Immature fruit
Cucurbita argyrosperma Huber	Pumpkin	Young/mature fruit and seed
Cucurbita ficifolia Bouché	Fig-leaf gourd	Fruit

BOTANICAL NAMES, COMMON NAMES, AND EDIBLE PLANT PARTS OF VEGETABLES—Continued

Botanical Name	Common Name	Edible Plant Part
Cucurbita maxima Duch.	Giant pumpkin, winter squash	Mature fruit and seed
Cucurbita moschata Duch. ex Poir.	Butternut squash, tropical pumpkin	Young and mature fruit
Cucurbita pepo L.	Summer squash, zucchini	Young fruit
Cucurbita pepo L.	Common field pumpkin	Mature fruit and seed
Cyclanthera pedata (L.) Schrader var. *pedata*	Pepino	Immature fruit
Lagenaria siceraria (Mol.) Standl.	Bottle gourd	Immature fruit, tender shoot and leaf
Luffa acutangula (L.) Roxb.	Angled loofah	Immature fruit
Luffa aegyptiaca Miller	Smooth loofah	Immature fruit and leaf
Momordica charantia L.	Bitter gourd	Immature fruit and young leaf
Praecitrullus fistulosus (Stocks) Pang.	Squash	Fruit
Sechium edule (Jacq.) Swartz.	Chayote	Fruit, tender shoot, leaf
Sicana odorifera (Vell.) Naudin	Casabanana	Immature/mature fruit
Telfairia occidentalis Hook. f.	Fluted gourd	Seed, leaf, tender shoot
Telfairia pedata (Smith ex Sims) Hook.	Oyster nut	Seed
Trichosanthes cucumerina L. var. *anguinea* (L.) Haines	Snake gourd	Immature fruit, leaf, and tender shoot
Trichosanthes cucumeroides (Ser.) Maxim.	Japanese snake gourd	Immature fruit
Trichosanthes dioica Roxb.	Pointed gourd	Immature fruit, tender shoot
Euphorbiaceae	SPURGE FAMILY	
Cnidoscolus aconitifolius (Miller) Johnston	Chaya	Leaf

Cnidoscolus chayamansa McVaughn	Chaya	Leaf
Codiaeum variegatum (L.) Blume	Croton	Young leaf
Manihot esculenta Crantz	Yuca	Root and leaf
Sauropus androgynus (L.) Merr.	Common sauropus	Leaf
Fabaceae	PEA FAMILY	
Arachis hypogaea L.	Peanut	Immature/mature seed
Bauhinia esculenta Burchell	Marama bean	Immature pod and root
Cajanus cajan (L.) Huth.	Cajan pea	Immature pod/leaf
Canavalia ensiformis (L.) DC.	Jack bean	Immature seed
Canavalia gladiata (Jacq.) DC.	Sword bean	Immature seed
Cicer arietinum L.	Garbanzo, chick pea	Seed
Cyamopsis tetragonoloba (L.) Taub.	Cluster bean	Immature pod and seed
Flemingia vestita Benth. ex Bak.	Flemingia	Tuber
Glycine max (L.) Merr.	Soybean	Immature and sprouted seed
Lablab purpurus (L.) Sweet.	Hyacinth	Immature seed
Lathyrus sativus L.	Chickling pea	Immature pod/seed
Lathyrus tuberosus L.	Groundnut	Tuber
Lens culinaris Medikus	Lentil	Immature pod, sprouted seed
Lupinus spp.	Lupin	Seed
Macrotyloma geocarpum (Harms) Marechal and Baudet	Hausa groundnut	Seed
Macrotyloma uniflorum (Lam.) Verdc.	Horse gram	Seed
Medicago sativa L.	Alfalfa	Leaf, young shoot, sprouted seed
Mucuna pruriens (L.) DC.	Buffalo bean	Seed
Neptunia oleracea Lour.	Water mimosa	Leaf and tender shoot
Pachyrhizus ahipa (Wedd.) Parodi	Yam bean	Root

BOTANICAL NAMES, COMMON NAMES, AND EDIBLE PLANT PARTS OF VEGETABLES—Continued

Botanical Name	Common Name	Edible Plant Part
Pachyrhizus erosus (L.) Urban	Jicama	Root, immature pod and seed
Pachyrhizus tuberosus (Lam.) Sprengel	Potato bean	Root and immature pod
Phaseolus acutifolius A. Gray	Tepary bean	Seed, immature pod
Phaseolus coccineus L.	Scarlet runner bean	Immature pod and seed
Phaseolus lunatus L.	Lima bean	Immature seed
Phaseolus vulgaris L.	French bean	Immature pod and seed
Pisum sativum L. ssp. *sativum*	Pea	Immature seed, tender shoot
Pisum sativum L. ssp. *sativum* f. *macrocarpon*	Snow pea	Immature pod
Psophocarpus tetragonolobus (L.) DC.	Goa bean	Immature pod, seed, leaf, root
Pueraria lobata (Willd.) Ohwi	Kudzu	Root, leaf, tender shoot
Sphenostylis stenocarpa (Hochst. ex. A. Rich.) Harms.	African yam bean	Tuber and seed
Tetragonolobus purpureus Moench	Asparagus pea	Immature pod
Trigonella foenum-graecum L.	Fenugreek	Leaf, tender shoot, immature pod
Vicia faba L.	Fava bean	Immature seed
Vigna aconitifolia (Jacq.) Maréchal	Moth bean	Immature pod and seed
Vigna angularis (Willd.) Ohwi & Ohashi	Adzuki bean	Seed
Vigna mungo (L.) Hepper	Black gram	Immature pod and seed
Vigna radiata (L.) Wilcz.	Mung bean	Immature pod, sprouted seed, seed

Vigna subterranea (L.) Verdn.	Madagascar groundnut	Immature/mature seed
Vigna umbellata (Thunb.) Ohwi & Ohashi	Rice bean	Seed
Vigna unguiculata (L.) Walp. subsp. *cylindrica* (L.) Van Eselt. ex Verdn.	Catjang	Immature pod and seed
Vigna unguiculata (L.) Walp. subsp. *sesquipedalis* (L.)	Asparagus bean	Immature pod and seed
Vigna unguiculata (L.) Walp. subsp. *unguiculata* (L.)	Southern pea	Immature pod and seed
Gnetaceae	GNETUM FAMILY	
Gnetum gnemon L.	Bucko	Leaf, tender shoot and fruit
Haloragaceae	WATER MILFOIL FAMILY	
Myriophyllum aquaticum (Vellozo) Verdc.	Parrot's feather	Shoot tip
Icacinaceae	ICACINA FAMILY	
Icacina senegalensis A. Juss.	False yam	Tuber
Lamiaceae	MINT FAMILY	
Lycopus lucidus Turcz.	Shiny bugleweed	Rhizome
Mentha pulegium L.	Pennyroyal mint	Leaf
Mentha spicata L. em. Harley	Spearmint	Leaf and inflorescence
Ocimum basilicum L.	Common basil	Leaf
Ocimum canum Sims.	Hoary basil	Young basil
Origanum vulgare L.	Marjoram	Flowering plant and inflorescence
Perilla frutescens (L.) Britt. var. *crispa* (Thunb.) Deane	Perilla	Leaf and seed
Plectranthus esculentus N.E. Br.	Kaffir potato	Tuber
Satureja hortensis L.	Savory	Leaf and young shoot
Solenostemon rotundifolius (Poir.) J. K. Morton	Hausa potato	Tuber
Stachys affinis Bunge	Japanese artichoke	Tuber

BOTANICAL NAMES, COMMON NAMES, AND EDIBLE PLANT PARTS OF VEGETABLES—Continued

Botanical Name	Common Name	Edible Plant Part
Malvaceae	MALLOW FAMILY	
Abelmoschus esculentus (L.) Moench	Okra	Immature fruit
Abelmoschus manihot (L.) Medikus	Hibiscus root	Leaf and tender shoot
Hibiscus acetosella Wel. ex Hiern	False roselle	Young leaf and shoot
Hibiscus sabdariffa L.	Jamaican sorrel	Calyx and leaf
Malva rotundifolia L.	Mallow	Leaf and young shoot
Moraceae	MULBERRY FAMILY	
Humulus lupulus L.	Hops	Tender shoot
Nelumbonaceae	LOTUS FAMILY	
Nelumbo nucifera Gaertn.	Lotus root	Rhizome, leaf
Nelumbo nucifera Gaertn.	Lotus seeds	Seed
Nyctaginaceae	FOUR O'CLOCK FAMILY	
Mirabilis expansa (Ruiz & Paron) Standley	Mauka	Tuber
Nymphaeaceae	WATER LILY FAMILY	
Euryale ferox Salisb.	Foxnut	Seed, tender shoot, root
Nymphaea nouchali Burm. f.	Water lily	Rhizome, flower stalk, seed
Onagraceae	EVENING PRIMROSE FAMILY	
Oenothera biennis L.	Evening primrose	Leaf and tender shoot
Orobanchaceae	BROOMRAPE FAMILY	
Orobanche crenata Forsskal.	Broomrape	Shoot
Oxalidaceae	OXALIS FAMILY	
Oxalis tuberosa Molina	Oka	Tuber

Passifloraceae	PASSION FLOWER FAMILY	
Passiflora biflora Lam.	Passion flower	Shoot, young leaf, flower
Pedaliaceae	PEDALIUM FAMILY	
Sesamum radiatum Schum. ex Thonn.	Gogoro	Young shoot
Phytolaccaceae	POKEWEED FAMILY	
Phytolacca acinosa Roxb.	Indian poke	Leaf and young shoot
Phytolacca americana L.	Poke	Leaf and young shoot
Phytolacca esculenta Van Houtte	Pokeweed	Leaf and young shoot
Phytolacca octandra L.	Inkweed	Leaf and young shoot
Plantaginaceae	PLAINTAIN FAMILY	
Plantago coronopus L. var. *sativa* Fiori	Buckshorn plantain	Leaf
Polygonaceae	BUCKWHEAT FAMILY	
Rheum rhabarbarum L.	Rhubarb	Petiole
Rumex acetosa L.	Sorrel	Leaf
Rumex patientia L.	Dock	Leaf
Rumex scutatus L.	French sorrel	Leaf
Portulacaceae	PURSLANE FAMILY	
Montia perfoliata (Donn. ex Willd.) Howell	Winter purslane	Leaf
Portulaca oleracea L.	Purslane	Leaf and young shoot
Talinum paniculatum (Jacq.) Gaertn.	Flameflower	Young shoot
Talinum triangulare (Jacq.) Willd.	Waterleaf	Leaf
Resedaceae	MIGNONETTE FAMILY	
Reseda odorata L.	Mignonette	Leaf and flower
Rosaceae	ROSE FAMILY	
Fragaria × *Ananassa* Duchesne.	Strawberry	Fruit
Saururaceae	LIZARD'S-TAIL FAMILY	
Houttuynia cordata Thunb.	Saururis	Leaf
Solanaceae	NIGHTSHADE FAMILY	
Capsicum annuum L. Grossum group	Bell pepper	Mature fruit

BOTANICAL NAMES, COMMON NAMES, AND EDIBLE PLANT PARTS OF VEGETABLES—Continued

Botanical Name	Common Name	Edible Plant Part
Capsicum annuum L. Longum group	Cayenne pepper	Mature fruit
Capsicum baccatum L. var. *baccatum*	Small pepper	Fruit
Capsicum chinense Jacq.	Scotch bonnet pepper, habanero pepper	Fruit
Capsicum frutescens L.	Tabasco pepper	Fruit
Capsicum pubescens Ruiz & Pavon	Rocoto	Fruit
Cyphomandra betacea (Cav.) Sendtner	Tamarillo	Ripe fruit
Lycium chinense Mill.	Box thorn	Leaf
Lycopersicon esculentum Mill.	Tomato	Ripe fruit
Lycopersicon pimpinellifolium (L.) Mill.	Currant tomato	Ripe fruit
Physalis alkekengi L.	Chinese lantern plant	Ripe fruit
Physalis ixocarpa Brot. ex Hornem.	Tomatillo	Unripe fruit
Physalis peruviana L.	Cape gooseberry	Ripe fruit
Solanum aethiopicum L.	Golden apple	Fruit and leaf
Solanum americanum Mill.	American black nightshade	Tender shoot, leaf, unripe fruit
Solanum gilo Raddi	Gilo	Young shoot
Solanum incanum L.	Garden egg	Unripe fruit
Solanum integrifolium Poir.	Scarlet eggplant	Immature fruit
Solanum macrocarpon L.	African eggplant	Leaf and fruit
Solanum melongena L.	Eggplant	Immature fruit
Solanum muricatum Ait.	Sweet pepino	Ripe fruit
Solanum nigrum L.	Black nightshade	Mature fruit, leaf, tender shoot

Solanum quitoense Lam.	Naranjillo	Ripe fruit
Solanum torvum Swartz	Pea eggplant	Tender shoot, immature fruit
Solanum tuberosum L.	Potato	Tuber
Tiliaceae	BASSWOOD FAMILY	
Corchorus olitorius L.	Jew's marrow	Leaf and tender shoot
Trapaceae	WATER CHESTNUT FAMILY	
Trapa bicornis Osbeck	Water chestnut	Seed
Trapa natans L.	Water chestnut	Seed
Tropaeolaceae	NASTURTIUM FAMILY	
Tropaeolum majus L.	Nasturtium	Leaf, flower
Tropaeolum tuberosum Ruiz & Pavon	Tuberous nasturtium	Tuber
Urticaceae	NETTLE FAMILY	
Pilea glaberrima (Blume) Blume	Pilea	Leaf
Pilea trinervia Wight	Pilea	Leaf
Urtica dioica L.	Stinging nettle	Leaf
Valerianaceae	VALERIAN FAMILY	
Valerianella eriocarpa Desv.	Italian corn-salad	Leaf
Valerianella locusta (L.) Laterrade em. Betcke	European corn-salad	Leaf
Violaceae	VIOLET FAMILY	
Viola tricolor L.	Violet	Flower, leaf
Vitaceae	GRAPE FAMILY	
Cissus javana DC.	Kangaroo vine	Leaf, young shoot

NAMES OF COMMON VEGETABLES IN NINE LANGUAGES

English	Danish	Dutch	French	German	Italian	Portuguese	Spanish	Swedish
Artichoke	artiskok	artisjok	artischaut	Artischocke	carciofo	alcachofra	alcachofa	kronärtskocka
Asparagus	asparges	asperge	asperge	Spargel	asparago	espargo	espárrago	sparris
Broad bean	hestebønne	tuinboon	feve	Puffbohne	fava maggiore	fava	haba	bondböna
Snap bean	bønne	boon	haricot	Bohne	fagiolino	feijão	ejote	böna
Beet	rødbede	kroot	betterave rouge	rote Rube	bietola da orta	beterraba de mesa	betabol	rödbeta
Broccoli	broccoli	broccoli	chou-brocoli	Brokkoli	cavolo broccolo	bróculo	brocoli	broccoli
Brussels sprouts	rosenkal	spruitkool	chou de Bruxelles	Rosenkohl	cavolo di Bruxelles	couve de Bruxelas	col de Bruselas	brysselkål
Cabbage	kål	kool	chou	Kohl	cavolo	couve	col, repollo	kål
Carrot	karot	peen	carotte	Karotte	carota	cenoura	zanahoria	morot
Cauliflower	blomkål	bloemkool	chou-fleur	Blumenkohl	cavolfiore	courve-flor	coliflor	blomkål
Celery	selleri	selderij	céleri	Sellerie	sedano da erbucci	aipo	apio	selleri
Celeriac	knoldselleri	knolselderij	céleri-rave	Knollensel-lerie	sedano rapa	aipo de cabega	apio nabo	rotselleri
Chicory	cikorie	cichorei	chicoree	Zichorien-wurzel	cicoria	chicoria do café	achicoria raíz	cikoria
Chinese cabbage	kinesisk kål	Chinese kool	chou de Chine	Chinakohl	cavolo cinese	couve da China	col de China	salladkål
Sweet corn	sukkermajs	suikermais	mais sucré	Zuchermais	mais dolce	milho doce	elate	sockermajs
Cucumber	agurk	komkommer	concombre	Gurke	cetriolino	pepino	pepino	gurka

Eggplant	aegplante	eierplant	aubergine	Eierfrucht	melanzana	beringela	berenjena	äggplanta
Endive	endivie	andijvie	chicorée frisée	Endivie	indivia	chicoria	escarola	endiviesallat
Horseradish	peberrod	mierikswortel	raifort	Meerrettich	barbfonte	rabano rüstico	rábana rústicana	pepparrot
Kale	grønkål	groene kool	chou vert	Grunkohl	cavolo a foglia riccia	couve galega frizada	sin cabeza	grönkål
Kohlrabi	knudekål	koolrabi	chou-rave	Kohlrabi	cavolo-rapa	couve-rabano	colirábano	kålrabbi
Leek	porre	prei	poireau	Breitlauch	porro	alho porro	puerro	purjolök
Lettuce	salat	sla	laitue	Salat	lattuga	alface	lechuga	sallad
Muskmelon	melon	meloen	melon	Melone	popone	melão	melón	melon
Onion	løg	ui	ognon	Zwiebel	cipolla	cebola	cebolla	lök
Parsley	persille	peterselie	persil	Petersilie	prezzemola comune	salsa frisada	perejil	persilja
Parsnip	pastinak	pastinaak	panais	Pastsinake	pastinaca	pastinaca	pastinaca	pasternacka
Pea	haveaert	erwt	pois	Erbse	pisello	ervilha	guisante	ärt
Pepper	spansk peber	spaanse peper	piment	Spanischer Pfeffer	peperone dolce	pimento	chile	paprika
Potato	kartoffel	aardappel	pomme de terre	Kartoffel	patata	batata	patata	potatis
Pumpkin	centner-graeskar	pompoen	potiron	Zentnerkür-bis	zucca gigante	abóbora	calabaza grande	jättepumpa
Radish	radis	radijs	radis	Radies	ravanello	rabanete	rábano	rädisa
Rhubarb	rabarber	rabarber	rhubarbe	Rhabarber	rabarbaro	ruibarbo	ruibarbo	rabarber
Rutabaga	kalrabi	koolraap	chou-navet	Kohlrübe	navone	rutabaga	colinabo	kålrot
Spinach	spinat	spinazie	épinard	Spinat	spinaci	espinafre	espinaca	spenat

NAMES OF COMMON VEGETABLES IN NINE LANGUAGES—Continued

English	Danish	Dutch	French	German	Italian	Portuguese	Spanish	Swedish
New Zealand spinach	Nyzeelandsk spinat	Nieuw-zeelandshe spinazie	tetragone	Neuzeeländer spinat	spinacio di Nuova Zelanda	espinafre da Nova Zelândia	espinaca Nueva Zelandia	Nyzeeländsk spenat
Strawberry	jordbaer	aardbei	fraise	Erdbeere	fragola	morango	fresa	jordgubbe
Summer squash	mandel-graeskar	pompoen	courge	Kürbis	zucca	abóbora porqueira	calabacita	matpumpa
Swiss chard	bladbede	snijbiet	poirée	Mangold	bietola de costa	acelga	acelga	mangold
Tomato	tomat	tomaat	tomate	Tomate	pomodoro	tomate	tomate	tomat
Turnip	majroe	raap	navet	Weissrübe	rapa bianca	nabo	nabo	rova
Watermelon	vandmelon	watermeloen	melon d'eau	Wasser-melone	melore d'acqua	melancia	sandia	vattenmelon

Adapted from P. J. Stadhouders (chief editor), *Elsevier's Dictionary of Horticultural and Agricultural Plant Production.* Elsevier Science Publishing Co., Inc., New York (1990).

U.S. VEGETABLE PRODUCTION STATISTICS: LEADING FRESH MARKET VEGETABLE STATES, 1995 [1]

	Harvested Acreage		Production		Value	
Rank	State	% of Total	State	% of Total	State	% of Total
1	California	40.2	California	46.1	California	52.1
2	Florida	11.0	Florida	10.2	Florida	12.0
3	Georgia	6.6	Arizona	7.4	Arizona	8.8
4	Texas	6.4	Georgia	5.6	Texas	4.8
5	Arizona	5.3	Texas	5.4	Georgia	4.2

Adapted from Vegetables, 1995 Summary. USDA, NASS Vg 1-2 (1996).

[1] Includes data for artichoke, asparagus,* lima bean, snap bean, broccoli,* brussels sprouts, cabbage, carrot, cauliflower,* celery, cucumber, eggplant, escarole/endive, garlic, honeydew melon, lettuce, muskmelon, onion, bell pepper, spinach, sweet corn, tomato, and watermelon.

*Includes fresh market and processing.

IMPORTANT STATES IN THE PRODUCTION OF U.S. FRESH MARKET VEGETABLES BY CROP VALUE, 1995

Crop	First	Second	Third
Artichoke[1]	California	—	—
Asparagus[1]	California	Washington	Michigan
Bean, lima	Georgia	—	—
Bean, snap	Florida	California	Georgia
Broccoli[1]	California	Arizona	Texas
Brussels sprouts[1]	California	—	—
Cabbage	California	Texas	New York
Carrot	California	Michigan	Colorado
Cauliflower[1]	California	Arizona	Oregon
Celery	California	Michigan	Texas
Cucumber	California	Florida	Georgia
Eggplant	Florida	New Jersey	—
Escarole/Endive	Florida	Ohio	New Jersey
Garlic	California	—	—
Honeydew melon	California	Texas	Arizona
Lettuce, head	California	Arizona	New Jersey
Lettuce, leaf	California	Arizona	Florida
Lettuce, romaine	California	Arizona	Florida
Muskmelon	California	Arizona	Georgia
Onion	California	Texas	Oregon
Pepper, bell	Florida	California	Texas
Spinach	California	New Jersey	Texas
Strawberry	California	Florida	North Carolina
Sweet corn	Florida	California	New York
Tomato	Florida	California	Georgia
Watermelon	California	Florida	Georgia

Adapted from Vegetables, 1995 Summary. USDA, NASS Vg 1-2 (1996).

[1] Includes fresh market and processing.

HARVESTED ACREAGE, PRODUCTION, AND VALUE OF U.S. FRESH MARKET VEGETABLES, 1993–1995 AVERAGE

Crop	Acres	Production (1000 cwt)	Value ($1000)
Artichoke	8,367	830	47,213
Asparagus[1]	77,747	2,151	174,851
Bean, lima	4,733	137	4,298
Bean, snap	87,147	4,222	157,067
Broccoli[1]	107,233	11,958	326,927
Brussels sprouts	4,100	692	18,895
Cabbage	76,747	24,969	264,554
Carrot	85,517	24,382	321,063
Cauliflower[1]	53,500	6,732	204,901
Celery	27,823	17,188	248,696
Cucumber	58,607	9,591	162,106
Eggplant	3,200	722	18,277
Escarole/Endive	3,700	529	14,252
Garlic	28,000	4,622	164,447
Honeydew melon	25,567	4,500	83,077
Lettuce, head	203,307	65,073	1,123,648
Lettuce, leaf	39,090	8,590	260,251
Lettuce, romaine	27,287	7,583	165,546
Muskmelon	104,893	19,478	327,019
Onion	159,043	61,874	698,118
Pepper, bell	64,283	14,362	434,548
Spinach	17,100	2,035	62,154
Strawberry	49,597	15,314	753,742
Sweet corn	218,233	20,781	368,891
Tomato	132,997	35,025	996,175
Watermelon	206,233	39,535	297,198

Adapted from Vegetables, 1995 Summary. USDA, NASS Vg 1-2 (1996).

[1] Includes fresh market and processing.

AVERAGE U.S. YIELDS OF FRESH MARKET VEGETABLES, 1993–1995

Crop	Yield (cwt/acre)
Artichoke	99
Asparagus[1]	27
Bean, lima	29
Bean, snap	48
Broccoli[1]	112
Brussels sprouts[1]	170
Cabbage	325
Carrot	285
Cauliflower[1]	126
Celery	618
Cucumber	163
Eggplant	227
Escarole/Endive	144
Garlic	165
Honeydew melon	174
Lettuce, head	320
Lettuce, leaf	220
Lettuce, romaine	278
Muskmelon	186
Onion	389
Pepper, bell	223
Spinach	119
Strawberry	309
Sweet corn	95
Tomato	263
Watermelon	192

Adapted from Vegetables, 1995 Summary. USDA, NASS Vg 1-2 (1996).

[1] Includes fresh market and processing.

LEADING PROCESSING VEGETABLE STATES, 1995 [1]

	Harvested Acreage		Production		Value	
Rank	State	% of Total	State	% of Total	State	% of Total
1	California	22.5	California	62.0	California	46.3
2	Wisconsin	17.7	Wisconsin	7.2	Washington	9.1
3	Minnesota	13.3	Washington	6.9	Wisconsin	9.1
4	Washington	10.0	Minnesota	4.8	Minnesota	6.3
5	Oregon	7.1	Oregon	4.2	Oregon	6.1

Adapted from Vegetables, 1995 Summary. USDA, NASS Vg 1-2 (1996).

[1] Includes lima bean, snap bean, beet, cabbage, carrot, sweet corn, cucumber for pickles, pea, spinach, and tomato.

HARVESTED ACREAGE, PRODUCTION, AND VALUE OF U.S. PROCESSING VEGETABLES, 1993-1995 AVERAGE

Crop	Acres	Production (tons)	Value ($1000)
Asparagus	77,747 [1]	45,957	49,048
Bean, lima	45,267	60,580	26,395
Bean, snap	210,257	721,997	124,803
Beet	9,140	135,603	7,859
Broccoli	107,233 [1]	70,493	25,877
Cabbage	6,140	164,450	7,068
Carrot	25,347	545,587	41,360
Cauliflower	53,500 [1]	43,153	19,615
Corn, sweet	490,690	3,258,793	234,785
Cucumber	114,027	605,260	132,907
Pea, green	274,003	440,083	114,635
Spinach	19,327	146,790	14,843
Strawberry	49,597 [1]	231,900	129,818
Tomato	330,503	10,831,646	649,610

Adapted from Vegetables, 1995 Summary. USDA, NASS Vg 1-2 (1996).

[1] Includes fresh market and processing.

IMPORTANT STATES IN THE PRODUCTION OF U.S. PROCESSING VEGETABLES BY CROP VALUE, 1995

Crop	First	Second	Third
Asparagus	Washington	Michigan	—
Bean, snap	Wisconsin	Oregon	Illinois
Beet	Wisconsin	New York	—
Broccoli	California	—	—
Cabbage	Wisconsin	New York	—
Carrot	Washington	California	Wisconsin
Corn, sweet	Washington	Wisconsin	Minnesota
Cucumber	Michigan	North Carolina	California
Pea, green	Minnesota	Washington	Wisconsin
Spinach	Texas	—	—
Strawberry	California	Oregon	Washington
Tomato	California	Ohio	Indiana

Adapted from Vegetables, 1995 Summary. USDA, NASS Vg 1-2 (1996).

AVERAGE U.S. YIELDS OF PROCESSING VEGETABLES, 1993–1995

Crop	Yield (tons/acre)
Bean, lima	1.33
Bean, snap	3.43
Beet	14.90
Cabbage	25.84
Carrot	21.60
Corn, sweet	6.62
Cucumber	5.31
Pea, green	1.62
Spinach	7.67
Tomato	32.73

Adapted from Vegetables, 1995 Summary. USDA, NASS Vg 1-2 (1996).

POTATO AND SWEET POTATO PRODUCTION STATISTICS: HARVESTED ACREAGE, YIELD, PRODUCTION, AND VALUE [1]

Crop	Acres	Yield (cwt/acre)	Production (1000 cwt)	Value ($1000)
Potato	1,349,850	332	448,309	2,397,640
Sweet Potato	81,500	150	12,224	182,390

Adapted from Potatoes, USDA National Agricultural Statistics Service Pot 6 (95) (1995) and Vegetables and Specialties. Situation and Outlook Yearbook. USDA Economic Research Service VGS-266 (1995).

[1] 1993–1994 average.

IMPORTANT STATES IN POTATO AND SWEET POTATO PRODUCTION BY CROP VALUE [1]

Rank	Potato	Sweet Potato
1	Idaho	North Carolina
2	Washington	Louisiana
3	California	California
4	Wisconsin	Texas
5	Oregon	Georgia

Adapted from Potatoes, USDA National Agricultural Statistics Service Pot 6 (95) (1995) and Vegetables and Specialties. Situation and Outlook Yearbook. USDA Economic Research Service VGS-266 (1995).

[1] 1993–1994 average.

UTILIZATION OF THE POTATO CROP, 1993–1994 AVERAGE

Item	Amount			
	1000 cwt	% of Total		
A. Sales	408,667	91		
1. Table stock	129,228		29	
2. Processing	251,740		56	
a. Chips and shoestrings	49,268			11
b. Dehydration	41,088			9
c. Frozen french fries	128,809			29
d. Other frozen products	25,776			6
e. Canned potatoes	2,191			<1
f. Other canned products	2,675			<1
g. Starch and flour	1,934			<1
3. Other sales	27,699		6	
a. Livestock feed	3,323			1
b. Seed	24,377			5
B. Nonsales	39,642	9		
1. Seed used on farms where grown	4,776			1
2. Household and feed used on farms where grown	1,167			<1
3. Shrinkage	33,699			8
Total production	448,309			

Adapted from Potatoes, USDA National Agricultural Statistics Service Pot 6 (95) (1995).

CONSUMPTION OF VEGETABLES: TRENDS IN PER CAPITA CONSUMPTION OF FRESH, CANNED, AND FROZEN VEGETABLES [1] (FRESH WEIGHT BASIS)

	Amount (lb)			
Period	Fresh	Canned	Frozen	Total
1947–1949 average	121	72	7	200
1957–1959 average	104	81	15	200
1965	98	85	18	201
1970	99	94	21	214
1975	98	101	20	219
1980	108	89	21	218
1985	103	95	20	218
1990	113	102	21	236
1995	114	111	23	248

Adapted from Vegetables Outlook and Situation Report, USDA TVS-233 (1984); Vegetable and Specialties, USDA TVS-260 (1993); and Vegetables and Specialties, USDA TVS-265 (1995).

[1] Excluding potatoes and melons.

PER CAPITA CONSUMPTION OF COMMERCIALLY PRODUCED VEGETABLES, 1995

Vegetable	Amount (lb)			
	Fresh	Canned	Frozen	Total
Artichoke, all	—	—	—	0.6
Asparagus	0.6	0.3	0.10	1.0
Bean, dry, all	—	—	—	7.8
Bean, snap	1.5	3.9	2.0	7.4
Broccoli	2.7	—	2.3	5.0
Brussels sprouts, all	—	—	—	0.4
Cabbage	9.7	1.3	—	11.0
Carrot	7.4	1.0	2.7	11.1
Cauliflower	1.2	—	0.6	1.8
Celery	6.5	—	—	6.5
Corn, sweet	7.5	10.7	9.8	28.0
Cucumber	5.3	4.7	—	10.0
Eggplant, all	—	—	—	0.4
Escarole/endive	0.2	—	0	0.2
Garlic, all	—	—	—	1.9
Honeydew melon	1.9	—	—	1.9
Lettuce, head	21.2	—	—	21.2
Lettuce, leaf & romaine	4.4	—	—	4.4
Mushroom, all	—	—	—	3.9
Muskmelon	8.8	—	—	8.8
Onion [1]	18.2	—	—	18.2
Pea, green	—	1.6	2.1	3.7
Pea & lentil, dry, all	—	—	—	0.5
Pepper, bell	6.2	—	—	6.2
Pepper, chile	—	6.5	—	6.5
Potato	49.2	33.1 [2]	56.9	139.2
Radish	0.4	—	—	0.4
Spinach	0.7	0.5	0.5	1.7
Strawberry [3]	3.6	—	1.6	5.2
Sweet potato, all	—	—	—	4.4
Tomato	15.1	79.0	—	94.1
Watermelon	14.7	—	—	14.7
Other vegetables	—	1.0	2.5	3.5

Adapted from Vegetables and Specialties, USDA VGS-265 (1995), Vegetables and Specialties, USDA VGS-266 (1995), and Diane Bertelson. The U.S. Strawberry Industry, USDA, ERS Stat. Bul. No. 914 (1995).

[1] Includes fresh and processed onion.

[2] Other processed potato.

[3] 1993 data.

TRENDS IN PER CAPITA CONSUMPTION OF POTATO, SWEET POTATO, DRY BEAN, AND DRY PEA

	Amount (lb)			
Period	Potato[1]	Sweet Potato[2]	Dry Bean	Dry Pea
1947–1949 average	114	13	6.7	0.6
1957–1959 average	107	8	7.7	0.6
1965	108	6	6.6	0.4
1970	118	6	5.9	0.3
1975	122	5	6.5	0.4
1980	116	5	5.4	0.4
1985	122	5	7.1	0.5
1990	128	5	6.4	0.5
1995	139	4	7.4	0.5

Adapted from Vegetable Outlook and Situation Report, USDA TVS-233 (1984); Vegetables and Specialties, USDA TVS-260 (1993); and Vegetables and Specialties, USDA TVS-265 (1995).

[1] Includes fresh and processed potato.

[2] Includes fresh and processed sweet potato.

COMPOSITION OF THE EDIBLE PORTIONS OF FRESH, RAW VEGETABLES

Vegetable	Amount/100 g Edible Portion										
	Water (%)	Energy (kcal)	Protein (g)	Fat (g)	Carbo-hydrate (g)	Fiber (g)	Ca (mg)	P (mg)	Fe (mg)	Na (mg)	K (mg)
Artichoke	84	51	2.7	0.2	11.9	1.1	48	77	1.6	80	339
Asparagus	92	22	3.1	0.2	3.7	0.8	22	52	0.7	2	302
Bean, green	90	31	1.8	0.1	7.1	1.1	37	38	1.0	6	209
Bean, lima	70	113	6.8	0.9	20.2	1.9	34	136	3.1	8	467
Beet greens	92	19	1.8	0.1	4.0	1.3	119	40	3.3	201	547
Beet roots	87	44	1.5	0.1	10.0	0.8	16	48	0.9	72	324
Broccoli	91	28	3.0	0.4	5.2	1.1	48	66	0.9	27	325
Brussels sprouts	86	43	3.4	0.3	9.0	1.5	42	69	1.4	25	389
Cabbage, common	93	24	1.2	0.2	5.4	0.8	47	23	0.6	18	246
Cabbage, red	92	27	1.4	0.3	6.1	1.0	51	42	0.5	11	206
Cabbage, savoy	91	27	2.0	0.1	6.1	0.8	35	42	0.4	28	230
Carrot	88	43	1.0	0.2	10.1	1.0	27	44	0.5	35	323
Cauliflower	92	24	2.0	0.2	4.9	0.9	29	46	0.6	15	355
Celery	95	16	0.7	0.1	3.6	0.7	36	26	0.5	88	284
Chicory, witloof	95	15	1.0	0.1	3.2	—	—	21	0.5	7	182
Chinese cabbage	94	16	1.2	0.2	3.2	0.6	77	29	0.3	9	238
Collards	94	19	1.6	0.2	3.8	0.6	117	16	0.6	28	148
Cucumber	96	13	0.5	0.1	2.9	0.6	14	17	0.3	2	149
Eggplant	92	26	1.1	0.1	6.3	1.0	36	33	0.6	4	219
Endive	94	17	1.3	0.2	3.4	0.9	52	28	0.8	22	314

Garlic	59	149	6.4	0.5	33.1	1.5	181	153	1.7	17	401
Kale	85	50	3.3	0.7	10.0	1.5	135	56	1.7	43	447
Kohlrabi	91	27	1.7	0.1	6.2	1.0	24	46	0.4	20	350
Leek	83	61	1.5	0.3	14.1	1.5	59	35	2.1	20	180
Lettuce, butterhead	96	13	1.3	0.2	2.3	—	—	—	0.3	5	257
Lettuce, crisphead	96	13	1.0	0.2	2.1	0.5	19	20	0.5	9	158
Lettuce, loose leaf	94	18	1.3	0.3	3.5	0.7	68	25	1.4	9	264
Lettuce, romaine	95	16	1.6	0.2	2.4	0.7	36	45	1.1	8	290
Melon, casaba	92	26	0.9	0.1	6.2	0.5	5	7	0.4	12	210
Melon, honeydew	90	35	0.5	0.1	9.2	0.6	6	10	0.1	10	271
Melon, other netted	90	35	0.9	0.3	8.4	0.4	11	17	0.2	9	309
Mushroom	92	25	2.1	0.4	4.7	0.8	5	104	1.2	4	370
Mustard greens	91	26	2.7	0.2	4.9	1.1	103	43	1.5	25	354
Okra	90	38	2.0	0.1	7.6	0.9	81	63	0.8	8	303
Onion, bunching	92	25	1.7	0.1	5.6	0.8	60	33	1.9	4	257
Onion, dry	91	34	1.2	0.3	7.3	0.4	25	29	0.4	2	155
Parsley	88	33	2.2	0.3	6.9	1.2	130	41	6.2	39	536
Parsnip	80	75	1.2	0.3	18.0	2.0	36	71	0.6	10	375
Pea, edible-podded	89	42	2.8	0.2	7.6	2.5	43	53	2.1	4	200
Pea, green	79	81	5.4	0.4	14.5	2.2	25	108	1.5	5	244
Pepper, hot, chili	88	40	2.0	0.2	9.5	1.8	18	46	1.2	7	340
Pepper, sweet	93	25	0.9	0.5	5.3	1.2	6	22	1.3	3	195
Potato	79	79	2.1	0.1	18.0	0.4	7	46	0.8	6	543
Pumpkin	92	26	1.0	0.1	6.5	1.1	21	44	0.8	1	340
Radish	95	17	0.6	0.5	3.6	0.5	21	18	0.3	24	232
Rhubarb	94	21	0.9	0.2	4.6	0.7	86	14	0.2	4	288
Rutabaga	90	36	1.2	0.2	8.1	1.1	47	58	0.5	20	337
Salsify	77	82	3.3	0.2	18.6	1.8	60	75	0.7	20	380
Southern pea	67	127	9.0	0.8	21.8	1.8	26	53	1.1	4	432

COMPOSITION OF THE EDIBLE PORTIONS OF FRESH, RAW VEGETABLES—Continued

Vegetable	Water (%)	Energy (kcal)	Protein (g)	Fat (g)	Carbohydrate (g)	Fiber (g)	Ca (mg)	P (mg)	Fe (mg)	Na (mg)	K (mg)
	Amount/100 g Edible Portion										
Spinach	92	22	2.9	0.4	3.5	0.9	99	49	2.7	79	558
Squash, butternut	86	45	1.0	0.1	11.7	1.4	48	33	0.7	4	352
Squash, Hubbard	88	40	2.0	0.5	8.7	1.4	14	21	0.4	7	320
Squash, scallop	94	18	1.2	0.2	3.8	0.6	19	36	0.4	1	182
Squash, summer	94	20	1.2	0.2	4.4	0.6	20	35	0.5	2	195
Squash, winter	89	37	1.5	0.2	8.8	1.4	31	32	0.6	4	350
Squash, zucchini	96	14	1.2	0.1	2.9	0.5	15	32	0.4	3	248
Strawberry	92	30	0.6	0.4	7.0	0.5	14	19	0.4	1	166
Sweet corn	76	86	3.2	1.2	19.0	0.7	2	89	0.5	15	270
Sweet potato	73	105	1.7	0.3	24.3	0.9	22	28	0.6	13	204
Swiss chard	93	19	1.8	0.2	3.7	0.8	51	46	1.8	213	379
Tomato, green	93	24	1.2	0.2	5.1	0.5	13	28	0.5	13	204
Tomato, ripe	94	19	0.9	0.2	4.3	0.5	7	23	0.5	8	207
Turnip greens	91	27	1.5	0.3	5.7	0.8	190	42	1.1	40	296
Turnip roots	92	27	0.9	0.1	6.2	0.9	30	27	0.3	67	191
Watermelon	93	26	0.5	0.2	6.4	—	7	10	0.5	1	100

Adapted from D. B. Haytowitz and R. H. Matthews, *Composition of Foods, Vegetables and Vegetable Products—Raw, Processed, Prepared*, USDA Agricultural Handbook 8-11 (1984) and S. E. Gebhardt, R. Cutrufelli, and R. H. Matthews, *Composition of Foods, Fruits and Fruit Juices—Raw, Processed, Prepared*, USDA Agricultural Handbook 8-9 (1982).

VITAMIN CONTENT OF FRESH RAW VEGETABLES

Vegetable	Amount/100 g Edible Portion					
	Vitamin A (IU)	Thiamine (mg)	Riboflavin (mg)	Niacin (mg)	Ascorbic Acid (mg)	Vitamin B_6 (mg)
Artichoke	185	0.08	0.06	0.76	10.8	0.11
Asparagus	897	0.11	0.12	1.14	33.0	0.15
Bean, green	668	0.08	0.11	0.75	16.3	0.07
Bean, lima	303	0.22	0.10	1.47	23.4	0.20
Beet greens	6,100	0.10	0.22	0.40	30.0	0.11
Beet roots	20	0.05	0.02	0.40	11.0	0.05
Broccoli	1,542	0.07	0.12	0.64	93.2	0.16
Brussels sprouts	883	0.14	0.09	0.75	85.0	0.22
Cabbage, common	126	0.05	0.03	0.30	47.3	0.10
Cabbage, red	40	0.05	0.03	0.30	57.0	0.21
Cabbage, savoy	1,000	0.07	0.03	0.30	31.0	0.19
Carrot	28,129	0.10	0.06	0.93	9.3	0.15
Cauliflower	16	0.08	0.06	0.63	71.5	0.23
Celery	127	0.03	0.03	0.30	6.3	0.03
Chicory, witloot	0	0.07	0.14	0.50	10.0	0.05
Chinese cabbage	1,200	0.04	0.05	0.40	27.0	0.23
Collards	3,330	0.03	0.06	0.37	23.3	0.07
Cucumber	45	0.03	0.02	0.30	4.7	0.05
Eggplant	70	0.09	0.02	0.60	1.6	0.09

VITAMIN CONTENT OF FRESH RAW VEGETABLES—Continued

Vegetable	Amount/100 g Edible Portion					
	Vitamin A (IU)	Thiamine (mg)	Riboflavin (mg)	Niacin (mg)	Ascorbic Acid (mg)	Vitamin B_6 (mg)
Endive	2,050	0.08	0.08	0.40	6.5	0.02
Garlic	0	0.20	0.11	0.70	31.2	—
Kale	8,900	0.11	0.13	1.00	120.0	0.27
Kohlrabi	36	0.05	0.02	0.40	62.0	0.15
Leek	95	0.06	0.03	0.40	12.0	—
Lettuce, butterhead	970	0.06	0.06	0.30	8.0	—
Lettuce, crisphead	330	0.05	0.03	0.19	3.9	0.04
Lettuce, loose leaf	1,900	0.05	0.08	0.40	18.0	0.06
Lettuce, romaine	2,600	0.10	0.10	0.50	24.0	—
Melon, casaba	30	0.06	0.02	0.40	16.0	—
Melon, honeydew	40	0.08	0.02	0.60	24.8	0.06
Melon, other netted	3,224	0.04	0.02	0.57	42.2	0.12
Mushroom	0	0.10	0.45	4.12	3.5	0.10
Mustard greens	5,300	0.08	0.11	0.80	70.0	—
Okra	660	0.20	0.06	1.00	21.1	0.22
Onion, bunching	5,000	0.07	0.14	0.20	45.0	—
Onion, dry	0	0.06	0.01	0.10	8.4	0.16
Parsley	5,200	0.08	0.11	0.70	90.0	0.16
Parsnip	0	0.09	0.05	0.70	17.0	0.09
Pea, edible-podded	145	0.15	0.08	0.60	60.0	0.16

Pea, green	640	0.27	0.13	2.09	40.0	0.17
Pepper, hot, chili	770	0.09	0.09	0.95	242.5	0.28
Pepper, sweet	530	0.09	0.05	0.55	128.0	0.16
Potato	—	0.09	0.04	1.48	19.7	0.26
Pumpkin	1,600	0.05	0.11	0.60	9.0	—
Radish	8	0.01	0.05	0.30	22.8	0.07
Rhubarb	100	0.02	0.03	0.30	8.0	0.09
Rutabaga	0	0.09	0.04	0.70	25.0	0.10
Salsify	0	0.08	0.22	0.50	8.0	—
Southern pea	817	0.11	0.15	1.45	2.5	0.07
Spinach	6,715	0.08	0.19	0.72	28.1	0.20
Squash, butternut	7,800	0.10	0.02	1.20	21.0	0.15
Squash, Hubbard	5,400	0.07	0.04	0.50	11.0	0.15
Squash, scallop	110	0.07	0.03	0.60	18.0	0.11
Squash, summer	196	0.06	0.04	0.55	14.8	0.11
Squash, winter	4,060	0.10	0.03	0.80	12.3	0.08
Squash, zucchini	340	0.07	0.03	0.40	9.0	0.09
Strawberry	27	0.02	0.07	0.23	56.7	0.06
Sweet corn	281	0.20	0.06	1.70	6.8	0.06
Sweet potato	20,063	0.07	0.15	0.67	22.7	0.26
Swiss chard	3,300	0.04	0.09	0.40	30.0	—
Tomato, green	642	0.06	0.04	0.50	23.4	—
Tomato, ripe	1,133	0.06	0.05	0.60	17.6	0.05
Turnip greens	7,600	0.07	0.10	0.60	60.0	0.38
Turnip roots	0	0.04	0.03	0.40	21.0	0.09
Watermelon	590	0.03	0.03	0.20	7	—

Adapted from D. B. Haytowitz and R. H. Matthews, *Composition of Foods, Vegetables and Vegetable Products—Raw, Processed, Prepared*, USDA Agricultural Handbook 8–11 (1984) and S. E. Gebhardt, R. Cutrufelli, and R. H. Matthews, *Composition of Foods, Fruits and Fruit Juices—Raw, Processed, Prepared*, USDA Agricultural Handbook 8–9 (1982).

Selection of the variety (technically, *cultivar*) to plant is one of the most important decisions the commercial vegetable grower must make each season. Each year seed companies and experiment stations release dozens of new varieties to compete with those already available. Glowing descriptions, tempting photographs, and sometimes exaggerated claims accompany the release of each new variety. Growers should evaluate some new varieties each year on a trial basis to observe performance on their own farms. A limited number of new varieties should be evaluated so that observations on plant performance and characteristics and yields can be noted and recorded. It is relatively easy to establish a trial but very time-consuming to make all the observations necessary to make a decision on adoption of a new variety. Some factors to consider before adopting a variety follow:

Yield: The variety should have the potential to produce crops at least equivalent to those already grown. Harvested yield is usually much less than potential yield because of market restraints.

Disease Resistance: The most economical and effective means of pest management is through the use of varieties with genetic resistance to disease. When all other factors are about equal, it would be prudent to select a variety with the needed disease resistance.

Horticultural Quality: Characteristics of the plant habit as related to climate and production practices and of the marketed plant product must be acceptable.

Adaptability: Successful varieties must perform well under the range of environmental conditions usually encountered on the individual farm.

Market Acceptability: The harvested plant product must have characteristics desired by the packer, shipper, wholesaler, retailer, and consumer. Included among these qualities are pack out, size, shape, color, flavor, and nutritional quality.

During the past few years there has been a decided shift to hybrid varieties in an effort by growers to achieve earliness, higher yields, better quality, and greater uniformity. Seed costs for hybrids are higher than for open-pollinated varieties.

Variety selection is a very dynamic process. Some varieties retain favor for many years, whereas others might be used only a few seasons if some special situation, such as plant disease or marketing change, develops. If a variety was released by the USDA or a university, many seed companies may have it available. Varieties developed by a seed company may be available only from that source, or may be distributed through many sources.

The Cooperative Exension Service in most states publishes annual or periodic lists of recommended varieties. These lists are usually available in county extension offices.

Adapted from D. N. Maynard, Variety Selection, p. 19 in Donald N. Maynard and George J. Hochmuth (eds.), Vegetable Production Guide for Florida. Fla. Coop. Ext. Ser. SP 170 (1995b).

PART 2

PLANT GROWING AND GREENHOUSE VEGETABLE PRODUCTION

TRANSPLANT PRODUCTION

Vegetable crops are established in the field by direct seeding or by use of vegetative propagules (see Part 3) or transplants. Transplants are produced in containers of various sorts in greenhouses, protected beds, and open fields. Either containerized or field-grown transplants can be used successfully. Generally containerized transplants get off to a faster start, but are more expensive.

Transplant production is a very specialized segment of the vegetable business which demands suitable facilities and careful attention to detail. For these reasons, many vegetable growers choose to purchase containerized or field-grown transplants from production specialists rather than grow them themselves.

RELATIVE EASE OF TRANSPLANTING VEGETABLES

Easy	Moderate	Require Special Care [1]
Beet	Celery	Sweet corn
Broccoli	Eggplant	Cucumber
Brussels sprouts	Onion	Muskmelon
Cabbage	Pepper	Summer squash
Cauliflower		Watermelon
Chard		
Lettuce		
Tomato		

[1] Containerized transplants are recommended.

ADVANTAGES AND DISADVANTAGES OF VARIOUS PLANT GROWING CONTAINERS

Container	Advantages	Disadvantages
Clay pot	Long life	Slow to work with, pots dry out, pots are heavy
Fiber block	Easily handled	May have slow root penetration
Fiber tray	Allows maximum use of space	Hard to handle when wet
Single peat pellet	No media preparation, low storage requirement	Requires individual handling in setup, limited sizes
Prespaced peat pellet	No media preparation, can be handled as a unit of 50	Limited to rather small sizes
Single peat pot	Good root penetration, easy to handle in field, available in large sizes	Difficult to separate, master container is required, dries out easily, may act as a wick in the field if not properly covered
Strip peat pots	Good root penetration, easy to handle in field, available in large sizes, saves setup and filling time	May be slow to separate in the field, dries out easily
Plastic flat with unit	Easily handled, reusable, good root penetration	Requires storage during off season, may be limited in sizes
Plastic pack	Easily handled	Roots may grow out of container causing handling problems, limited in sizes, requires some setup labor
Plastic pot	Reusable, good root penetration	Requires handling as single plant
Polyurethane foam flat	Easily handled, requires less media than similar sizes of other containers, comes in many sizes, reusable	Requires regular fertilization, plants grow slowly at first because cultural systems use low levels of nitrogen

ADVANTAGES AND DISADVANTAGES OF VARIOUS PLANT GROWING CONTAINERS—Continued

Container	Advantages	Disadvantages
Soil band	Good root penetration	Requires extensive labor to setup
Soil block	Excellent root penetration	Expensive machinery
Expanded polystyrene	Lightweight, easy to handle, variable cell sizes and shapes, reusable, automation compatible	Need sterilization between uses, moderate investment
Injection-molded trays	Variable cell sizes, reusable, long life, compatible for automation	Large investment, need sterilization between uses
Vacuum-formed tray	Low capital investment, automation incompatible due to damage to tray	Short life span, need sterilization between uses

Adapted in part from D. C. Sanders and G. R. Hughes (eds.), Production of Commercial Vegetable Transplants, North Carolina Agricultural Extension Service AG-337 (1984).

1. *Media.* Field soil alone usually is not a desirable seeding medium, because it may crust or drain poorly under greenhouse conditions. Adding sand or sand and peat may produce a very good seeding mixture. Many growers use artificial mixes (see page 52) because of the difficulty of obtaining field soil that is free from pests and contaminating chemicals.

   A desirable seeding mix should provide good drainage but retain moisture well enough to prevent rapid fluctuations, have good aeration, be low in soluble salts, and be free from insects, diseases, and weed seeds.
2. *Seeding.* Adjust seeding rates to account for the stated germination percentages and variations in soil temperatures. Excessively thick stands result in spindly seedlings and poor stands are wasteful of valuable bench or bed space.

   Seeding depth should be carefully controlled; most seeds should be planted from 1/4 to 1/2 in. deep. Exceptions are celery, which should only be 1/8 in. deep, and the vine crops, sweet corn, and beans, which can be seeded 1 in. or deeper.
3. *Moisture.* Maintain soil moisture in the desirable range by thorough watering after seeding and careful periodic watering as necessary. A combination of "spot watering" of dry areas and overall watering is usually necessary. Do not overwater.
4. *Temperature.* Be certain to maintain the desired temperature. Cooler than optimum temperatures may encourage disease and warmer temperatures result in spindly seedlings.
5. *Disease control.* Use diseasefree or treated seed to prevent early disease problems. Containers should be new or diseasefree. A diseasefree seeding medium is essential. Maintain a strict sanitation program to prevent introduction of diseases. Carefully control watering and relative humidity. Use approved fungicides as drenches or sprays when necessary.
6. *Transplanting.* Start transplanting when seedlings show the first true leaves to that transplanting can be completed before the seedlings become large and overcrowded.

APPROXIMATE SEED REQUIREMENTS FOR PLANT GROWING

Vegetable	Plants/oz of Seed	Seed Required to Produce 10,000 Transplants
Asparagus	550	1¼ lb
Broccoli	5,000	2 oz
Brussels sprouts	5,000	2 oz
Cabbage	5,000	2 oz
Cauliflower	5,000	2 oz
Celery	15,000	1 oz
Sweet corn	100	6¼ lb
Cucumber	500	1¼ lb
Eggplant	2,500	4 oz
Lettuce	10,000	1 oz
Muskmelon	500	1¼ lb
Onion	4,000	3 oz
Pepper	1,500	7 oz
Summer squash	200	3¼ lb
Tomato	4,000	3 oz
Watermelon	200	3¼ lb

To determine seed requirements per acre:

$$\frac{\text{Desired plant population}}{10{,}000} \times \text{seed required for 10,000 plants}$$

Example 1: To grow enough broccoli for a population of 20,000 plants/acre:

$$\frac{20{,}000}{10{,}000} \times 2 = 4 \text{ oz seed}$$

Example 2: To grow enough summer squash for a population of 3600 plants/acre:

$$\frac{3600}{10{,}000} \times 3\tfrac{1}{4} \text{ lb} = 1\tfrac{1}{4} \text{ lb approximately}$$

RECOMMENDATIONS FOR TRANSPLANT PRODUCTION

Crop [1]	Cell Size (inches)	Seed Required for 10,000 Transplants	Seeding Depth (inches)	Optimum Germination Temperature (°F)	Germination (days) [2]	pH Tolerance [3]	Time Required (weeks)
Broccoli	0.8–1.0	2 oz	¼	85	4	6.0–6.8	5–7
Brussels sprouts	0.8–1.0	2 oz	¼	80	5	5.5–6.8	5–7
Cabbage	0.8–1.0	2 oz	¼	85	4	6.0–6.8	5–7
Cauliflower	0.8–1.0	2 oz	¼	80	5	6.0–6.8	5–7
Celery	0.5–0.8	1 oz	⅛–¼	70	7	6.0–6.8	5–7
Collards	0.8–1.0	2 oz	¼	85	5	5.5–6.8	5–7
Cucumber	1.0	1¼ lb	½	90	3	5.5–6.8	2–3
Eggplant	1.0	4 oz	¼	85	5	6.0–6.8	5–7
Lettuce	0.5–0.8	1 oz	⅛	75	2	6.0–6.8	4
Muskmelon	1.0	1¼ lb	½	90	3	6.0–6.8	4–5
Onion	0.5–0.8	3 oz	¼	75	4	6.0–6.8	10–12
Pepper	0.5–0.8	7 oz	¼	85	8	5.5–6.8	5–7
Squash	0.5–0.8	3¼ lb	½	90	3	5.5–6.8	3–4
Tomato	1.0	3 oz	¼	85	5	5.5–6.8	5–7
Watermelon	1.0	3¼ lb	½	90	3	5.0–6.8	3–4

Adapted from C. S. Vavrina. Transplant Production. In D. N. Maynard and G. J. Hochmuth (eds.), Commercial Vegetable Production Guide for Florida, Fla. Coop. Ext. Serv. SP-170 (1996).

[1] Other crops can be grown as transplants by matching seed types and growing according to the above specifications (example: endive = lettuce). Sweet corn can be transplanted, but tap root is susceptible to breakage.

[2] Under optimum germination temperatures.

[3] Plug pH will increase over time with alkaline irrigation water.

SOILLESS MIXES FOR TRANSPLANT PRODUCTION

Most commercial transplant producers use some type of soilless media for growing vegetable transplants. Most media used employs various mixtures of sphagnum peat and vermiculite or perlite and growers might incorporate some fertilizer materials as the final media is blended. For small growers or on-farm use, similar types of media can be purchased premixed and bagged. Most of the currently used media mixes are based on variations of the Cornell mix recipe below:

CORNELL PEAT-LITE MIXES

Component	Amount (cu yd)
Spagnum peat	0.5
Horticultural vermiculite	0.5

Additions for Specific Uses (amount/cu yd)

Addition	Seedling or Bedding Plants	Greenhouse Tomatoes: Liquid Feed	Greenhouse Tomatoes: Slow-Release Feed
Ground limestone (lb)	5	10	10
20% superphosphate (lb)	1–2	2.5	2.5
Calcium or potassium nitrate (lb)	1	1.5	1.5
Trace element mix (oz)	2	2	2
Osmocote (lb)	0	0	10
Mag Amp (lb)	0	0	5
Wetting agent (oz)	3	3	3

Adapted from J. W. Boodley and R. Sheldrake, Jr., Cornell Peat-lite Mixes for Commercial Plant Growing. New York Agr. Expt. Sta. Agr. Info. Bul. 43 (1982).

STERILIZATION OF PLANT GROWING SOILS

Agent	Method	Recommendation
Heat	Steam	30 min at 180°F
	Aerated steam	30 min at 160°F
	Electric	30 min at 180°F
Chemical	Chloropicrin	3–5 cc/cu ft of soil. Cover for 1–3 days. Aerate for 14 days or until no odor is detected before using.
	Vapam	1 qt/100 sq ft. Allow 7–14 days before use.
	Methyl bromide	1 lb/cu yd of soil or 2 lb/100 sq ft. Cover with gasproof cover for 24–48 hr. Aerate for 24–48 hr before use.

General suggestions: Methyl bromide is effective for soils in flats and containers; chloropicrin or methyl bromide for bulk soils; chloropicrin, methyl bromide, or Vapam for other situations.

Caution: Chemical fumigants are highly toxic. Follow manufacturer's recommendations on the label.

Soluble salts, manganese, and ammonium usually increase after heat sterilization. Delay using heat-sterilized soil for at least 2 weeks to avoid problems with these toxic materials.

Adapted from K. F. Baker (ed.), The UC System for Producing Healthy Container Grown Plants, California Agr. Expt. Sta. Manual 23 (1972).

TEMPERATURES REQUIRED TO DESTROY PESTS IN COMPOST SOIL

Pests	30-min Temperature (°F)
Nematodes	120
Damping-off organisms	130
Most pathogenic bacteria and fungi	150
Soil insects and most viruses	160
Most weed seeds	175
Resistant weeds and resistant viruses	212

Adapted from K. F. Baker (ed.), The UC System for Producing Healthy Container Grown Plants, California Agr. Expt. Sta. Manual 23 (1972).

FERTILIZER FORMULATIONS FOR TRANSPLANT FERTILIZATION BASED ON NITROGEN AND POTASSIUM CONCENTRATIONS

	N and K_2O Concentrations (ppm)			
Fertilizer	50	100	200	400
	oz/100 gal.[1]			
20-20-20	3.3	6.7	13.3	26.7
15-0-15	4.5	8.9	17.8	35.6
20-10-20	3.3	6.7	13.3	26.7
Ammonium nitrate	1.4	2.9	5.7	11.4
+ potassium nitrate	1.5	3.0	6.1	12.1
Calcium nitrate	3.0	6.0	12.0	24.0
+ potassium nitrate	1.5	3.0	6.0	12.0
Ammonium nitrate	1.2	2.5	4.9	9.9
+ potassium nitrate	1.5	3.0	6.0	12.0
+ monoammonium phosphate	0.5	1.1	2.2	4.3

Adapted from P. V. Nelson. Fertilization. pp. 151–176. In: E. J. Holcomb (ed.). *Bedding Plants IV. A Manual on the culture of Bedding Plants as a Greenhouse Crop*, Ball Publishing, Batavia, IL (1994). Used with permission.

[1] 1.0 oz. in 100 gals. is equal to 7.5 g. in 100 liters.

ELECTRICAL CONDUCTIVITY (EC) IN SOIL AND PEAT-LITE MIXES

Mineral Soils	Peat-lite Mixes		Interpretations
(mS)[1]			
2.0+	3.5+	Excessive	Plants may be severely injured.
1.76 to 2.0	2.25 to 3.5	Very high	Plants may grow adequately, but range is near danger zone, especially if soil dries.
1.26 to 1.75	1.76 to 2.25	High	Satisfactory for established plants. May be too high for seedlings and cuttings.
0.51 to 1.25	1.0 to 1.76	Medium	Satisfactory for general plant growth. Excellent range for constant fertilization program.
0.0 to 0.50	0.0 to 1.0	Low	Low EC does no harm, but may indicate low nutrient concentration.

Adapted from R. W. Langhans and E. T. Paparozzi. pp. 139–150. In: E. J. Holcomb (ed.). *Bedding Plants IV. A Manual on the Culture of Bedding Plants as a Greenhouse Crop*, Ball Publishing, Batavia, IL (1994). Used with permission.

[1] EC of soil determined from one part dry soil to two parts water. EC of mix determined from level tsp dry mix to 40 ml water.

MAXIMUM ACCEPTABLE WATER QUALITY INDICES FOR BEDDING PLANTS

Variable	Plug Production	Finish Flats and Pots
pH [1] (acceptable range)	5.5 to 7.5	5.5 to 7.5
Alkalinity [2]	1.5 me/l (75 ppm)	2.0 me/l (100 ppm)
Hardness [3]	3.0 me/l (150 ppm)	3.0 me/l (150 ppm)
EC	1.0 mS	1.2 mS
Ammonium-N	20 ppm	40 ppm
Boron	0.5 ppm	0.5 ppm

Adapted from P. V. Nelson. Fertilization. pp. 151–176. In: E. J. Holcomb (ed.). *Bedding Plants IV. A Manual on the Culture of Bedding Plants as a Greenhouse Crop*, Ball Publishing, Batavia, IL (1994). Used with permission.

[1] pH not very important alone; alkalinity level more important.

[2] Moderately higher alkalinity levels are acceptable when lower amounts of limestone are incorporated into the substrate during its formulation. Very high alkalinity levels require acid injection into water source.

[3] High hardness values are not a problem if calcium and magnesium concentrations are adequate and soluble salt level is tolerable.

There are two systems for application of water (and fertilizer solutions) to transplants produced in commercial operations: overhead sprinklers and sub-irrigation. Sprinkler systems apply water or nutrient solution by overhead water sprays from various types of sprinkler or emitter applicators. Advantages of sprinklers include the ability to apply chemicals to foliage and the ability to leach excessive salts from media. Disadvantages include high investment cost and maintenance requirements. Chemical and water application can be variable in poorly maintained systems and nutrients can be leached if excess amounts of water are applied. One type of sub-irrigation uses a trough of nutrient solution in which the transplant trays are periodically floated, sometimes called ebb and flow. Water and soluble nutrients are absorbed by the media and move upward into the media. Advantages of this system include uniform application of water and nutrient solution to all flats in a trough or basin. Sub-irrigation with recirculation of the nutrient solution minimizes the potential for pollution because all nutrients are kept in an enclosed system. Challenges with sub-irrigation include the need for care to avoid contamination of the entire trough with a disease organism. In addition, sub-irrigation systems restrict the potential to vary nutrient needs of different crops or developmental stages of transplants within a specific sub-irrigation trough.

With either production system, transplant growers need to exercise care in application of water and nutrients to the crop. Excessive irrigation can leach nutrients. Irrigation and fertilization programs are linked. Changes in one program can affect the efficiency of the other program. Excessive fertilization can lead to soluble salt injury and excessive nitrogen application can lead to overly vegetative transplants.

DIAGNOSIS AND CORRECTION OF TRANSPLANT DISORDERS

Symptoms	Possible Causes [1]	Corrective Measures
1. Spindly growth	Shade, cloudy weather, excessive watering, excessive temperature	Provide full sun, reduce temperature, restrict watering, ventilate or reduce night temperature, fertilize less frequently, provide adequate space
2. Stunted plants	Low fertility	Apply fertilizer frequently in low concentration
A. Purple leaves	Phosphorus deficiency	Apply a soluble, phosphorus-rich fertilizer at 50 ppm P every irrigation for up to one week
B. Yellow leaves	Nitrogen deficiency	Apply N fertilizer solution at 50 to 75 ppm each irrigation for one week. Wash the foliage with water after application
C. Wilted shoots	*Pythium* root rot, flooding damage, soluble salt damage to roots	Check for *Pythium* or other disease organism. Reduce irrigation amounts and reduce fertilization
D. Discolored roots	High soluble salts from overfertilization. High soluble salts from poor soil sterilization	Leach the soil by excess watering. Do not sterilize at temperatures above 160°F. Leach soils before planting when soil tests indicate high amounts of soluble salts
E. Normal roots	Low temperature	Maintain suitable day and night temperature
3. Tough, woody plants	Overhardening	Apply starter solution (10–55–10 or 15–30–15 at 1 oz/gal to each 6–12 sq ft of bench area) 3–4 days before transplanting

DIAGNOSIS AND CORRECTION OF TRANSPLANT DISORDERS—Continued

Symptoms	Possible Causes [1]	Corrective Measures
4. Water-soaked and decayed stems near the soils urface	Damping-off	Use a sterile, well-drained medium. Adjust watering and ventilation practices to provide a less moist environment. Use approved fungicidal drenches
5. Poor root growth	Poor soil aeration. Poor soil drainage. Low soil fertility. Excess soluble salts. Low temperature. Residue from chemical sterilization. Herbicide residue	Determine the cause and take corrective measures
6. Green algae or mosses growing on soil surface	High soil moisture, especially in shade or during cloudy periods	Adjust watering and ventilation practices to provide a less moist environment. Use a better drained medium

[1] Possible causes are listed here; however, more than one factor may lead to the same symptom. Therefore, plant producers should thoroughly evaluate all possible causes of a specific disorder.

SUGGESTIONS FOR MINIMIZING DISEASES IN VEGETABLE TRANSPLANTS

Successful vegetable transplant production depends on attention to disease control. With the lack of labeled chemical pesticides, growers must focus on cultural and greenhouse management strategies to minimize opportunities for disease organisms to attack the transplant crop.

Greenhouse environment: Transplant production houses should be located at least several miles from any vegetable production field to avoid the entry of disease-causing agents in the house. Weeds around the greenhouse should be removed and the area outside the greenhouse free of weeds or volunteer vegetable plants or discarded transplants.

Media and water: All media and irrigation water should be pathogen-free. If media is to be blended on-site, all mixing equipment and surfaces must be routinely sanitized. Irrigation water should be drawn from pathogen-free sources. Water from ponds or recycling reservoirs should be avoided.

Planting material: Only pathogen-free seed or plant plugs should be brought into the greenhouse to initiate a new transplant crop. Transplant producers should not accept seeds of unknown quality for use in transplant production. This can be a problem especially when producing small batches of transplants from small packages of seed, e.g., for a variety trial.

Cultural practices: Attention must be given to transplant production practices such as fertilization, irrigation, temperature, etc. so that plant vigor is optimum. Free moisture, from sprinkler irrigation or condensation, on plants should be avoided. Ventilation of houses by exhaust fans and horizontal air-flow fans will help reduce free moisture on plants. Growers should follow a strict sanitation program that will prevent introduction of disease organisms into the house. Weeds under benches must be removed. Outside visitors to the greenhouse should be strictly minimized and all visitors and workers should walk through a disinfecting foot bath. All plant material and soil mix remaining between transplant crops should be removed from the house.

One aspect of transplant quality involves transplants of size and height that are optimum for efficient handling in the field during transplantation and for rapid establishment. Traditional means for controlling plant height included withholding water and nutrients and/or application of growth regulator chemicals. Today growth regulator chemicals are not being labeled for vegetable transplant production. Plant height control research is focusing on nutrient management, temperature manipulation, light quality, and mechanical conditioning of plants.

Nutrient management: Nitrogen applied in excess often causes transplants to grow tall rapidly. Using low-N solutions with 30 to 50 parts per million (ppm) nitrogen will help control plant height when frequent (daily) irrigations are needed. Higher concentrations of N might be needed when irrigations are infrequent (every 3 to 4 days). Often, an intermediate N concentration (e.g., 80 ppm) is chosen for the entire transplant life cycle and often an excessive growth rate results. Irrigation frequency should guide the N concentration.

Moisture stress: Withholding water is a time-tested method of reducing plant height, but transplants can be damaged by drought. Sometimes transplants growing in styrofoam trays along the edge of a greenhouse walkway will dry out faster than the rest of the transplants in the greenhouse. These "dry" plants are always shorter compared to the other transplants. Overwatering transplants should therefore be avoided and careful attention should be given to irrigation timing.

Light intensity: Transplants grown under reduced light intensity will stretch, therefore growers must give attention to maximizing light intensity in the greenhouse. Aged polyethylene greenhouse covers should be replaced and greenhouse roofs and sides should be cleaned periodically, especially in winter. Supplementing light intensity for some transplant crops with lights might be justified.

Temperature reduction: Transplants grown under cooler temperatures (e.g., 50°F) will be shorter than plants grown under warmer temperatures. Where possible, greenhouse temperatures can be reduced or plants can be moved outdoors. Under cool temperatures, the transplant production cycle will be longer by several days and increased crop turnaround time might be unacceptable. For some crops, such as tomato, growing transplants under cool temperatures might lead to fruit quality problems, e.g., catfacing of fruits.

Mechanical conditioning: Shaking or brushing transplants frequently results in shorter transplants. Transplants can be brushed by several physical methods, for example, by brushing a plastic rod over the tops of the plants. This technique obviously should be practiced on dry plants only to avoid spreading disease organisms.

Day/night temperature management: The difference between the day and night temperatures (DIF) can be employed to help control plant height. With a negative DIF, the day temperature is cooler than night temperature. Plants grown with a positive DIF are taller than plants grown with a zero or negative DIF. This system is not used during germination, but rather is initiated when the first true leaves appear. The DIF system rquires the capability to control the greenhouse temperature and would be most applicable to temperature regions in winter and spring seasons when day temperatures are cool and greenhouses can be heated.

VEGETABLE TRANSPLANT RESPONSE TO THE DIFFERENCE IN DAY AND NIGHT TEMPERATURE (DIF)

Common Name	Scientific Name	Response to DIF[1]
Broccoli	*Brassica oleracea,* Italica Group	3
Brussels sprouts	*Brassica oleracea,* Gemmifera Group	3
Cabbage	*Brassica oleracea,* Capitata Group	3
Cauliflower	*Brassica oleracea,* Botrytis Group	3
Cucumber	*Cucumis sativus*	1–2
Eggplant	*Solanum melongena*	3
Muskmelon	*Cucumis melo*	3
Pepper	*Capsicum annuum*	0–1
Squash	*Cucurbita spp.*	2
Tomato	*Lycopersicon esculentum*	2
Watermelon	*Citrullus lanatus*	3

From E. J. Holcomb (ed.). *Bedding Plants IV.* Ball Publishing, Batavia, IL. (1994), original source: J. E. Erwin and R. D. Heins. Temperature Effects on Bedding Plant Growth, Bulletin 42:1–18, Minnesota Commercial Flower Growers Association (1993). Used with permission.

[1] Response is 0 = no response; 3 = strong response.

Objective: To prepare plants to withstand stress conditions in the field. These may be low temperatures, high temperatures, drying winds, low soil moisture, or injury to the roots in transplanting. Growth rates decrease during hardening, and the energy otherwise used in growth is stored in the plant to aid in resumption of growth after transplanting.

Methods: Any treatment that restricts growth will increase hardiness. Cool-season crops generally develop hardiness in proportion to the severity of the treatment and length of exposure, and will when well-hardened withstand subfreezing temperatures. Warm-season crops, even when hardened, will not withstand temperatures much below freezing.

1. *Water supply.* Gradually reduce water by watering lightly at less frequent intervals. Do not allow the plants to dry out suddenly with severe wilting.
2. *Temperature.* Expose plants to lower temperatures (5–10°F) than those used for optimum growth. High day temperatures may reverse the effects of cool nights, making temperature management difficult. Do not expose biennials to prolonged cool temperatures, for this induces bolting.
3. *Fertility.* Do not fertilize, particularly with nitrogen, immediately before or during the initial stages of hardening. Apply a starter solution or liquid fertilizer 1 or 2 days before field setting and/or with the transplanting water. (See page 65).
4. *Combinations.* Restricting water and lowering temperatures and fertility, used in combination, are perhaps more effective than any single approach.

Duration: Seven to ten days is usually sufficient to effect the hardening process. Do not impose conditions so severe that plants will be overhardened in case of delayed planting because of poor weather.

Overhardened plants require too much time to resume growth, and early yields may be lower.

PRETRANSPLANT HANDLING OF CONTAINERIZED TRANSPLANTS

Field performance of transplants is related not only to production techniques in the greenhouse, but also to handling techniques before field planting. In the containerized tray production system, plants can be delivered to the field in the trays if the transplant house is near the production fields. For long-distance transport, the plants are usually pulled from the trays and packed in boxes. Tomato plants left in trays until field planting tend to have more rapid growth rates and larger fruit yields than when transplants were pulled from the trays and packed in boxes. Storage of pulled and packed tomato plants also reduced yields of large fruits compared to plants kept in the trays. If pulled plants must be stored prior to planting, storage temperatures should be selected to avoid chilling or overheating of transplants. Transplants that must be stored for short periods can be kept successfully at 50 to 55°F.

STARTER SOLUTIONS FOR FIELD TRANSPLANTING[1]

Materials	Quantity to Use in Transplanter Tank
Readily Soluble Commercial Mixtures	
8–24–8, 11–48–0 23–21–17, 13–26–13 6–25–15, 10–52–17	(Follow manufacturer's directions) Usually 3 lb/50 gal of water
Straight Nitrogen Chemicals	
Ammonium sulfate, calcium nitrate, or sodium nitrate	2½ lb/50 gal of water
Ammonium nitrate	1½ lb/50 gal of water
Commercial Solutions	
30% nitrogen solution	1½ pt/50 gal of water
8–24–0 solution (N and P_2O_5)	2 qt/50 gal of water
Regular Commercial Fertilizer Grades	
4–8–12, 5–10–5, 5–10–10, etc.:	
1 lb/gal for stock solution; stir well and let settle	5 gal of stock solution with 45 gal of water

[1] Apply at a rate of about ½ pt/plant.

Although most vegetables can be grown successfully in greenhouses, only a very few are grown commercially. Tomato, cucumber, and lettuce are the three most commonly grown vegetables in commercial greenhouses. Some general cultural management principles are discussed here.

Sanitation

There is no substitute for good sanitation for preventing insect and disease outbreaks in greenhouse crops.

To keep greenhouses clean, remove and destroy all dead plants, unnecessary mulch material, flats, weeds, and so on. Burn or bury all plant refuse. Do not contaminate streams or water supplies with plant refuse. Weeds growing in and near the greenhouse after the cropping period should be destroyed. Do not attempt to overwinter garden or house plants in the greenhouses. Pests will also be maintained and will be ready for an early invasion of vegetable crops. To prevent disease organisms from carrying over on the structure of the greenhouse and on the heating pipes and walks, spray with formaldehyde (3 gal of 37% formalin in 100 gal of water). Immediately after spraying, close up the greenhouse for 4–5 days, then ventilate. CAUTION: Wear a respirator when spraying with formaldehyde.

A 15- to 20-ft strip of carefully maintained lawn or bare ground around the greenhouse will help decrease trouble from two-spotted mites or other pests. To reduce entry of whiteflies, leafhoppers, and apids from weeds and other plants near the greenhouses, spray the area growth occasionally with a labeled insecticide.

Monitoring Pests

Insects such as greenhouse or silverleaf whiteflies, thrips, and leaf miners are attracted to shades of yellow and will fly toward that color. Thus insect traps can be made by painting pieces of board with the correct shade of yellow pigment and then covering the paint with a sticky substance. Similar traps are available commercially from several sources. By placing a number of traps within the greenhouse range, it is possible to check infestations daily and be aware of early infestations. Control programs can then be commenced while populations are low.

Two-spotted mites cannot be trapped in this way, but infestations usually begin in localized areas first. Check leaves daily and begin control measures as soon as the first infested areas are noted.

Spacing

Good-quality container-grown transplants should be set in arrangements to allow about 4 sq ft/plant for tomato, 5 sq ft/plant for American-type cucumber, and 7–9 sq ft/plant for European-type cucumber. Lettuce requires 36–81 sq in./plant.

Temperature

Greenhouse tomato varieties may vary in their temperature requirements, but most varieties perform well at a day temperature of 70–75°F and a night temperature of 62–64°F. Temperatures for cucumber seedlings should be 72–76°F day and 68°F night. In a few weeks, night temperature can be gradually lowered to 62–64°F. Night temperatures for lettuce can be somewhat lower than those used for tomato and cucumber.

In northern areas, provisions should be made to heat water to be used in greenhouses to about 70°F.

Pruning and Tying

Greenhouse tomatoes and cucumbers are usually pruned to a single stem by frequent removal of axillary shoots or suckers. Other pruning systems are possible and are sometimes used. Various tying methods are used; a common method is to train the pruned plant around a string suspended from an overhead wire.

Pollination

Greenhouse tomatoes must be pollinated by hand or with bumblebees to assure a good set of fruit. This involves tapping or vibrating each flower cluster to transfer the pollen grains from the anther to the stigma. This should be done daily as long as there are open blossoms on the flower cluster. The pollen is transferred most readily during sunny periods and with the most difficulty during dark, cloudy days. The electric or battery-operated hand vibrator is the most widely accepted tool for vibrating tomato flower clusters. Most red-fruited varieties pollinate more easily than pink-fruited varieties and can often be pollinated satisfactorily by "tapping" the overhead support wires, or by shaking flowers by using the air stream from a motor-driven backpack duster. Modern growers now use bumblebees for pollinating tomato. Specially reared hives of bumblebees are purchased by the grower for pollination.

Pollination of European seedless cucumbers causes off-shape fruit, so bees must be prevented from entering the greenhouse. To help overcome this, gynoecious cultivars have been developed that bear almost 100% female flowers. Only completely gynoecious cultivars are now recommended for commercial production.

American-type cucumbers require bees for pollination. One colony of honeybees per house should be provided. It is advisable to shade colonies from the afternoon sun, and to avoid excessively high temperatures and humidities. Honeybees fly well in glass and polyethylene plastic houses, but fail to work under certain other types of plastic. Under these conditions, crop failures may occur through lack of pollination.

Adapted from Ontario Ministry of Agriculture Publication 356 (1985–1986) and from G. Hochmuth (ed.). Florida Greenhouse Vegetable Production Handbook, Volume 3. Greenhouse Vegetable Crop Production Guide.Fla. Coop.Ext. Circ. SP 48 (1991).

CARBON DIOXIDE ENRICHMENT OF GREENHOUSE ATMOSPHERES

The beneficial effects of adding carbon dioxide (CO_2) to the northern greenhouse environment are well established. The crops that respond most consistently to supplement CO_2 are cucumber, lettuce, and tomato, although almost all other greenhouse crops will also benefit. CO_2 enrichment of southern greenhouses probably has little benefit due to frequent ventilation requirements under the warm temperatures.

Outside air contains about 340 parts per million (ppm) of CO_2 by volume. Most plants grow well at this level, but if levels are higher, the plants will respond by producing more sugars. During the day, in a closed greenhouse, the plants use the CO_2 in the air and reduce the level below the normal 340 ppm. This is the point at which CO_2 addition is most important. Most crops respond to CO_2 additions up to about 1300 ppm. Somewhat lower concentrations are adequate for seedlings or when growing conditions are less than ideal.

Carbon dioxide can be obtained by burning natural gas, propane, or kerosene, and also directly from containers of pure CO_2. Each source has potential advantages and disadvantages. When natural gas, propane, or kerosene is burned, not only is CO_2 produced, but also heat, which can supplement the normal heating system. Incomplete combustion or contaminated fuels may cause plant damage. Most sources of natural gas and propane have sufficiently low levels of impurities, but you should notify your supplier of your intention to use the fuel for CO_2 addition. Sulfur levels in the fuel should not exceed 0.02% by weight.

A number of commercial companies have burners available for natural gas, propane, and liquid fuels. The most important feature of a burner should be that it burns the fuel completely.

Because photosynthesis occurs only during daylight hours, CO_2 addition is not required at night, but supplementation is recommended during dull days. Supplementation should start approximately one hour before sunrise and the system should be shut off one hour before sunset. If supplemental lighting is used at night, intermittent addition of CO_2 or the use of a CO_2 controller may be helpful.

When ventilators are opened, it is not possible to maintain high CO_2 levels. However, it is often during these hours (high light intensity and temperature) that CO_2 supplementation is beneficial. Because it is impossible to maintain optimal levels, it is suggested to maintain at least ambient. A CO_2 controller, whereby the CO_2 concentration can be maintained at any level above ambient is therefore very useful.

One very important factor is an adequate distribution system. The distribution of CO_2 mainly depends on the air movement in the greenhouse(s), for CO_2 does not travel very far by diffusion. That means that if a single source of CO_2 is used for a large surface area or several connecting greenhouses, a distribution system must be installed. Air circulation (horizontal fans or fanjet system) that moves a large volume of air will provide uniform distribution within the greenhouse.

Adapted from Ontario Ministry of Agriculture and Food AGDEX 290/27 (1984) and from G. Hochmuth (ed.). Florida Greenhouse Vegetable Production Handbook, Volume 3. Greenhouse Vegetable Crop Production Guide. Fla. Coop. Ext. Circ. SP 48 (1991).

SOILLESS CULTURE OF GREENHOUSE VEGETABLES

Well-managed field soils supply crops with sufficient water and appropriate concentrations of the 13 essential inorganic elements. A combination of desirable soil chemical, physical, and biotic characteristics provide conditions for extensive rooting, which results in anchorage, the third general quality provided to crops by soil.

When field soils are used in the greenhouse for repeated intensive crop culture, desirable soil characteristics deteriorate rapidly. Diminishing concentrations of essential elements and impaired physical properties are restored as in the field by applications of lime, fertilizer, and organic matter. Deterioration of the biotic quality of the soil by increased pathogenic microorganism and nematode populations has been restricted mostly by steam sterilization.

Even with the best management, soils may deteriorate in quality over time. In addition, the costs—particularly of steam sterilization—of maintaining greenhouse soils in good condition have escalated so that soilless culture methods are competitive, or perhaps more economically favorable than soil culture. Accordingly, there has been a considerable shift from soil culture to soilless culture in greenhouses in recent years. Liquid and media systems are used.

Liquid Soilless Culture

The nutrient-film technique (NFT) is the most commonly used liquid system.

NFT growing systems consist of a series of narrow channels through which nutrient solution is recirculated from a supply tank. A plumbing system of plastic tubing and a submersible pump in the tank are the basic components. The channels are generally constructed of opaque plastic film or plastic pipe; asphalt-coated wood and fiberglass also have been used. The basic characteristic of all NFT systems is the shallow depth of solution that is maintained in the channels. Flow is usually continuous, but sometimes systems are operated intermittently by supplying solution a few minutes every hour. The purpose of intermittent flow is to assure adequate aeration of the root systems. This also reduces the energy required; but under rapid growth conditions, plants could experience water stress if the flow period is too short or infrequent. Therefore, intermittent flow management seems better adapted to mild temperature periods or to plantings during the early stages of development. Capillary matting is sometimes used in the bottom of NFT channels, principally to avoid the side-to-side meandering of the solution stream around young root systems, but it also acts as a reservoir by retaining nutrients and water during periods when flow ceases.

NFT channels are frequently designed for a single row of plants with a channel width of 6–8 inches. Wider channels of 12–15 inches have been used to accommodate two rows of plants, but meandering of the shallow solution stream becomes a greater problem with greater width. To minimize this problem, small dams can be created at intervals down the channel by placing thin wooden sticks crossways in the stream, or the channel may be lined with capillary matting. The channels should be sloped 4–6 inches per 100 feet to maintain gravity flow of the solution. Flow rate into the channels should be in the range of 1–2 qt/min.

Channel length should be limitd to a maximum of 100 feet in order to minimize increased solution temperature on bright days. The ideal solution temperature for tomato is 68–77°F. Temperatures below 59° or above 86°F decrease plant growth and tomato yield. Channels of black plastic film increase solution temperature on sunny days. During cloudy weather, it may be necessary to heat the solution to the recommended temperature. Solution temperatures in black plastic channels can be decreased by shading or painting the surfaces white or silver. As an alternative to channels lined with black polyethylene, 4- to 6-in. PVC pipe may be used. Plant holes are spaced appropriately along the pipe. The PVC system is permanent once it is constructed compared to the polyethylene-lined channels, which must be replaced for each crop. Initial costs are higher for the PVC and sanitation between crops may be more difficult. In addition, PVC pipe systems are subject to root flooding if root masses clog pipes.

Solid Soilless Culture

Lightweight media in containers or bags and rockwool mats are the most commonly used media culture systems.

Media Culture

Soilless culture in bags, pots, or troughs with a lightweight medium is the simplest, most economical, and easiest to manage of all soilless systems. The most common media used in containerized systems of soilless culture are perlite, peat-lite, or a mixture of bark and wood chips. Container types range from long wooden troughs in which one or two rows of plants are grown, to polyethylene bags or rigid plastic pots containing one to three plants. Bag or pot systems using bark chips or peat-lite are in common use throughout the United States and offer some major advantages over other types of soilless culture: (1) these materials have excellent retention qualities for nutrients and water; (2) containers of medium are readily moved in or out of the greenhouse whenever necessary or desirable; (3) they are lightweight and easily handled; (4) the medium is useful for several successive crops; (5) the containers are significantly less expensive and less time-consuming to install; and (6) in comparison with recirculated hydroponic systems, the nutrient-solution system is less complicated and less expensive to manage. From a plant nutrition standpoint, the latter advantage is of significant importance. In a recirculated system the solution is continuously changing in its concentration because of differential plant uptake. In the bag or pot system, the solution is not recirculated. Nutrient solution is supplied from a fertilizer proportioner or large supply tank to the surface of the medium in a sufficient quantity to wet the medium. Any excess is drained away from the system through drain holes in the base of the containers. Thus, the concentration of nutrients in solution supplied to the plants is the same at each application. This eliminates the need to sample and analyze the solution periodically to determine the kind of necessary adjustments and avoids the possibility of solution excess or deficiencies.

In the bag or pot system, the volume of medium per container varies from about 1/2 cu ft in vertical polyethylene bags or pots to 2 cu ft in lay-flat bags. In the vertical bag system, 4-mil black polyethylene bags with prepunched drain holes at the bottom are common. One, but sometimes two, tomato or cucumber plants are grown in each bag. Lay-flat bags accommodate two or three plants. In either case, the bags are aligned in rows with spacing appropriate to the type of crop being grown. It is good practice to place vertical bags or pots on a narrow sheet of plastic film to prevent root contact or penetration into the underlying soil. Plants in lay-flat bags, which have drainage slits (or overflow ports) cut along the sides an inch or so above the base, would also benefit from a protective plastic sheet beneath them.

Nutrient solution is delivered to the containers by supply lines of black polyethylene tubing, spaghetti tubing, spray sticks, or ring drippers in the containers. The choice of application system is important in order to provide proper wetting of the medium at each irrigation. Texture and porosity of the growing medium and the surface area to be wetted are important considerations in making the choice. Spaghetti tubing provides a point-source wetting pattern, which might be appropriate for fine-textured media that allow water to be conducted laterally with ease. In lay-flat bags, single spaghetti tubes at individual plant holes will provide good wetting of peat-lite. In a vertical bag containing a porous medium, a spray stick with a 90-degree spray pattern will do a good job of irrigation if it is located to wet the majority of the surface. Ring drippers are also a good choice for vertical bags although somewhat more expensive. When choosing an application system for bag or container culture, remember that the objective of irrigation is to distribute nutrient solution uniformly so that all of the medium is wet.

Rockwool and Perlite Culture

Rockwool is made by melting various types of rocks at very high temperatures. The resulting fibrous particles are formed into growing blocks or mats that are sterile and free of organic matter. The growing mats have a very high water-holding capacity, no buffering capacity, and an initial pH of 7–8.5, which is lowered quickly with application of slightly acidic nutrient solutions. Uncovered mats, which are covered with polyethylene during setup, or polyethylene enclosed mats can be purchased. The mats are 8–12 in. wide, 36 in. long, and 3 in. thick. Perlite, a volcanic mineral, is heated and expanded into small, granular particles. Perlite has a high water-holding capacity, but provides good aeration.

The greenhouse floor should be carefully leveled, and covered with 3-mil black/white polyethylene which will restrict weed growth and act as a light reflector with the white side up. The mats are placed end-to-end to form a row; single or double rows are spaced for the crop and greenhouse configuration.

A complete nutrient solution made with good-quality water is used for initial soaking of the mats. Large volumes are necessary because of the high water-holding capacity of the mats. Drip-irrigation tubing or spaghetti tubing arranged along the plant row are used for initial soaking and later for fertigation. After soaking, uncovered mats are covered with polyethylene and drainage holes are made in the bagged mats.

Cross-slits, corresponding in size to the propagating blocks, are made in the polyethylene mat cover at desired in-row plant spacings; usually two plants are grown in each 30-in. long mat. The propagating blocks containing the transplant are placed on the mat, and the excess polyethylene from the cross-slit is arranged around the block. Frequent irrigation is required until plant roots are established in the mat; thereafter fertigation is applied 4–10 times a day depending upon the growing conditions and stage of crop growth. The mats are leached with good-quality water when samples taken from the mats with a syringe have increased conductivity readings.

Adapted in part from H. Johnson, Jr., G. J. Hochmuth, and D. N. Maynard, Soilless Culture of Greenhouse Vegetables, Florida Cooperative Extension Bulletin 218 (1985) and from G. Hochmuth (ed.), Florida Greenhouse Vegetable Production Handbook, Volume 3. Greenhouse Vegetable Crop Production Guide, Fla. Coop. Ext. Circ. SP 48 (1991).

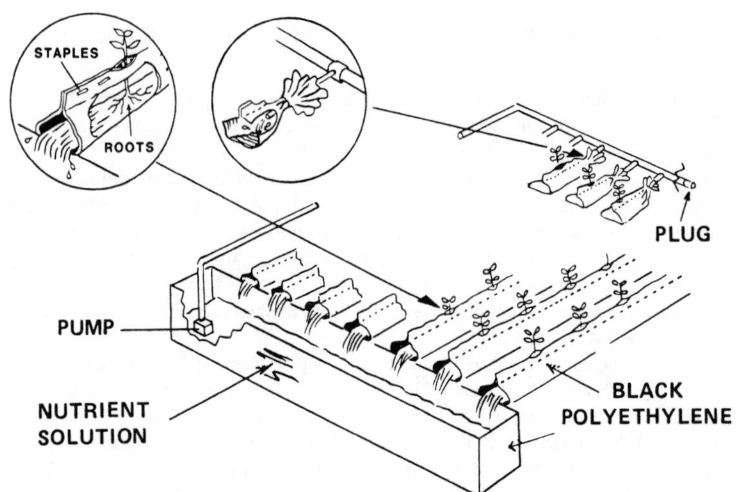

NFT culture system using polyethylene film to hold plants and supply nutrient solution through a recirculation system (From Florida Cooperative Extension Bulletin 218).

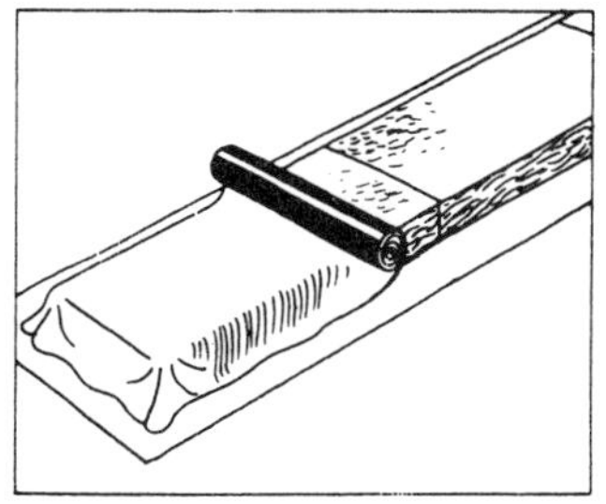

Arranged mats are covered with white/black polyethylene.

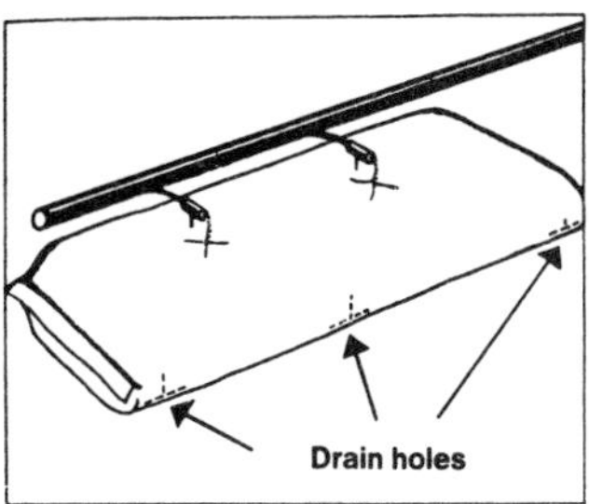

Irrigation system and drainage holes for rockwool mats enclosed in a polyethylene bag.

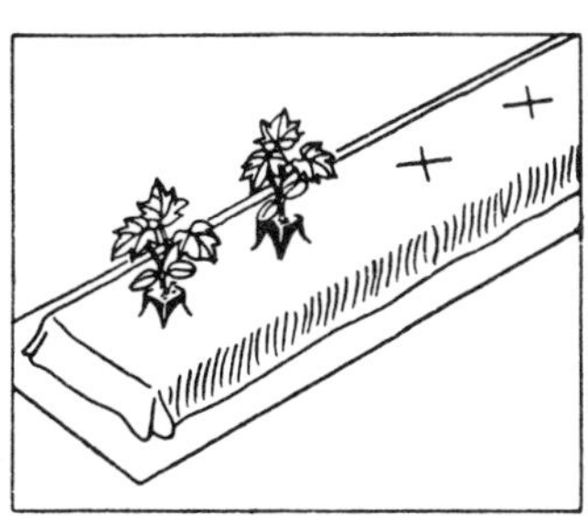

Cross-slits are made to accommodate transplants in propagation blocks.

Ordinarily, two plants are placed in each 30-in.-long mat.

Fertigation supplied by spaghetti tubing to each plant.

Fertigation supplied by drip irrigation tubing.

Removal of sample from rockwool mat with a syringe for conductivity determination.

Adapted from GRODAN® Instructions for cultivation—cucumbers, Grodania A/S, Denmark and used with permission.

NUTRIENT SOLUTIONS FOR SOILLESS CULTURE

Because the water and/or media used for soilless culture of greenhouse vegetables is devoid of essential elements, they must be supplied in a nutrient solution.

Commercially available fertilizer mixtures may be used, or nutrient solutions can be prepared from individual chemical salts. The most widely used and generally successful nutrient solution is one developed by D. R. Hoagland and D. I. Arnon at the University of California. Many commercial mixtures are based on their formula.

Detailed directions for preparation of Hoagland's nutrient solutions, which are suitable for experimental or commercial use, and the formulas for several nutrient solutions that are suitable for commercial use follow.

Salt	Stock Solution (g to make 1 liter)	Final Solution (ml to make 1 liter)
	Solution 1	
$Ca(NO_3)_2 \cdot 4H_2O$	236.2	5
KNO_3	101.1	5
KH_2PO_4	136.1	1
$MgSO_4 \cdot 7H_2O$	246.5	2
	Solution 2	
$Ca(NO_3)_2 \cdot 4H_2O$	236.2	4
KNO_3	101.1	6
$NH_4H_2PO_4$	115.0	1
$MgSO_4 \cdot 7H_2O$	246.5	2

Micronutrient Solution

Compound	Amount (g) Dissolved in 1 Liter of Water
H_3BO_3	2.86
$MnCl_2 \cdot 4H_2O$	1.81
$ZnSO_4 \cdot 7H_2O$	0.22
$CuSO_4 \cdot 5H_2O$	0.08
$H_2MoO_4 \cdot H_2O$	0.02

Iron Solution

Iron chelate, such as Sequestrene 330, made to stock solution containing 1 g actual iron/liter. Sequestrene 330 is 10% iron; thus 10 g/liter are required. The amounts of other chelates will have to be adjusted on the basis of their iron content.

Procedure: To make 1 liter of Solution 1, add 5 ml $Ca(NO_3)_2 \cdot 4H_2O$ stock solution, 5 ml KNO_3, 1 ml KH_2PO_4, ml $MgSO_4 \cdot 7H_2O$, 1 ml micronutrient solution, and 1 ml iron solution to 800 ml distilled water. Make up to 1 liter. Some plants grow better on Solution 2, which is prepared in the same way.

Adapted from D. R. Hoagland and D. I. Arnon, The Water-culture Method for Growing Plants Without Soil, California Agricultural Experiment Station Circular 347 (1950).

SOME NUTRIENT SOLUTIONS FOR COMMERCIAL GREENHOUSE VEGETABLE PRODUCTION

These solutions are designed to be supplied directly to greenhouse vegetable crops.

JOHNSON'S SOLUTION

Compound	Amount (g/100 gal of water)
Potassium nitrate	95
Monopotassium phosphate	54
Magnesium sulfate	95
Calcium nitrate	173
Chelated iron (FeDTPA)	9
Boric acid	0.5
Manganese sulfate	0.3
Zinc sulfate	0.04
Copper sulfate	0.01
Molybdic acid	0.005

	N	P	K	Ca	Mg	S	Fe	B	Mn	Zn	Cu	Mo
ppm	105	33	138	85	25	33	2.3	0.23	0.26	0.024	0.01	0.007

JENSEN'S SOLUTION

Compound	Amount (g/100 gal of water)
Magnesium sulfate	187
Monopotassium phosphate	103
Potassium nitrate	77
Calcium nitrate	189
Chelated iron (FeDTPA)	9.6
Boric acid	1.0
Manganese chloride	0.9
Cupric chloride	0.05
Molybdic acid	0.02
Zinc sulfate	0.15

	N	P	K	Ca	Mg	S	Fe	B	Mn	Zn	Cu	Mo
ppm	106	62	156	93	48	64	3.8	0.46	0.81	0.09	0.05	0.03

Adapted from H. Johnson, Jr., G. J. Hochmuth, and D. N. Maynard, Soilless Culture of Greenhouse Vegetables, Fla. Coop. Ext. Bul. 218 (1985).

NUTRIENT SOLUTION FORMULATION FOR TOMATO GROWN IN PERLITE OR ROCKWOOL IN FLORIDA

	Stage of Growth				
	1 Transplant to First Cluster	2 First Cluster to Second	3 Second Cluster to Third	4 Third Cluster to Fifth	5 Fifth Cluster to Termination
Stock A	3.3 pts Phosphorus [1]	3.3 pts Phosphorus	3.3 pts Phosphorus	3.3 pts Phosphorus	3.3 pts Phosphorus
	6 lb. KCl	6 lb. KCl	6 lb. KCl	6 lb. KCl	6 lb. KCl
	10 lb. $MgSO_4$	10 lb. $MgSO_4$	10 lb. $MgSO_4$	12 lb. $MgSO_4$	12 lb. $MgSO_4$
			2 lb. KNO_3	2 lb. KNO_3	6 lb. KNO_3
					1 lb. NH_4NO_3
	10 g $CuSO_4$	10 g $CuSO_4$	10 g $CuSO_4$	10 g $CuSO_4$	10 g $CuSO_4$
	35 g $MnSO_4$	35 g $MnSO_4$	35 g $MnSO_4$	35 g $MnSO_4$	35 g $MnSO_4$
	10 g $ZnSO_4$	10 g $ZnSO_4$	10 g $ZnSO_4$	10 g $ZnSO_4$	10 g $ZnSO_4$
	40 g Solubor	40 g Solubor	40 g Solubor	40 g Solubor	40 g Solubor
	3 ml Molybdenum [2]	3 ml Molybdenum	3 ml Molybdenum	3 ml Molybdenum	3 ml Molybdenum

NUTRIENT SOLUTION FORMULATION FOR TOMATO GROWN IN PERLITE OR ROCKWOOL IN FLORIDA—Continued

	Stage of Growth				
	1 Transplant to First Cluster	2 First Cluster to Second	3 Second Cluster to Third	4 Third Cluster to Fifth	5 Fifth Cluster to Termination
Stock B	2.1 gal. $Ca(NO_3)_2$ [3] or 11.5 lb. dry $Ca(NO_3)_2$ 0.7 lb. Fe 330 [4]	2.4 gal. $Ca(NO_3)_2$ 13.1 lb. dry $Ca(NO_3)_2$ 0.7 lb. Fe 330	2.7 gal. $Ca(NO_3)_2$ 14.8 lb. dry $Ca(NO_3)_2$ 0.7 lb. Fe 330	3.3 gal. $Ca(NO_3)_2$ 18.0 lb. dry $Ca(NO_3)_2$ 0.7 lb. Fe 330	3.3 gal. $Ca(NO_3)_2$ 18.0 lb. dry $Ca(NO_3)_2$ 0.7 lb. Fe 330

Adapted from G. Hochmuth (ed.), Florida Greenhouse Vegetable Production Handbook, Volume 3, Florida Cooperative Extension Service SP-48 (1991).

[1] Phosphorus from phosphoric acid (13 lb/gal. specific wt., 23% P).

[2] Molybdenum from liquid sodium molybdate (11.4 lb/gal. specific wt., 17% Mo).

[3] Liquid $Ca(NO_3)_2$ from a 7-0-0-11 (N-P_2O_5-K_2O-Ca) solution.

[4] Iron as Sequestrene 330 (10% Fe).

RECOMMENDED NUTRIENT SOLUTION CONCENTRATIONS FOR TOMATO GROWN IN ROCKWOOL OR PERLITE IN FLORIDA

Nutrient	Stage of Growth				
	1 Transplant to First Cluster	2 First Cluster to Second	3 Second Cluster to Third	4 Third Cluster to Fifth	5 Fifth Cluster to Termination
	Final delivered nutrient solution concentration (ppm)				
N	70	80	100	120	150
P	50	50	50	50	50
K	120	120	150	150	200
Ca	150	150	150	150	150
Mg	40	40	40	50	50
S	50	50	50	60	60
Fe	2.8	2.8	2.8	2.8	2.8
Cu	0.2	0.2	0.2	0.2	0.2
Mn	0.8	0.8	0.8	0.8	0.8
Zn	0.3	0.3	0.3	0.3	0.3
B	0.7	0.7	0.7	0.7	0.7
Mo	0.05	0.05	0.05	0.05	0.05

Adapted from G. Hochmuth (ed.), Florida Greenhouse Vegetable Production Handbook, Volume 3, Florida Cooperative Extension Service SP-48 (1991).

APPROXIMATE NORMAL TISSUE COMPOSITION OF HYDROPONICALLY GROWN GREENHOUSE VEGETABLES [1]

Element	Tomato	Cucumber
K	5–8%	8–15%
Ca	2–3%	1–3%
Mg	0.4–1.0%	0.3–0.7%
NO_3-N	14,000–20,000 ppm	10,000–20,000 ppm
PO_4-P	6000–8000 ppm	8000–10,000 ppm
Fe	40–100 ppm	90–120 ppm
Zn	15–25 ppm	40–50 ppm
Cu	4–6 ppm	5–10 ppm
Mn	25–50 ppm	50–150 ppm
Mo	1–3 ppm	1–3 ppm
B	20–60 ppm	40–60 ppm

Adapted from H. Johnson, Hydroponics: A Guide to Soilless Culture Systems, University of California Division of Agricultural Science Leaflet 2947 (1977).

[1] Values are for recently expanded leaves, 5th or 6th from the growing tip, petiole analysis for macronutrients, leaf blade analysis for micronutrients. Expressed on a dry weight basis.

SUFFICIENCY NUTRIENT RANGES FOR SELECTED GREENHOUSE VEGETABLE CROPS USING DRIED MOST RECENTLY MATURED WHOLE LEAVES

	Beginning of Harvest Season		Just Before Harvest
Element	Tomato	Cucumber	Lettuce
		percent	
N	3.5–4.0	2.5–5.0	2.1–5.6
P	0.4–0.6	0.5–1.0	0.5–0.9
K	2.8–4.0	3.0–6.0	4.0–8.0
Ca	0.5–2.0	0.8–6.0	0.9–2.0
Mg	0.4–1.0	0.4–0.8	0.4–0.8
S	0.4–0.8	0.4–0.8	0.2–0.5
		parts per million	
B	35–60	40–100	25–65
Cu	8–20	4–10	5–18
Fe	50–200	90–150	50–200
Mn	50–125	50–300	25–200
Mo	1–5	1–3	0.5–3.0
Zn	25–60	50–150	30–200

Adapted from G. Hochmuth (ed.), Florida Greenhouse Vegetable Production Handbook, Volume 3. Greenhouse Vegetable Crop Production Guide. Fla. Coop. Ext. Circ. SP 48 (1991).

PART 3

FIELD PLANTING

TEMPERATURES FOR VEGETABLES

SCHEDULING SUCCESSIVE PLANTINGS

TIME REQUIRED FOR SEEDLING EMERGENCE

SEED REQUIRED

PLANTING RATES FOR LARGE SEEDS

SPACING OF VEGETABLES

PRECISION SEEDING

SEED PRIMING

VEGETATIVE PROPAGATION

POLYETHYLENE MULCHES

ROW COVERS

WINDBREAKS

COOL-SEASON AND WARM-SEASON VEGETABLES

Vegetables generally can be divided into two broad groups. Cool-season vegetables develop edible vegetative parts, such as roots, stems, leaves, and buds or immature flower parts. Sweet potato and other tropical root crops (root used) and New Zealand spinach (leaf and stem used) are exceptions to this rule. Warm-season vegetables develop edible immature and mature fruits. Pea and broad bean are exceptions, being cool-season crops.

Cool-season crops generally differ from warm-season crops in the following respects:

1. They are hardy or frost tolerant.
2. Seeds germinate at cooler soil temperatures.
3. Root systems are shallower.
4. Plant size is smaller.
5. Some, the biennials, are susceptible to premature seed stalk development from exposure to prolonged cool weather.
6. They are stored near 32°F, except for the white potato. Sweet corn is the only warm-season crop held at 32°F after harvest.
7. The harvested product is not subject to chilling injury at temperatures between 32 and 50°F, as is the case with some of the warm-season vegetables.

CLASSIFICATION OF VEGETABLE CROPS ACCORDING TO THEIR ADAPTATION TO FIELD TEMPERATURES

Cool-season Crops

Hardy [1]		Half-hardy [1]
Asparagus	Kohlrabi	Beet
Broad bean	Leek	Carrot
Broccoli	Mustard	Cauliflower
Brussels sprouts	Onion	Celery
Cabbage	Parsley	Chard
Chive	Pea	Chicory
Collards	Radish	Chinese cabbage
Garlic	Rhubarb	Globe artichoke
Horseradish	Spinach	Endive
Kale	Turnip	Lettuce
		Parsnip
		Potato
		Salsify

Warm-season Crops

Tender [1]	Very Tender [1]
Cowpea	Cucumber
New Zealand spinach	Eggplant
Snap bean	Lima bean
Soybean	Muskmelon
Sweet corn	Okra
Tomato	Pepper, hot
	Pepper, sweet
	Pumpkin
	Squash
	Sweet potato
	Watermelon

Adapted from A. A. Kader, J. M. Lyons, and L. L. Morris, Postharvest Responses of Vegetables to Preharvest Field Temperatures, *HortScience* 9:523–529 (1974).

[1] Relative resistance to frost and light freezes.

GROWING DEGREE DAY BASE TEMPERATURES

Crop	Base Temperature (°F) [1]
Asparagus	40
Bean, snap	50
Beet	40
Broccoli	40
Carrot	38
Collards	40
Cucumber	55
Eggplant	60
Lettuce	40
Muskmelon	50
Onion	35
Okra	60
Pea	40
Pepper	50
Potato	40
Squash	45
Strawberry	39
Sweet corn	48
Sweet potato	60
Tomato	51
Watermelon	55

Adapted from D. C. Sanders, H. J. Kirk, and C. Van Den Brink. Growing Degree Days in North Carolina. N.C. Agr. Ext. Serv. AG-236 (1980).

[1] Temperature below which growth is negligible.

APPROXIMATE MONTHLY TEMPERATURES FOR BEST GROWTH AND QUALITY OF VEGETABLE CROPS

Some crops can be planted as temperatures approach the proper range. Cool-season crops grown in the spring must have time to mature before warm weather. Fall crops can be started in hot weather to ensure a sufficient period of cool temperature to reach maturity. Within a crop, varieties may differ in temperature requirements; hence this listing provides general rather than specific guidelines.

Temperatures (°F)			
Optimum	Minimum	Maximum	Vegetable
55–75	45	85	Chicory, chive, garlic, leek, onion, salsify, scolymus, scorzonera, shallot
60–65	40	75	Beet, broad bean, broccoli, Brussels sprouts, cabbage, chard, collards, horseradish, kale, kohlrabi, parsnip, radish, rutabaga, sorrel, spinach, turnip
60–65	45	75	Artichoke, cardoon, carrot, cauliflower, celeriac, celery, Chinese cabbage, endive, Florence fennel, lettuce, mustard, parsley, pea, potato
60–70	50	80	Lima bean, snap bean
60–75	50	95	Sweet corn, Southern pea, New Zealand spinach
65–75	50	90	Chayote, pumpkin, squash
65–75	60	90	Cucumber, muskmelon
70–75	65	80	Sweet pepper, tomato
70–85	65	95	Eggplant, hot pepper, martynia, okra, roselle, sweet potato, watermelon

SOIL TEMPERATURE CONDITIONS FOR VEGETABLE SEED GERMINATION[1]

Vegetable	Minimum (°F)	Optimum Range (°F)	Optimum (°F)	Maximum (°F)
Asparagus	50	60–85	75	95
Bean	60	60–85	80	95
Bean, lima	60	65–85	85	85
Beet	40	50–85	85	95
Cabbage	40	45–95	85	100
Carrot	40	45–85	80	95
Cauliflower	40	45–85	80	100
Celery	40	60–70	70[2]	85[2]
Chard, Swiss	40	50–85	85	95
Corn	50	60–95	95	105
Cucumber	60	60–95	95	105
Eggplant	60	75–90	85	95
Lettuce	35	40–80	75	85
Muskmelon	60	75–95	90	100
Okra	60	70–95	95	105
Onion	35	50–95	75	95
Parsley	40	50–85	75	90
Parsnip	35	50–70	65	85
Pea	40	40–75	75	85
Pepper	60	65–95	85	95
Pumpkin	60	70–90	90	100
Radish	40	45–90	85	95
Spinach	35	45–75	70	85
Squash	60	70–95	95	100
Tomato	50	60–85	85	95
Turnip	40	60–105	85	105
Watermelon	60	70–95	95	105

[1] Compiled by J. F. Harrington, Department of Vegetable Crops, University of California, Davis.
[2] Daily fluctuation to 60°F or lower at night is essential.

SCHEDULING SUCCESSIVE PLANTINGS

Successive plantings are necessary to ensure a continuous supply of produce. This seemingly easy goal is in fact extremely difficult to achieve because of interrupted planting schedules, poor stands, and variable weather conditions.

Maturity can be predicted in part by use of "days to harvest" or "heat units." Additional flexibility is provided by using varieties that differ in time and heat units to reach maturity. Production for fresh market entails the use of days to harvest while some processing crops may be scheduled using the heat unit concept.

Fresh Market Crops

Sweet corn is used as an example, since it is an important fresh-market crop in many parts of the country and requires several plantings to obtain a season-long supply.

Step 1. Select varieties suitable for your area which mature over a period of time. We will illustrate with five fictitious varieties maturing in 68–84 days from planting with 4-day intervals between varieties.

Step 2. Make the first planting as early as possible in your area.

Step 3. Construct a table like the one following and calculate the time of the next planting, so that the earliest variety used matures 4 days after "Late" in the first planting. We chose to use "Mainseason" as the earliest variety in the second planting; thus 88 days − 80 days = 8 days elapsed time before the second and subsequent plantings.

Step 4. As sometimes happens, the third planting was delayed 4 days by rain. To compensate for this delay, "Midseason" is selected as the earliest variety in the third planting to provide corn 96 days after the first planting.

EXAMPLES OF SWEET CORN PLANTINGS

		Time (days)		
Planting	Variety	To Maturity	From First Planting	To Next Planting
First	Early	68	68	
	Second Early	72	72	
	Midseason	76	76	
	Mainseason	80	80	
	Late	84	84	
				8
Second	Mainseason	80	88	
	Late	84	92	
				12
Third	Midseason	76	96	
	Mainseason	80	100	
	Late	84	104	

Adapted from H. Tiessen, Scheduled Planting of Vegetable Crops, Ontario Ministry of Agriculture and Food AGDEX 250/22 (1980).

Processing Crops

The heat unit system is used to schedule plantings and harvests for some processing crops, most notably pea and sweet corn. The use of this system implies that accumulated temperatures over a selected base temperature are a more accurate means of measuring growth than a time unit such as days.

In its simplest form heat units are calculated as follows:

$$\frac{\text{Maximum + minimum daily temperature}}{2} - \text{base temperature}$$

The base temperature is 40°F for pea and 50°F for sweet corn. A number of variations to this basic formula have been proposed to further extend its usefulness.

Heat unit requirements to reach maturity have been determined for most processing pea and sweet corn varieties and many snap bean varieties. Processors using the heat unit system assist growers in scheduling plantings to coincide with plant operating capacity.

DAYS REQUIRED FOR SEEDLING EMERGENCE AT VARIOUS SOIL TEMPERATURES FROM SEED PLANTED ½ IN. DEEP

The days from planting to emergence constitute the time interval when a preemergence weed control treatment can be used safely and effectively. More days are required with deeper seeding because of cooler temperatures and the greater distance of growth.

	Soil Temperature (°F)								
Vegetable	32	41	50	59	68	77	86	95	104
Asparagus	NG	NG	53	24	15	10	12	20	28
Bean, lima	—	—	NG	31	18	7	7	NG	—
Bean snap	NG	NG	NG	16	11	8	6	6	NG
Beet	—	42	17	10	6	5	5	5	—
Cabbage	—	—	15	9	6	5	4	—	—
Carrot	NG	51	17	10	7	6	6	9	NG
Cauliflower	—	—	20	10	6	5	5	—	—
Celery	NG	41	16	12	7	NG	NG	NG	—
Corn, sweet	NG	NG	22	12	7	4	4	3	NG
Cucumber	NG	NG	NG	13	6	4	3	3	—
Eggplant	—	—	—	—	13	8	5	—	—
Lettuce	49	15	7	4	3	2	3	NG	NG
Muskmelon	—	—	—	—	8	4	3	—	—
Okra	NG	NG	NG	27	17	13	7	6	7
Onion	136	31	13	7	5	4	4	13	NG
Parsley	—	—	29	17	14	13	12	—	—

DAYS REQUIRED FOR SEEDLING EMERGENCE AT VARIOUS SOIL TEMPERATURES FROM SEED PLANTED ½ IN. DEEP—Continued

	Soil Temperature (°F)								
Vegetable	32	41	50	59	68	77	86	95	104
Parsnip	172	57	27	19	14	15	32	NG	NG
Pea	—	36	14	9	8	6	6	—	—
Pepper	NG	NG	NG	25	13	8	8	9	NG
Radish	NG	29	11	6	4	4	3	—	—
Spinach	63	23	12	7	6	5	6	NG	NG
Tomato	NG	NG	43	14	8	6	6	9	NG
Turnip	NG	NG	5	3	2	1	1	1	3
Watermelon	—	NG	—	—	12	5	4	3	—

Adapted from J. F. Harrington and P. A. Minges, Vegetable Seed Germination, California Agricultural Extension Mimeo Leaflet (1954).

NG = No germination, — = not tested.

APPROXIMATE NUMBER OF SEEDS PER UNIT WEIGHT AND FIELD SEEDING RATES FOR TRADITIONAL PLANT DENSITIES

Vegetable	Seeds	Unit Weight	Field Seeding[1] (lb/acre)
Asparagus[2]	14,000–20,000	lb	2–3
Bean, baby lima	1,200–1,500	lb	60
Bean, fordhook lima	400–600	lb	85
Bean, bush snap	1,600–2,000	lb	75–90
Bean, pole snap	1,600–2,000	lb	20–45
Beet	24,000–26,000	lb	10–15
Broad bean	300–800	lb	60–80
Broccoli[3]	9,000	oz	½–1½
Brussels sprouts[3]	9,000	oz	½–1½
Cabbage[3]	9,000	oz	½–1½
Cardoon	11,000	lb	4–5
Carrot	300,000–400,000	lb	2–4
Cauliflower[3]	9,000	oz	½–1½
Celeriac	72,000	oz	1–2
Celery[3]	72,000	oz	1–2
Chicory	27,000	oz	3–5
Chinese cabbage	9,000	oz	1–2
Collards	9,000	oz	2–4
Corn salad	13,000	oz	10
Cucumber	15,000–16,000	lb	3–5
Dandelion	35,000	oz	2
Eggplant[3]	6,500	oz	2
Endive	25,000	oz	3–4
Florence fennel	7,000	oz	3
Kale	9,000	oz	2–4
Kohlrabi	9,000	oz	3–5
Leek[3]	200,000	lb	4
Lettuce, head[3]	20,000–25,000	oz	1–3
Lettuce, leaf	25,000–30,000	oz	1–3
Muskmelon[3]	16,000–20,000	lb	2
Mustard	15,000	oz	3–5
New Zealand spinach	5,600	lb	15
Okra	8,000	lb	6–8
Onion, bulb[3]	130,000	lb	3–4
Onion, bunching	180,000–200,000	lb	3–4
Parsley	250,000	lb	20–40
Parsnip	192,000	lb	3–5
Pea	1,500–2,500	lb	80–250
Pepper[3]	4,200–4,600	oz	24

APPROXIMATE NUMBER OF SEEDS PER UNIT WEIGHT AND FIELD SEEDING RATES FOR TRADITIONAL PLANT DENSITIES—Continued

Vegetable	Seeds	Unit Weight	Field Seeding[1] (lb/acre)
Pumpkin	1,500–4,000	lb	2–4
Radish	40,000–50,000	lb	10–20
Roselle	900–1,000	oz	3–5
Rutabaga	150,000–190,000	lb	1–2
Salsify	1,900	oz	8–10
Sorrel	30,000	oz	2–3
Southern pea	3,600	lb	20–40
Soybean	4,000	lb	20–40
Spinach	45,000	lb	10–15
Squash, summer	3,500–4,500	lb	4–6
Squash, winter	1,600–4,000	lb	2–4
Swiss chard	25,000	lb	6–8
Sweet corn, Su, Se	1,800–2,500	lb	12–15
Sweet corn, sh	3,000–5,000	lb	12–15
Tomato[3]	10,000–12,000	oz	½–1
Turnip	150,000–200,000	lb	1–2
Watermelon, small seed[3]	8,000–10,000	lb	1–3
Watermelon, large seed[3]	3,000–5,000	lb	2–4

[1] Actual seeding rates are adjusted to desired plant populations, germination percentage of the seed lot, and weather conditions that influence germination.
[2] 6–8 lbs/acre for crown production.
[3] Transplants are used frequently, instead of direct field seeding. See pages 50–51 for seeding rates for transplants.

Weigh out a 1-oz sample of the seed lot and count the number of seeds.

The following table gives the approximate pounds of seed per acre for certain between-row and in-row spacings of lima bean, pea, snap bean, and sweet corn. These are based on 100% germination. If the seed germinates only 90%, for example, then divide the pounds of seed by 0.90 to get the planting rate. Do the same with other germination percentages.

Example: 30 seeds/oz to be planted in 22-in. rows at 1-in. spacing between seeds.

$$\frac{595}{0.90} = 661 \text{ lb/acre}$$

Only precision planting equipment would begin to approach as exact a job of spacing as this table indicates. Moreover, field conditions such as soil structure, temperature, and moisture will affect germination and final stand.

PLANTING RATES FOR LARGE SEEDS

No. of Seeds/oz	Spacing Between Rows (in.): 18						20						22					
	Spacing Between Seeds in Row (in.): 1	2	3	4	5	6	1	2	3	4	5	6	1	2	3	4	5	6
	Seed Needed (lb/acre)																	
30	726	364	242	182	146	121	655	328	218	164	131	109	595	298	198	149	119	98
40	545	273	182	136	110	90	491	246	163	123	99	82	446	223	148	112	90	74
50	440	220	146	110	88	74	396	198	132	99	79	66	361	180	120	90	72	60
60	354	178	118	90	76	59	318	159	106	80	64	53	289	145	97	73	58	48
70	312	156	104	78	62	56	281	140	94	70	56	47	256	128	85	64	51	43
80	272	136	90	68	54	46	245	123	82	62	49	41	223	112	74	56	45	37
90	242	120	82	60	48	40	218	109	73	55	44	37	198	99	66	50	40	33
100	216	108	72	54	42	38	198	99	66	50	39	33	181	90	60	45	35	30
110	198	99	66	50	40	34	173	89	59	44	35	30	161	80	54	40	32	27
120	180	90	60	45	36	30	162	81	54	40	33	27	148	74	49	37	30	25
130	168	84	56	42	34	28	152	76	51	38	31	25	138	69	46	34	28	23
140	156	78	52	38	30	26	141	70	47	35	28	24	128	64	43	32	25	22
150	146	73	49	36	28	24	131	66	44	33	26	22	119	60	40	30	24	20

PLANTING RATES FOR LARGE SEEDS—Continued

No. of Seeds/oz	*Spacing Between Rows (in.):* 24						30						36					
	Spacing Between Seeds in Row (in.): 1	2	3	4	5	6	1	2	3	4	5	6	1	2	3	4	5	6
	Seed Needed (lb/acre)																	
30	545	273	182	136	109	91	437	219	146	109	88	73	363	182	121	91	73	61
40	408	204	136	102	82	68	328	164	106	82	66	54	272	136	91	68	55	45
50	330	165	110	82	66	55	265	132	88	66	53	44	220	110	73	55	44	37
60	265	133	88	67	57	44	212	106	71	59	43	35	177	89	59	45	38	29
70	234	117	78	59	47	39	188	94	63	47	38	31	156	78	52	39	31	26
80	204	102	68	51	41	34	164	82	53	41	33	27	136	68	45	34	27	23
90	181	90	61	45	36	30	146	73	49	37	29	25	121	60	41	30	24	20
100	162	81	55	40	32	28	131	67	44	33	27	22	108	54	37	27	21	19
110	148	74	49	37	30	25	119	60	40	30	24	20	99	49	33	25	20	17
120	135	68	45	34	27	23	108	54	36	27	22	18	90	45	30	23	18	15
130	126	63	42	32	25	21	101	51	34	25	20	17	84	42	28	21	17	14
140	117	58	39	29	23	20	94	47	32	23	19	16	78	39	26	19	15	13
150	109	55	38	27	22	18	88	44	29	22	18	15	73	37	24	18	14	12

SPACING OF VEGETABLES AND PLANT POPULATIONS

Spacing for vegetables is determined by the equipment used to plant, maintain, and harvest the crop as well as by the area required for growth of the plant without undue competition from neighboring plants. Previously row spacings were dictated almost entirely by the space requirement of cultivating equipment. Many of the traditional row spacings can be traced back to the horse cultivator.

Modern herbicides have largely eliminated the need for extensive cultivation in many crops; thus row spacings need not be related to cultivation equipment. Instead the plant's space requirement can be used as the determining factor.

Invariably, plant populations increase when this approach is used. A more uniform product with a higher proportion of marketable vegetables as well as higher total yields result from the closer plant spacings. The term "high-density production" has been developed to describe vegetable spacings designed to satisfy the plant's space requirement.

HIGH-DENSITY SPACING OF VEGETABLES

Vegetable	Spacing (in.)	Plant Population (plants/acre)
Snap bean	3 × 12	174,000
Beet	2 × 12	261,000
Carrot	1½ × 12	349,000
Cauliflower	12 × 18	29,000
Cabbage	12 × 18	29,000
Cucumber (processing)	3 × 20	104,000
Lettuce	12 × 18	29,000
Onion	1 × 12	523,000

TRADITIONAL PLANT AND ROW SPACINGS FOR VEGETABLES

Vegetable	Between Plants in Row (in.)	Between Rows (in.)
Artichoke	48–72	84–96
Asparagus	9–15	48–72
Bean, broad	8–10	20–48
Bean, bush	2–4	18–36
Bean, lima, bush	3–6	18–36
Bean, lima, pole	8–12	36–48
Bean, pole	6–9	36–48
Beet	2–4	12–30
Broccoli	12–24	18–36
Broccoli raab	3–4	24–36
Brussels sprouts	18–24	24–40
Cabbage	12–24	24–36
Cardoon	12–18	30–42
Carrot	1–3	16–30
Cauliflower	14–24	24–36
Celeriac	4–6	24–36
Celery	6–12	18–40
Chard, Swiss	12–15	24–36
Chervil	6–10	12–18
Chicory	4–10	18–24
Chinese cabbage	10–18	18–36
Chive	12–18	24–36
Collards	12–24	24–36
Corn	8–12	30–42
Cress	2–4	12–18
Cucumber	8–12	36–72
Dandelion	3–6	14–24
Dasheen (taro)	24–30	42–48
Eggplant	18–30	24–48
Endive	8–12	18–24
Florence fennel	4–12	24–42
Garlic	1–3	12–24
Horseradish	12–18	30–36
Jerusalem artichoke	15–18	42–48
Kale	18–24	24–36
Kohlrabi	3–6	12–36
Leek	2–6	12–36
Lettuce, cos	10–14	16–24

TRADITIONAL PLANT AND ROW SPACINGS FOR VEGETABLES—Continued

Vegetable	Between Plants in Row (in.)	Between Rows (in.)
Lettuce, head	10–15	16–24
Lettuce, leaf	8–12	12–24
Muskmelon and other melons	12	60–84
Mustard	5–10	12–36
New Zealand spinach	10–20	36–60
Okra	8–24	42–60
Onion	1–4	16–24
Parsley	4–12	12–36
Parsley, Hamburg	1–3	18–36
Parsnip	2–4	18–36
Pea	1–3	24–48
Pepper	12–24	18–36
Potato	6–12	30–42
Pumpkin	36–60	72–96
Radish	½–1	8–18
Radish, storage type	4–6	18–36
Rhubarb	24–48	36–60
Roselle	24–46	60–72
Rutabaga	5–8	18–36
Salsify	2–4	18–36
Scolymus	2–4	18–36
Scorzonera	2–4	18–36
Shallot	4–8	36–48
Sorrel	½–1	12–18
Southern pea	3–6	18–42
Spinach	2–6	12–36
Squash, bush	24–48	36–60
Squash, vining	36–96	72–96
Strawberry	10–24	24–64
Sweet potato	10–18	36–48
Tomato, flat	18–48	36–60
Tomato, staked	12–24	36–48
Tomato, processing	2–10	42–60
Turnip	2–6	12–36
Turnip greens	1–4	6–12
Watercress	1–3	6–12
Watermelon	24–36	72–96

LENGTH OF ROW PER ACRE AT VARIOUS ROW SPACINGS

Distance Between Rows (in.)	Row Length (ft/acre)	Distance Between Rows (in.)	Row Length (ft/acre)
6	87,120	40	13,068
12	43,560	42	12,445
15	34,848	48	10,890
18	29,040	60	8,712
20	26,136	72	7,260
21	24,891	84	6,223
24	21,780	96	5,445
30	17,424	108	4,840
36	14,520	120	4,356

NUMBER OF PLANTS PER ACRE AT VARIOUS SPACINGS

In order to obtain other spacings, divide 43,560, the number of square feet per acre, by the product of the between-rows and in-the-row spacings, each expressed as feet; that is, 43,560 divided by 0.75 (36 × 3 in. or 3 × 0.25 ft) = 58,080.

Spacing (in.)	Plants	Spacing (in.)	Plants	Spacing (ft)	Plants
12 × 1	522,720	30 × 3	69,696	6 × 1	7260
12 × 3	174,240	30 × 6	34,848	6 × 2	3630
12 × 6	87,120	30 × 12	17,424	6 × 3	2420
12 × 12	43,560	30 × 15	13,939	6 × 4	1815
	418,176	30 × 18	11,616	6 × 5	1452
15[1] × 1	139,392	30 × 24	8,712	6 × 6	1210
15 × 3	69,696		58,080		6223
15 × 6	34,848	36 × 3	29,040	7 × 1	3111
15 × 12		36 × 6	14,520	7 × 2	2074
		36 × 12		7 × 3	

Spacing (in.)	Plants	Spacing (in.)	Plants	Spacing (ft)	Plants
18[1] × 3	116,160	36 × 18	9,680	7 × 4	1556
18 × 6	58,080	36 × 24	7,260	7 × 5	1244
18 × 12	29,040	36 × 36	4,840	7 × 6	1037
18 × 14	24,891			7 × 7	889
18 × 18	19,360	40 × 6	26,136		
		40 × 12	13,068	8 × 1	5445
20[1] × 3	104,544	40 × 18	8,712	8 × 2	2722
20 × 6	52,272	40 × 24	6,534	8 × 3	1815
20 × 12	26,136			8 × 4	1361
20 × 14	22,402	42 × 6	24,891	8 × 5	1089
20 × 18	17,424	42 × 12	12,445	8 × 6	907
		42 × 18	8,297	8 × 8	680
21[1] × 3	99,564	42 × 24	6,223		
21 × 6	49,782	42 × 36	4,148	10 × 2	2178
21 × 12	24,891			10 × 4	1089
21 × 14	21,336	48 × 6	21,780	10 × 6	726
21 × 18	16,594	48 × 12	10,890	10 × 8	544
		48 × 18	7,260	10 × 10	435
24 × 3	87,120	48 × 24	5,445		
24 × 6	43,560	48 × 36	3,630		
24 × 12	21,780	48 × 48	2,722		
24 × 18	14,520				
24 × 24	10,890	60 × 12	8,712		
		60 × 18	5,808		
		60 × 24	4,356		
		60 × 36	2,904		
		60 × 48	2,178		
		60 × 60	1,742		

[1] Equivalent to double rows on beds at 30, 36, 40, and 42 in. centers, respectively.

High-density plantings, high costs of hand thinning, and erratic performance of mechanical thinners have resulted in the development of precision seeding techniques. The success of precision seeding depends on having seeds with nearly 100% germination and on exact placement of each seed.

Some of the advantages of precision seeding are:

- Reduced seed costs. Only the seed that is needed is sown.
- Greater crop uniformity. Each seed is spaced equally, fewer harvests are necessary, and/or greater yield is obtained at harvest.
- Improved yields. Each plant has an equal chance to mature; yields can increase 20% to 50%.
- Improved plant stands. Seeds are dropped shorter distances, resulting in less scatter and a uniform depth of planting.
- Thinning can be reduced or eliminated.

Some precautions must be taken to ensure the proper performance of precision seeding equipment:

1. A fine, smooth seedbed is required for uniform seeding depth.
2. Seed must have high germination.
3. Seed must be uniform in size; this can be achieved by seed sizing or seed coating.
4. Seed must be of regular shape; irregular seeds such as carrot, lettuce, and onion must be coated for satisfactory precision seeding. Seed size is increased two to five times with clay or proprietary coatings.

Several types of equipment are available for precision seeding of vegetables.

Belt type—represented by the StanHay seeder. Circular holes punched in a belt accommodate the seed size. Holes are spaced along the belt at specified intervals. Coated seed usually improves the uniformity obtained with this type of seeder.

Plate type—represented by the John Deere 33 or Earth Way. Seeds drop into a notch in a horizontal plate and are transported to the drop point. The plate is vertical in the Earth Way and catches seed in a pocket in a plastic plate. Most spacing is achieved by gearing the rate of turn of the plate.

Vacuum type—represented by the Gaspardo, Heath, Monosem, StanHay, and several other seeders. Seed is drawn against holes in a vertical plate and is agitated to remove excess seed. Various spacings are achieved through a combination of gears and number of holes per plate. Coated seed should not be used in these planters.

Spoon type—represented by the Nibex. Seed is scooped up out of a reservoir by small spoons (sized for the seed) and then carried to a drop shoot where the spoon turns and drops the seed. Spacing is achieved by spoon number and gearing.

Pneumatic type—represented by the International Harvester cyclo planter. Seed is held in place against a drum until the air pressure is broken. Then it drops in tubes and is blown to the soil. This planter is recommended only for larger vegetable seed.

Grooved cylinder type—represented by the Gramor seeder. This seeder requires round seed or seed that is made round by coating. Seven seeds fall from a supply tube into a slot at the top of a metal case into a metal cylinder. The cylinder turns slowly. As it reaches the bottom of the case, the seeds drop out of a diagonal slot. The seed is placed in desired increments by a combination of forward speed and turning rate. This planter can be used with seed as small as pepper seed but it works best with coated seed.

Guidelines for Operation and Maintenance of Equipment

1. Check the planter for proper operation and replace worn parts during the off-season.
2. Thoroughly understand the contents of the manufacturer's manual.
3. Make certain that the operator is trained to use the equipment and check its performance.
4. Double check your settings to be sure that you have the desired spacing and depth.
5. Make a trial run before moving to the field.
6. Operate the equipment at the recommended tractor speed.
7. Check the seed drop of each unit periodically during the planting operation.

Adapted in part from Precision Planting Program, Asgrow Seed Co., Kalamazoo, MI and Sanders, D. C. and J. R. Schultheis. Precision Seeding. p. 10. In D. C. Sanders (ed.), A Guide to Intensive Vegetable Systems. North Carolina Cooperative Extension AG-502 (1993).

NUMBER OF SEEDS PLANTED PER MINUTE AT VARIOUS SPEEDS AND SPACINGS [1]

Planter Speed (mph)	In-row Spacing (in.) 2	3	4	6
2.5	1320	880	660	440
3.0	1584	1056	792	528
4.0	2112	1408	1056	704
5.0	2640	1760	1320	880

Adapted from Precision Planting Program, Asgrow Seed Co., Kalamazoo, MI.

[1] For most conditions, a planter speed of 2–3 mph will result in the greatest precision.

SEED PRIMING

Seed priming is a physiologically based seed enhancement technique designed to improve the germination characteristics of seeds. Germination speed, uniformity, and seedling vigor are all improved by priming. These benefits are especially pronounced under adverse temperature and/or moisture conditions.

The commercial applications of seed priming have been expanding rapidly in recent years. Important vegetable crops that are now enhanced through priming include brassicas, carrot, celery, cucurbits, lettuce, onion, pepper, and tomato More crop species are being added on an ongoing basis.

Priming is accomplished by partially hydrating seed and maintaining it under defined moisture, temperature, and aeration conditions for a prescribed period of time. In this state, the seed is metabolically active. In an optimally hydrated, metabolically active state, important germination steps can be accomplished within the seed. These include repair of membranes and/or genetic material, development of immature embryos, alteration of tissues covering the embryo, and destruction or removal of dormancy blocks.

At the conclusion of the process, the seed is redried to its storage moisture level. The gains made in priming are not lost during storage. Primed seed is physiologically closer to germination than nonprimed seed. When planted at a later date, primed seed starts at this advanced state and moves directly into the final stages of germination and growth.

There are several commercial methods of seed priming. All are based on the basic principles of hydrated seed physiology. They differ in the methods used to control hydration, aeration, temperature, and dehydration. The most important commercial priming methods include:

Liquid Osmotic. In this approach, seed is bubbled in a solution of known osmotic concentration (accomplished with various salts or organic osmotic agents). The osmotic properties of the solution control water uptake by the seed. The bubbling is necessary to provide sufficient oxygen to keep the seed alive during the process. The temperature of the solution is controlled throughout the process. After priming is completed, the seeds are removed, washed and dried.

Membrane and/or Flat Media Osmotic. This method is a variation of liquid osmotic priming. With this method, the seed is placed on a porous membrane suspended on the surface of the osmotic solution. This method addresses some of the aeration concerns associated with liquid osmotic priming, but is limited by practical considerations to smaller seed lots.

Drum Hydration. With this method, seeds are placed in a rotating drum and controlled quantities of water are sprayed onto the seed, bringing it to the desired moisture level. Drum rotation provides the necessary aeration to the seeds, and temperature and air flow are controlled throughout the process. After the priming period, the seed is dried by flushing air through the drum. Drum priming is a patented technology.

Solid Matrix Priming (SMP). With the SMP method, water uptake is controlled by suspending seed in a defined medium (or matrix) of solids (organic and/or inorganic) of known water holding properties. The seed and matrix compete for available water, coming to equilibrium at precisely the right point for priming to occur. Aeration and temperature are precisely controlled throughout the process. After the process is complete, the seed and matrix are separated. The seed is dried back to its original moisture. The SMP method is a patented technology.

In maintaining processing conditions during priming, it is important to prevent the seed from progressing too far through the germination process. If germination is allowed to progress beyond the early stages, it is too late to return to a resting state. The seed is "committed" to growth and cannot be redried without damage and/or reduced shelf life.

Priming alters many basic characteristics of germination and seedling emergence as indicated below:

Germination Speed. Primed seed has already accomplished the early stages of germination and begins growing much more rapidly. The total time required is cut approximately in half. This is especially important with slow-germinating species such as celery or carrot.

Increased Temperature Range. Primed seed will emerge under both cooler and warmer temperatures than unprimed seed. Generally the temperature range is extended by 5° to 8°F in both directions.

More Uniform Emergence. The distribution of germination times within most seed lots is greatly reduced resulting in improved uniformity.

Germination at Reduced Seed Water Content. Primed seed will germinate at a lower seed water content than unprimed seed.

Control of Dormancy Mechanisms. In many cases, priming overcomes dormancy mechanisms that slow germination.

Germination Percentages. An increase in the germination percentage occurs in many instances with individual seed lots as a result of the priming process. The increase is generally due to repair of weak or abnormal seeds within the lot.

Considerations with Primed Seed

Shelf Life of Primed Seed. Shelf life is a complicated subject and is influenced by many different factors. The most important factors include crop species, seed lot quality, seed moisture content in storage, transportation and storage conditions (especially temperature), the degree to which a lot has been primed, and subsequent seed treatments (fungicides, film coating, pelleting).

Assuming proper transportation and storage conditions and no other complicating factors (such as coating), deterioration in seed lot performance is rarely experienced during the growing season for which a lot was primed (generally 4 months). In most cases (assuming the same qualifiers listed above), lot performance is maintained for much longer.

As storage time increases, the risk of loss also increases. Most lots are stable, but a percentage deteriorate rapidly. Not only is the priming effect lost, but generally a significant percentage of the lot dies. Screening methods to predict high risk lots are needed. The results of research in this area are promising, but a usable method of predicting deterioration is not yet available.

Seed only should be primed for planting during the immediate growing season. Priming seed for planting in subsequent years is discouraged. In cases where primed seed must be held for extended periods, the seed should be retested before planting to assess whether deterioration may have occurred.

Treating, Coating and Pelleting Primed Seed. The compatibility of primed seed with any subsequent seed treatment, coating or pelleting must be determined on a case-by-case basis. The germination characteristics may be influenced. In some cases, priming is performed to improve the vigor of lots that would otherwise not tolerate the stress of coating or pelleting. In other cases, primed seeds may be more sensitive than unprimed seeds and experience deterioration. Combinations must be tested after priming, on a case-by-case basis, before other commercial treatments are performed.

Transport and Storage Conditions. Exposure to high temperatures, even for brief periods, can induce rapid deterioration of all seeds. The risk is greater with primed seeds. In storage and transport, it is important to maintain seeds that have been enhanced under dry, cool conditions (temperatures of 70°F or less are recommended). Unfavorable conditions may negatively influence shelf life.

Adapted from John A. Eastin and John S. Vendeland. Kamterter Products, Inc., Lincoln, NB. Presented at Florida Seed Association Seminar (1996).

Plant Part	Temperature (°F)	Relative Humidity (%)	Comments
Asparagus crowns	30–32	85–90	Roots may be trimmed to 8 in. Prevent heating and excessive drying
Garlic bulbs	50	50–65	Fumigate for mites, if present. Hot-water-treat (120°F for 20 min) for control of stem and bulb nematode immediately before planting
Horseradish roots	32	85–90	Pit storage is used in cold climates
Onion sets	32	70–75	Sets may be cured naturally in the field, in trays, or artificially with warm, dry air
Potato tubers	36–40 (extended storage) 45–50 (short storage)	90	Cure at 60–65°F and 90–95% relative humidity for 10–14 days. Move to 60–65°F 10–14 days before planting
Rhubarb crowns	32–35	80–85	Field storage is satisfactory in cold climates
Strawberry plants	30–32	85–90	Store in crates lined with 1.5-mil polyethylene
Sweet potato roots	55–60	85–90	Cures roots at 85°F and 85–90% relative humidity for 6–8 days before storage
Witloof chicory roots	32	90–95	Prevent excessive drying

FIELD REQUIREMENTS FOR VEGETATIVELY PROPAGATED CROPS

Vegetable	Plant Parts	Quantity/acre [1]
Artichoke	Root sections	807–1,261
Asparagus	Crowns	5,808–10,890
Dasheen	Corms (2–5 oz)	9–18 cwt
Garlic	Cloves	8–20 cwt
Jerusalem artichoke	Tubers (2 oz)	10–12 cwt
Horseradish	Root cuttings	9,000–11,000
Onion	Sets	5–10 cwt
Potato	Tubers or tuber sections	13–26 cwt
Rhubarb	Crown divisions	4,000–5,000
Strawberry	Plants	6,000–50,000
Sweet potato	Roots for bedding	5–6 cwt

[1] Varies with field spacing, size of individual units, and vigor of stock.

SEED POTATOES REQUIRED PER ACRE, WITH VARIOUS PLANTING DISTANCES AND SIZES OF SEED PIECE

	Seed Piece Weights				
Spacing of Rows and Seed Pieces	1 oz	1¼ oz	1½ oz	1¾ oz	2 oz
	(Pounds of Seed/Acre)				
Rows 30 in. Apart					
8-in. spacing	1632	2040	2448	2856	3270
10-in. spacing	1308	1638	1956	2286	2614
12-in. spacing	1089	1361	1632	1908	2178
14-in. spacing	936	1164	1398	1632	1868
16-in. spacing	816	1020	1224	1428	1632
Rows 32 in. Apart					
8-in. spacing	1530	1914	2298	2682	3066
10-in. spacing	1224	1530	1836	2142	2448
12-in. spacing	1020	1278	1536	1788	2040

SEED POTATOES REQUIRED PER ACRE, WITH VARIOUS PLANTING DISTANCES AND SIZES OF SEED PIECE—Continued

Spacing of Rows and Seed Pieces	Seed Piece Weights				
	1 oz	1¼ oz	1½ oz	1¾ oz	2 oz
	(Pounds of Seed/Acre)				
Rows 32 in. Apart					
14-in. spacing	876	1092	1314	1530	1752
16-in. spacing	768	960	1152	1344	1536
Rows 34 in. Apart					
8-in. spacing	1440	1800	2160	2520	2880
10-in. spacing	1152	1440	1728	2016	2304
12-in. spacing	960	1200	1440	1680	1920
14-in. spacing	822	1026	1236	1440	1644
16-in. spacing	720	900	1080	1260	1440
Rows 36 in. Apart					
8-in. spacing	1362	1704	2040	2382	2724
10-in. spacing	1086	1362	1632	1902	2178
12-in. spacing	906	1134	1362	1590	1812
14-in. spacing	780	972	1164	1362	1554
16-in. spacing	678	852	1020	1188	1362
18-in. spacing	606	756	906	1056	1212
Rows 42 in. Apart					
18-in. spacing	516	648	780	906	1038
24-in. spacing	390	486	582	678	780
30-in. spacing	312	390	468	546	624
36-in. spacing	258	324	390	456	516
Rows 48 in. Apart					
18-in. spacing	456	570	678	792	906
24-in. spacing	342	426	510	594	678
30-in. spacing	270	342	408	474	546
36-in. spacing	228	282	342	396	456

Polyethylene mulch has been used commercially on vegetables since the early 1960s. Currently, polyethylene mulch is used on thousands of acres of vegetables in the United States. Florida and California lead in use with about 100,000 acres of mulched vegetables in each state.

Types of Mulch

Basically, three major colors of mulch are used commercially: black, clear, and white (or white-on-black). Black mulch is used most widely because it suppresses weed growth, resulting in less chemical usage and is useful for cool seasons because it warms the soil by contact. Clear polyethylene is used widely in the northern United States because it promotes warmer soil temperatures (by the greenhouse effect) than black mulch. Clear mulch requires use of labeled fumigants or herbicides underneath to prevent weed growth. White or white-on-black mulch is used for fall crops which are established under hot summer conditions. Soils under white mulch or white-on-black mulch remain cooler because less radiant energy is absorbed by the mulch. Some growers create their own "white" mulch by painting the surface of black-mulched beds with white latex paint.

Benefits of Mulch

Increases Early Yields. The largest benefit from polyethylene mulch is the increase in soil temperature in the bed, which promotes faster crop development and earlier yields.

Aids Moisture Retention. Mulch reduces evaporation from the bed soil surface. As a result, a more uniform soil moisture regime is maintained and the frequency of irrigation is reduced slightly. Irrigation is still mandatory for mulched crops so that the soil under the mulch doesn't dry out excessively. Tensiometers placed in the bed between plants can help indicate when irrigation is needed.

Inhibits Weed Growth. Black and white-on-black mulches greatly inhibit light penetration to the soil. Therefore, weed seedlings cannot survive under the mulch. Nutgrass can still be a problem, however. The nuts provide enough energy for the young nutgrass to puncture the mulch and emerge. Other pests, such as soilborne pathogens, insects, and nematodes, are not reduced by most mulches. Some benefit has been shown from high temperatures under clear mulch (solarization), but the cost is prohibitive for commercial use at this time. Currently, the best measure for nutgrass and pest control under the mulch is labeled fumigation.

Reduces Fertilizer Leaching. Fertilizer placed in the bed under the mulch is less subject to leaching by rainfall. As a result, the fertilizer program is more efficient and the potential exists for reducing traditional amounts of fertilizer. Heavy rainfall that floods the bed can still result in fertilizer leaching. This fertilizer can be replaced if the grower is using drip irrigation, or it can be replaced with a liquid fertilizer injection wheel.

Decreases Soil Compaction. Mulch acts as a barrier to the action of rainfall, which can cause soil crusting, compaction, and erosion. Less-compacted soil provides a better environment for seedling emergence and root growth.

Protects Fruits. Mulch reduces rain-splashed soil deposits on fruits. In addition, mulch reduces fruit rot caused by soil-inhabiting organisms, because there is a protective barrier between the fruit and the organism.

Aids Fumigation. Mulches increase the effectiveness of soil fumigant chemicals. Acting as a barrier to gas escape, mulches help keep gaseous fumigants in the soil.

Negative Aspects of Mulch

Mulch Removal and Disposal. The biggest problems associated with mulch use are removal and disposal. Since most mulches are not biodegradable, they must be removed from the field after use. This usually involves some hand labor, although mulch lifting and removal machines are available. Some growers have been burning the mulch, but the buried edges still must be removed by hand. Disposal also presents a problem because of the quantity of waste generated.

Specialized equipment. The mulch cultural system requires a small investment in some specialized equipment, including a bed press, mulch layer, and mulch transplanter or plug-mix seeder. Vacuum seeders are also available for seeding through mulch. This equipment is not very expensive, is easily obtained, and some can even be manufactured on the farm.

Mulch Application

Mulch is applied by machine for commercial operations. Machines that prepare beds, fertilize, fumigate, and mulch in separate operations or in combination are available. The best option is to complete all of these operations in one pass across the field. In general, all chemicals and fertilizers are applied to the soil before mulching.

When laying mulch, be sure the bed is pressed firmly and that the mulch is in tight contact with the bed. This helps transfer heat from mulch to bed and reduces flapping in the wind, which results in tears and blowing of mulch from the bed. The mulch layer should be adjusted so that the edges are buried sufficiently to prevent uplifting by wind.

Degradable Mulches

Degradable plastic mulches have many of the properties and provide the usual benefits of standard polyethylene mulches. One important difference is that degradable mulches begin to break down after the film has received a predetermined amount of ultraviolet (UV) light.

When a film has received sufficient UV light, it becomes brittle and develops cracks, tears, and holes. Small sections of film may tear off and be blown around by the wind. Finally, the film breaks down into small flakes and disintegrates into the soil. The edges covered by the soil retain their strength and break down only after being disced to the surface where they are exposed to UV light.

The use of long-lasting degradable mulches formulated for long-season crops, such as peppers, will result in some plastic residue fragments remaining in the soil for the next crop. This residue is primarily the edges of film that were covered with soil. Seeding early crops in a field that had a long-term, degradable mulch the previous season should be avoided. Most plastic fragments should break down and disappear into the soil by the end of the growing season after the mulch was used.

Factors affecting the time and rate of breakdown:

- The formulation and manufacturing of the film, i.e., short-, intermediate-, or long-lasting film.
- Factors that influence the amount of UV light received by the mulch film and, thus, the breakdown include the growth habit of the crop (vine or upright), the time of year the film is applied, the time between application and planting, crop vigor, and double- or single-row planting. Weed growth, mowing off the crop, and length of time the mulch is left in the field after harvest also influence time and extent of breakdown.
- High temperatures can increase the rate of breakdown, and wind can rapidly enlarge tears and holes in film that is breaking down.
- Other factors, including depressions in the bed, footprints, animal and tire tracks, trickle irrigation tubes under the film, and stress on the plastic resulting from making holes for plants and planting, all weaken the film and increase the rate of breakdown.

Suggestions for using degradable mulches:

- Select the proper mulch formulation for the crop to be grown. Consult the company representative.
- Make uniform beds, free from depressions and footprints. Apply long-term mulches 1 to 2 weeks before planting. This will allow mulch to receive UV light and initiate the breakdown process. Apply short-duration films a few days to immediately before planting.
- Minimize damage to the film and avoid unnecessary footprints, especially during planting and early in the growing season.
- Maintain clean weed control between mulch strips. Shading from weed growth can slow the rate of mulch breakdown.
- Lift the soil-covered edges before final harvest or as soon as possible after harvest. This will expose some of the covered edges to UV light and start the breakdown process.
- Mow down crop immediately after the last harvest to allow UV light to continue the breakdown process.
- When film is brittle, disk the beds. Then, angle or cross-disk to break mulch (especially the edges) into small fragments.
- Plant a cover crop to trap larger fragments and prevent them from blowing around. Plant a border strip of a tall-growing grass around the field to prevent fragments from blowing into neighboring areas.

Adapted from G. J. Hochmuth. Polyethylene Mulching for Early Vegetable Production in North Florida. Fla. Coop. Ext. Serv. Circ. 805 (1990) and E. R. Kee, P. Mulrooney, D. Caron, and J. Whalen. Commercial Vegetable Production. Del. Coop. Ext. Bull. 137 (1995).

Row covers have been used for many years for early growth enhancement of certain vegetables in a few production areas such as San Diego County, California. New materials and methods have been developed recently which make the use of row covers a viable production practice wherever vegetables are seeded or transplanted when temperatures are below optimum and early production is desired. Row covers, when properly used, will result in earlier harvest and perhaps greater total production. There are two general types of row covers—supported and floating; many variations of the row cover concept are possible, depending on the needs of the individual grower. Row covers generally work best when used in conjunction with black polyethylene-mulched rows or beds.

Supported Row Covers

Clear polyethylene, 5–6 ft wide and 1 to 1½ mils thick, is the most convenient material to use and is generally used just once. Slitted row covers have slits 5 in. long and ¾ in. apart in two rows. The slits, arranged at the upper sides of the constructed supported row cover, provide ventilation; otherwise the cover would have to be manually opened and closed each day. Hoops of no. 8 or no. 9, are cut 63 in. long for 5-ft. wide polyethylene.

Hoops are installed over the polyethylene-mulched crop so that the center of the hoop is 14–16 in. above the row. The slitted row cover can be mechanically applied over the hoops with a high-clearance tractor and a modified mulch applicator.

Floating Row Covers

Floating row covers are made of spun-bonded polyester and polypropylene. The material appears very similar to the fabrics used in the clothing industry for interlining, interfacing, and other uses. It is white or off-white, porous to air and water, very lightweight (0.6 oz/sq yd) and transmits about 80% of the light. The material comes in rolls 67 in. wide and 250–2500 ft long. One-piece blankets are also available. With care, the spun-bonded fabrics can be used two to three or more times.

Immediately after planting (seeds or transplants) the spun-bonded fabric is laid directly over the row, and the edges are secured with soil, boards, bricks, or wire pins. Because the material is of such light weight, the plants will push up the fabric as the plants grow. Accordingly, enough slack should be provided to allow for the plants to reach maximum size during the time the material is left over the plants. For bean or tomato, about 12 in. of slack should be left. For a crop such as cucumber, 8 in. is sufficient.

Floating covers can be left over vegetables for 3–8 weeks, depending on the crop and the weather. For tomato and pepper, it can be left on for about 1 month but should be removed (at least partially) when the temperature under the covers reaches 86°F and is likely to remain that high for several hours.

The blossoms of muskmelon can withstand very high temperatures, but the cover must be removed when the first female flowers appear so that bees can begin pollination.

Frost Protection

Frost protection with slitted and floating covers is not as good as with solid plastic covers. A maximum of 3–4°F is all that can be expected, whereas with solid covers, frost protection of 5–7°F has been attained. Row covers should not be viewed merely as a frost-protection system but as a growth-intensifying system during cool spring weather. Therefore, do not attempt to plant very early and hope to be protected against heavy frosts. An earlier planting date of 10 days to 2 weeks would be more reasonable. The purpose of row covers is to increase productivity through an economical increase of early and perhaps total production per unit area.

Adapted from O. S. Wells and J. B. Loy, Row Covers for Intensive Vegetable Production, New Hampshire Cooperative Extension Service (1985).

Windbreaks are important considerations in an intensive vegetable production system. Use of windbreaks can result in increased yield and earlier crop production.

Young plants are most susceptible to wind damage and "sand blasting." Rye or other tall-growing grass strips between rows can provide protection from wind and wind-borne sand. Windbreaks can improve early plant growth and earlier crop production, particularly with melons, cucumbers, squash, peppers, eggplant, tomatoes, and okra.

A major benefit of a windbreak is improved use of moisture. Reducing the wind speed reaching the crop reduces both the direct evaporation from the soil and the moisture transpired by the crop. This moisture advantage also improves conditions for seed germination. Seeds germinate more rapidly and young plants establish root systems more quickly. Improved moisture conditions continue to enhance crop growth and development throughout the growing season.

The type and height of the windbreak determine its effect. Windbreaks can be living or nonliving. Rye strips are suggested for intensive vegetable production based on economics. In general, windbreaks should be as close as economically viable, for example, every three or four beds of melons. The windbreak should be planted perpendicular to the prevailing wind direction. Rye strips should be planted prior to the crop to be protected so as to obtain good plant establishment and to provide adequate time for plant growth prior to beginning the next production season. Fertilization and pest management of rye windbreaks may be necessary to encourage growth to the desired height.

Adapted from J. R. Schultheis, D. C. Sanders, and K. B. Perry. Windbreaks and Drive Rows. p. 9. In D. C. Sanders (ed.), A Guide to Intensive Vegetable Systems. N. C. Coop. Ext. AG-502 (1993).

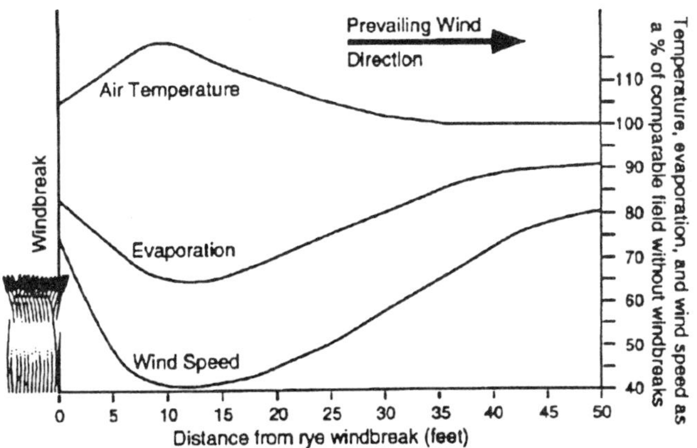

Air temperature, evaporation rate, and wind speed changes with distance from the windbreak. Variables are expressed as percent of their level if the windbreak was not present.

PART 4

SOILS AND FERTILIZERS

ORGANIC MATTER

SOIL-IMPROVING CROPS

MANURES

SOIL TEXTURE

SOIL REACTION

SALINITY

FERTILIZERS

FERTILIZER CONVERSION FACTORS

NUTRIENT ABSORPTION

PLANT ANALYSIS

SOIL TESTS

FERTILIZER APPLICATION RATES

NUTRIENT DEFICIENCIES

MICRONUTRIENTS

FERTILIZER DISTRIBUTORS

FUNCTION OF ORGANIC MATTER IN SOIL

Rapid decomposition of fresh organic matter contributes most effectively to the physical condition of a soil. Plenty of moisture, nitrogen, and a warm temperature speed up the rate of decomposition.

Organic matter serves as a source of energy for soil microorganisms and as a source of plant nutrients.

Organic matter holds the minerals absorbed from the soil against loss by leaching until they are released by the action of microorganisms.

Bacteria thriving on the organic matter produce complex carbohydrates that cement soil particles together into aggregates.

Acids produced in the decomposition of organic matter may make available mineral nutrients of the soil to crop plants.

The entrance and percolation of water into and through the soil are facilitated. This reduces losses of soil by erosion.

Penetration of roots through the soil is improved by good structure brought about by the decomposition of organic matter.

The water-holding capacity of sands and sandy soils may be increased by the incorporation of organic matter. Aggregation in heavy soils may improve drainage.

It is seldom possible to make a large permanent increase in the organic-matter content of a soil.

ORGANIC SOIL AMENDMENTS

Animal manures, sludges, and plant materials have been used commercially for decades for vegetable production. Today, society demands efficient use of natural materials so that recycling of wastes into agriculture is viewed as important. Many municipalities are producing solid waste materials that can be used on the farm as soil amendments and sources of mineral nutrients for plants. The technology of compost production and utilization is still developing. One challenge for the grower is to locate compost sources that can produce a product of consistent chemical and physical quality. Incompletely composted waste, sometimes called "green" compost, can reduce crop growth because nitrogen is "robbed" or used by the microorganisms to decompose the organic matter in the compost. Growers contemplating use of soil amendments will need to thoroughly investigate the quality of the product, including testing for nutrient content.

ENVIRONMENTAL ASPECTS OF ORGANIC SOIL AMENDMENTS

Although the addition of organic matter, such as manures, to the soil can have beneficial effects on crop performance, there are some potential negative effects. As the nitrogen is released from the organic matter, it can be subject to leaching. Heavy applications of manure could contribute to groundwater pollution unless a crop is planted soon to utilize the nitrogen. This potential can be especially great for southern climates where nitrogen release can be rapid, and most nitrogen is released in the first season after application. Plastic mulch placed over the manured soil will reduce the potential for nitrate leaching. In today's environmentally aware world, manures must be used carefully to manage the released nutrients.

TYPICAL COMPOSITION OF MANURES

Manures vary greatly in their nutrient content. The kind of feed used, the percentage and type of litter or bedding, the moisture content, and the age and degree of decomposition or drying all modify the composition. In the case of the commercially dried, pulverized manures, some nitrogen is lost in the process. The following data are representative analyses from widely scattered reports.

		Approximate Composition (% dry weight)		
Source	Dry Matter (%)	N	P_2O_5	K_2O
Dairy	15–25	0.6–2.1	0.7–1.1	2.4–3.6
Feedlot	20–40	1.0–2.5	0.9–1.6	2.4–3.6
Horse	15–25	1.7–3.0	0.7–1.2	1.2–2.2
Poultry	20–30	2.0–4.5	4.5–6.0	1.2–2.4
Sheep	25–35	3.0–4.0	1.2–1.6	3.0–4.0
Swine	20–30	3.0–4.0	0.4–0.6	0.5–1.0

NITROGEN LOSSES FROM ANIMAL MANURE TO THE AIR BY METHOD OF APPLICATION

Application Method	Type of Manure	Nitrogen Loss (%) [1]
Broadcast without incorporation	Solid	15–30
	Liquid	10–25
Broadcast with incorporation	Solid	1–5
	Liquid	1–5
Injection (Knifing)	Liquid	0–2
Irrigation	Liquid	30–40

Adapted from D. E. Chaney, L. E. Drinkwater, and G. S. Pettygrove. Organic Soil Amendments and Fertilizers. University of California Division of Agriculture and Natural Resources Publication 21505 (1992).

[1] Loss within 3 days of application.

Under most environments the nutrients in organic materials become available to plants slowly. However, mineralization of nutrients in organic matter can be rapid under warm, humid conditions. For example, in Florida most usable nitrogen can be made available from poultry manure during one season. There is considerable variation in nutrient content among samples of organic soil amendments. Commercial manure products should have a summary of the chemical analyses provided on the container. Growers should have any organic soil amendment tested for nutrient content so that fertilization programs can be planned. The data below are representative of many noted in the literature and in reports of state analytical laboratories.

	Percentage on a Dry Weight Basis		
Organic Materials	N	P_2O_5	K_2O
Bat guano	10.0	4.0	2.0
Blood	13.0	2.0	1.0
Bone meal, raw	3.0	22.0	—
Bone meal, steamed	1.0	15.0	—
Castor bean meal	5.5	2.0	1.0
Cottonseed meal	6.6	3.0	1.5
Fish meal	10.0	6.0	—
Garbage tankage	2.5	2.0	1.0
Peanut meal	7.0	1.5	1.2
Sewage sludge	1.5	1.3	0.4
Sewage sludge, activated	6.0	3.0	0.2
Soybean meal	7.0	1.2	1.5
Tankage	7.0	10.0	1.5

Materials	Moisture (%)	Approximate Pounds per Ton of Dry Material N	P_2O_5	K_2O
Alfalfa hay	10	50	11	50
Alfalfa straw	7	28	7	36
Barley hay	9	23	11	33
Barley straw	10	12	5	32
Bean straw	11	20	6	25
Beggarweed hay	9	50	12	56
Buckwheat straw	11	14	2	48
Clover hay				
Alyce	11	35	—	—
Bur	8	60	21	70
Crimson	11	45	11	67
Ladino	12	60	13	67
Sweet	8	60	12	38
Cowpea hay	10	60	13	36
Cowpea straw	9	20	5	38
Field pea hay	11	28	11	30
Field pea straw	10	20	5	26
Horse bean hay	9	43	—	—
Lezpedeza hay	11	41	8	22
Lezpedeza straw	10	21	—	—
Oat hay	12	26	9	20
Oat straw	10	13	5	33
Ryegrass hay	11	26	11	25
Rye hay	9	21	8	25
Rye straw	7	11	4	22
Sorghum stover, Hegari	13	18	4	—
Soybean hay	12	46	11	20
Soybean straw	11	13	6	15
Sudan grass hay	11	28	12	31
Sweet corn fodder	12	30	8	24
Velvet bean hay	7	50	11	53
Vetch hay				
Common	11	43	15	53
Hairy	12	62	15	47
Wheat hay	10	20	8	35
Wheat straw	8	12	3	19

Adapted from *Morrison Feeds and Feeding*, Morrison Publishing Co., Ithaca, NY (1948).

SEED REQUIREMENTS OF SOIL-IMPROVING CROPS AND AREAS OF ADAPTATION

Soil-Improving Crops	Seed (lb/acre)	U.S. Area Where Crop is Adapted
Winter Cover Crops		
Legumes		
Berseem (*Trifolium alexandrinum*)	15	West and southeast
Black medic (*Medicago lupulina*)	15	All
Black lupine (*Lupinus hirsutus*)	70	All
Clover		
Crimson (*Trifolium incarnatum*)	15	South and southeast
Bur, California (*Medicago hispida*)	25	South
Southern (*M. arabica*) unhulled	100	Southeast
Tifton (*M. rigidula*) unhulled	100	Southeast
Sour (*Melilotus indica*)	20	South
Sweet, hubam (*Melilotus alba*)	20	All
Fenugreek (*Trigonella foenum-graecum*)	30	Southwest
Field pea (*Pisum sativum*)		
Canada	80	All
Austrian winter	70	All
Horse bean (*Vicia faba*)	100	Southwest and southeast
Rough pea (*Lathyrus hirsutus*)	60	Southwest and southeast
Vetch		
Bitter (*Vicia ervilia*)	30	West and southeast
Common (*V. sativa*)	50	West and southeast
Hairy (*V. villosa*)	30	All
Hungarian (*V. pannonica*)	50	West and southeast
Monantha (*V. articulata*)	40	West and southeast
Purple (*V. bengalensis*)	40	West and southeast
Smooth (*V. villosa* var. *glabrescens*)	30	All
Woollypod (*V. dasycarpa*)	30	Southeast
Nonlegumes		
Barley (*Hordeum vulgare*)	75	All
Mustard (*Brassica nigra*)	20	All
Oat (*Avena sativa*)	75	All
Rape (*Brassica napus*)	20	All
Rye (*Secale cereale*)	75	All
Wheat (*Triticum sativum*)	75	All

SEED REQUIREMENTS OF SOIL-IMPROVING CROPS AND AREAS OF ADAPTATION—Continued

Soil-Improving Crops	Seed (lb/acre)	U.S. Area Where Crop is Adapted
	Summer Cover Crops	
Legumes		
Alfalfa (*Medicago sativa*)	20	All
Beggarweed (*Desmodium purpureum*)	10	Southeast
Clover		
Alyce (*Alysicarpus vaginalis*)	20	Southeast
Crimson (*Trifolium incartum*)	15	Southeast
Red (*T. pratense*)	10	All
Cowpea (*Vigna sinensis*)	90	South and southwest
Hairy indigo (*Indigofera hirsuta*)	10	Southern tier
Lezpedeza		
Common (*Lezpedeza striata*)	25	Southeast
Korean (*L. stipulacea*)	20	Southeast
Sesbania (*Sesbania exaltata*)	30	Southwest
Soybean (*Glycine max*)	75	All
Sweet clover, white (*Melilotus alba*)	20	All
Sweet clover (*M. officinalis*)	20	All
Velvet bean (*Stizolobium deeringianum*)	100	Southeast
Nonlegumes		
Buckwheat (*Fagopyrum esculentum*)	75	All
Pearl millet (*Pennisetum glaucum*)	25	Southern and southeast
Sorghum, Hegari (*Sorghum vulgare*)	40	Western half
Sudan grass (*Sorghum vulgare* var. *sudanese*)	25	All

Adapted from Growing Summer Cover Crops, USDA Farmer's Bulletin 2182 (1967); P. R. Henson and E. A. Hollowell, Winter Annual Legumes for the South, USDA Farmers Bulletin 2146 (1960); and P. R. Miller, W. A. Williams, and B. A. Madson. Covercrops for California Agriculture. Univ. of Calif. Div. Agr. and Nat. Res. Pub. 21471 (1989).

DECOMPOSITION OF SOIL-IMPROVING CROPS

The normal carbon:nitrogen (C:N) ratio in soils is about 10:1. Turning under organic matter alters this ratio because most organic matter is richer in carbon than in nitrogen. Unless the residue contains at least 1.5% nitrogen, the decomposing organisms will utilize soil nitrogen as the energy source for the decomposition process. Soil organisms can tie up as much as 25 lb of nitrogen per acre from the soil in the process of decomposition of carbon-rich fresh organic matter.

A soil-improving crop should be fertilized adequately with nitrogen. This fertilization will increase the nitrogen content somewhat and improve layer decomposition. Nitrogen may have to be added as the soil-improving crop is incorporated into the soil. This speeds the decomposition and prevents a temporary shortage of nitrogen for the succeeding vegetable crop.

As a general rule, about 20 lb of nitrogen should be added for each ton of dry matter for a nonlegume green-manure crop.

APPROXIMATE CARBON TO NITROGEN RATIOS OF COMMON ORGANIC MATERIALS

Material	C:N Ratio
Alfalfa	12:1
Sweet clover, young	12:1
Sweet clover, mature	24:1
Rotted manure	20:1
Oat straw	75:1
Corn stalks	80:1
Timothy straw	80:1
Sawdust	300:1

SOIL TEXTURE

The particles of a soil are classified by size into sand, silt, and clay. The classification of soil-particle sizes is shown in the table.

Soil-Particle Size Classes (diameter, mm)

	2.0	0.02	0.002	0
Gravel	Sand	Silt	Clay	
Particles visible with the naked eye		Particles visible under microscope	Particles visible under electron microscope	

The percentage of sand, silt, and clay may be plotted on the diagram to determine the textural class of that soil.

Example: A soil containing 13% clay, 41% silt, and 46% sand would have a loam texture.

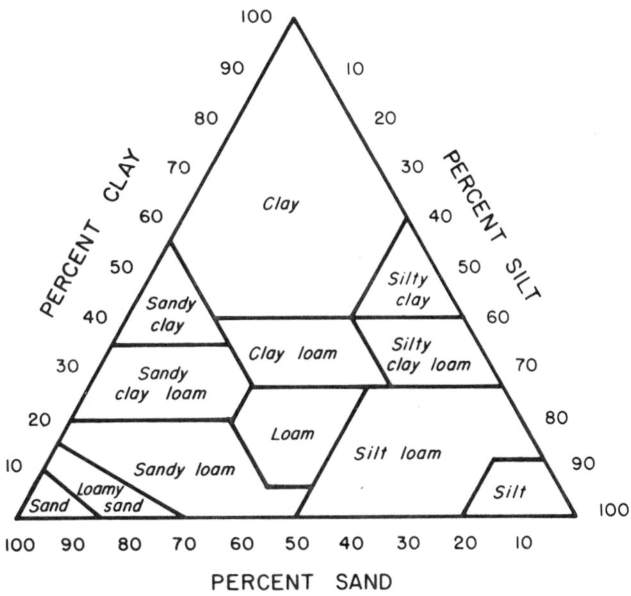

Soil textural triangle. From Soil Conservation Service, *Soil Survey Manual*, USDA Agricultural Handbook 18 (1951).

RELATIVE TOLERANCE OF VEGETABLE CROPS TO SOIL ACIDITY

Vegetables in the slightly tolerant group can be grown successfully on soils that are on the alkaline side of neutrality. They do well up to pH 7.6 if there is no deficiency of essential nutrients. Vegetables in the very tolerant group will grow satisfactorily at a soil pH as low as 5.0. For the most part even the most tolerant crops grow better at pH 6.0–6.8 than in more acid soils. Calcium, phosphorus, magnesium, and molybdenum are the nutrients most likely to be deficient in acid soils.

Slightly Tolerant (pH 6.8–6.0)	Moderately Tolerant (pH 6.8–5.5)	Very Tolerant (pH 6.8–5.0)
Asparagus	Bean	Chicory
Beet	Bean, lima	Dandelion
Broccoli	Brussels sprouts	Endive
Cabbage	Carrot	Fennel
Cauliflower	Collards	Potato
Celery	Corn	Rhubarb
Chard, Swiss	Cucumber	Shallot
Chinese cabbage	Eggplant	Sorrel
Cress	Garlic	Sweet potato
Leek	Gherkin	Watermelon
Lettuce	Horseradish	
Muskmelon	Kale	
New Zealand spinach	Kohlrabi	
Okra	Mustard	
Onion	Parsley	
Orach	Pea	
Parsnip	Pepper	
Salsify	Pumpkin	
Soybean	Radish	
Spinach	Rutabaga	
Watercress	Squash	
	Strawberry	
	Tomato	
	Turnip	

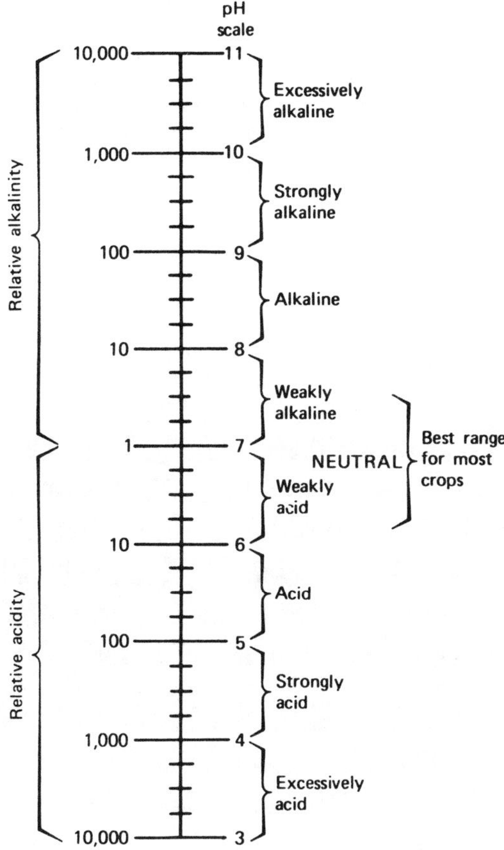

Relation Between pH, Alkalinity, Acidity, and Plant Growth.

Soil reaction affects plants by influencing the availability of nutrients. Changes in soil reaction caused by liming or by the use of sulfur and acid-forming fertilizers may increase or decrease the supply of the nutrients available to the plants.

The general relationship between soil reaction and availability of plant nutrients in organic soils differs from that in mineral soils. The diagrams depict nutrient availability for both mineral and organic soils. The width of the band indicates the availability of the nutrient. It does not indicate the actual amount present.

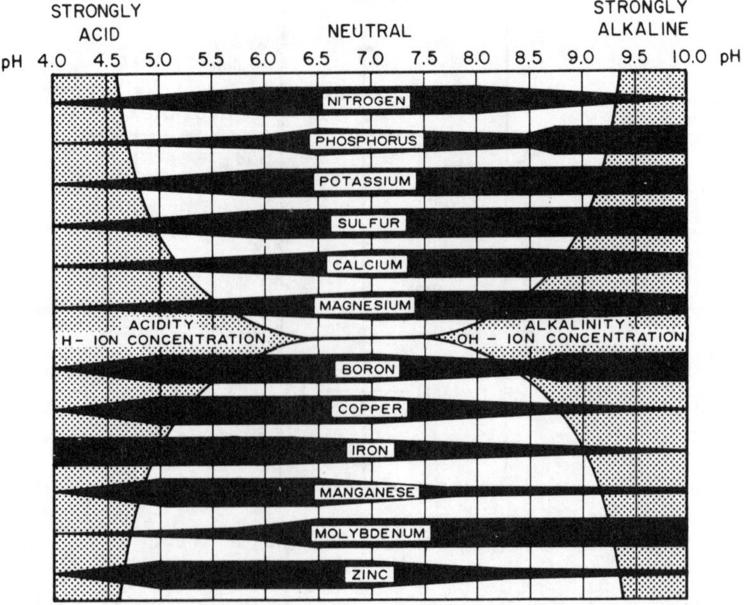

Influence of pH on the availability of plant nutrients in organic soils; widest parts of the shaded areas indicate maximum availability of each element.

Adapted from R. E. Lucas and J. F. Davis, Relationships Between pH Values of Organic Soils and Availability of 12 Plant Nutrients, *Soil Science* 92:177–182 (1961).

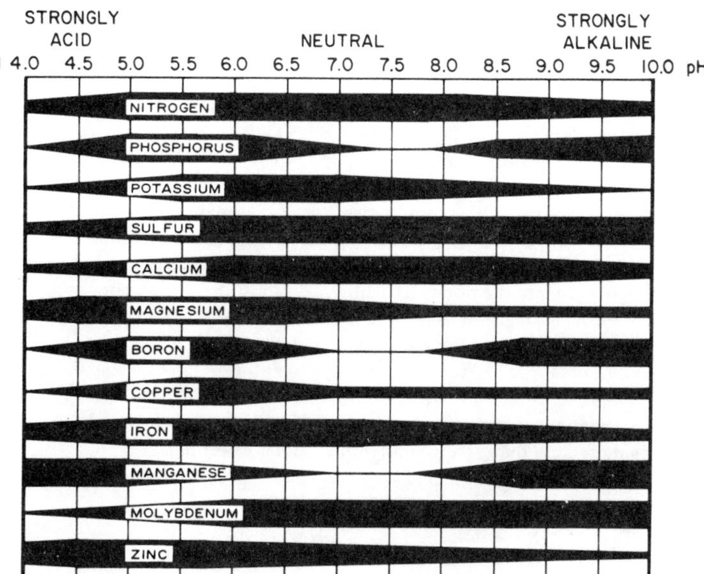

Influence of pH on the availability of plant nutrients in mineral soils; widest parts of the shaded areas indicate maximum availability of each element.

Adapted from L. B. Nelson (ed.), *Changing Patterns in Fertilizer Use*, Soil Science Society of America, Madison, WI (1968).

CORRECTION OF SOIL ACIDITY

Liming materials are used to change an unfavorable acidic soil reaction to a pH more favorable for crop production. However, soil types differ in their response to liming, a property referred to as the soil's pH buffering capacity. Acidic soil reaction is caused by hydrogen ions present in the soil solution ("active acidity") and attached to soil particles or organic matter ("potential acidity"). Active acidity can be neutralized rapidly, whereas potential acidity is neutralized over time as the potential acidity is released. Soils vary in their relative content of these sources of acidity. Due to this complexity in soil pH, it is difficult to provide a rule of thumb for rates of liming materials. Most soil testing laboratories now use a lime requirement test to estimate the potential acidity and therefore provide a more accurate liming recommendation than could be done before. The lime requirement test treats the soil sample with a buffer solution to estimate the potential acidity, and thus provides a more accurate lime recommendation than can usually be obtained by treating the soil sample with water only. Soils with similar amounts of active acidity might have different amounts of potential acidity and thus require different lime recommendations even though the rule-of-thumb approach might have given similar lime recommendations. Soils with large potential acidity (clays and mucks) will require more lime than sandy soils with a similar water pH.

COMMON LIMING MATERIALS

Materials	Chemical Formula	Pure $CaCO_3$ Equivalent (%)	Liming Material (lb) Necessary to Equal 100 lb of Limestone
Burned lime	CaO	150	64
Hydrated lime	$Ca(OH)_2$	120	82
Dolomitic limestone	$CaCO_3$, $MgCO_3$	104	86
Limestone	$CaCO_3$	95	100
Marl	$CaCO_3$	95	100
Shell, oyster, etc.	$CaCO_3$	95	100

COMMON ACIDIFYING MATERIALS [1]

Material	Chemical Formula	Sulfur (%)	Acidifying Material (lb) Necessary to Equal 100 lb of Soil Sulfur
Soil sulfur	S	99.0	100
Sulfuric acid (98%)	H_2SO_4	32.0	306
Sulfur dioxide	SO_2	50.0	198
Lime-sulfur solution (32° Baumé)	CaS_x + water	24.0	417
Iron sulfate	$FeSO_4 \cdot 7H_2O$	11.5	896
Aluminum sulfate	$Al_2(SO_4)_3$	14.4	694

[1] Certain fertilizer materials also markedly increase soil acidity when used in large quantities (see page 142).

APPROXIMATE QUANTITY OF SOIL SULFUR NEEDED TO INCREASE SOIL ACIDITY TO ABOUT pH 6.5

Change in pH Desired	Sulfur (lb/acre) Sands	Loams	Clays
8.5–6.5	2000	2500	3000
8.0–6.5	1200	1500	2000
7.5–6.5	500	800	1000
7.0–6.5	100	150	300

EFFECT OF SOME FERTILIZER MATERIALS ON THE SOIL REACTION

Materials	N (%)	Pounds of Limestone ($CaCO_3$) Per lb of N	Pounds of Limestone ($CaCO_3$) Per 100 lb of the Fertilizer Material
		Needed to Counteract the Acidity Produced	
Acidity-Forming			
Ammonium nitrate	33.5	1.80	60
Monoammonium phosphate	11	5.35	59
Ammonium phosphate sulfate	16	5.35	88
Ammonium sulfate	21	5.35	110
Anhydrous ammonia	82	1.80	148
Aqua ammonia	24	1.80	44
Aqua ammonia	30	1.80	54
Diammonium phosphate	16–18	1.80	70
Liquid phosphoric acid	52 (P_2O_5)	—	110
Urea	46	1.80	84
		Equivalents Produced	
Alkalinity-Forming			
Calcium cyanamide	22	2.85	63
Calcium nitrate	15.5	1.35	20
Potassium nitrate	13	1.80	23
Sodium nitrate	16	1.80	29
Neutral			
Ammonium nitrate-lime	Potassium sulfate		
Calcium sulfate (gypsum)	Superphosphate		
Potassium chloride			

Based on the method of W. H. Pierre, Determination of Equivalent Acidity and Basicity of Fertilizers, Industrial Engineering Chemical Analytical Edition, 5:229–234 (1933).

RELATIVE SALT EFFECTS OF FERTILIZER MATERIALS ON THE SOIL SOLUTION

When fertilizer materials are placed close to seeds or plants they may increase the osmotic pressure of the soil solution and cause injury to the crop. The term "salt index" refers to the effect of a material in relation to that produced by sodium nitrate, which is given a rating of 100. The "partial index" shows the relationships per unit (20 lb) of the actual nutrient supplied. Any material with a high salt index must be used with great care.

Material	Salt Index	Partial Salt Index per Unit of Plant Food
Anhydrous ammonia	47.1	0.572
Ammonium nitrate	104.7	2.990
Ammonium nitrate–lime (Cal-Nitro)	61.1	2.982
Ammonium sulfate	69.0	3.253
Calcium carbonate (limestone)	4.7	0.083
Calcium nitrate	52.5	4.409
Calcium sulfate (gypsum)	8.1	0.247
Diammonium phosphate	29.9	1.614 [1]
		0.637 [2]
Dolomite (calcium and magnesium carbonates)	0.8	0.042
Monoammonium phosphate	34.2	2.453 [1]
		0.485 [2]
Monocalcium phosphate	15.4	0.274
Nitrogen solution, 37%	77.8	2.104
Potassium chloride, 50%	109.4	2.189
Potassium chloride, 60%	116.3	1.936
Potassium nitrate	73.6	5.336 [1]
		1.580 [3]
Potassium sulfate	46.1	0.853
Sodium chloride	153.8	2.899
Sodium nitrate	100.0	6.060
Sulfate of potash–magnesia	43.2	1.971
Superphosphate, 20%	7.8	0.390
Superphosphate, 45%	10.1	0.224
Urea	75.4	1.618

Adapted from L. F. Rader, L. M. White, and C. W. Whittaker, The Salt Index—A Measure of the Effect of Fertilizers on the Concentrationof the Soil Solution, *Soil Science* 55:201–218 (1943).

[1] N. [2] P_2O_5. [3] K_2O.

RELATIVE SALT TOLERANCE OF VEGETABLES

The indicated salt tolerances are based on growth rather than yield. With most crops there is little difference in salt tolerance among varieties. Boron tolerances may vary depending upon climate, soil condition, and crop varieties.

Vegetable	Maximum Soil Salinity Without Yield Loss (Threshold) (dS/m)	Decrease in Yield at Soil Salinities Above the Threshold (% per dS/m)
Sensitive crops		
Bean	1.0	19
Carrot	1.0	14
Strawberry	1.0	33
Onion	1.2	16
Moderately sensitive		
Turnip	0.9	9
Radish	1.2	13
Lettuce	1.3	13
Pepper	1.5	14
Sweet potato	1.5	11
Broad bean	1.6	10
Corn	1.7	12
Potato	1.7	12
Cabbage	1.8	10
Celery	1.8	6
Spinach	2.0	8
Cucumber	2.5	13
Tomato	2.5	10
Broccoli	2.8	9
Squash, scallop	3.2	16
Moderately tolerant		
Beet	4.0	9
Squash, zucchini	4.7	9

Adapted from E. V. Maas, Crop Tolerance, *California Agriculture* (October, 1984).

Note: 1 decisiemens per meter (dS/m) = 1 mmho/cm
= approximately 640 mg/liter salt

SOIL SALINITY

With an increase in soil salinity plant roots extract water less easily from the soil solution. This situation is more critical under hot and dry than under humid conditions. High soil salinity may result also in toxic concentrations of ions in plants. Soil salinity is determined by finding the electrical conductivity of the soil saturation extract (ECe). The electrical conductivity is measured in millimhos per centimeter (mmho/cm). One mmho/cm is equivalent to 1 decisiemens per meter (dS/m) and, on the average, to 640 ppm of salt.

CROP RESPONSE TO SALINITY

Salinity (expressed as ECe, mmho/cm, or as dS/m)	Crop Responses
0–2	Salinity effects mostly negligible
2–4	Yields of very sensitive crops may be restricted
4–8	Yields of many crops restricted
8–16	Only tolerant crops yield satisfactorily
Above 16	Only a few very tolerant crops yield satisfactorily

Adapted from Leon Bernstein, Salt Tolerance of Plants, USDA Agricultural Information Bulletin 283 (1970).

Grade or *analysis* means the minimum guarantee of the percentage of total nitrogen (N), available phosphoric acid (P_2O_5), and water-soluble potash (K_2O) in the fertilizer.

Example: 20–0–20 or 5–15–5.

Ratio is the grade reduced to its simplest terms.

Example: A 20–0–20 has a ratio of 1–0–1, as does a 10–0–10.

Formula shows the actual pound and percentage composition of the various ingredients or compounds that are mixed together to make up a ton of fertilizer.

An *open-formula mix* carries the formula as well as the grade on the tag attached to each bag.

Carrier, simple, or *source* is the material or compound in which a given plant nutrient is found or supplied.

Example: Ammonium nitrate and urea are sources or carriers that supply nitrogen.

Unit means 1% of 1 ton or 20 lb. On the basis of a ton, the units per ton are equal to the percentage composition or the pounds per 100 lb.

Example: Ammonium sulfate contains 21% nitrogen, or 21 lb of nitrogen/100 lb, or 21 units of nitrogen in a ton.

Primary nutrient refers to nitrogen, phosphorus, and potassium, which are used in considerable quantities by crops.

Secondary nutrient refers to calcium, magnesium, and sulfur, which are used in moderate quantities by crops.

Micronutrient, trace, or *minor element* refers to the essential plant nutrients used in relatively small quantities.

APPROXIMATE COMPOSITION OF SOME CHEMICAL FERTILIZER MATERIALS [1]

Fertilizer Material	Total Nitrogen (% N)	Available Phosphorus (% P_2O_5)	Water-Soluble Potassium (% K_2O)
Nitrogen			
Ammonium nitrate	33.5	—	—
Ammonium nitrate-lime (A-N-L, Cal-Nitro)	20.5	—	—
Monoammonium phosphate	11.0	48.0	—
Ammonium phosphate-sulfate	16.0	20.0	—
Ammonium sulfate	21.0	—	—
Anhydrous ammonia	82.0	—	—
Aqua ammonia	20.0	—	—
Calcium cyanamide	21.0	—	—
Calcium nitrate	15.5	—	—
Calcium ammonium nitrate	17.0	—	—
Diammonium phosphate	16–18	46.0–48.0	—
Potassium nitrate	13.0	—	44.0
Sodium nitrate	16.0	—	—
Urea	46.0	—	—
Urea formaldehyde	38.0	—	—
Phosphorus			
Phosphoric acid solution	—	52.0–54.0	—
Normal (single) superphosphate	—	18.0–20.0	—
Concentrated (triple or treble) superphosphate	—	45.0–46.0	—
Monopotassium phosphate	—	53.0	—
Potassium			
Potassium chloride	—	—	60.0–62.0
Potassium nitrate	13.0	—	44.0
Potassium sulfate	—	—	50.0–53.0
Sulfate of potash-magnesia	—	—	26.0
Monopotassium phosphate	—	—	34.0

[1] See page 142 for effect of these materials on soil reaction.

SOLUBILITY OF FERTILIZER MATERIALS

Solubility of fertilizer materials is an important factor in preparing starter solutions, foliar sprays, and for solutions to be knifed into the soil or injected into an irrigation system. Hot water may be needed to get the chemicals dissolved.

Material	Solubility in Cold Water (lb/100 gal)
Primary Nutrients	
Ammonium nitrate	984
Ammonium sulfate	592
Calcium cyanamide	Decomposes
Calcium nitrate	851
Diammonium phosphate	358
Monoammonium phosphate	192
Potassium nitrate	108
Sodium nitrate	608
Superphosphate, single	17
Superphosphate, treble	33
Urea	651
Secondary and Micronutrients	
Ammonium molybdate	Decomposes
Borax	8
Calcium chloride	500
Copper oxide	Insoluble
Copper sulfate	183
Ferrous sulfate	242
Magnesium sulfate	592
Maganese sulfate	876
Sodium chloride	300
Sodium molybdate	467
Zinc sulfate	625

CONVERSION FACTORS FOR FERTILIZER MATERIALS

Multiply	By	To Obtain Equivalent Nutrient
Ammonia—NH_3	4.700	Ammonium nitrate—NH_4NO_3
Ammonia—NH_3	3.879	Ammonium sulfate—$(NH_4)_2SO_4$
Ammonia—NH_3	0.823	Nitrogen—N
Ammonium nitrate—NH_4NO_3	0.350	Nitrogen—N
Ammonium sulfate—$(NH_4)_2SO_4$	0.212	Nitrogen—N
Borax—$Na_2B_4O_7 \cdot 10H_2O$	0.114	Boron—B
Boric acid—H_3BO_3	0.177	Boron—B
Boron—B	8.813	Borax—$Na_2B_4O_7 \cdot 10H_2O$
Boron—B	5.716	Boric acid—H_3BO_3
Calcium—Ca	1.399	Calcium oxide—CaO
Calcium—Ca	2.498	Calcium carbonate—$CaCO_3$
Calcium—Ca	1.849	Calcium hydroxide—$Ca(OH)_2$
Calcium—Ca	4.296	Calcium sulfate—$CaSO_4 \cdot 2H_2O$ (gypsum)
Calcium carbonate—$CaCO_3$	0.400	Calcium—Ca
Calcium carbonate—$CaCO_3$	0.741	Calcium hydroxide—$Ca(OH)_2$
Calcium carbonate—$CaCO_3$	0.560	Calcium oxide—CaO
Calcium carbonate—$CaCO_3$	0.403	Magnesia—MgO
Calcium carbonate—$CaCO_3$	0.842	Magnesium carbonate—$MgCO_3$
Calcium hydroxide—$Ca(OH)_2$	0.541	Calcium—Ca
Calcium hydroxide—$Ca(OH)_2$	1.351	Calcium carbonate—$CaCO_3$
Calcium hydroxide—$Ca(OH)_2$	0.756	Calcium oxide—CaO
Calcium oxide—CaO	0.715	Calcium—Ca
Calcium oxide—CaO	1.785	Calcium carbonate—$CaCO_3$
Calcium oxide—CaO	1.323	Calcium hydroxide—$Ca(OH)_2$
Calcium oxide—CaO	3.071	Calcium sulfate—$CaSO_4 \cdot 2H_2O$ (gypsum)
Gypsum—$CaSO_4 \cdot 2H_2O$	0.326	Calcium oxide—CaO
Gypsum—$CaSO_4 \cdot 2H_2O$	0.186	Sulfur—S
Magnesia—MgO	2.480	Calcium carbonate—$CaCO_3$
Magnesia—MgO	0.603	Magnesium—Mg

Multiply	By	To Obtain Equivalent Nutrient
Magnesia—MgO	2.092	Magnesium carbonate—$MgCO_3$
Magnesia—MgO	2.986	Magnesium sulfate—$MgSO_4$
Magnesia—MgO	6.114	Magnesium sulfate—$MgSO_4 \cdot 7H_2O$ (Epsom salts)
Magnesium—Mg	4.116	Calcium carbonate—$CaCO_3$
Magnesium—Mg	1.658	Magnesia—MgO
Magnesium—Mg	3.466	Magnesium carbonate—$MgCO_3$
Magnesium—Mg	4.951	Magnesium sulfate—$MgSO_4$
Magnesium—Mg	10.136	Magnesium sulfate—$MgSO_4 \cdot 7H_2O$ (Epsom salts)
Magnesium carbonate—$MgCO_3$	1.187	Calcium carbonate—$CaCO_3$
Magnesium carbonate—$MgCO_3$	0.478	Magnesia—MgO
Magnesium carbonate—$MgCO_3$	0.289	Magnesium—Mg
Magnesium sulfate—$MgSO_4$	0.335	Magnesia—MgO
Magnesium sulfate—$MgSO_4$	0.202	Magnesium—Mg
Magnesium sulfate—$MgSO_4 \cdot 7H_2O$ (Epsom salts)	0.164	Magnesia—MgO
Magnesium sulfate—$MgSO_4 \cdot 7H_2O$ (Epsom salts)	0.099	Magnesium—Mg
Manganese—Mn	2.749	Manganese(ous) sulfate—$MnSO_4$
Manganese—Mn	4.060	Manganese(ous) sulfate—$MnSO_4 \cdot 4H_2O$
Manganese(ous) sulfate—$MnSO_4$	0.364	Manganese—Mn
Manganese(ous) sulfate—$MnSO_4 \cdot 4H_2O$	0.246	Manganese—Mn
Nitrate—NO_3	0.226	Nitrogen—N
Nitrogen—N	1.216	Ammonia—NH_3
Nitrogen—N	2.856	Ammonium nitrate—NH_4NO_3
Nitrogen—N	4.716	Ammonium sulfate—$(NH_4)_2SO_4$
Nitrogen—N	4.426	Nitrate—NO_3
Nitrogen—N	6.068	Sodium nitrate—$NaNO_3$
Nitrogen—N	6.250	Protein
Phosphoric acid—P_2O_5	0.437	Phosphorus—P

Multiply	By	To Obtain Equivalent Nutrient
Phosphorus—P	2.291	Phosphoric acid—P_2O_5
Potash—K_2O	1.583	Potassium chloride—KCl
Potash—K_2O	2.146	Potassium nitrate—KNO_3
Potash—K_2O	0.830	Potassium—K
Potash—K_2O	1.850	Potassium sulfate—K_2SO_4
Potassium—K	1.907	Potassium chloride—KCl
Potassium—K	1.205	Potash—K_2O
Potassium—K	2.229	Potassium sulfate—K_2SO_4
Potassium chloride—KCl	0.632	Potash—K_2O
Potassium chloride—KCl	0.524	Potassium—K
Potassium nitrate—KNO_3	0.466	Potash—K_2O
Potassium nitrate—KNO_3	0.387	Potassium—K
Potassium sulfate—K_2SO_4	0.540	Potash—K_2O
Potassium sulfate—K_2SO_4	0.449	Potassium—K
Sodium nitrate—$NaNO_3$	0.165	Nitrogen—N
Sulfur—S	5.368	Calcium sulfate—$CaSO_4 \cdot 2H_2O$ (gypsum)
Sulfur—S	2.497	Sulfur trioxide—SO_3
Sulfur—S	3.059	Sulfuric acid—H_2SO_4
Sulfur trioxide—SO_3	0.401	Sulfur—S
Sulfuric acid—H_2SO_4	0.327	Sulfur—S

Examples: 80 lb of ammonia (NH_3) contains the same amount of N as 310 lb of ammonium sulfate [$(NH_4)_2SO_4$] $80 \times 3.88 = 310$. 1000 lb of calcium carbonate multiplied by 0.400 equals 400 lb of calcium. A material contains 20% phosphoric acid. This percentage (20) multiplied by 0.437 equals 8.74% phosphorus.

AMOUNT OF CARRIERS NEEDED TO SUPPLY A CERTAIN AMOUNT OF NUTRIENT PER ACRE [1]

Nutrients (lb/acre):	20	40	60	80	100	120	160	200
% Nutrient in Carrier	Carriers Needed (lb)							
3	667	1333	2000					
4	500	1000	1500	2000				
5	400	800	1200	1600	2000			
6	333	667	1000	1333	1667	2000		
7	286	571	857	1142	1429	1714		
8	250	500	750	1000	1250	1500	2000	
9	222	444	667	889	1111	1333	1778	
10	200	400	600	800	1000	1200	1600	2000
11	182	364	545	727	909	1091	1455	1818
12	166	333	500	666	833	1000	1333	1666
13	154	308	462	615	769	923	1231	1538
15	133	267	400	533	667	800	1067	1333
16	125	250	375	500	625	750	1000	1250
18	111	222	333	444	555	666	888	1111
20	100	200	300	400	500	600	800	1000
21	95	190	286	381	476	571	762	952
25	80	160	240	320	400	480	640	800
30	67	133	200	267	333	400	533	667
34	59	118	177	235	294	353	471	588
42	48	95	143	190	238	286	381	476
45	44	89	133	178	222	267	356	444
48	42	83	125	167	208	250	333	417
50	40	80	120	160	200	240	320	400
60	33	67	100	133	167	200	267	333

[1] This table can be used in determining the acre rate for applying a material in order to supply a certain number of pounds of a nutrient.

Example: A carrier provides 34% of a nutrient. To get 200 lb of the nutrient, 588 lb of the material is needed; and for 60 lb of the nutrient, 177 lb of carrier is required.

APPROXIMATE RATES OF MATERIALS TO PROVIDE CERTAIN QUANTITIES OF NITROGEN PER ACRE

	N (lb/acre):	15	30	45	60	75	100
Fertilizer Material	% N	Material to Apply (lb/acre)					
Solids							
Ammonium nitrate	33	45	90	135	180	225	300
Ammonium phosphate (48% P_2O_5)	11	135	270	410	545	680	910
Ammonium phosphate—sulfate (20% P_2O_5)	16	95	190	280	375	470	625
Ammonium sulfate	21	70	140	215	285	355	475
Calcium nitrate	15.5	95	195	290	390	485	645
Potassium nitrate	13	115	230	345	460	575	770
Sodium nitrate	16	95	190	280	375	470	625
Urea	46	35	65	100	130	165	215
Liquids							
Anhydrous ammonia (approx. 5 lb/gal) [1]	82	20	35	55	75	90	120
Aqua ammonium phosphate (24% P_2O_5; approx. 10 lb/gal)	8	190	375	560	750	940	1250
Aqua ammonia (approx. 7½ lb/gal) [1]	20	75	150	225	300	375	500
Nitrogen solution (approx. 11 lb/gal)	32	50	100	150	200	250	330

[1] To avoid burning, especially on alkaline soils, these materials must be placed deeper and further away from the plant row than you would place dry fertilizers.

RATES OF APPLICATION FOR CERTAIN NITROGEN SOLUTIONS

Nitrogen (lb/acre)	Nitrogen Solution Needed (gal/acre)		
	21% Solution	32% Solution	41% Solution
20	8.9	5.6	5.1
25	11.1	7.1	6.4
30	13.3	8.5	7.7
35	15.6	9.9	9.0
40	17.8	11.3	10.3
45	20.0	12.7	11.5
50	22.2	14.1	12.8
55	24.4	15.5	14.1
60	26.7	16.5	15.4
65	28.9	18.4	16.7
70	31.1	19.8	17.9
75	33.3	21.2	19.2
80	35.6	22.6	20.5
85	37.8	24.0	21.8
90	40.0	25.4	23.1
95	42.2	26.8	24.4
100	44.4	28.2	25.6
110	48.9	31.1	28.2
120	53.3	33.9	30.8
130	57.8	36.7	33.3
140	62.2	39.6	35.9
150	66.7	42.4	38.5
200	88.9	56.5	51.3

Adapted from C. W. Gandt, W. C. Hulburt, and H. D. Brown, Hose Pump for Applying Nitrogen Solutions, USDA Farmer's Bulletin 2096 (1956).

Many states issue suggested rates of application of fertilizers for specific vegetables. These recommendations are sometimes made according to the type of soil, that is, light or heavy, sands, loams, clays, peats, and mucks. Other factors often used in establishing these rates are whether manure or soil-improving crops are employed and whether an optimum moisture supply can be maintained. The nutrient requirements of the crop to be grown must be considered, as well as the past fertilizer and cropping history. The season of the year will affect nutrient availability. Broad recommendations are at best only a point from which to make adjustments to suit your conditions. Each field may require a different fertilizer program for the same vegetable.

Calibrated soil testing can provide an estimate of the concentration of essential elements that will be available to the crop during the season and predict the amount of fertilizer needed to produce a crop. Various extraction solutions are used by soil testing labs around the country to estimate the nutrient supplying capacity of the soil, and not all solutions are calibrated for all soils. Therefore, growers must exercise care in selecting a lab to analyze soil samples, and use only those labs that employ analytical procedures calibrated with yield response in specific soil types and growing regions. Even though several labs might differ in lab procedures, if all procedures are calibrated, then fertilizer recommendations should be similar. If unclear about specific soil testing practices, growers should consult their Cooperative Extension Service and the specific analytical lab.

Phosphorus. This element is not very mobile in most agricultural soils. Phosphorus is fixed in soils with basic reactions and large quantities of calcium, or in acidic soils containing aluminum or iron. Even though phosphorus can be fixed, if a calibrated soil test predicts no response to phosphorus fertilization, then growers need not add large amounts of phosphorus because enough phosphorus will be made available to the crop during the growing season even though the soil has a high phosphorus fixing capacity. Sometimes crops might respond to small amounts of starter phosphorus supplied to high phosphorus testing soils in cold planting seasons.

Potassium. Although not generally considered a mobile element in soils, potassium can leach in coarse, sandy soils. Clay soils and loamy soils often contain adequate amounts of available potassium and may not need fertilization with potassium. Coarse, sandy soils usually test medium or low in extractable potassium and respond to potassium fertilization.

Nitrogen. Most soil testing labs have no calibrated soil test for nitrogen because nitrogen is highly mobile in most soils and predicting a crop's response to nitrogen fertilization from a soil test is risky. However, some labs do predict N supplying capacity of a soil from a determination of soil organic matter. Estimates vary from 20 to 40 lb of nitrogen made available during the season for each percent soil organic matter. Another soil nitrogen estimation procedure being used by some labs is the presidedress soil nitrate test. This test predicts the likelihood of need for sidedressed nitrogen during the season but is relatively insensitive for predicting exact amounts of sidedress nitrogen.

PREDICTED RESPONSES OF CROPS TO RELATIVE AMOUNTS OF EXTRACTED PLANT NUTRIENTS BY SOIL TEST

Soil Test Interpretation	Predicted Crop Response
Very high	No crop response predicted to fertilization with a particular element
High	No crop response predicted to fertilization with a particular element
Medium	75 to 100% of maximum expected yield predicted without fertilization
Low	50 to 75% of maximum expected yield predicted without fertilization
Very low	25 to 50% of maximum expected yield predicted without fertilization

APPROXIMATE CROP CONTENT OF NUTRIENT ELEMENTS

Sometimes crop removal values are used to estimate fertilizer needs by crops. Removal values are obtained by analyzing plants and fruits for nutrient content and then expressing the results on an acre basis. It is risky to relate fertilizer requirements on specific soils to generalized listings of crop removal values. A major problem is that crop removal values are usually derived from analyzing plants grown on fertile soils where much of the nutrient content of the crop is supplied from soil reserves rather than from fertilizer application. Since plants can absorb larger amounts of specific nutrients than they require, crop removal values can overestimate the true crop nutrient requirement of a crop. The crop content (removal) values presented in the table are presented for information purposes and are not suggested for use in formulating fertilizer recommendations.

APPROXIMATE ACCUMULATION OF NUTRIENTS BY SOME VEGETABLE CROPS

Vegetable	Yield (cwt/acre)	Nutrient Absorption (lb/acre)		
		N	P	K
Broccoli	100 heads	20	2	45
	Other	145	8	165
		165	10	210
Brussels sprouts	160 sprouts	150	20	125
	Other	85	9	110
		235	29	235
Carrot	500 roots	80	20	200
	Tops	65	5	145
		145	25	345
Celery	1000 tops	170	35	380
	Roots	25	15	55
		195	50	435
Honeydew melon	290 fruits	70	8	65
	Vines	135	15	95
		205	23	160
Lettuce	350 plants	95	12	170
Muskmelon	225 fruits	95	17	120
	Vines	60	8	35
		155	25	155
Onion	400 bulbs	110	20	110
	Tops	35	5	45
		145	25	155
Pea, shelled	40 peas	100	10	30
	Vines	70	12	50
		170	22	80

APPROXIMATE ACCUMULATION OF NUTRIENTS BY SOME VEGETABLE CROPS—Continued

Vegetable	Yield (cwt/acre)	Nutrient Absorption (lb/acre)		
		N	P	K
Pepper	225 fruits	45	6	50
	Plants	95	6	90
		140	12	140
Potato	400 tubers	150	19	200
	Vines	60	11	75
		210	30	275
Snap bean	100 beans	120	10	55
	Plants	50	6	45
		170	16	100
Spinach	200 plants	100	12	100
Sweet corn	130 ears	55	8	30
	Plants	100	12	75
		155	20	105
Sweet potato	300 roots	80	16	160
	Vines	60	4	40
		140	20	200
Tomato	600 fruits	100	10	180
	Vines	80	11	100
		180	21	280

PLANT ANALYSIS GUIDE FOR SAMPLING TIME, PLANT PART, AND NUTRIENT LEVELS OF VEGETABLE CROPS (DRY-WEIGHT BASIS)

Crop	Time of Sampling	Plant Part	Source	Nutrient[1]	Nutrient Level: Deficient	Nutrient Level: Sufficient
Asparagus	Midgrowth of fern	4-in. tip section of new fern branch	NO_3	N, ppm	100	500
			PO_4	P, ppm	800	1,600
				K, %	1	3
Bean, bush snap	Midgrowth	Petiole of 4th leaf from tip	NO_3	N, ppm	2,000	3,000
			PO_4	P, ppm	1,000	2,000
				K, %	3	5
	Early bloom	Petiole of 4th leaf from tip	NO_3	N, ppm	1,000	1,500
			PO_4	P, ppm	800	1,500
				K, %	2	4
Broccoli	Midgrowth	Midrib of young, mature leaf	NO_3	N, ppm	7,000	9,000
			PO_4	P, ppm	2,500	4,000
				K, %	3	5
	First buds	Midrib of young, mature leaf	NO_3	N, ppm	5,000	7,000
			PO_4	P, ppm	2,500	4,000
				K, %	2	4
Brussels sprouts	Midgrowth	Midrib of young, mature leaf	NO_3	N, ppm	5,000	7,000
			PO_4	P, ppm	2,000	3,500
				K, %	3	5

	Late growth	Midrib of young, mature leaf	NO_3	N, ppm	2,000	3,000
			PO_4	P, ppm	1,000	3,000
				K, %	2	4
Cabbage	At heading	Midrib of wrapper leaf	NO_3	N, ppm	5,000	7,000
			PO_4	P, ppm	2,500	3,500
				K, %	2	4
Chinese cabbage	At heading	Midrib of wrapper leaf	NO_3	N, ppm	8,000	10,000
			PO_4	P, ppm	2,000	3,000
				K, %	4	7
Carrot	Midgrowth	Petiole of young, mature leaf	NO_3	N, ppm	5,000	7,500
			PO_4	P, ppm	2,000	3,000
				K, %	4	6
Cauliflower	Buttoning	Midrib of young, mature leaf	NO_3	N, ppm	5,000	7,000
			PO_4	P, ppm	2,500	3,500
				K, %	2	4
Celery	Midgrowth	Petiole of newest fully elongated leaf	NO_3	N, ppm	5,000	7,000
			PO_4	P, ppm	2,500	3,000
				K, %	4	7
	Near maturity	Petiole of newest fully elongated leaf	NO_3	N, ppm	4,000	6,000
			PO_4	P, ppm	2,000	3,000
				K, %	3	5
Cucumber, pickling	Early fruit set	Petiole of 6th leaf from tip	NO_3	N, ppm	5,000	7,500
			PO_4	P, ppm	1,500	2,500
				K, %	3	5

PLANT ANALYSIS GUIDE FOR SAMPLING TIME, PLANT PART, AND NUTRIENT LEVELS OF VEGETABLE CROPS (DRY-WEIGHT BASIS)—Continued

Crop	Time of Sampling	Plant Part	Source	Nutrient[1]	Nutrient Level	
					Deficient	Sufficient
Cucumber, slicing	Early harvest period	Petiole of 6th leaf from growing tip	NO_3	N, ppm	5,000	7,500
			PO_4	P, ppm	1,500	2,500
				K, %	4	7
Eggplant	At first harvest	Petiole of young, mature leaf	NO_3	N, ppm	5,000	7,500
			PO_4	P, ppm	2,000	3,000
				K, %	4	7
Garlic	Early growth (prebulbing)	Newest fully elongated leaf	PO_4	P, ppm	2,000	3,000
				K, %	3	4
	Midseason (bulbing)	Newest fully elongated leaf	PO_4	P, ppm	2,000	3,000
				K, %	2	3
	Late season (postbulbing)	Newest fully elongated leaf	PO_4	P, ppm	2,000	3,000
				K, %	1	2
Lettuce	At heading	Midrib of wrapper leaf	NO_3	N, ppm	4,000	6,000
			PO_4	P, ppm	2,000	3,000
				K, %	2	4

	At harvest	Midrib of wrapper leaf	NO_3	N, ppm	3,000	5,000
			PO_4	P, ppm	1,500	2,500
				K, %	1.5	2.5
Muskmelon	Early growth (short runners)	Petiole of 6th leaf from growing tip	NO_3	N, ppm	8,000	12,000
			PO_4	P, ppm	2,000	3,000
				K, %	4	6
	Early fruit	Petiole of 6th leaf from growing tip	NO_3	N, ppm	5,000	8,000
			PO_4	P, ppm	1,500	2,500
				K, %	3	5
	First mature fruit	Petiole of 6th leaf from growing tip	NO_3	N, ppm	2,000	3,000
			PO_4	P, ppm	1,000	2,000
				K, %	2	4
	Early growth	Blade of 6th leaf from growing tip	NO_3	N, ppm	2,000	3,000
			PO_4	P, ppm	1,500	2,300
				K, %	1	2.5
	Early fruit	Blade of 6th leaf from growing tip	NO_3	N, ppm	1,000	1,500
			PO_4	P, ppm	1,300	1,700
				K, %	1	2.0
	First mature fruit	Blade of 6th leaf from growing tip	NO_3	N, ppm	500	800
			PO_4	P, ppm	1,000	1,500
				K, %	1	1.8
Onion	Early season	Tallest leaf	PO_4	P, ppm	1,000	2,000
				K, %	3	4.5
	Midseason	Tallest leaf	PO_4	P, ppm	1,000	2,000
				K, %	2	4
	Late season	Tallest leaf	PO_4	P, ppm	1,000	2,000
				K, %	2	3

PLANT ANALYSIS GUIDE FOR SAMPLING TIME, PLANT PART, AND NUTRIENT LEVELS OF VEGETABLE CROPS (DRY-WEIGHT BASIS)—Continued

Crop	Time of Sampling	Plant Part	Source	Nutrient[1]	Nutrient Level: Deficient	Nutrient Level: Sufficient
Pepper, chili	Early growth first bloom	Petiole of young, mature leaf	NO_3	N, ppm	5,000	7,000
			PO_4	P, ppm	2,000	2,500
				K, %	3	5
	Early fruit set	Petiole of young, mature leaf	NO_3	N, ppm	1,000	1,500
			PO_4	P, ppm	1,500	2,000
				K, %	2	4
	Fruits, full size	Petiole of young, mature leaf	NO_3	N, ppm	750	1,000
			PO_4	P, ppm	1,500	2,000
				K, %	1.5	3
	Early growth first bloom	Blade of young, mature leaf	NO_3	N, ppm	1,500	2,000
			PO_4	P, ppm	1,500	2,000
				K, %	3	5
	Early fruit set	Blade of young, mature leaf	NO_3	N, ppm	500	800
			PO_4	P, ppm	1,500	2,000
				K, %	2	4
Pepper, sweet	Early growth, first flower	Petiole of young, mature leaf	NO_3	N, ppm	8,000	10,000
			PO_4	P, ppm	2,000	3,000
				K, %	4	6

Crop	Time of Sampling	Plant Part	Nutrient Form		Deficient	Sufficient
	Early fruit set, 1 in. diameter	Petiole of young, mature leaf	NO_3	N, ppm	5,000	7,000
			PO_4	P, ppm	1,500	2,500
				K, %	3	5
	Fruit ¾ size	Petiole of young, mature leaf	NO_3	N, ppm	3,000	5,000
			PO_4	P, ppm	1,200	2,000
				K, %	2	4
	Early growth, first flower	Blade of young, mature leaf	NO_3	N, ppm	2,000	3,000
			PO_4	P, ppm	1,800	2,500
				K, %	3	5
	Early fruit set, 1 in. diameter	Blade of young, mature leaf	NO_3	N, ppm	1,500	2,000
			PO_4	P, ppm	1,500	2,000
				K, %	2	4
Potato	Early season	Petiole of 4th leaf from growing tip	NO_3	N, ppm	8,000	12,000
			PO_4	P, ppm	1,200	2,000
				K, %	9	11
	Midseason	Petiole of 4th leaf from growing tip	NO_3	N, ppm	6,000	9,000
			PO_4	P, ppm	800	1,600
				K, %	7	9
	Late season	Petiole of 4th leaf from growing tip	NO_3	N, ppm	3,000	5,000
			PO_4	P, ppm	500	1,000
				K, %	4	6
Spinach	Midgrowth	Petiole of young, mature leaf	NO_3	N, ppm	4,000	6,000
			PO_4	P, ppm	2,000	3,000
				K, %	2	4
Summer squash (zucchini)	Early bloom	Petiole of young, mature leaf	NO_3	N, ppm	12,000	15,000
			PO_4	P, ppm	4,000	6,000
				K, %	6	10

PLANT ANALYSIS GUIDE FOR SAMPLING TIME, PLANT PART, AND NUTRIENT LEVELS OF VEGETABLE CROPS (DRY-WEIGHT BASIS)—Continued

Crop	Time of Sampling	Plant Part	Source	Nutrient[1]	Nutrient Level	
					Deficient	Sufficient
Sweet corn	Tasseling	Midrib of 1st leaf above primary ear	NO_3	N, ppm	500	1,000
			PO_4	P, ppm	500	1,000
				K, %	2	4
Sweet potato	Midgrowth	Petiole of 6th leaf from the growing tip	NO_3	N, ppm	1,500	2,500
			PO_4	P, ppm	1,000	2,000
				K, %	3	5
Tomato, cherry	Early fruit set	Petiole of 4th leaf from the growing tip	NO_3	N, ppm	8,000	10,000
			PO_4	P, ppm	2,000	3,000
				K, %	4	7
	Fruit ½ in. diameter	Petiole of 4th leaf from growing tip	NO_3	N, ppm	5,000	7,000
			PO_4	P, ppm	2,000	3,000
				K, %	3	5
	At first harvest	Petiole of 4th leaf from growing tip	NO_3	N, ppm	1,000	2,000
			PO_4	P, ppm	2,000	3,000
				K, %	2	4

Tomato, processing and determinate, fresh market	Early bloom	Petiole of 4th leaf from growing tip	NO_3	N, ppm	8,000	12,000
			PO_4	P, ppm	2,000	3,000
				K, %	3	6
	Fruit 1 in. diameter	Petiole of 4th leaf from growing tip	NO_3	N, ppm	4,000	6,000
			PO_4	P, ppm	1,500	2,500
				K, %	2	4
	First color	Petiole of 4th leaf from growing tip	NO_3	N, ppm	2,000	3,000
			PO_4	P, ppm	1,000	2,000
				K, %	1	3
Tomato, fresh market nondeterminate	Early bloom	Petiole of 4th leaf from growing tip	NO_3	N, ppm	10,000	14,000
			PO_4	P, ppm	2,500	3,000
				K, %	4	7
	Fruit 1 in. diameter	Petiole of 4th leaf from growing tip	NO_3	N, ppm	8,000	12,000
			PO_4	P, ppm	2,500	3,000
				K, %	3	5
	Full ripe fruit	Petiole of 4th leaf from growing tip	NO_3	N, ppm	4,000	6,000
			PO_4	P, ppm	2,000	2,500
				K, %	2	4
Watermelon	Early fruit set	Petiole of 6th leaf from growing tip	NO_3	N, ppm	5,000	7,500
			PO_4	P, ppm	1,500	2,500
				K, %	3	5

Adapted from H. M. Reisenauer (ed.), Soil and Plant Tissue Testing in California, University of California Division of Agricultural Science Bulletin 1879 (1983).

[1] Two percent acetic acid-soluble NO_3–N and PO_4–P and total K (dry-weight basis). Updated 1995 personal communication T. K. Hartz, University of California, Davis. Values represent conventionally fertilized crops. Organically managed crops may show lower petiole-nitrate (NO_3–N) concentrations. Total macronutrient concentrations of whole leaves is the preferred method of evaluating nutrient sufficiency under organic fertility management.

TOTAL NUTRIENT ANALYSES FOR DIAGNOSIS OF THE NUTRIENT LEVEL OF VEGETABLE CROPS

Crop	Time of Sampling	Plant Part	Nutrient	Nutrient Level (% dry weight)	
				Deficient	Sufficient
Asparagus	Early fern growth	4 in. tip section of new fern branch	N	4.00	5.00
			P	0.20	0.40
			K	2.00	4.00
	Mature fern	4 in. tip section of new fern branch	N	3.00	4.00
			P	0.20	0.40
			K	1.00	3.00
Bean, bush snap	Full bloom	Petiole: recent fully exposed trifoliate leaf	N	1.50	2.25
			P	0.15	0.30
			K	1.00	2.50
	Full bloom	Blade: recent fully exposed trifoliate leaf	N	1.25	2.25
			P	0.25	0.40
			K	0.75	1.50
Bean, lima	Full bloom	Oldest trifoliate leaf	N	2.50	3.50
			P	0.20	0.30
			K	1.50	2.25
Celery	Midgrowth	Petiole	N	1.00	1.50
			P	0.25	0.55
			K	4.00	5.00

Garlic	Early season (prebulbing)	Newest fully elongated leaf	N	4.00	5.00
			P	0.20	0.30
			K	3.00	4.00
	Midseason (bulbing)	Newest fully elongated leaf	N	3.00	4.00
			P	0.20	0.30
			K	2.00	3.00
	Late season (postbulbing)	Newest fully elongated leaf	N	2.00	3.00
			P	0.20	0.30
			K	1.00	2.00
Lettuce	At heading	Leaves	N	1.50	3.00
			P	0.20	0.35
			K	2.50	5.00
	Nearly mature	Leaves	N	1.25	2.50
			P	0.15	0.30
			K	2.50	5.00
Muskmelon	Early growth	Petiole of 6th leaf from growing tip	N	2.50	3.50
			P	0.30	0.60
			K	4.00	6.00
	Early fruit	Petiole of 6th leaf from growing tip	N	2.00	3.00
			P	0.20	0.35
			K	3.00	5.00
	First mature fruit	Petiole of 6th leaf from growing tip	N	1.50	2.00
			P	0.15	0.30
			K	2.00	4.00
Onion	Early season	Tallest leaf	N	3.00	4.00
			P	0.10	0.20
			K	3.00	4.00

TOTAL NUTRIENT ANALYSES FOR DIAGNOSIS OF THE NUTRIENT LEVEL OF VEGETABLE CROPS—Continued

Crop	Time of Sampling	Plant Part	Nutrient	Nutrient Level (% dry weight)	
				Deficient	Sufficient
Onion (*continued*)	Midseason	Tallest leaf	N	2.50	3.00
			P	0.10	0.20
			K	2.50	4.00
	Late season	Tallest leaf	N	2.00	2.50
			P	0.10	0.20
			K	2.00	3.00
Pepper, sweet	Full bloom	Blade and petiole	N	3.00	4.00
			P	0.15	0.25
			K	1.50	2.50
	Full bloom, fruit ¾ size	Blade and petiole	N	2.50	3.50
			P	0.12	0.20
			K	1.00	2.00
Potato	Early, plants 12 in. tall	Petiole of 4th leaf from tip	N	2.50	3.50
			P	0.20	0.30
			K	9.00	11.00
	Midseason	Petiole of 4th leaf from tip	N	2.25	2.75
			P	0.10	0.20
			K	7.00	9.00

	Late, nearly mature	Petiole of 4th leaf from tip	N	1.50	2.25
			P	0.08	0.15
			K	4.00	6.00
	Early, plants 12 in. tall	Blade of 4th leaf from tip	N	4.00	6.00
			P	0.30	0.60
			K	3.50	5.00
	Midseason	Blade of 4th leaf from tip	N	3.00	5.00
			P	0.20	0.40
			K	2.50	3.50
	Late, nearly mature	Blade of 4th leaf from tip	N	2.00	4.00
			P	0.10	0.20
			K	1.50	2.50
Southern pea (cowpea)	Full bloom	Blade and petiole	N	2.00	3.50
			P	0.20	0.30
			K	1.00	2.00
Spinach	Midgrowth	Mature leaf blade and petiole	N	2.00	4.00
			P	0.20	0.40
			K	3.00	6.00
	At harvest	Mature leaf blade and petiole	N	1.50	3.00
			P	0.20	0.35
			K	2.00	5.00
Sweet corn	Tasseling	Sixth leaf from base of plant	N	2.75	3.50
			P	0.18	0.28
			K	1.75	2.25
	Silking	Leaf opposite first ear	N	1.50	2.00
			P	0.20	0.30
			K	1.00	2.00

TOTAL NUTRIENT ANALYSES FOR DIAGNOSIS OF THE NUTRIENT LEVEL OF VEGETABLE CROPS—Continued

Crop	Time of Sampling	Plant Part	Nutrient	Nutrient Level (% dry weight)	
				Deficient	Sufficient
Tomato (determinate)	Flowering	Leaf blade and petiole	N	2.50	3.50
			P	0.20	0.30
			K	1.50	2.50
	First ripe fruit	Leaf blade and petiole	N	1.50	2.50
			P	0.15	0.25
			K	1.00	2.00

Adapted from H. M. Reisenauer (ed.), Soil and Plant Tissue Testing in California, University of California Division of Agricultural Science Bulletin 1879 (1983). Updated 1995, personal communication T. K. Hartz, University of California, Davis.

CRITICAL (DEFICIENCY) VALUES, ADEQUATE RANGES, HIGH VALUES, AND TOXICITY VALUES FOR PLANT NUTRIENT CONTENT FOR VEGETABLES

Crop	Plant Part[1]	Time of Sampling	Status	% N	% P	% K	% Ca	% Mg	% S	ppm Fe	ppm Mn	ppm Zn	ppm B	ppm Cu	ppm Mo
Bean, snap	MRM trifoliate leaf	Before bloom	Deficient	<3.0	0.25	2.0	0.8	0.20	0.20	25	20	20	15	5	—
			Adequate range	3.0	0.25	2.0	0.8	0.20	0.40	25	20	20	15	5	0.4
				4.0	0.45	3.0	1.5	0.45	0.40	200	100	40	40	10	1.0
			High	>4.1	0.46	3.1	1.6	0.45	0.40	200	100	40	40	10	—
			Toxic (>)	—	—	—	—	—	—	—	1000	—	150	—	—
	MRM trifoliate leaf	First bloom	Deficient	<3.0	0.25	2.0	0.8	0.25	0.20	25	20	20	15	5	—
			Adequate range	3.0	0.25	2.0	0.8	0.26	0.21	25	20	20	15	5	0.4
				4.0	0.45	3.0	1.5	0.45	0.40	200	100	40	40	10	1.0
			High	>4.1	0.46	3.1	1.6	0.45	0.40	200	100	40	40	10	—
			Toxic (>)	—	—	—	—	—	—	—	1000	—	150	—	—
	MRM trifoliate	Full bloom	Deficient	<2.5	0.20	1.5	0.8	0.25	0.20	25	20	20	15	5	—
			Adequate range	2.5	0.20	1.6	0.8	0.26	0.21	25	20	20	15	5	0.4
				4.0	0.40	2.5	1.5	0.45	0.40	200	100	40	40	10	1.0
			High	>4.1	0.41	2.5	1.6	0.45	0.40	200	100	40	40	10	—
			Toxic (>)	—	—	—	—	—	—	—	1000	—	150	—	—

CRITICAL (DEFICIENCY) VALUES, ADEQUATE RANGES, HIGH VALUES, AND TOXICITY VALUES FOR PLANT NUTRIENT CONTENT FOR VEGETABLES—Continued

Crop	Plant Part[1]	Time of Sampling	Status	%						ppm					
				N	P	K	Ca	Mg	S	Fe	Mn	Zn	B	Cu	Mo
Beet, table	Leaf blades	5 weeks	Deficient	<3.0	0.22	2.0	1.5	0.25	—	40	30	15	30	5	0.05
		after seeding	Adequate	3.0	0.25	2.0	1.5	0.25	0.60	40	30	15	30	5	0.20
			range	5.0	0.40	6.0	2.0	1.00	0.80	200	200	30	80	10	0.60
			High	>5.0	0.40	6.0	2.0	1.00	—	—	—	—	80	10	—
			Toxic (>)	—	—	—	—	—	—	—	—	—	650	—	—
	Leaf	9 weeks	Deficient	<2.5	0.20	1.7	1.5	0.30	—	—	—	15	30	5	0.05
	blades	after seeding	Adequate	2.6	0.20	1.7	1.5	0.30	0.60	—	70	15	60	5	0.60
			range	4.0	0.30	4.0	3.0	1.00	0.80	—	200	30	80	10	—
			High	>4.0	0.30	4.0	3.0	1.00	—	—	—	—	80	10	—
			Toxic (>)	—	—	—	—	—	—	—	—	—	650	—	—
Broccoli	MRM	Heading	Deficient	<3.0	0.30	1.1	0.8	0.23	0.20	40	20	25	20	3	0.04
	leaf		Adequate	3.0	0.30	1.5	1.2	0.23	—	40	25	45	30	5	0.04
			range	4.5	0.50	4.0	2.5	0.40	—	300	150	95	50	10	0.16
			High	>4.5	0.50	4.0	2.5	0.40	—	300	150	100	100	10	—
Brussels	MRM	At early	Deficient	<2.2	0.20	2.4	0.4	0.20	0.20	50	20	20	20	4	0.04
sprouts	leaf	sprouts	Adequate	2.2	0.20	2.4	0.4	0.20	0.20	50	20	20	30	5	0.16
			range	5.0	0.60	3.5	2.0	0.40	0.80	150	200	80	70	10	0.16
			High	>5.0	0.60	3.5	2.0	0.40	0.80	150	200	80	70	—	—

Cabbage	MRM	5 weeks	Deficient	<3.2	0.30	2.8	0.5	0.25	—	30	20	30	20	3	0.3
	leaf	after	Adequate	3.2	0.30	2.8	1.1	0.25	0.30	30	20	30	20	3	0.3
		transplanting	range	6.0	0.60	5.0	2.0	0.60	—	60	40	50	40	7	0.6
			High	>6.0	0.60	5.0	2.0	0.60	—	100	40	50	40	10	—
	MRM	8 weeks	Deficient	<3.0	0.30	2.0	0.5	0.20	—	30	20	30	20	3	0.3
	leaf	after	Adequate	3.0	0.30	2.0	1.5	0.25	0.30	30	20	30	20	3	0.3
		transplanting	range	6.0	0.60	4.0	2.0	0.60	—	60	40	50	40	7	0.6
			High	>6.0	0.60	4.0	2.0	0.60	—	100	40	50	40	10	—
	Wrapper	Heads	Deficient	<3.0	0.30	1.7	0.5	0.25	—	20	20	20	30	4	0.3
	leaf	½ grown	Adequate	3.0	0.30	2.3	1.5	0.25	0.30	20	20	20	30	4	0.3
			range	4.0	0.50	4.0	2.0	0.45	—	40	40	30	50	8	0.6
			High	>4.0	0.50	4.0	2.0	0.45	—	100	40	40	50	10	—
	Wrapper	At harvest	Deficient	<1.8	0.26	1.2	0.5	0.25	—	20	20	20	30	4	0.3
	leaf		Adequate	1.8	0.26	1.5	1.5	0.25	0.30	20	20	20	30	4	0.3
			range	3.0	0.40	3.0	2.0	0.45	—	40	40	30	50	8	0.6
			High	>3.0	0.40	3.0	2.0	0.45	—	100	40	40	50	10	—
Carrot	MRM	60 days	Deficient	<1.8	0.20	2.0	1.0	0.15	—	30	30	20	20	4	—
	leaf	after seeding	Adequate	1.8	0.20	2.0	2.0	0.20	—	30	30	20	20	4	—
			range	2.5	0.40	4.0	3.5	0.50	—	60	60	60	40	10	—
			High	>2.5	0.40	4.0	3.5	0.50	—	60	100	60	40	10	—
	MRM	Harvest	Deficient	<1.5	0.18	1.0	1.0	0.25	—	20	30	20	20	4	—
	leaf		Adequate	1.5	0.18	1.4	1.0	0.40	—	20	30	20	20	4	—
			range	2.5	0.40	4.0	1.5	0.50	—	30	60	60	40	10	—
			High	>2.5	0.40	4.0	1.5	0.50	—	60	100	60	40	10	—
Cauliflower	MRM	Buttoning	Deficient	<3.0	0.40	2.0	0.8	0.25	0.60	30	30	30	30	5	—
	leaf		Adequate	3.0	0.40	2.0	0.8	0.25	0.60	30	30	30	30	5	—
			range	5.0	0.70	4.0	2.0	0.60	1.00	60	80	50	50	10	—
			High	>5.0	0.70	4.0	2.0	0.60	—	100	100	50	50	10	—

CRITICAL (DEFICIENCY) VALUES, ADEQUATE RANGES, HIGH VALUES, AND TOXICITY VALUES FOR PLANT NUTRIENT CONTENT FOR VEGETABLES—Continued

Crop	Plant Part[1]	Time of Sampling	Status	%						ppm					
				N	P	K	Ca	Mg	S	Fe	Mn	Zn	B	Cu	Mo
Cauliflower (*Continued*)	MRM leaf	Heading	Deficient	<2.2	0.30	1.5	1.0	0.25	—	30	50	30	30	5	—
			Adequate	2.2	0.30	1.5	1.0	0.25	—	30	50	30	30	5	—
			range	4.0	0.70	3.0	2.0	0.60	—	60	80	50	50	10	—
			High	>4.0	0.70	3.0	2.0	0.60	—	100	100	50	50	10	—
Celery	Outer petiole	6 weeks after transplanting	Deficient	<1.5	0.30	6.0	1.3	0.30	—	20	5	20	15	4	—
			Adequate	1.5	0.30	6.0	1.3	0.30	—	20	5	20	15	4	—
			range	1.7	0.60	8.0	2.0	0.60	—	30	10	40	25	6	—
			High	>1.7	0.60	8.0	2.0	0.60	—	100	20	60	25	—	—
	Outer petiole	At maturity	Deficient	<1.5	0.30	5.0	1.3	0.30	—	20	5	20	20	1	—
			Adequate	1.5	0.30	5.0	1.3	0.30	—	20	5	20	20	1	—
			range	1.7	0.60	7.0	2.0	0.60	—	30	10	40	40	3	—
			High	>1.7	0.60	7.0	2.0	0.60	—	100	20	60	40	3	—
Chinese cabbage (heading)	Oldest undamaged leaf	8-leaf stage	Deficient	<4.5	0.50	7.5	4.5	0.35	—	—	8	30	15	5	—
			Adequate	4.5	0.50	7.5	4.5	0.35	—	—	14	30	15	5	—
			range	5.0	0.60	8.5	5.0	0.45	—	—	20	50	25	10	—
			High	>5.0	0.60	8.5	5.0	0.45	—	—	20	50	25	10	—
	Oldest undamaged leaf	At maturity	Deficient	<3.5	0.30	3.0	—	0.40	—	—	7	20	30	4	—
			Adequate	3.5	0.30	3.0	3.7	0.40	—	—	13	20	30	4	—
			range	4.0	0.60	6.5	6.0	0.50	—	—	19	40	50	6	—
			High	>4.0	0.60	6.5	6.0	0.50	—	—	20	40	50	6	—

Collards	Tops	Young plants	Deficient	<4.0	0.30	3.0	1.0	0.40	—	40	40	25	25	5	—
			Adequate	4.0	0.30	3.0	1.0	0.40	—	40	40	25	25	5	—
			range	5.0	0.60	5.0	2.0	1.00	—	100	100	50	50	10	—
			High	>5.0	0.60	5.0	2.0	1.00	—	100	100	50	50	10	—
	MRM	Harvest	Deficient	<3.0	0.25	2.5	1.0	0.35	—	40	40	20	25	5	—
	leaf		Adequate	3.0	0.25	2.5	1.0	0.35	—	40	40	20	25	5	—
			range	5.0	0.50	4.0	2.0	0.10	—	100	100	40	50	10	—
			High	>5.0	0.50	4.0	2.0	0.10	—	100	100	40	50	10	—
Cucumber	MRM	Before bloom	Deficient	<3.5	0.30	1.6	2.0	0.58	0.30	40	30	20	20	5	0.2
	leaf		Adequate	3.5	0.30	1.6	2.0	0.58	0.30	40	30	20	20	5	0.3
			range	6.0	0.60	3.0	4.0	0.70	0.80	100	100	50	60	20	1.0
			High	>6.0	0.60	3.0	4.0	0.70	0.80	100	100	50	60	20	2.0
	MRM	Early bloom	Deficient	<2.5	0.25	1.6	1.3	0.30	0.30	40	30	20	20	5	0.2
	leaf		Adequate	2.5	0.25	1.6	1.3	0.30	0.30	40	30	20	20	5	0.3
			range	5.0	0.60	3.0	3.5	0.60	0.80	100	100	50	60	20	1.0
			High	>5.0	0.60	3.0	3.5	0.60	0.80	100	100	50	60	20	2.0
			Toxic (>)	—	—	—	—	—	—	—	900	950	150	—	—
Eggplant	MRM	Early fruit	Deficient	<4.2	0.30	3.5	0.8	0.25	0.40	50	50	20	20	5	0.5
	leaf	set	Adequate	4.2	0.30	3.5	0.8	0.25	0.40	50	50	20	20	5	0.5
			range	5.0	0.60	5.0	1.5	0.60	0.60	100	100	40	40	10	0.8
			High	>6.0	0.60	5.0	1.5	0.60	0.60	100	100	40	40	10	0.8
Endive	Oldest	8-leaf	Deficient	<4.5	0.45	4.5	2.0	0.25	—	—	15	30	25	5	—
	undamaged	stage	Adequate	4.5	0.45	4.5	2.0	0.25	—	—	15	30	25	5	—
	leaf		range	6.0	0.80	6.0	4.0	0.60	—	—	25	50	35	10	—
			High	>6.0	0.80	6.0	4.0	0.60	—	—	25	50	35	10	—
	Oldest	Maturity	Deficient	<3.5	0.40	4.0	1.8	0.30	—	—	15	20	30	5	—
	undamaged		Adequate	3.5	0.40	6.0	1.8	0.30	—	—	15	20	30	5	—
	leaf		range	3.5	0.60	6.0	3.0	0.40	—	—	20	40	40	10	—
			High	>4.2	0.60	6.0	3.0	0.40	—	—	20	40	40	10	—

CRITICAL (DEFICIENCY) VALUES, ADEQUATE RANGES, HIGH VALUES, AND TOXICITY VALUES FOR PLANT NUTRIENT CONTENT FOR VEGETABLES—Continued

Crop	Plant Part[1]	Time of Sampling	Status	%						ppm					
				N	P	K	Ca	Mg	S	Fe	Mn	Zn	B	Cu	Mo
Escarole	Oldest	8-leaf	Deficient	<4.2	0.45	5.7	1.7	0.25	—	—	15	30	20	4	—
	undamaged	stage	Adequate	4.2	0.45	5.7	1.7	0.25	—	—	15	30	20	4	—
	leaf		range	5.0	0.60	6.5	2.2	0.35	—	—	25	50	30	6	—
			High	>5.0	0.60	6.5	2.2	0.35	—	—	25	50	30	6	—
	Oldest	Maturity	Deficient	<3.0	0.35	5.5	2.0	0.25	—	—	15	20	30	4	—
	undamaged		Adequate	3.0	0.35	5.5	2.0	0.25	—	—	15	20	30	4	—
	leaf		range	4.5	0.45	6.5	3.0	0.35	—	—	25	50	45	6	—
			High	>4.5	0.45	6.5	3.0	0.35	—	—	25	50	45	6	—
Lettuce,	Oldest	8-leaf	Deficient	<4.0	0.40	5.0	1.0	0.40	—	50	10	40	15	5	0.1
Boston	undamaged	stage	Adequate	4.0	0.40	5.0	1.7	0.40	—	50	10	40	15	5	0.1
	leaf		range	6.0	0.60	6.0	2.0	0.60	—	100	20	60	25	10	0.2
			High	>6.0	0.60	6.0	2.0	0.60	—	100	20	60	25	10	0.4
			Toxic (>)	—	—	—	—	—	—	—	250	—	100	—	—
	Oldest	Maturity	Deficient	<3.0	0.35	5.0	1.0	0.30	—	50	10	20	15	5	0.1
	undamaged		Adequate	3.0	0.35	5.0	1.7	0.30	—	50	10	20	15	5	0.1
	leaf		range	4.0	0.45	6.0	2.0	0.60	—	100	20	40	25	10	0.2
			High	>4.0	0.45	6.0	2.0	0.60	—	100	20	40	25	10	0.4
			Toxic (>)	—	—	—	—	—	—	—	250	—	100	—	—

Lettuce,	Oldest	8-leaf	Deficient	<4.0	0.50	4.0	1.7	0.30	—	40	10	40	20	5	—
cos	undamaged	stage	Adequate	4.0	0.50	4.0	1.7	0.30	—	40	10	40	20	5	—
	leaf		range	5.0	0.60	6.0	2.0	1.70	—	100	20	60	40	10	—
			High	>5.0	0.60	6.0	2.0	1.70	—	100	20	60	40	10	—
	Oldest	Maturity	Deficient	<3.0	0.40	4.0	1.7	0.30	—	20	10	20	20	5	—
	undamaged		Adequate	3.0	0.40	4.0	1.7	0.30	—	20	10	20	20	5	—
	leaf		range	4.0	0.60	6.0	2.0	0.70	—	50	20	40	40	10	—
			High	>4.0	0.60	6.0	2.0	0.70	—	50	20	40	40	10	—
Lettuce,	MRM	8-leaf	Deficient	<4.0	0.40	5.0	1.0	0.30	—	50	20	25	15	5	—
crisphead		stage	Adequate	4.0	0.40	5.0	1.0	0.30	0.30	50	20	25	15	5	—
			range	5.0	0.60	7.0	2.0	0.50	0.50	150	40	50	30	10	—
			High	>5.0	0.60	7.0	2.0	0.50	—	150	40	50	30	10	—
	Wrapper	Heads	Deficient	<2.5	0.40	4.5	1.4	0.30	—	50	20	25	15	5	—
	leaf	½ size	Adequate	2.5	0.40	4.5	1.4	0.30	0.30	50	20	25	15	5	—
			range	4.0	0.60	8.0	2.0	0.70	0.50	150	40	50	30	10	—
			High	>4.0	0.60	8.0	2.0	0.70	—	150	40	50	30	10	—
	Wrapper	Maturity	Deficient	<2.0	0.25	2.5	1.4	0.30	—	50	20	25	15	5	—
	leaf		Adequate	2.0	0.25	2.5	1.4	0.30	0.30	50	20	25	15	5	—
			range	3.0	0.50	5.0	2.0	0.70	0.50	150	40	50	30	10	—
			High	>3.0	0.50	5.0	2.0	0.70	—	150	40	50	30	10	—
Lettuce,	Oldest	8-leaf	Deficient	<5.0	0.35	5.0	2.0	0.25	—	—	15	20	30	5	—
romaine	undamaged	stage	Adequate	5.0	0.35	5.0	2.0	0.25	—	—	15	20	30	5	—
	leaf		range	6.0	0.80	6.0	3.0	0.35	—	—	25	50	45	10	—
			High	>6.0	0.80	6.0	3.0	0.35	—	—	25	50	45	10	—
	Oldest	Maturity	Deficient	<3.5	0.35	5.0	2.0	0.25	—	—	15	20	30	5	0.1
	undamaged		Adequate	3.5	0.35	5.0	2.0	0.25	—	—	15	20	30	5	0.1
	leaf		range	4.5	0.60	6.0	3.0	0.40	—	—	25	50	45	10	0.4
			High	>4.5	0.60	6.0	3.0	0.40	—	—	25	50	45	10	—

CRITICAL (DEFICIENCY) VALUES, ADEQUATE RANGES, HIGH VALUES, AND TOXICITY VALUES FOR PLANT NUTRIENT CONTENT FOR VEGETABLES—Continued

				%						ppm					
Crop	Plant Part[1]	Time of Sampling	Status	N	P	K	Ca	Mg	S	Fe	Mn	Zn	B	Cu	Mo
Muskmelon	MRM leaf	12-inch vines	Deficient	<4.0	0.40	5.0	3.0	0.35	—	40	20	20	20	5	0.6
			Adequate	4.0	0.40	5.0	3.0	0.35	0.20	40	20	20	20	5	0.6
			range	5.0	0.70	7.0	5.0	0.45	0.50	100	100	60	80	10	1.0
			High	>5.0	0.70	7.0	5.0	0.45	—	100	100	60	80	10	1.0
			Toxic (>)	—	—	—	—	—	—	—	900	—	150	—	—
	MRM leaf	Early fruit set	Deficient	<3.5	0.25	1.8	1.8	0.30	—	40	20	20	20	5	0.6
			Adequate	3.5	0.25	1.8	1.8	0.30	0.20	40	20	20	20	5	0.6
			range	4.5	0.40	4.0	5.0	0.40	0.50	100	100	60	80	10	1.0
			High	>4.5	0.40	4.0	5.0	0.40	—	100	100	60	80	10	1.0
			Toxic (>)	—	—	—	—	—	—	—	900	—	150	—	—
Okra	MRM leaf	30 days after seeding	Deficient	<3.5	0.30	2.0	0.5	0.25	—	50	30	30	25	5	—
			Adequate	3.5	0.30	2.0	0.5	0.25	—	50	30	30	25	5	—
			range	5.0	0.60	3.0	0.8	0.50	—	100	100	50	50	10	—
			High	>5.0	0.60	3.0	0.8	0.50	—	100	100	50	50	10	—
	MRM leaf	Prior to harvest	Deficient	<2.5	0.30	2.0	1.0	0.25	—	50	30	30	25	5	—
			Adequate	2.5	0.30	2.0	1.0	0.25	—	50	30	30	25	5	—
			range	3.0	0.60	3.0	1.5	0.50	—	100	100	50	50	10	—
			High	>3.0	0.60	3.0	1.5	0.50	—	100	100	50	50	10	—

Onion, sweet	MRM	Just prior	Deficient	<2.0	0.20	1.5	0.6	0.15	0.20	—	10	15	10	5	—
	leaf	to bulb	Adequate	2.0	0.20	1.5	0.6	0.15	0.20	—	10	15	10	5	—
		initiation	range	3.0	0.50	3.0	0.8	0.30	0.60	—	20	20	25	10	—
			High	>3.0	0.50	3.0	0.8	0.30	0.60	—	20	20	25	10	—
			Toxic (>)	—	—	—	—	—	—	—	—	—	100	—	—
Pepper	MRM	Prior to	Deficient	<4.0	0.30	5.0	0.9	0.35	0.30	30	30	25	20	5	—
	leaf	blossoming	Adequate	4.0	0.30	5.0	0.9	0.35	0.30	30	30	25	20	5	—
			range	5.0	0.50	6.0	1.5	0.60	0.60	150	100	80	50	10	—
			High	>5.0	0.50	6.0	1.5	0.60	0.60	150	100	80	50	10	—
			Toxic (>)	—	—	—	—	—	—	—	—	—	350	—	—
	MRM	First	Deficient	<3.0	0.30	2.5	0.9	0.30	0.30	30	30	25	20	5	—
	leaf	blossoms	Adequate	3.0	0.30	2.5	0.9	0.30	0.30	30	30	25	20	5	—
		open	range	5.0	0.50	5.0	1.5	0.50	0.60	150	100	80	50	10	—
			High	>5.0	0.50	5.0	1.5	0.50	0.60	150	100	80	50	10	—
			Toxic (>)	—	—	—	—	—	—	—	1000	—	350	—	—
	MRM	Early fruit	Deficient	<2.9	0.25	2.5	1.0	0.30	0.30	30	30	25	20	5	—
	leaf	set	Adequate	2.9	0.25	2.5	1.0	0.30	0.30	30	30	25	20	5	—
			range	4.0	0.40	4.0	1.5	0.40	0.40	150	100	80	50	10	—
			High	>4.0	0.40	4.0	1.5	0.40	0.40	150	100	80	50	10	—
			Toxic (>)	—	—	—	—	—	—	—	—	—	350	—	—
	MRM	Early harvest	Deficient	<2.5	0.20	2.0	1.0	0.30	0.30	30	30	25	20	5	0.1
	leaf		Adequate	2.5	0.20	2.0	1.0	0.30	0.30	30	30	25	20	5	0.1
			range	3.0	0.40	3.0	1.5	0.40	0.40	150	100	80	50	10	0.2
			High	>3.0	0.40	3.0	1.5	0.40	0.40	150	100	80	50	10	—
			Toxic (>)	—	—	—	—	—	—	—	—	—	350	—	—

CRITICAL (DEFICIENCY) VALUES, ADEQUATE RANGES, HIGH VALUES, AND TOXICITY VALUES FOR PLANT NUTRIENT CONTENT FOR VEGETABLES—Continued

Crop	Plant Part[1]	Time of Sampling	Status	%						ppm					
				N	P	K	Ca	Mg	S	Fe	Mn	Zn	B	Cu	Mo
Potato	MRM	Plants	Deficient	<3.0	0.20	3.5	0.6	0.30	0.25	40	30	30	20	5	0.1
	leaf	8 to 10 in. tall	Adequate	3.0	0.20	3.5	0.6	0.30	0.25	40	30	30	20	5	0.1
			range	6.0	0.80	6.0	2.0	0.60	0.50	150	60	60	60	10	0.2
			High	>6.0	0.80	6.0	2.0	0.60	0.50	150	60	60	60	10	—
	MRM	First	Deficient	<3.0	0.20	3.0	0.6	0.25	0.20	40	30	30	20	5	0.1
	leaf	blossom	Adequate	3.0	0.20	3.0	0.6	0.25	0.20	40	30	30	20	5	0.1
			range	4.0	0.50	5.0	2.0	0.60	0.50	150	100	60	30	10	0.2
			High	>4.0	0.50	5.0	2.0	0.60	0.50	150	100	60	30	10	—
	MRM	Tubers	Deficient	<2.0	0.20	2.5	0.6	0.25	0.20	40	20	30	20	5	0.1
	leaf	½ grown	Adequate	2.0	0.20	2.5	0.6	0.25	0.20	40	20	30	20	5	0.1
			range	4.0	0.40	4.0	2.0	0.60	0.50	150	100	60	30	10	0.2
			High	>4.0	0.40	4.0	2.0	0.60	0.50	150	100	60	30	10	—
	MRM	At tops-down	Deficient	<2.0	0.16	1.5	0.6	0.20	0.20	40	20	30	20	5	0.1
	leaf		Adequate	2.0	0.16	1.5	0.6	0.20	0.20	40	20	30	20	5	0.1
			range	3.0	0.40	3.0	2.0	0.50	0.50	150	100	60	30	10	0.2
			High	>3.0	0.40	3.0	2.0	0.50	0.50	150	100	60	30	10	—
Pumpkin	MRM	5 weeks	Deficient	<3.0	0.30	2.3	0.9	0.35	0.20	40	40	20	25	5	0.3
	leaf	after seeding	Adequate	3.0	0.30	2.3	0.9	0.35	0.20	40	40	20	25	5	0.3
			range	6.0	0.50	4.0	1.5	0.60	0.40	100	100	50	40	10	0.5
			High	>6.0	0.50	4.0	1.5	0.60	0.40	100	100	50	40	10	—

	MRM leaf	8 weeks from seeding	Deficient	<3.0	0.25	2.0	0.9	0.30	0.20	40	40	20	20	5	0.3
			Adequate	3.0	0.25	2.0	0.9	0.30	0.20	40	40	20	20	5	0.3
			range	4.0	0.40	3.0	1.5	0.50	0.40	100	100	50	40	10	0.5
			High	>4.0	0.40	3.0	1.5	0.50	0.40	100	100	50	40	10	—
Radish	MRM leaf	At harvest	Deficient	<3.0	0.25	1.5	1.0	0.30	—	30	20	30	15	3	0.1
			Adequate	3.0	0.25	1.5	1.0	0.30	—	30	20	30	15	3	0.1
			range	4.5	0.40	3.0	2.0	0.50	—	50	40	50	30	10	2.0
			High	>4.5	0.40	3.0	2.0	0.50	—	50	40	50	30	10	2.0
			Toxic (>)	—	—	—	—	—	—	—	—	—	85	—	—
Southern pea	MRM leaf	Before bloom	Deficient	<3.5	0.30	2.0	1.0	0.30	—	30	30	20	15	5	—
			Adequate	3.5	0.30	2.0	1.0	0.30	—	30	30	20	15	5	—
			range	5.0	0.80	4.0	1.5	0.50	—	100	100	40	25	10	—
			High	>5.0	0.80	4.0	1.5	0.50	—	100	100	40	25	10	—
	MRM leaf	First bloom	Deficient	<2.5	0.20	2.0	1.0	0.30	—	30	30	20	15	5	4.0
			Adequate	2.5	0.20	2.0	1.0	0.30	—	30	30	20	15	5	4.0
			range	4.0	0.40	4.0	1.5	0.50	—	100	100	40	25	10	6.0
			High	>4.0	0.40	4.0	1.5	0.50	—	100	100	40	25	10	6.0
Spinach	MRM leaf	30 days after seeding	Deficient	<3.0	0.30	3.0	0.6	1.00	—	—	50	50	20	5	0.1
			Adequate	3.0	0.30	3.0	0.6	1.00	—	—	50	50	20	5	0.1
			range	4.5	0.50	4.0	1.0	1.60	—	—	100	70	40	7	1.0
			High	>5.0	0.50	4.0	1.0	1.60	—	—	100	70	40	7	1.0
	MRM leaf	Harvest	Deficient	<3.0	0.25	2.5	0.6	1.00	—	—	30	50	20	5	0.1
			Adequate	3.0	0.25	2.5	0.6	1.00	—	—	30	50	20	5	0.1
			range	4.0	0.50	3.5	1.0	1.60	—	—	50	70	40	7	1.0
			High	>4.0	0.50	4.0	1.0	1.60	—	—	80	70	40	7	1.0

CRITICAL (DEFICIENCY) VALUES, ADEQUATE RANGES, HIGH VALUES, AND TOXICITY VALUES FOR PLANT NUTRIENT CONTENT FOR VEGETABLES—Continued

Crop	Plant Part[1]	Time of Sampling	Status	%						ppm					
				N	P	K	Ca	Mg	S	Fe	Mn	Zn	B	Cu	Mo
Squash	MRM	Early fruit	Deficient	<3.0	0.25	2.0	1.0	0.30	0.20	40	40	20	25	5	0.3
			Adequate	3.0	0.25	2.0	1.0	0.30	0.20	40	40	20	25	5	0.3
			range	5.0	0.50	3.0	2.0	0.50	0.50	100	100	50	40	20	0.5
			High	>5.0	0.50	3.0	2.0	0.50	0.50	100	100	50	40	20	0.5
Strawberry	MRM	Transplants	Deficient	<2.8	0.25	1.5	0.3	0.30	—	50	30	25	25	5	—
	leaf		Adequate	2.8	0.25	1.5	0.3	0.30	—	50	30	25	25	5	—
			range	3.5	0.40	3.0	1.5	0.60	—	100	100	40	40	10	—
			High	>3.5	0.40	3.0	1.5	0.60	—	100	100	40	40	10	—
	MRM	Initial	Deficient	<3.0	0.20	1.5	0.4	0.25	—	50	30	20	20	5	—
	leaf	flower	Adequate	3.0	0.20	1.5	0.4	0.25	—	50	30	20	20	5	—
			range	4.0	0.40	3.0	1.5	0.50	—	100	100	40	40	10	—
			High	>4.0	0.40	3.0	1.5	0.50	—	100	100	40	20	10	—
	MRM	Initial	Deficient	<3.0	0.20	1.5	0.4	0.25	—	50	30	20	20	5	—
	leaf	harvest	Adequate	3.0	0.20	1.5	0.4	0.25	—	50	30	20	20	5	—
			range	3.5	0.40	2.5	1.5	0.50	—	100	100	40	40	10	—
			High	>3.5	0.40	2.5	1.5	0.50	—	100	100	40	40	10	—
			Toxic (>)	—	—	—	—	—	—	—	800	—	—	—	—

	MRM leaf	Midseason	Deficient	<2.8	0.20	1.1	0.4	0.20	0.8	50	25	20	20	5	0.5
			Adequate	2.8	0.20	1.1	0.4	0.20	0.8	50	25	20	20	5	0.5
			range	3.0	0.40	2.5	1.5	0.40	1.0	100	100	40	40	10	0.8
			High	>3.0	0.40	2.5	1.5	0.40	1.0	100	100	40	40	10	0.8
			Toxic (>)	—	—	—	—	—	—	—	800	—	—	—	—
	MRM leaf	End of season	Deficient	<2.5	0.20	1.1	0.4	0.20	—	50	25	20	20	5	—
			Adequate	2.5	0.20	1.1	0.4	0.20	—	50	25	20	20	5	—
			range	3.0	0.30	2.0	1.5	0.40	—	100	100	40	40	10	—
			High	>3.0	0.30	2.0	1.5	0.40	—	100	100	40	40	10	—
Sweet corn	Whole seedlings	3-leaf stage	Deficient	<3.0	0.35	2.5	0.6	0.25	0.4	50	40	30	10	5	0.1
			Adequate	3.0	0.35	2.5	0.6	0.25	0.4	50	40	30	10	5	0.1
			range	4.0	0.50	4.0	0.8	0.50	0.6	100	100	40	30	10	0.2
			High	>4.0	0.50	4.0	0.8	0.50	0.6	100	100	40	30	10	0.2
			Toxic (>)	—	—	—	—	—	—	—	—	—	100	—	—
	Whole seedlings	6-leaf stage	Deficient	<3.0	0.25	2.5	0.5	0.25	0.4	50	40	30	10	5	0.1
			Adequate	3.0	0.25	2.5	0.5	0.25	0.4	50	40	30	10	5	0.1
			range	4.0	0.50	4.0	0.8	0.50	0.6	100	100	40	30	10	0.2
			High	>4.0	0.50	4.0	0.8	0.50	0.6	100	100	40	30	10	0.2
			Toxic (>)	—	—	—	—	—	—	—	—	—	100	—	—
	MRM leaf	30 inches tall	Deficient	<2.5	0.20	2.5	0.5	0.20	0.2	40	40	25	10	4	0.1
			Adequate	2.5	0.20	2.5	0.5	0.20	0.2	40	40	25	10	4	0.1
			range	4.0	0.40	4.0	0.8	0.40	0.4	100	100	40	30	10	0.2
			High	>4.0	0.40	4.0	0.8	0.40	0.4	100	100	40	30	10	0.2
			Toxic (>)	—	—	—	—	—	—	—	—	—	100	—	—
	MRM leaf	Just prior to tassel	Deficient	<2.5	0.20	2.0	0.3	0.15	0.2	30	30	20	10	4	0.1
			Adequate	2.5	0.20	2.0	0.3	0.15	0.2	30	30	20	10	4	0.1
			range	4.0	0.40	3.5	0.6	0.40	0.4	100	100	40	20	10	0.2
			High	>4.0	0.40	3.5	0.6	0.40	0.4	100	100	40	20	10	0.2
			Toxic (>)	—	—	—	—	—	—	—	—	—	100	—	—

CRITICAL (DEFICIENCY) VALUES, ADEQUATE RANGES, HIGH VALUES, AND TOXICITY VALUES FOR PLANT NUTRIENT CONTENT FOR VEGETABLES—Continued

				%						ppm					
Crop	Plant Part[1]	Time of Sampling	Status	N	P	K	Ca	Mg	S	Fe	Mn	Zn	B	Cu	Mo
Sweet corn	Ear	Tasseling	Deficient	<1.5	0.20	1.2	0.3	0.15	0.20	30	20	20	10	4	0.1
(Continued)	leaf		Adequate	1.5	0.20	1.2	0.3	0.15	0.20	30	20	20	10	4	0.1
			range	2.5	0.40	2.0	0.6	0.40	0.40	100	100	40	20	10	0.2
			High	>2.5	0.40	2.0	0.6	0.40	0.40	100	100	40	20	10	0.2
Sweet potato	MRM	Early	Deficient	<4.0	0.30	2.5	0.8	0.40	0.20	40	40	25	20	5	—
	leaf	vining	Adequate	4.0	0.30	2.5	0.8	0.40	0.20	40	40	25	20	5	—
			range	5.0	0.50	4.0	1.6	0.80	0.60	100	100	50	50	10	—
			High	>5.0	0.50	4.0	1.6	0.80	0.60	100	100	50	50	10	—
	MRM	Midseason	Deficient	<3.0	0.20	2.0	0.8	0.25	0.20	40	40	25	25	5	—
	leaf	before root	Adequate	3.0	0.20	2.0	0.8	0.25	0.20	40	40	25	25	5	—
		enlargement	range	4.0	0.30	4.0	1.8	0.50	0.40	100	100	40	40	10	—
			High	>4.0	0.30	4.0	1.8	0.50	0.40	100	100	40	40	10	—
	MRM	Root	Deficient	<3.0	0.20	2.0	0.8	0.25	0.20	40	40	25	20	5	—
	leaf	enlargement	Adequate	3.0	0.20	2.0	0.8	0.25	0.20	40	40	25	20	5	—
			range	4.0	0.30	4.0	1.6	0.50	0.60	100	100	50	50	10	—
			High	>4.0	0.30	4.0	1.6	0.50	0.60	100	100	50	50	10	—
	MRM	Just before	Deficient	<2.8	0.20	2.0	0.8	0.25	0.20	40	40	25	20	5	—
	leaf	harvest	Adequate	2.8	0.20	2.0	0.8	0.25	0.20	40	40	25	20	5	—
			range	3.5	0.30	4.0	1.6	0.50	0.60	100	100	50	50	10	—
			High	>3.5	0.30	4.0	1.6	0.50	0.60	100	100	50	50	10	—

Tomato	MRM	5-leaf	Deficient	<3.0	0.30	3.0	1.0	0.30	0.30	40	30	25	20	5	0.2
	leaf	stage	Adequate	3.0	0.30	3.0	1.0	0.30	0.30	40	30	25	20	5	0.2
			range	5.0	0.60	5.0	2.0	0.50	0.80	100	100	40	40	15	0.6
			High	>5.0	0.60	5.0	2.0	0.50	0.80	100	100	40	40	15	0.6
	MRM	First	Deficient	<2.8	0.20	2.5	1.00	0.30	0.30	40	30	25	20	5	0.2
	leaf	flower	Adequate	2.8	0.20	2.5	1.00	0.30	0.30	40	30	25	20	5	0.2
			range	4.0	0.40	4.0	2.00	0.50	0.80	100	100	40	40	15	0.6
			High	>4.0	0.40	4.0	2.00	0.50	0.80	100	100	40	40	15	0.6
			Toxic (>)	—	—	—	—	—	—	—	1500	300	250	—	—
	MRM	Early	Deficient	<2.5	0.20	2.5	1.0	0.25	0.30	40	30	20	20	5	0.2
	leaf	fruit set	Adequate	2.5	0.20	2.5	1.0	0.25	0.30	40	30	20	20	5	0.2
			range	4.0	0.40	4.0	2.0	0.50	0.60	100	100	40	40	10	0.6
			High	>4.0	0.40	4.0	2.0	0.50	0.60	100	100	40	40	10	0.6
			Toxic (>)	—	—	—	—	—	—	—	—	—	250	—	—
	MRM	First ripe	Deficient	<2.0	0.20	2.0	1.0	0.25	0.30	40	30	20	20	5	0.2
	leaf	fruit	Adequate	2.0	0.20	2.0	1.0	0.25	0.30	40	30	20	20	5	0.2
			range	3.5	0.40	4.0	2.0	0.50	0.60	100	100	40	40	10	0.6
			High	>3.5	0.40	4.0	2.0	0.50	0.60	100	100	40	40	10	0.6
	MRM	During	Deficient	<2.0	0.20	1.5	1.0	0.25	0.30	40	30	20	20	5	0.2
	leaf	harvest	Adequate	2.0	0.20	1.5	1.0	0.25	0.30	40	30	20	20	5	0.2
		period	range	3.0	0.40	2.5	2.0	0.50	0.60	100	100	40	40	10	0.6
			High	>3.0	0.40	2.5	2.0	0.50	0.60	100	100	40	40	10	0.6
Turnip	MRM	Hypocotyl	Deficient	<3.0	0.25	2.5	0.8	0.25	0.20	30	30	20	20	5	—
greens	leaf	1-inch	Adequate	3.0	0.25	2.5	0.8	0.25	0.20	30	30	20	20	5	—
		diameter	range	5.0	0.80	4.0	1.5	0.60	0.60	100	100	40	40	10	—
			High	>5.0	0.80	4.0	1.5	0.60	0.60	100	100	40	40	10	—

CRITICAL (DEFICIENCY) VALUES, ADEQUATE RANGES, HIGH VALUES, AND TOXICITY VALUES FOR PLANT NUTRIENT CONTENT FOR VEGETABLES—Continued

Crop	Plant Part[1]	Time of Sampling	Status	%						ppm					
				N	P	K	Ca	Mg	S	Fe	Mn	Zn	B	Cu	Mo
Watermelon	MRM	Layby	Deficient	<3.0	0.25	3.0	1.0	0.25	0.20	30	20	20	20	5	—
	leaf	(last	Adequate	3.0	0.25	3.0	1.0	0.25	0.20	30	20	20	20	5	—
		cultivation)	range	4.0	0.50	4.0	2.0	0.50	0.40	100	100	40	40	10	—
			High	>4.0	0.50	4.0	2.0	0.50	0.40	100	100	40	40	10	—
			Toxic (>)	—	—	—	—	—	—	—	800	—	—	—	—
	MRM	First	Deficient	<2.5	0.25	2.7	1.0	0.25	0.20	30	20	20	20	5	—
	leaf	flower	Adequate	2.5	0.25	2.7	1.0	0.25	0.20	30	20	20	20	5	—
			range	3.5	0.50	3.5	2.0	0.50	0.40	100	100	40	40	10	—
			High	>3.5	0.50	3.5	2.0	0.50	0.40	100	100	40	40	10	—
	MRM	First	Deficient	<2.0	0.25	2.3	1.0	0.25	0.20	30	20	20	20	5	—
	leaf	fruit	Adequate	2.0	0.25	2.3	1.0	0.25	0.20	30	20	20	20	5	—
			range	3.0	0.50	3.5	2.0	0.50	0.40	100	100	40	40	10	—
			High	>3.0	0.50	3.5	2.0	0.50	0.40	100	100	40	40	10	—

MRM	Harvest	Deficient	<2.0	0.25	2.0	1.0	0.25	0.20	30	20	20	20	3	—
leaf	period	Adequate	2.0	0.25	2.0	1.0	0.25	0.20	30	20	20	20	3	—
		range	3.0	0.50	3.0	2.0	0.50	0.40	100	100	40	40	10	—
		High	>3.0	0.50	3.0	2.0	0.50	0.40	100	100	40	40	10	—

Adapted from G. Hochmuth, D. Maynard, C. Vavrina, and E. Hanlon. Plant Tissue Analysis and Interpretation for Vegetable Crops in Florida. Fla. Coop. Ext. Serv. Special Series SSVEC-42, 1991.

[1] MRM leaf is the most recently matured whole leaf plus petiole.

UNIVERSITY OF FLORIDA GUIDELINES FOR LEAF PETIOLE FRESH SAP NITRATE-NITROGEN AND POTASSIUM TESTING

Crop	Development Stage/Time	Fresh Petiole Sap Concentration (ppm)	
		NO_3-N	K
Eggplant	First fruit (two inches long)	1200–1600	4500–5000
	First harvest	1000–1200	4000–4500
	Mid harvest	800–1000	3500–4000
Pepper	First flower buds	1400–1600	3200–3500
	First open flowers	1400–1600	3000–3200
	Fruits half-grown	1200–1400	3000–3200
	First harvest	800–1000	2400–3000
	Second harvest	500–800	2000–2400
Potato	Plants eight inches tall	1200–1400	4500–5000
	First open flowers	1000–1400	4500–5000
	50% flowers open	1000–1200	4000–4500
	100% flowers open	900–1200	3500–4000
	Tops falling over	600–900	2500–3000
Strawberry[1]	November	800–900	3000–3500
	December	600–800	3000–3500
	January	600–800	2500–3000
	February	300–500	2000–2500
	March	200–500	1800–2500
	April	200–500	1500–2000
Tomato	First buds	1000–1200	3500–4000
	First open flowers	600–800	3500–4000
	Fruits one-inch diameter	400–600	3000–3500
	Fruits two-inch diameter	400–600	3000–3500
	First harvest	300–400	2500–3000
	Second harvest	200–400	2000–2500
Watermelon	Vines 6 inches in length	1200–1500	4000–5000
	Fruit 2 inches in length	1000–1200	4000–5000
	Fruits one-half mature	800–1000	3500–4000
	At first harvest	600–800	3000–3500

Adapted from G. Hochmuth, Plant Petiole Sap-testing Guide for Vegetable Crops, Fla. Coop. Ext. Serv. Circ. 1144 (1994).

[1] Annual-hill production system.

SOIL TESTING

Analyses for total amounts of nutrients in the soil are of limited value in predicting fertilizer needs. Consequently, various methods and extractants have been developed to estimate the available soil nutrients and to serve as a basis for predicting fertilizer needs. Proper interpretation of the results of soil analysis is essential in recommending fertilizer needs.

INTERPRETATION OF SOIL TEST RESULTS FOR PHOSPHORUS BY THE OLSON BICARBONATE EXTRACTION, FOR POTASSIUM AND MAGNESIUM BY AMMONIUM ACETATE EXTRACTION, AND FOR ZINC BY DPTA EXTRACTION

	Amount in Soil (ppm)			
Nutrient Need	Phosphorus[1] (PO_4-P)	Potassium[2] (K)	Magnesium[2] (Mg)	Zinc[3] (Zn)
Deficient levels for most vegetables	0–10	0–60	0–25	0–0.3
Deficient for susceptible vegetables	10–20	60–120	25–50	0.3–0.6
A few susceptible crops may respond	20–40	120–200	50–100	0.6–1.0
No crop response	Above 40	Above 200	Above 100	Above 1.0
Levels are excessive and could cause problems	Above 150	Above 2000	Above 1000	Above 3.0

Adapted from H. M. Reisenauer (ed.), Soil and Plant Tissue Testing in California, University of California Division of Agricultural Science Bulletin 1879 (1976).

[1] Olson (0.5*M*, pH 8.5) sodium bicarbonate extractant.

[2] Exchangeable with 1*N* ammonium acetate extractant.

[3] DPTA extractable Zn.

INTERPRETATION OF SOIL TEST RESULTS OBTAINED BY THE DOUBLE-ACID (0.05*N* HCl, 0.025*N* H_2SO_4) SOIL EXTRACTION

Relative Level in Soil	Amount (lb/acre)			
	Phosphorus (P)	Potassium (K)	Magnesium (Mg)	Calcium (Ca)
Very low	0–13	0–29	0–35	0–400
Low	14–27	30–70	36–70	401–800
Medium	28–45	71–134	71–125	801–1200
High	46–89	135–267	126–265	1201–1600
Very high	90+	268+	266+	1601+

Adapted from Commercial Vegetable Production Recommendations, Maryland Cooperative Extension Service Bul. 137 (1989).

INTERPRETATION OF THE MEHLICH-1 EXTRACTANT USED BY THE UNIVERSITY OF FLORIDA

	ppm (soil)				
Element	Very Low	Low	Medium	High	Very High
P	<10	10–15	16–30	31–60	>60
K	<20	20–35	36–60	61–125	>125
Mg		<15	15–30	>30	

Micronutrients	Soil pH (mineral soils only)		
	5.5–5.9	6.0–6.4	6.5–7.0
	ppm (soil)		
Test level below which there may be a crop response to applied *copper*	0.1–0.3	0.3–0.5	0.5
Test level above which *copper* toxicity may occur	2.0–3.0	3.0–5.0	5.0
Test level below which there may be a crop response to applied *manganese*	3.0–5.0	5.0–7.0	7.0–9.0
Test level below which there may be a crop response to applied *zinc*	0.5	0.5–1.0	1.0–3.0

Adapted from G. Hochmuth and E. Hanlon, IFAS Standardized Fertilization Recommendations for Vegetable Crops. Fla. Coop. Ext. Serv. Circ. 1152 (1995).

GUIDE FOR DIAGNOSING NUTRIENT STATUS OF CALIFORNIA SOILS FOR VEGETABLE CROPS [1]

Vegetable	Nutrient [1]	Vegetable Yield Response to Fertilizer Application: Likely (soil ppm less than)	Vegetable Yield Response to Fertilizer Application: Not Likely (soil ppm more than)
Lettuce	P	15	25
	K	50	80
	Zn	0.5	1.0
Muskmelon	P	8	12
	K	80	100
	Zn	0.4	0.6
Onion	P	8	12
	K	80	100
	Zn	0.5	1.0
Potato (mineral soils)	P	12	25
	K	100	150
	Zn	0.3	0.7
Tomato	P	8	12
	K	100	150
	Zn	0.3	0.7
Warm-season vegetables	P	8	12
	K	50	70
	Zn	0.2	0.5
Cool-season vegetables	P	20	30
	K	50	80
	Zn	0.5	1.0

Adapted from Soil and Plant Tissue Testing in California, University of California Division Agricultural Science Bulletin 1879 (1983). Updated 1996, personal communication T. K. Hartz, University of California, Davis.

[1] Soil extracts:

PO_4-P: 0.5*M* pH 8.5 sodium bicarbonate ($NaHCO_3$).

K: 1.0*M* ammonium acetate (NH_4OAc).

Zn: 0.005*M* diethylenetriaminepentaacetic acid (DTPA).

CONVERSION OF FERTILIZER RATES OF APPLICATION ON A PER-ACRE BASIS TO RATES BASED ON LINEAR BED FEET FOR FULL-BED MULCHED CROPS

Typical bed spacing for mulched vegetables grown in Florida:

Vegetable	Typical Spacing (ft)	Rows of Plants per Bed	Vegetable	Typical Spacing (ft)	Rows of Plants per Bed
Broccoli	6	2	Muskmelon	5	1
Cabbage	6	2	Pepper	6	2
Cauliflower	6	2	Summer Squash	6	2
Cucumber	6	2	Strawberry	4	2
Eggplant	6	1	Tomato	6	1
Lettuce	4	2	Watermelon	8	1

CONVERSION OF FERTILIZER RATES OF APPLICATION ON A PER-ACRE BASIS TO RATES BASED ON LINEAR BED FEET FOR FULL-BED MULCHED CROPS—Continued

Spacing between the centers of two adjacent beds.

Typical Bed Spacing (ft)	Recommended Fertilizer (N, P_2O_5, or K_2O) (lb/A)								
	20	40	60	80	100	120	140	160	180
	Resulting Fertilizer Rate (N, P_2O_5, or K_2O) (lb/100 LBF)								
3	0.14	0.28	0.41	0.55	0.69	0.83	0.96	1.10	1.24
4	0.18	0.37	0.55	0.73	0.92	1.10	1.29	1.47	1.65
5	0.23	0.46	0.69	0.92	1.15	1.38	1.61	1.84	2.07
6	0.28	0.55	0.83	1.10	1.38	1.65	1.93	2.20	2.48
8	0.37	0.73	1.10	1.47	1.84	2.20	2.57	2.94	3.31

To determine the correct fertilization rate in lb of nutrient per 100 linear bed feet (LBF), choose the crop and its typical bed spacing. Locate that typical bed spacing value in the bottom part of the table. Then locate the desired value for recommended fertilizer rate. Read down the column under recommended fertilizer rate until you reach the value in the row containing the typical bed spacing.

Adapted from G. J. Hochmuth. Soil and Fertilizer Management for Vegetable Production in Florida. pp. 2–17. In: D. N. Maynard and G. J. Hochmuth (eds.). Vegetable Production Guide for Florida. Fla. Coop. Ext. Serv. Circ. SP-170 (1995).

RATES OF FERTILIZERS RECOMMENDED FOR VEGETABLE CROPS IN MID-ATLANTIC STATES BASED ON SOIL ANALYSES[1]

Vegetable	Amount N (lb/acre)	Amount P_2O_5 (lb/acre)			Amount K_2O (lb/acre)		
		Low Soil P	High Soil P	Very High Soil P	Low Soil K	High Soil K	Very High Soil K
Asparagus	50	200	50	0	200	50	0
Bean (snap)	40–80	80	40	20	80	40	20
Beet	75–100	150	50	0	150	50	0
Broccoli	150–200	200	50	0	200	50	0
Cabbage	100–150	200	50	0	200	50	0
Carrot	50–80	150	50	0	150	50	0
Cauliflower	100–150	200	50	0	200	50	0
Celery	125–150	250	100	0	250	100	0
Cucumber	100–125	150	50	25	200	100	25
Eggplant	125–150	250	100	0	250	100	0
Lettuce (iceberg)	60–80	200	100	0	200	100	0
Leek	100–125	200	100	0	200	100	0
Muskmelon	75–100	150	50	25	200	100	25
Onion	75–100	200	50	0	200	50	0
Pea	40–60	120	40	0	120	40	0
Pepper	100–130	200	100	0	200	100	0
Potato	125–150	200	100	50	300	100	50
Pumpkin	50–75	150	50	0	200	100	0

RATES OF FERTILIZERS RECOMMENDED FOR VEGETABLE CROPS IN MID-ATLANTIC STATES BASED ON SOIL ANALYSES [1]—Continued

		Amount P_2O_5 (lb/acre)			Amount K_2O (lb/acre)		
Vegetable	Amount N (lb/acre)	Low Soil P	High Soil P	Very High Soil P	Low Soil K	High Soil K	Very High Soil K
Spinach	100–125	200	100	0	200	100	0
Squash (summer)	75–100	150	50	0	200	100	0
Strawberry	150–200	150	50	0	150	50	0
Sweet corn	125–150	160	80	20	160	80	20
Sweet potato	50–75	200	50	0	300	100	0
Tomato	80–90	200	100	0	300	100	0
Watermelon	125–150	150	50	0	200	100	0

Adapted from Commercial Vegetable Production Recommendations, Maryland Cooperative Extension Service EB-236 rev. (1994).

[1] A common recommendation is to broadcast and work deeply into the soil one-third to one-half of the fertilizer at planting and to apply the balance as a side-dressing in one or two applications after the crop is fully established.

RATES OF FERTILIZERS RECOMMENDED FOR VEGETABLE CROPS IN FLORIDA ON SANDY SOILS BASED ON MEHLICH-I SOIL TEST RESULTS

Vegetable	N (lb/acre)	P_2O_5 (lb/acre) [1] Soil P			K_2O (lb/acre) [1] Soil K		
		Very Low	Low	Medium	Very Low	Low	Medium
Bean	90	120	100	80	120	100	80
Beet	120	120	100	80	120	100	80
Broccoli	175	150	120	100	150	120	100
Cabbage	150	150	120	80	150	120	80
Carrot	150	150	120	100	150	120	100
Cauliflower	175	150	120	100	150	120	100
Celery	200	200	150	100	250	150	100
Chinese cabbage	150	150	120	80	150	120	80
Collards	150	150	120	80	150	120	80
Cucumber	150	120	100	80	120	100	80
Eggplant	160	160	130	100	160	130	100
Lettuce	150	150	120	80	150	120	80
Muskmelon	150	150	120	80	150	120	80
Mustard	120	150	120	100	150	120	100
Okra	120	150	120	100	150	120	100
Onion	150	150	120	80	150	120	80
Parsley	120	150	120	100	150	120	100
Pea (southern)	60	80	80	60	80	80	60
Pepper	175	160	130	100	160	130	100

RATES OF FERTILIZERS RECOMMENDED FOR VEGETABLE CROPS IN FLORIDA ON SANDY SOILS BASED ON MEHLICH-I SOIL TEST RESULTS—Continued

Vegetable	N (lb/acre)	P_2O_5 (lb/acre) [1] Soil P			K_2O (lb/acre) [1] Soil K		
		Very Low	Low	Medium	Very Low	Low	Medium
Potato	175	120	120	60	140	140	140
Radish	90	120	100	80	120	100	80
Spinach	90	120	100	80	120	100	80
Squash	120	120	100	80	120	100	80
Strawberry	150	150	120	100	150	120	100
Sweet corn	150	120	100	80	120	100	80
Sweet potato	160	120	100	80	120	100	80
Tomato	175	150	120	100	225	150	100
Watermelon	150	150	120	80	150	120	80

Adapted from G. Hochmuth and E. Hanlon, IFAS Standardized Fertilization Recommendations for Vegetable Crops, Fla. Coop. Ext. Serv. Circ. 1152 (1995).

[1] No P or K recommended for soils testing high except for potato, which receives no P but receives 140 lb K_2O/acre.

FERTILIZATION RECOMMENDATIONS FOR NEW ENGLAND VEGETABLES

Crop	Nitrogen	Soil Phosphorus					Soil Potassium				
		Very Low	Low	Medium	High	Very High	Very Low	Low	Medium	High	Very High
	(lb/acre)	P_2O_5 (lb/acre)					K_2O (lb/acre)				
Asparagus, established	75	200	175	150	100	50	300	250	200	150	75
Bean	50	100	75	50	25	25	100	75	50	50	25
Beet, Swiss Chard	100–130	150	125	100	50	0	300	200	100	50	0
Carrot, Parsnip	110–150	150	100	75	50	25	400	350	250	150	0–75
Celery	180	200	150	100	50	0	300	240	180	120	0–60
Cole crops	160	200	170	130	100	20	175	150	125	50	0
Sweet Corn, early	130	110	80	40	40	40	200	160	130	30	0
Sweet Corn, main	160	110	80	40	20	0	200	160	130	30	0
Cucumber	130	150	120	100	80	40	200	150	100	80	40
Eggplant	110	200	150	100	50	0	200	150	100	50	0
Gourd	90	125	100	75	50	0	150	125	100	75	0
Lettuce, Endive, Escarole	75–120	190	165	140	90	40	190	165	140	90	40
Muskmelon	130	150	120	100	80	40	200	150	100	80	40
Onion	130	175	150	100	50	0	175	150	100	50	0

FERTILIZATION RECOMMENDATIONS FOR NEW ENGLAND VEGETABLES—Continued

		Soil Phosphorus					Soil Potassium				
Crop	Nitrogen	Very Low	Low	Medium	High	Very High	Very Low	Low	Medium	High	Very High
	(lb/acre)	P_2O_5 (lb/acre)					K_2O (lb/acre)				
Pea	75	150	100	75	50	25	150	100	75	50	0
Pepper	140	200	150	100	50	20	200	150	100	50	0
Potato	120–180	300	250	200	180	150	250	225	200	180	150
Pumpkin, Squash	130	150	125	100	70	40	200	150	100	70	40
Radish	50	125	100	75	50	25	125	100	75	50	25
Rutabaga, Turnip	50	100	75	50	25	0	100	75	50	25	0
Spinach	90–110	150	120	100	60	30	200	150	100	50	0
Tomato	140–160	200	150	100	50	0	250	200	150	100	0
Watermelon	130	150	120	100	80	40	200	150	100	80	40

Adapted from D. Ferro (ed.). New England Vegetable Management Guide. Coop. Ext. Services of New England States (1996).

FERTILIZER RATES RECOMMENDED FOR VEGETABLE CROPS IN NEW YORK

Vegetable	Amount (lb/acre)[1]		
	N	P_2O_5	K_2O
Asparagus	50–75	0–160	0–200
Bean	30–40	0–100	0–80
Beet	150–175	0–200	50–400
Broccoli	120–150	0–160	0–200
Brussels sprouts	120–150	0–160	0–200
Cabbage	120–150	0–160	0–200
Carrot	120–150	0–160	0–200
Cauliflower	120–150	0–160	0–200
Celery	180	0–200	60–300
Cucumber	120–140	0–160	0–160
Eggplant	130	0–200	0–200
Endive	100–130	0–160	0–200
Lettuce	100–130	0–160	0–200
Muskmelon	120–140	0–160	0–160
Onion	100–110	0–200	0–200
Parsnip	120–150	0–160	0–160
Pea	40–50	0–120	0–160
Pepper	130	0–200	0–200
Potato	150	120–300	50–300
Pumpkin	120–140	0–160	0–160
Radish	60	0–125	0–200
Rhubarb	50–80	0–160	0–200
Rutabaga	130	0–125	0–200
Spinach	130	50–170	0–200
Squash, summer	120–140	0–160	0–160
Squash, winter	120–140	0–160	0–160
Sweet corn	120–140	0–160	0–160
Tomato	130	0–200	0–240
Turnip	130	0–125	0–200
Watermelon	120–140	0–160	0–160

Adapted from Vegetable Production Handbook, Cornell Cooperative Extension Service (1994).

[1] Total amounts are listed; application may be broadcast and plow down, broadcast and disk in, band, or side-dress. Actual rate of fertilization depends on soil type, previous cropping history, and soil test results.

A KEY TO NUTRIENT-DEFICIENCY SYMPTOMS

Nutrient	Plant Symptoms	Occurrence
Primary		
Nitrogen	Stems are thin, erect, and hard. Leaves are smaller than normal, pale green or yellow; lower leaves are affected first, but all leaves may be deficient in severe cases. Plants grow slowly	Excessive leaching on light soils
Phosphorus	Stems are thin and shortened. Leaves develop purple coloration, first on undersides and later throughout. Plants grow slowly, and maturity is delayed	On acid soils. Temporary deficiencies on cold, wet soils
Potassium	Older leaves develop gray or tan areas near the margins. Eventually a scorch around the entire leaf margin may occur. Chlorotic areas may develop throughout leaf	Excessive leaching on light soils
Secondary and Micronutrients		
Boron	Growing points die; stems are shortened and hard; leaves are distorted. Specific deficiencies include browning of cauliflower, cracked stem of celery, blackheart of beet, and internal browning of turnip	On soils with a pH above 6.8 or on crops with a high boron requirement
Calcium	Stem elongation restricted by death of the growing point. Root tips die and root growth is restricted. Specific deficiencies include blossom-end rot of tomato, brownheart of escarole, celery blackheart, and carrot cavity spot	On acid soils, following leaching rains, on soils with very high potassium levels, or on very dry soils

Nutrient	Plant Symptoms	Occurrence
Secondary and Micronutrients (Continued)		
Copper	Yellowing of leaves. Leaves may become elongated. Onion bulbs are soft, with thin, pale-yellow scales	Most cases of copper deficiency occur on muck or peat soils
Iron	Distinct yellow or white areas appear between the veins on the youngest leaves	On soils with a pH above 6.8
Magnesium	Initially, older leaves show yellowing between the veins; continued deficiency causes younger leaves to become affected. Older leaves may fall with prolonged deficiency	On acid soils, on soils with very high potassium levels, or on very light soils subject to leaching
Manganese	Yellow mottled areas, not as intense as with iron deficiency, appear on the youngest leaves. This finally results in an overall pale appearance. In beet, foliage becomes densely red. Onion and corn show narrow stripping of yellow	On soils with a pH above 6.7
Molybdenum	Pale, distorted, very narrow leaves with some interveinal yellowing on older leaves. Whiptail of cauliflower; small, open, loose curds	On very acid soils
Zinc	Small reddish-brown spots on cotyledon leaves of bean. Green and yellow broad stripping at base of leaves of corn. Interveinal yellowing with marginal burning on beet	On wet soils in early spring; often related to heavy phosphorus fertilization

INTERPRETATION OF MICRONUTRIENT SOIL TESTS

Element	Method	Range in Critical Level (ppm) [1]
Boron (B)	Hot H_2O	0.1–0.7
Copper (Cu)	$NH_4C_2H_3O_2$ (pH 4.8)	0.2
	0.5*M* EDTA	0.75
	0.43*N* HNO_3	3–4
	Biological assay	2–3
Iron (Fe)	$NH_4C_2H_3O_2$ (pH 4.8)	2
	DTPA + $CaCl_2$ (pH 7.3)	2.5–4.5
Manganese (Mn)	0.05*N* HCl + 0.025*N* H_2SO_4	5–9
	0.1*N* H_3PO_4 and 3*N* $NH_4H_2PO_4$	15–20
	Hydroquinone + $NH_4C_2H_3O_2$	25–65
	H_2O	2
Molybdenum (Mo)	$(NH_4)_2C_2O_4$ (pH 3.3)	0.04–0.2
Zinc (Zn)	0.1*N* HCl	1.0–7.5
	Dithizone + $NH_4C_2H_3O_2$	0.3–2.3
	EDTA + $(NH_4)_2CO_3$	1.4–3.0
	DTPA + $CaCl_2$ (pH 7.3)	0.5–1.0

Reprinted with permission from S. S. Mortvedt, P. M. Giordano, and W. L. Lindsay (eds.), *Micronutrients in Agriculture*, Soil Science Society of America, Madison, WI (1972).

[1] Deficiencies are likely to occur when concentrations are below the critical level.

MANGANESE RECOMMENDATIONS FOR RESPONSIVE CROPS GROWN ON MINERAL SOILS IN MICHIGAN

	Soil pH						
Soil Test	6.2	6.4	6.6	6.8	7.0	7.2	7.4
ppm[1]	Band Applied Mn (lb/acre)						
2	2	3	4	5	7	8	9
4	1	2	3	5	6	7	8
8	0	1	2	3	5	6	7
12	0	0	1	2	3	4	6
16	0	0	0	1	2	3	4
20	0	0	0	0	0	2	3
24	0	0	0	0	0	0	1

Adapted from D. D. Warncke, D. R. Christenson, L. W. Jacobs, M. L. Vitosh, and B. H. Zandstra, Fertilizer Recommendations for Vegetable Crops in Michigan, Mich. Coop. Ext. Serv. Bul. E550B (1992).

[1] 0.1*N* HCl extractant.

MANGANESE RECOMMENDATIONS FOR RESPONSIVE CROPS GROWN ON ORGANIC SOILS IN MICHIGAN

	Soil pH						
Soil Test	5.8	6.0	6.2	6.4	6.6	6.8	7.0
ppm[1]	Band Applied Mn (lb/acre)						
2	2	4	5	7	9	10	12
4	1	3	5	6	8	10	11
8	0	1	3	5	7	8	10
12	0	0	2	4	6	7	9
16	0	0	1	3	4	6	8
20	0	0	0	1	3	5	6
24	0	0	0	0	2	4	5
28	0	0	0	0	1	2	4
32	0	0	0	0	0	1	3
36	0	0	0	0	0	0	1

Adapted from D. D. Warncke, D. R. Christenson, L. W. Jacobs, M. L. Vitosh, and B. H. Zandstra, Fertilizer Recommendations for Vegetable Crops in Michigan, Mich. Coop. Ext. Serv. Bul. E550B (1992).

[1] 0.1*N* HCl extractant.

ZINC RECOMMENDATIONS FOR RESPONSIVE CROPS GROWN ON MINERAL AND ORGANIC SOILS IN MICHIGAN

Soil Test	Soil pH			
	6.7	7.0	7.3	7.6
ppm[1]	Band Applied Zn (lb/acre)[2]			
1	1	3	4	6
2	1	2	4	5
4	0	1	3	4
6	0	0	2	4
8	0	0	1	3
10	0	0	0	2
12	0	0	0	1

Adapted from D. D. Warncke, D. R. Christenson, L. W. Jacobs, M. L. Vitosh, and B. H. Zandstra, Fertilizer Recommendations for Vegetable Crops in Michigan, Mich. Coop. Ext. Serv. Bul. E550B (1992).

[1] 0.1*N* HCl extractant.

[2] Rates may be divided by 5 when chelates are used.

COPPER RECOMMENDATIONS FOR CROPS GROWN ON ORGANIC SOILS IN MICHIGAN

	Crop Response		
Soil Test	Low	Medium	High
ppm[1]	Cu (lb/acre)		
1	3	4	6
4	3	4	5
8	2	3	4
12	1	2	3
16	1	2	2
20	1	1	2
24	0	1	1

Adapted from D. D. Warncke, D. R. Christenson, L. W. Jacobs, M. L. Vitosh, and B. H. Zandstra, Fertilizer Recommendations for Vegetable Crops in Michigan, Mich. Coop. Ext. Serv. Bul. E550B (1992).

[1] 0.1*N* HCl extractant.

RELATIVE RESPONSE OF VEGETABLES TO MICRONUTRIENTS [1]

Vegetable	Response to Micronutrient					
	Manganese	Boron	Copper	Zinc	Molybdenum	Iron
Asparagus	Low	Low	Low	Low	Low	Medium
Bean	High	Low	Low	High	Medium	High
Beet	High	High	High	Medium	High	High
Broccoli	Medium	High	Medium	—	High	High
Cabbage	Medium	Medium	Medium	Low	Medium	Medium
Carrot	Medium	Medium	Medium	Low	Low	—
Cauliflower	Medium	High	Medium	—	High	High
Celery	Medium	High	Medium	—	Low	—
Cucumber	High	Low	Medium	—	—	—
Lettuce	High	Medium	High	Medium	High	—
Onion	High	Low	High	High	High	—
Pea	High	Low	Low	Low	Medium	—
Potato	High	Low	Low	Medium	Low	—
Radish	High	Medium	Medium	Medium	Medium	—
Spinach	High	Medium	High	High	High	High
Sweet corn	High	Medium	Medium	High	Low	Medium
Tomato	Medium	Medium	High	Medium	Medium	High
Turnip	Medium	High	Medium	—	Medium	—

Adapted from M. L. Vitosh, D. D. Warncke, and R. E. Lucas, Secondary and Micronutrients for Vegetables and Field Crops, Michigan Extension Bulletin E-486 (1994).

[1] The crops listed will respond as indicated to applications of the respective micronutrient when that micronutrient concentration in the soil is low.

BORON REQUIREMENTS OF VEGETABLES ARRANGED IN APPROXIMATE ORDER OF DECREASING REQUIREMENTS

High Requirement (more than 0.5 ppm in soil)	Medium Requirement (0.1–0.5 ppm in soil)	Low Requirement (less than 0.1 ppm in soil)
Beet	Tomato	Corn
Turnip	Lettuce	Pea
Cabbage	Sweet potato	Bean
Broccoli	Carrot	Lima bean
Cauliflower	Onion	Potato
Asparagus		
Radish		
Brussels sprouts		
Celery		
Rutabaga		

Adapted from K. C. Berger, Boron in Soils and Crops, *Advances in Agronomy*, Vol. 1, Academic Press, New York (1949), pp. 321–351.

RELATIVE TOLERANCE OF VEGETABLES TO BORON, ARRANGED IN ORDER OF INCREASING SENSITIVITY TO BORON

Tolerant	Semitolerant	Sensitive
Asparagus	Celery	Jerusalem artichoke
Artichoke	Potato	Bean
Beet	Tomato	
Muskmelon	Radish	
Broad bean	Corn	
Onion	Pumpkin	
Turnip	Bell pepper	
Cabbage	Sweet potato	
Lettuce	Lima bean	
Carrot		

Adapted from L. V. Wilcox, Determining the Quality of Irrigation Water, USDA Agricultural Information Bulletin 197 (1958).

SOIL AND FOLIAR APPLICATION OF SECONDARY AND TRACE NUTRIENTS

Vegetables differ in their requirements for these secondary nutrients. Availability in the soil is influenced by soil reaction and soil type. Use higher rates on muck and peat soils than on mineral soils and lower rates for band application than for broadcast. Foliar applications is one means of correcting an evident deficiency that appears while the crop is growing.

Nutrient	Nutrient Application Rate (per acre basis)	Nutrient Source	Composition
Boron	0.5–3.5 lb (soil)	Borax ($Na_2B_4O_7 \cdot 10H_2O$)	11% B
		Boric acid (H_3BO_3)	17% B
		Sodium pentaborate ($Na_2B_{10}O_{16} \cdot 10H_2O$)	18% B
		Sodium tetraborate ($Na_2B_4O_7$)	21% B
Calcium	2–5 lb (foliar)	Calcium chloride ($CaCl_2$)	36% Ca
		Calcium nitrate ($CaNO_3 \cdot 2H_2O$)	20% Ca
		Liming materials and gypsum supply calcium when used as soil amendments	
Copper	2–6 lb (soil)	Cupric chloride ($CuCl_2$)	47% Cu
		Copper sulfate ($CuSO_4 \cdot H_2O$)	35% Cu
		Copper sulfate ($CuSO_4 \cdot 5H_2O$)	25% Cu
		Cupric oxide (CuO)	80% Cu
		Cuprous oxide (Cu_2O)	89% Cu
		Copper chelates	8–13% Cu

SOIL AND FOLIAR APPLICATION OF SECONDARY AND TRACE NUTRIENTS—Continued

Nutrient	Nutrient Application Rate (per acre basis)	Nutrient Source	Composition
Iron	2–4 lb (soil)	Ferrous sulfate ($FeSO_4 \cdot 7H_2O$)	20% Fe
	0.5–1 lb (foliar)	Ferric sulfate [$Fe_2(SO_4)_3 \cdot 9H_2O$]	20% Fe
		Ferrous carbonate ($FeCO_3 \cdot H_2O$)	42% Fe
		Iron chelates	5–12% Fe
Magnesium	25–30 lb (soil)	Magnesium sulfate ($MgSO_4 \cdot 7H_2O$)	10% Mg
	2–4 lb (foliar)	Magnesium oxide (MgO)	55% Mg
		Dolomitic limestone	11% Mg
		Magnesium chelates	2–4% Mg
Manganese	20–100 lb (soil)	Manganese sulfate ($MnSO_4 \cdot 3H_2O$)	27% Mn
	2–5 lb (foliar)	Manganous oxide (MnO)	41–68% Mn
		Manganese chelates (Mn EDTA)	12% Mn
Molybdenum	25–400 g (soil)	Ammonium molybdate [$(NH_4)_6MO_7O_{24} \cdot 4H_2O$]	54% Mo
	25 g (foliar)	Sodium molybdate ($Na_2MoO_4 \cdot 2H_2O$)	39% Mo
Sulfur	20–50 lb (soil)	Sulfur (S)	100% S
		Ammonium sulfate [$(NH_4)_2SO_4$]	24% S
		Potassium sulfate (K_2SO_4)	18% S
		Calcium sulfate ($CaSO_4$)	16–18% S
		Ferric sulfate [$Fe_2(SO_4)_3$]	18–19% S
Zinc	2–10 lb (soil)	Zinc oxide (ZnO)	80% Zn
	0.25 lb (foliar)	Zinc sulfate ($ZnSO_4 \cdot 7H_2O$)	23% Zn
		Zinc chelates (Na_2Zn EDTA)	14% Zn

BORON RECOMMENDATIONS BASED ON SOIL TESTS FOR VEGETABLE CROPS

Interpretation of Boron Soil Tests				
ppm	lb/acre	Relative Level	Crops That Often Need Additional Boron	Boron Recommendation (lb/acre)
0.0–0.35	0.0–0.70	Low	Broccoli, cauliflower, celery	3
			Asparagus, beet, cabbage, carrot, eggplant, horseradish, rutabaga, squash, sweet corn, tomato, turnip	2
			Pepper, sweet potato	1
0.36–0.70	0.71–1.40	Medium	Broccoli, cauliflower, celery	1½
			Asparagus, beet, cabbage, carrot, eggplant, horseradish, rutabaga, squash, sweet corn, tomato, turnip	1
>0.70	>1.40	High	All crops	0

Adapted from Commercial Vegetable Production Recommendations, Maryland Cooperative Extension Service EB-236 rev. (1994).

TOLERANCE OF VEGETABLES TO A DEFICIENCY OF MAGNESIUM IN THE SOIL

Tolerant	Not Tolerant
Bean	Cabbage
Beet	Corn
Chard	Cucumber
Lettuce	Eggplant
Pea	Muskmelon
Radish	Pepper
Sweet potato	Potato
	Pumpkin
	Rutabaga
	Tomato
	Watermelon

Adapted from W. S. Ritchie and E. B. Holland, Minerals in Nutrition, Massachusetss Agricultural Experiment Station Bulletin 374 (1940).

Each time a distributor is used it is wise to check it to ensure that the proper quantity of fertilizer is being supplied. Fertilizers vary greatly in the way they flow through the equipment. Movement is influenced by the humidity of the atmosphere as well as the degree of granulation of the material.

Adjustment of Row Crop Distributor

1. Disconnect from one hopper, the downspout or tube to the furrow opener for a row.
2. Attach a can just below the fertilizer hopper.
3. Fill the hopper under which the can is placed.
4. Engage the fertilizer attachment and drive the tractor the suggested distance, according to the number of inches between rows.

Distance Between Rows (in.)	Distance to Pull the Distributor (ft)
20	261
24	218
30	174
36	145
38	138
40	131
42	124

5. Weigh the fertilizer in the can. Each pound in it equals 100 lb/acre. Each tenth of a pound equals 10 lb/acre.
6. Adjust the distributor for the rate of application desired, and then adjust the other distributor or distributors to the same setting.

Adjustment of Grain-Drill-Type Distributor

1. Remove four downspouts or tubes.
2. Attach a paper bag to each of the four outlets.
3. Fill the part of the drill over the bagged outlets.
4. Engage the distributor and drive the tractor the suggested distance, according to the inches between the drill rows.

Adjustment of Grain-Drill-Type Distributor

Distance Between Drill Rows (in.)	Distance to Pull the Drill (ft)
7	187
8	164
10	131
12	109
14	94

5. Weigh total fertilizer in the four bags. Each pound equals 100 lb/acre. Each tenth of a pound equals 10 lb/acre.

CALIBRATION OF FERTILIZER DRILLS

Set drill at opening estimated to give the desired rate of application. Mark level of the fertilizer in the hopper. Operate the drill for 100 ft. Weigh a pail full of fertilizer. Refill hopper to marked level and again weigh pail. The difference is the pounds of fertilizer used in 100 ft. Consult the column under the row spacing you are using. The left-hand column opposite the amount you used will then show the rate in pounds per acre at which the fertilizer has been applied. Adjust setting of the drill if necessary and recheck.

Distance Between Rows (in.):	18	20	24	36	48
Rate (lb/acre)	Approximate Amount of Fertilizer (lb/100 ft of row)				
250	0.9	1.1	1.4	1.7	2.3
500	1.7	2.3	2.9	3.5	4.6
750	2.6	3.4	4.3	5.2	6.9
1000	3.5	4.6	5.8	6.9	9.2
1500	5.2	6.8	8.6	10.4	13.8
2000	6.8	9.2	11.6	13.0	18.4
3000	10.5	14.0	17.5	21.0	28.0

PART 5
WATER AND IRRIGATION

ROOTING OF VEGETABLES

SOIL MOISTURE

SURFACE IRRIGATION

OVERHEAD IRRIGATION

DRIP OR TRICKLE IRRIGATION

WATER QUALITY

SUGGESTIONS ON SUPPLYING WATER TO VEGETABLES

Plants in hot, dry areas lose more moisture into the air than those in cooler, more humid areas. Vegetables utilize and evaporate more water in the later stages of growth when size and leaf area are greater. The root system becomes deeper and more widespread as the plant ages.

Some vegetables, especially lettuce and sweet corn, have sparse root systems that do not come into contact with all the soil moisture in their root-depth zone. Cool-season vegetables normally root to a shallower depth than do warm-season vegetables and perennials.

When applying water, use enough to bring the soil-moisture content of the effective rooting zone of the crop up to field capacity. This is the quantity of water that the soil will hold against the pull of gravity.

The frequency of irrigation will depend on the total supply of available moisture reached by the roots and the rate of water use. The first is affected by soil type, depth of wetted soil, and the depth and dispersion of roots. The latter is influenced by weather conditions and the age of the crops. Add water when the moisture in the root zone has been used to about the halfway point in the range of available moisture. Do not wait until vegetables show signs of wilting or develop color or texture changes that indicate they are not growing rapidly.

A general rule is that vegetables will need about an average of 1 in. of water per week from rain or supplemental irrigation in order to grow vigorously. In arid regions about 2 in./week is required. These amounts of water may vary from 0.5 in./week early in the season to more than 1.0 inch later in the season.

ROOTING DEPTH OF VEGETABLES

The depth of rooting of vegetables is influenced by the soil profile. If there is a clay pan, hard pan, compacted layer, or other dense formation, the normal depth of rooting is not possible. Also, some transplanted vegetables may not develop root systems as deep as those of seeded crops. Although vegetables may root as deep as 18 to 24 inches, most of the active root system may be between 8 and 12 inches.

CHARACTERISTIC MAXIMUM ROOTING DEPTHS OF VARIOUS VEGETABLES

Shallow (18–24 in.)	Moderately Deep (36–48 in.)	Deep (More than 48 in.)
Broccoli	Bean, bush	Artichoke
Brussels sprouts	Bean, pole	Asparagus
Cabbage	Beet	Bean, lima
Cauliflower	Carrot	Parsnip
Celery	Chard	Pumpkin
Chinese cabbage	Cucumber	Squash, winter
Corn	Eggplant	Sweet potato
Endive	Muskmelon	Tomato
Garlic	Mustard	Watermelon
Leek	Pea	
Lettuce	Pepper	
Onion	Rutabaga	
Parsley	Squash, summer	
Potato	Turnip	
Radish		
Spinach		
Strawberry		

DETERMINING MOISTURE IN SOIL BY APPEARANCE OR FEEL

A shovel will serve to obtain a soil sample from a shallow soil or when a shallow-rooted crop is being grown. A soil auger or soil tube is necessary to draw samples from great depths in the root zone.

Squeeze the soil sample in the hand and compare its behavior with those of the soils listed in the Practical Soil-Moisture Interpretation Chart to get a rough idea of its moisture content.

PRACTICAL SOIL-MOISTURE INTERPRETATION CHART

Amount of Readily Available Moisture Remaining for the Plant	Sand (gritty when moist, almost like beach sand)	Sandy Loam (gritty when moist; dirties fingers; contains some silt and clay)	Clay Loam (sticky and plastic when moist)	Clay (very sticky when moist; behaves like modeling clay)
Close to 0%. Little or no moisture available	Dry, loose, single-grained; flows through fingers	Dry, loose, flows through fingers	Dry clods that break down into powdery condition	Hard, baked, cracked surface. Hard clods difficult to break, sometimes has loose crumbs on surface
50% or less. Approaching time to irrigate	Still appears to be dry; will not form a ball with pressure	Still appears to be dry; will not form a ball	Somewhat crumbly, but will hold together with pressure	Somewhat pliable; will ball under pressure
50–75%. Enough available moisture	Same as sand under 50%	Tends to ball under pressure but seldom will hold together	Forms a ball, somewhat plastic; will sometimes stick slightly with pressure	Forms a ball; will ribbon out between thumb and forefinger
75% to field capacity. Plenty of available moisture	Tends to stick together slightly, sometimes forms a very weak ball under pressure	Forms weak ball, breaks easily, will not become slick	Forms a ball and is very pliable; becomes slick readily if high in clay	Easily ribbons out between fingers; feels slick

At field capacity. Soil will not hold any more water (after draining)	Upon squeezing, no free water appears; moisture is left on hand	Same as sand	Same as sand	Same as sand
Above field capacity. Unless water drains out, soil will be water-logged	Free water appears when soil is bounced in hand	Free water will be released with kneading	Can squeeze out free water	Puddles and free water form on surface

Adapted from R. W. Harris, and R. H. Coppock (eds.), Saving Water in Landscape Irrigation, University of California Division of Agricultural Science Leaflet 2976 (1978).

APPROXIMATE SOIL-WATER CHARACTERISTICS FOR TYPICAL SOIL CLASSES

Characteristic	Sandy Soil	Loamy Soil	Clayey Soil
Dry weight 1 cu ft	90 lb	80 lb	75 lb
Field capacity—% of dry weight	10%	20%	35%
Permanent wilting percentage	5%	10%	19%
Percent available water	5%	10%	16%
Water available to plants			
lb/cu ft	4 lb	8 lb	12 lb
in./ft depth	¾ in.	1½ in.	2¼ in.
gal/cu ft	½ gal	1 gal	1½ gal
Approximate depth of soil that will be wetted by each 1 in. of water applied if half the available water has been used	24 in.	16 in.	11 in.
Suggested lengths of irrigation runs	330 ft	660 ft	1320 ft

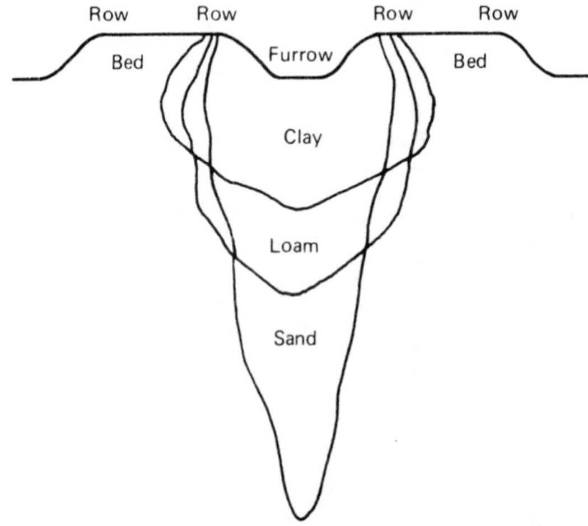

Arrangement of beds for furrow irrigation. Beds intended for two rows are usually on 36-, 40-, or 42-in. centers, with the surface 4–6 in. above the bottom of the furrow. The depth of penetration of an equal quantity of water varies with the class of soil as indicated.

RATES OF WATER APPLICATION FOR VARIOUS IRRIGATION METHODS

The infiltration rate has an important bearing on the rapidity with which water should be applied by any method of irrigation.

Normally, sandy soils have a high infiltration rate and clay soils have a low one. The rate is affected by soil texture, structure, dispersion, and the depth of the water table. The longer the water is allowed to run, the more the infiltration rate decreases.

With furrows, use a flow of water initially two to three times that indicated to fill the run as quickly as possible. Then cut back the flow to the indicated amount. This prevents excessive penetration at the head and equalizes the application of water throughout the whole furrow.

APPROXIMATE FLOW OF WATER PER FURROW AFTER IT HAS REACHED END OF THE FURROW

	Slope of Land (%):	0–0.2	0.2–0.5	0.5–1
Infiltration Rate of Soil (in./hr)	Length of Furrow (ft)	Flow of Water per Furrow (gal/min)		
High (1.5 or more)	330	9	4	3
	660	20	9	7
	1320	45	20	15
Medium (0.5–1.5)	330	4	3	1.5
	660	10	7	3.5
	1320	25	15	7.5
Low (0.1–0.5)	330	2	1.5	1
	660	4	3.5	2
	1320	9	7.5	4

SUGGESTED MAXIMUM WATER INFILTRATION RATES FOR VARIOUS SOIL TYPES

Soil Type	Infiltration Rate [1] (in./hr)
Sand	2.0
Loamy sand	1.8
Sandy loam	1.5
Loam	1.0
Silt and clay loam	0.5
Clay	0.2

[1] Assumes a full crop cover. For bare soil reduce the rate by one-half.

PERCENT OF AVAILABLE WATER DEPLETED FROM SOILS AT VARIOUS TENSIONS

Tension—less than—(bars) [1]	Loamy Sand	Sandy Loam	Loam	Clay
0.3	55	35	15	7
0.5	70	55	30	13
0.8	77	63	45	20
1.0	82	68	55	27
2.0	90	78	72	45
5.0	95	88	80	75
15.0	100	100	100	100

Adapted from Cooperative Extension, University of California Soil and Water Newsletter No. 26 (1975).

[1] 1 bar = 100 kilopascals

SPRINKLER IRRIGATION: APPROXIMATE APPLICATION OF WATER

Slope of Land (%):	0–5	5–12
Infiltration Rate of Soil (in./hr)	Approximate Application (in./hr)	
High (1.5 or more)	1.0	0.75
Medium (0.5–1.5)	0.5	0.40
Low (0.1–0.5)	0.2	0.15

BASIN IRRIGATION: APPROXIMATE AREA

Quantity of Water to be Supplied:	450 gal/min or 1 cu ft/sec	900 gal/min or 2 cu ft/sec
Infiltration Rate of Soil (in./hr)	Approximate Area (acre/basin)	
High (1.5 or more)	0.1	0.2
Medium (0.5–1.5)	0.2	0.4
Low (0.1–0.5)	0.5	1.0

VOLUME OF WATER APPLIED FOR VARIOUS FLOW RATES AND TIME PERIODS

	Volume (acre-in.) Applied			
Flow Rate (gpm)	1 hr	8 hr	12 hr	1 Day
25	0.06	0.44	0.66	1.33
50	0.11	0.88	1.33	2.65
100	0.22	1.77	2.65	5.30
200	0.44	3.54	5.30	10.60
300	0.66	5.30	7.96	15.90
400	0.88	7.07	10.60	21.20
500	1.10	8.84	13.30	26.50
1000	2.21	17.70	26.50	53.00
1500	3.32	26.50	39.80	79.60
2000	4.42	35.40	53.00	106.00

Adapted from A. Smajstrla and D. S. Harrison, Florida Cooperative Extension, Agricultural Engineering Fact Sheet AE18 (1982).

APPROXIMATE TIME REQUIRED TO APPLY VARIOUS DEPTHS OF WATER PER ACRE WITH DIFFERENT FLOWS[1]

Flow of Water			Approximate Time Required per Acre for a Depth of:							
			1 in.		2 in.		3 in.		4 in.	
gpm	sec-ft	Approximate acre-in./hr	hr	min	hr	min	hr	min	hr	min
50	0.11	1/8	9	03	18	06	27	09	36	12
100	0.22	1/4	4	32	9	03	13	35	18	06
150	0.33	5/16	3	01	6	02	9	03	12	04
200	0.45	7/16	2	16	4	32	6	47	9	03
250	0.56	9/16	1	49	3	37	5	26	7	14
300	0.67	11/16	1	31	3	01	4	32	6	02
350	0.78	3/4	1	18	2	35	3	53	5	10
400	0.89	7/8	1	08	2	16	3	24	4	32
450	1.00	1	1	00	2	01	3	01	4	01
500	1.11	1 1/8		54	1	49	2	43	3	37
550	1.23	1 3/16		49	1	39	2	28	3	18
600	1.34	1 5/16		45	1	31	2	16	3	01
650	1.45	1 7/16		42	1	24	2	05	2	48

APPROXIMATE TIME REQUIRED TO APPLY VARIOUS DEPTHS OF WATER PER ACRE WITH DIFFERENT FLOWS[1]—Continued

Flow of Water			Approximate Time Required per Acre for a Depth of:							
			1 in.		2 in.		3 in.		4 in.	
gpm	sec-ft	Approximate acre-in./hr	hr	min	hr	min	hr	min	hr	min
700	1.56	$1\frac{9}{16}$		39	1	18	1	56	2	35
750	1.67	$1\frac{21}{32}$		36	1	12	1	49	2	24
800	1.78	$1\frac{3}{4}$		34	1	08	1	42	2	16
850	1.89	$1\frac{7}{8}$		32	1	04	1	36	2	08
900	2.01	2		30	1	00	1	31	2	01
950	2.12	$2\frac{3}{32}$		29		57	1	26	1	54
1000	2.23	$2\frac{3}{16}$		27		54	1	21	1	49
1050	2.34	$2\frac{5}{16}$		26		52	1	18	1	44
1100	2.45	$2\frac{7}{16}$		25		49	1	14	1	38
1150	2.56	$2\frac{1}{2}$		24		47	1	11	1	34
1200	2.67	$2\frac{5}{8}$		23		45	1	08	1	31
1300	2.90	$2\frac{7}{8}$		21		42	1	03	1	24
1400	3.12	$3\frac{1}{16}$		20		39		58	1	18
1500	3.34	$3\frac{5}{16}$		18		36		54	1	12

[1] If a sprinkler system is used, the time required should be increased by 2–10% to compensate for the water that will evaporate before reaching the soil.

TO DETERMINE THE WATER NEEDED TO WET VARIOUS DEPTHS OF SOIL

Example: You wish to wet a loam soil to a 12-in. depth when half the available water in that zone is gone. Move across the chart from the left on the 12-in. line. Stop when you reach the diagonal line marked "loams." Move upward from that point to the scale at the top of the chart. You will see that about ¾ in. of water is needed.

Depth of water required, inches, based on depletion of about half the available water in the effective root zone.

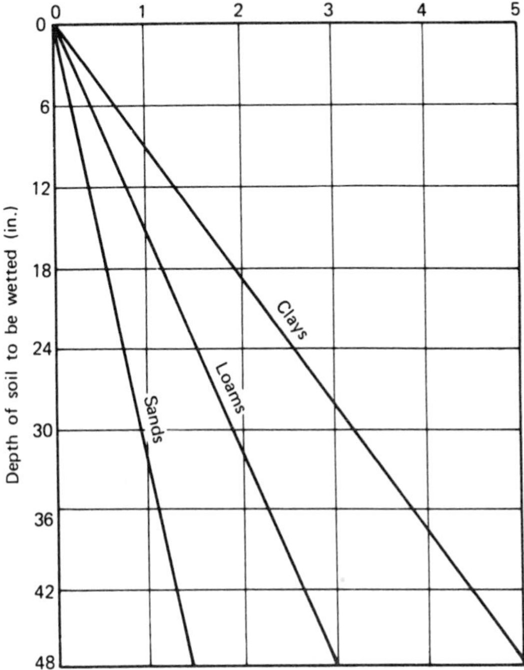

Chart for determining the amount of water needed to wet various depths of soil.

Siphons of metal, plastic, or rubber can be used to carry water from a ditch to the area or furrow to be irrigated.

The inside diameter of the pipe and the head—the vertical distance from the surface of the water in the ditch to the surface of the water on the outlet side—determine the rate of flow.

When the outlet is not submerged, the head is measured to the center of the siphon outlet. You can determine how many gallons per minute are flowing through each siphon from the chart below.

Example: You have a head of 4 in. and are using 2-in. siphons. Follow the 4-in. line across the chart until you reach the curve for 2-in. siphons. Move straight down to the scale at the bottom. You will find that you are putting on about 28 gal/minute.

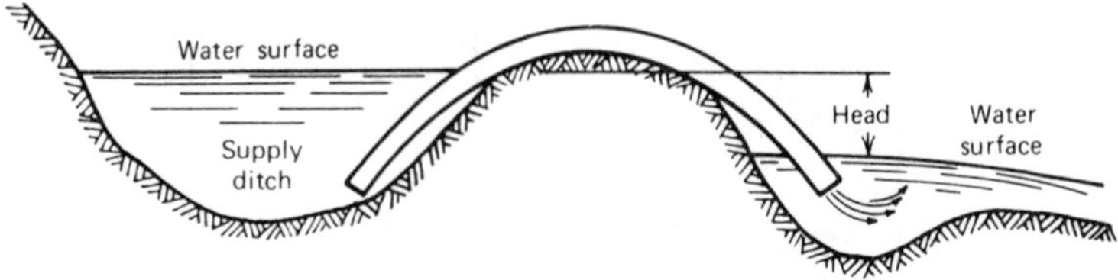

Method of measuring the head for water carried from a supply ditch to a furrow by means of a siphon. Adapted from University of California Division of Agricultural Science Leaflet 2956 (1977).

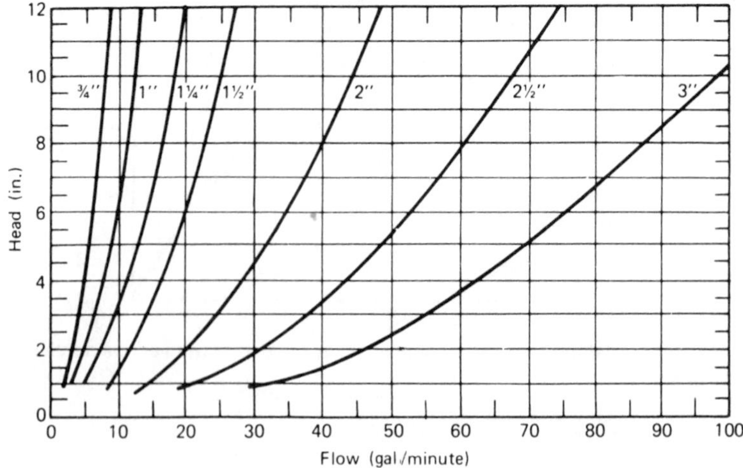

Chart for determining the flow of water through small siphons. Adapted from University of California Division of Agricultural Science Leaflet 2956 (1977).

There are certain limitations to the method of applying fertilizer solutions or soluble fertilizers in water supplied by furrow irrigation. You do not get uniform distribution of the fertilizer over the whole irrigated area. More of the dissolved material may enter the soil near the head than at the end of the furrow. You must know how long it will be necessary to run water in order to irrigate a certain area so as to meter out the fertilizer solution properly. Soils vary considerably in their ability to absorb water.

Fertilizer solutions can be dripped from containers into the water. Devices are available that meter dry fertilizer materials into the irrigation water where they dissolve.

The rate of flow of dry soluble fertilizer or of fertilizer solutions into an irrigation head ditch can be calculated as follows:

$$\frac{\text{Area to be irrigated (acres/hr)} \times \text{amount of nutrient wanted (lb/acre)}}{\text{nutrients in solution (lb/gal)}} = \text{flow rate of fertilizer solution (gal/hr)}$$

$$\frac{\text{Area to be irrigated (acres)} \times \text{amount of soluble fertilizer (lb/acre or gal/acre)}}{\text{time of irrigation (hr)}} = \text{flow rate of fertilizer solution (lb/hr or gal/hr)}$$

Knowing the gallons of solution per hour that are to be added to the irrigation water, you can adjust the flow from the tank as directed by the following table.

RATE OF FLOW OF FERTILIZER SOLUTIONS

Amount of Solution Desired (gal/hr)	Approximate Time (sec) to Fill a 4-oz Jar	Approximate Time (sec) to Fill an 8-oz Jar
½	225	450
1	112	224
2	56	112
3	38	76
4	28	56
5	22	44
6	18	36
7	16	32
8	14	28
9	12	24
10	11	22
12	9	18
14	8	16
16	7	14
18	6	12
20	5.5	11

Each irrigation system presents a separate engineering problem. The advice of a competent engineer is essential. Many factors must be taken into consideration in developing a plan for the equipment:

Water supply available at period of greatest use.
Distance from source of water to field to be irrigated.
Height of field above water source and topography of the land.
Type of soil (rate at which it will absorb water and its water-holding capacity).
Area to be irrigated.
Desired frequency of irrigation.
Quantity of water to be applied.
Time in which application is to be made.
Type of power available.
Normal wind velocity and direction.
Possible future expansion of the installation.

Specific details of the plan must then include the following:

Size of power unit and pump to do the particular job.
Pipe sizes and lengths for mains and laterals.
Operating pressures of sprinklers.
Size and spacing of sprinklers.
Friction losses in the system.

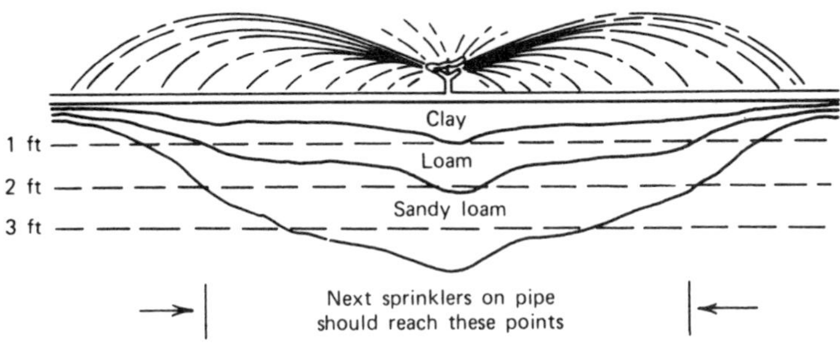

To avoid uneven water distribution, there should be enough distance between sprinklers to allow a 40% overlap in diameter of the area they are to cover. The diagram shows the approximate depth of penetration of available water from a 3-in. irrigation on various classes of soil.

ACREAGE COVERED BY MOVES OF PIPE OF VARIOUS LENGTHS

Lateral Move of Pipe (ft)	Length of Sprinkler Pipe (ft)	Area Covered per Move (acres)
20	2640	1.21
20	1320	0.61
20	660	0.30
20	330	0.15
30	2640	1.82
30	1320	0.91
30	660	0.46
30	330	0.23
40	2640	2.42
40	1320	1.21
40	660	0.61
40	330	0.30
50	2640	3.03
50	1320	1.52
50	660	0.76
50	330	0.38
60	2640	3.64
60	1320	1.82
60	660	0.91
60	330	0.46
80	2640	4.85
80	1320	2.42
80	660	1.21
80	330	0.61
100	2640	6.06
100	1320	3.03
100	660	1.52
100	330	0.76

To determine the output per sprinkler you need to put on your desired rate of application:

$$\frac{\text{Distance between sprinklers (ft)} \times \text{distance between line settings (ft)} \times \text{precipitation rate (in./hr)}}{96.3}$$

= sprinkler rate (gal/minute)

Example: $\dfrac{30 \times 50 \times 0.4}{96.3} = 6.23$ gal/minute per sprinkler

To determine the rate at which you are applying water:

$$\frac{\text{Sprinkler rate (gal/minute)} \times 96.3}{\text{Distance between sprinklers (ft)} \times \text{distance between line settings (ft)}} = \text{precipitation rate (in./hr)}$$

Manufacturer's specifications give the gallons per minute for each type of sprinkler at various pressures.

Example: $\dfrac{10 \times 96.3}{40 \times 50} = 0.481$ in./hr

PRECIPITATION RATES FOR VARIOUS NOZZLE SIZES, PRESSURE, AND SPACINGS

Nozzle Size (in.)	Pressure (psi)	Discharge[1] (gpm)	Diameter of Spray[2] (ft)	Precipitation Rate at Spacings (in./hr)[1]		
				30 × 40 ft	30 × 45 ft	40 × 40 ft
1/16	45	0.76	60–72	0.061		
1/16	50	0.80	61–73	0.064		
1/16	55	0.85	62–74	0.068		
1/16	60	0.88	63–75	0.071		
1/16	65	0.93	64–76	0.075		
5/64	45	1.19	59–73	0.095	0.085	
5/64	50	1.25	62–72	0.100	0.089	
5/64	55	1.30	64–74	0.104	0.094	0.079
5/64	60	1.36	67–76	0.110	0.097	0.082
5/64	65	1.45	68–77	0.116	0.103	0.087
3/32	45	1.72	68–76	0.138	0.123	0.103
3/32	50	1.80	69–77	0.145	0.128	0.108
3/32	55	1.88	70–78	0.151	0.134	0.113
3/32	60	1.98	71–79	0.159	0.141	0.119
3/32	65	2.08	72–80	0.167	0.148	0.125
7/64	45	2.32	71–78	0.186	0.165	0.140
7/64	50	2.44	72–80	0.196	0.174	0.147
7/64	55	2.56	74–81	0.205	0.182	0.154

7/64	60	2.69	76–82	0.216	0.192	0.161
7/64	65	2.79	77–83	0.224	0.199	0.168
1/8	45	3.04	76–82	0.244	0.217	0.183
1/8	50	3.22	78–82		0.230	0.193
1/8	55	3.39	79–83		0.242	0.204
1/8	60	3.55	80–84		0.253	0.213
1/8	65	3.70	81–85			0.222

Adapted from A. W. Marsh et al., Solid Set Sprinklers for Starting Vegetable Crops, University of California Division of Agricultural Science Leaflet 2265 (1977).

[1] Three-digit numbers are shown here only to indicate the progression as nozzle size and pressure increase.

[2] Range of diameters of spray for different makes and models of sprinklers.

GUIDE FOR SELECTING SIZE OF ALUMINUM PIPE FOR SPRINKLER LATERAL LINES

Sprinkler Discharge (gpm)	Maximum Number of Sprinklers to Use on Single Lateral Line: 30-ft Sprinkler Spacing for Pipe Diameter (in.): 2	3	4	40-ft Sprinkler Spacing for Pipe Diameter (in.): 2	3	4
0.75	47	95	200	43	85	180
1.00	40	80	150	36	72	125
1.25	34	69	118	31	62	104
1.50	30	62	100	28	56	92
1.75	27	56	92	25	50	83
2.00	25	51	84	23	46	76
2.25	23	47	78	21	43	71
2.50	21	44	73	19	40	66
2.75	20	42	68	18	38	62
3.00	19	40	65	17	36	58
3.25	18	38	62	16	34	56
3.50	17	36	59	15	32	53
3.75	16	34	56	14	31	51
4.00	16	33	54	14	30	48

Adapted from A. W. Marsh et al., Solid Set Sprinklers for Starting Vegetable Crops, University of California Division of Agricultural Science Leaflet 2265 (1977).

GUIDE TO MAIN-LINE PIPE SIZES [1]

Distance (ft)	Water Flow (gpm) for Pipe Diameter (in.): 200	400	600	800	1000	1200	1400	1600	1800
200	3	4	5	5	6	6	6	7	7
400	4	5	5	6	6	7	7	8	8
600	4	5	6	7	7	7	8	8	8
800	4	5	6	7	7	8	8	8	10
1000	5	6	6	7	8	8	8	10	10
1200	5	6	7	7	8	8	10	10	10

Adapted from A. W. Marsh et al., Solid Set Sprinklers for Starting Vegetable Crops, University of California Division of Agricultural Science Leaflet 2265 (1977).

[1] Using aluminum pipe (C = 120) with pressure losses ranging from 5 to 15 psi, average about 10.

CONTINUOUS POWER OUTPUT REQUIRED AT TRACTOR POWER TAKEOFF TO PUMP WATER

		Flow (gpm)								
		100	200	300	400	500	600	700	800	1000
Pressure[1] (psi)	Head[1] (ft)	Horsepower Required [2]								
50	116	3.9	7.8	11.7	16	20	23	27	31	39
55	128	4.3	8.7	13	17	22	26	30	35	43
60	140	4.7	9.5	14	19	24	28	33	38	47
65	151	5.1	10	15	20	25	30	36	41	51
70	162	5.5	11	16	22	27	33	38	44	55
75	173	5.8	12	17	23	29	35	41	47	58
80	185	6.2	12	19	25	31	37	44	50	62

Adapted from A. W. Marsh et al., Solid Set Sprinklers for Starting Vegetable Crops, University of California Division of Agricultural Science Leaflet 2265 (1977).

[1] Including nozzle pressure, friction loss, and elevation lift.

[2] Pump assumed to operate at 75% efficiency.

FLOW OF WATER REQUIRED TO OPERATE SOLID SET SPRINKLER SYSTEMS

	Area Irrigated per Set (acres)									
	4		8		12		16		20	
Irrigation rate (in./hr)	gpm[1]	cfs[2]	gpm	cfs	gpm	cfs	gpm	cfs	gpm	cfs
0.06	108	0.5	217	0.5	326	1.0	435	1.0	543	1.5
0.08	145	0.5	290	1.0	435	1.0	580	1.5	725	2.0
0.10	181	0.5	362	1.0	543	1.5	724	2.0	905	2.5
0.12	217	0.5	435	1.0	652	1.5	870	2.0	1086	2.5
0.15	271	1.0	543	1.5	815	2.0	1086	2.5	1360	3.5
0.20	362	1.0	724	2.0	1086	2.5	1448	2.5	1810	4.5

Adapted from A. W. Marsh et al., Solid Set Sprinklers for Starting Vegetable Crops, University of California Division of Agricultural Science Leaflet 2265 (1977).

[1] Gallons per minute pumped into the sprinkler system to provide an average precipitation rate as shown. Pump must have this much or slightly greater capacity.

[2] Cubic feet per second—the flow of water to the next larger 1/2 cfs that must be ordered from the water district, assuming that the district accepts orders only in increments of 1/2 cfs. Actually, 1/2 cfs = 225 gpm.

Anhydrous ammonia, aqua ammonia, and nitrogen solutions containing free ammonia should not be applied by sprinkler irrigation because of the excessive loss of the volatile ammonia. Ammonium nitrate, ammonium sulfate, calcium nitrate, sodium nitrate, and urea are all suitable materials for use through a sprinkler system. The water containing the ammonia salts should not have a reaction that is on the alkaline side of neutrality or the loss of ammonia will be considerable.

It is best to put phosphorus fertilizers directly in the soil by a band application. Potash fertilizers can be used in sprinkler lines. However, a soil application ahead of or at planting time will usually prove adequate and can be made efficiently at that time.

Manganese, boron, or copper can be applied through the sprinkler system. See pages 213–214 for possible rates of application.

The fertilizing material is dissolved in a tank of water. Calcium nitrate, ammonium sulfate, and ammonium nitrate will dissolve completely. The solution can then be introduced into the water line, either by suction or by pressure from a pump. See page 148 for relative solubility of fertilizer materials.

Introduce the fertilizer into the line slowly, taking 10–20 min to complete the operation.

After enough of the fertilizer solution has passed into the pipe lines, shut the valve if suction by pump has been used. This prevents unpriming the pump. Then run the system for 10–15 min to wash the fertilizer off the leaves. This will also flush out the lines, valves, and pump if one has been used to force or suck the solution into the main line.

AMOUNT OF FERTILIZER TO USE FOR EACH SETTING OF THE SPRINKLER LINE

Length of Line (ft)	Lateral Move of Line (ft)	Nutrient per Setting of Sprinkler Line (lb): 10	20	30	40	50	60	70	80	90	100
		Nutrient Application Desired (lb/acre)									
330	40	3	6	9	12	15	18	21	24	27	30
	60	4	9	12	18	22	27	31	36	40	45
	80	6	12	18	24	30	36	42	48	54	60
660	40	6	12	18	24	30	36	42	48	54	60
	60	9	18	24	36	45	54	63	72	81	90
	80	12	24	36	48	60	72	84	96	108	120
990	40	9	18	24	36	45	54	63	72	81	90
	60	13	27	40	54	67	81	94	108	121	135
	80	18	36	54	72	90	108	126	144	162	180
1320	40	12	24	36	48	60	72	84	96	108	120
	60	18	36	54	72	90	108	126	144	162	180
	80	24	48	72	96	120	144	168	192	216	240

It is necessary to calculate the actual pounds of a fertilizing material that must be dissolved in the mixing tank in order to supply a certain number of pounds of the nutrient to the acre at each setting of the sprinkler line. This is done as follows. To apply 40 lb of nitrogen to the acre when the sprinkler line is 660 ft long and will be moved 80 ft, if sodium nitrate is used, divide 48 (as shown in the table) by 0.16 (the percentage of nitrogen in sodium nitrate). This equals 300 lb, which must be dissolved in the tank and applied at each setting of the pipe. Do the same with ammonium nitrate: divide 48 by 0.33, which equals about 145 lbs.

SPRINKLER IRRIGATION FOR COLD PROTECTION

Sprinklers are often used to protect vegetables from freezing. Sprinkling provides cold protection because the latent heat of fusion is released when water changes from liquid to ice. When water is freezing, its temperature is near 32°F. The heat liberated as the water freezes maintains the temperature of the vegetable near 32°F even though the surroundings may be colder. As long as there is a mixture of both water and ice present, the temperature remains near 32°F. For all of the plant to be protected, it must be covered or encased in the freezing ice-water mixture. Enough water must be applied so that the latent heat released will compensate for the heat losses.

APPLICATION RATE RECOMMENDED FOR COLD PROTECTION UNDER DIFFERENT WIND AND TEMPERATURE CONDITIONS

Minimum Temperature Expected (°F)	Wind Speed (mph)		
	0–1	2–4	5–8
	(inches per hour)		
27	0.10	0.10	0.10
26	0.10	0.10	0.14
24	0.10	0.16	0.30
22	0.12	0.24	0.50
20	0.16	0.30	0.60

Adapted from D. S. Harrison, J. F. Gerber, and R. E. Choate, Sprinkler Irrigation for Cold Protection, Florida Cooperative Extension Circular 348 (1974).

Drip or trickle irrigation refers to the frequent slow application of water directly to the base of the plants. Vegetables are usually irrigated by double-wall or by thin-wall tubing to supply a uniform rate along the entire row.

Pressure in the drip lines varies from 8 to 10 psi and about 12 psi in the submains. Length of the drip lines may be as long as 600 ft but 200–250 ft is more common. Rate of water application is about 1/4 to 1/2 gpm/100 ft of row. One acre of plants in rows 100 ft long and 4 ft apart will use about 30 gpm of water. Unless clear sediment-free water is available, it is necessary to install a filter in the main line in order to prevent clogging of the small pores in the drip lines.

Drip irrigation allows for considerable saving in water application, particularly during early plant growth. Because water is applied only next to plants in the row, the aisles between rows remain dry.

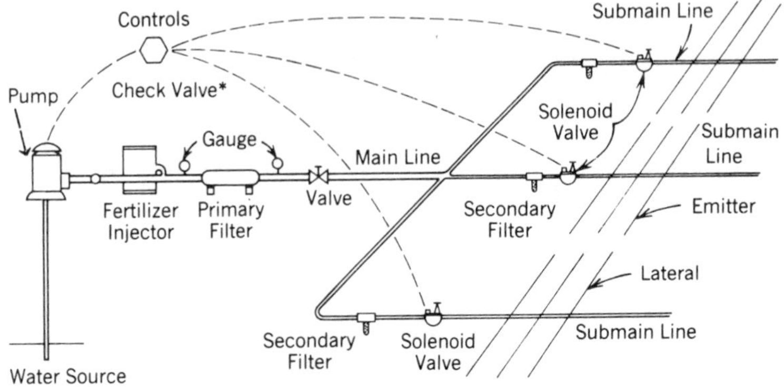

*A backflow preventer or vacuum breaker is required in some areas.

Drip or trickle irrigation system components.

VOLUME OF WATER TO APPLY (GALLONS) BY DRIP IRRIGATION PER 100 LINEAR FEET OF BED FOR A GIVEN WETTED SOIL VOLUME, AVAILABLE WATER-HOLDING CAPACITY, AND AN ALLOWABLE DEPLETION OF 1/2 [1]

Wetted Soil Volume Per 100 ft (cubic ft)	Available Water-Holding Capacity (inches of water per foot of soil)							
	0.25	0.50	0.75	1.00	1.25	1.50	1.75	2.00
	(gallons per 100 linear bed feet)							
25	2.2	4.3	6.5	8.7	10.8	13.0	15.2	17.3
50	4.3	8.7	13.0	17.3	21.6	26.0	30.3	34.6
75	6.5	13.0	19.5	26.0	32.5	39.0	45.5	51.9
100	8.7	17.3	26.0	34.6	43.3	51.9	60.6	69.3
125	10.8	21.6	32.5	43.3	54.1	64.9	75.8	86.6
150	13.0	26.0	39.0	51.9	64.9	77.9	90.9	103.9
175	15.2	30.3	45.5	60.6	75.8	90.9	106.1	121.2
200	17.3	34.6	51.9	69.3	86.6	103.9	121.2	138.5
225	19.5	39.0	58.4	77.9	97.4	116.9	136.4	155.8
250	21.6	43.3	64.9	86.6	108.2	129.9	151.5	173.1
275	23.8	47.6	71.4	95.2	119.0	142.8	166.7	190.5
300	26.0	51.9	77.9	103.9	129.9	155.8	181.8	207.8
350	30.3	60.6	90.9	121.2	151.5	181.8	212.1	242.4
400	34.6	69.3	103.9	138.5	173.1	207.8	242.4	277.0
450	39.0	77.9	116.9	155.8	194.8	233.8	272.7	311.7
500	43.3	86.6	129.9	173.1	216.4	259.7	303.0	346.3
550	47.6	95.2	142.8	190.5	238.1	285.7	333.3	380.9
600	51.9	103.9	155.8	207.8	259.7	311.7	363.6	415.6
700	60.6	121.2	181.8	242.4	303.0	363.6	424.2	484.8
800	69.3	138.5	207.8	277.0	346.3	415.6	484.8	554.1
900	77.9	155.8	233.8	311.7	389.6	467.5	545.4	623.3

Adapted from G. A. Clark, C. D. Stanley, and A. G. Smajstrla, Micro-irrigation on Mulched Bed Systems: Components, System Capacities and Management. Fla. Coop. Ext. Serv. Bul. 245 (1988).

[1] An irrigation application efficiency of 90% was assumed.

DISCHARGE PER GROSS ACRE (GPM/ACRE) FOR DRIP IRRIGATION BASED ON IRRIGATED LINEAR BED FEET AND EMITTER DISCHARGE

Linear Bed Feet Per Acre	Emitter Discharge (gpm/100 ft)						
	0.25	0.30	0.40	0.50	0.75	1.00	1.50
	(gallons per minute/acre)						
3,000	7.5	9.0	12.0	15.0	22.5	30.0	45.0
3,500	8.8	10.5	14.0	17.5	26.3	35.0	52.5
4,000	10.0	12.0	16.0	20.0	30.0	40.0	60.0
4,500	11.3	13.5	18.0	22.5	33.8	45.0	67.5
5,000	12.5	15.0	20.0	25.0	37.5	50.0	75.0
5,500	13.8	16.5	22.0	27.5	41.3	55.0	82.5
6,000	15.0	18.0	24.0	30.0	45.0	60.0	90.0
6,500	16.3	19.5	26.0	32.5	48.8	65.0	97.5
7,000	17.5	21.0	28.0	35.0	52.5	70.0	105.0
7,500	18.8	22.5	30.0	37.5	56.3	75.0	112.5
8,000	20.0	24.0	32.0	40.0	60.0	80.0	120.0
8,500	21.3	25.5	34.0	42.5	63.8	85.0	127.5
9,000	22.5	27.0	36.0	45.0	67.5	90.0	135.0
9,500	23.8	28.5	38.0	47.5	71.3	95.0	142.5
10,000	25.0	30.0	40.0	50.0	75.0	100.0	150.0

Adapted from G. A. Clark, C. D. Stanley, and A. G. Smajstrla. Micro-irrigation on Mulched Bed Systems: Components, System Capacities and Management. Fla. Coop. Ext. Serv. Bul. 245 (1988).

VOLUME OF WATER (GALLONS OF WATER PER ACRE PER MINUTE) DELIVERED UNDER VARIOUS BED SPACINGS WITH ONE TAPE LATERAL PER BED AND FOR SEVERAL EMITTER FLOW RATES

Bed Spacing (in.)	Drip Tape Per Acre (ft)	Emitter Flow Rate (gal. per min. per 100 ft)			
		0.50	0.40	0.30	0.25
		(gallons per acre/minute)			
24	21,780	108.9	87.1	65.3	54.5
30	17,420	87.1	69.7	52.3	43.6
36	14,520	72.6	58.1	43.6	36.6
42	12,450	62.2	49.8	37.3	31.1
48	10,890	54.5	43.6	32.7	27.2
54	9,680	48.4	38.7	29.0	24.2
60	8,710	43.6	34.9	26.1	21.8
72	7,260	36.3	29.0	21.8	18.2
84	6,220	31.1	24.9	18.7	15.6
96	5,450	27.2	21.8	16.3	13.6
108	4,840	24.2	19.4	14.5	12.1
120	4,360	21.8	17.4	13.1	10.0

VOLUME OF AVAILABLE WATER IN THE WETTED CYLINDRICAL DISTRIBUTION PATTERN UNDER A DRIP IRRIGATION LINE BASED UPON THE AVAILABLE WATER-HOLDING CAPACITY OF THE SOIL

	Wetted Radius (inches)[1]				
Available Water (%)	6	9	12	15	18
	(gallons available water per 100 emitters)				
3	9	20	35	55	79
4	12	26	47	74	106
5	15	33	59	92	132
6	18	40	71	110	159
7	21	46	82	129	185
8	24	53	94	147	212
9	26	60	106	165	238
10	29	66	118	184	265
11	32	73	129	202	291
12	35	79	141	221	318
13	38	86	153	239	344
14	41	93	165	257	371
15	44	99	176	276	397

Adapted from G. A. Clark and A. G. Smajstrla. Application Volumes and Wetted Patterns for Scheduling Drip Irrigation in Florida Vegetable Production. Fla. Coop. Ext. Serv. Circ. 1041 (1993).

[1] For a one-foot depth of wetting.

MAXIMUM APPLICATION TIMES FOR DRIP-IRRIGATED VEGETABLE PRODUCTION ON SANDY SOILS WITH VARIOUS WATER-HOLDING CAPACITIES

Available Water-Holding Capacity (inches water per inch of soil)	Tubing Flow Rate (gpm per 100 ft)				
	0.2	0.3	0.4	0.5	0.6
	(maximum minutes per application) [1]				
0.02	41	27	20	16	14
0.03	61	41	31	24	20
0.04	82	54	41	33	27
0.05	102	68	51	41	34
0.06	122	82	61	49	41
0.07	143	95	71	57	48
0.08	163	109	82	65	54
0.09	184	122	92	73	61
0.10	204	136	102	82	68
0.11	224	150	112	90	75
0.12	245	163	122	98	82

Adapted from C. D. Stanley and G. A. Clark. Maximum Application Times for Drip Irrigated Vegetable Production as Influenced by Soil Type or Tubing Emission Characteristics. Fla. Coop. Ext. Serv. Drip Tip No. 9305 (1993).

[1] Assumes 10-inch deep root zone and irrigation at 50% soil moisture depletion.

TREATING IRRIGATION SYSTEMS WITH CHLORINE

Chlorine can be used in irrigation systems to control the growth of algae and other microorganisms such as bacteria and fungi. These organisms are found in surface and ground water and can proliferate with the nutrients present in the water inside the drip tube. Filtration alone cannot remove all of these contaminants. Hypochlorous acid is the agent responsible for controlling microorganisms in drip tubes and is more active at slightly acidic water conditions. Chlorine gas, solid (calcium hypochlorite), or liquid (sodium hypochlorite) are sources of chlorine; however, all forms might not be legal for injecting into irrigation systems. For example, only sodium hypochlorite is legal for use in Florida.

When sodium hypochlorite is injected, the pH of the water will rise. The resulting chloride and sodium ions are not detrimental to crops at typical injection rates. Chlorine materials should be injected at a rate to provide one to two parts per million free residual chlorine at the most distant part of the irrigation system.

In addition to controlling microorganisms, hypochlorous acid also reacts with iron in solution to oxidize the ferrous form to the ferric form, which will precipitate as ferric hydroxide. If irrigation water contains iron, this reaction with injected chlorine should occur before the filter system so that the precipitate can be removed.

Adapted from G. A. Clark and A. G. Smajstrla. Treating Irrigation Systems with Chlorine. Fla. Coop. Ext. Serv. Circ. 1039 (1992).

METHODS OF INJECTING FERTILIZER AND OTHER CHEMICAL SOLUTIONS INTO IRRIGATION PIPELINE

There are four principal methods used to inject fertilizers and other solutions into drip-irrigation systems: (1) pressure differential; (2) the venturi (vacuum); (3) centrifugal pumps; and (4) positive displacement pumps. It is essential that irrigation systems equipped with a chemical injection system have a vacuum breaker (anti-siphon device) and a backflow preventer (check valve) installed upstream from the injection point. The vacuum-breaking valve and backflow preventer will prevent chemical contamination of the water source in case of a water pressure loss or power failure. Operators may need a license to chemigate in some states. Local backflow regulations should be consulted prior to chemigation to insure compliance.

REQUIRED VOLUME (GAL) OF CHEMICAL MIXTURE TO PROVIDE A DESIRED LEVEL OF AN ACTIVE CHEMICAL FOR DIFFERENT CONCENTRATIONS (LB/GAL) OF THE CHEMICAL IN THE STOCK SOLUTION

Mass of Chemical Desired (lb)	S_{mx} Mass of Chemical (lb) Per Gallon of Stock Solution							
	0.2	0.4	0.6	0.8	1.0	2.0	3.0	4.0
	(gallons of stock solution)							
20	100	50	33	25	20	10	7	5
40	200	100	67	50	40	20	13	10
60	300	150	100	75	60	30	20	15
80	400	200	133	100	80	40	27	20
100	500	250	167	125	100	50	33	25
150	750	375	250	188	150	75	50	38
200	1000	500	333	250	200	100	67	50
250	1250	625	417	313	250	125	83	63
300	1500	750	500	375	300	150	100	75
350	1750	875	583	438	350	175	117	88
400	2000	1000	667	500	400	200	133	100
450	2250	1125	750	563	450	225	150	113
500	2500	1250	833	625	500	250	167	125

Adapted from G. A. Clark, D. Z. Haman, and F. S. Zazueta. Injection of Chemicals into Irrigation Systems: Rates, Volumes, and Injection Periods. Fla. Coop. Ext. Serv. Bul. 250 (1990).

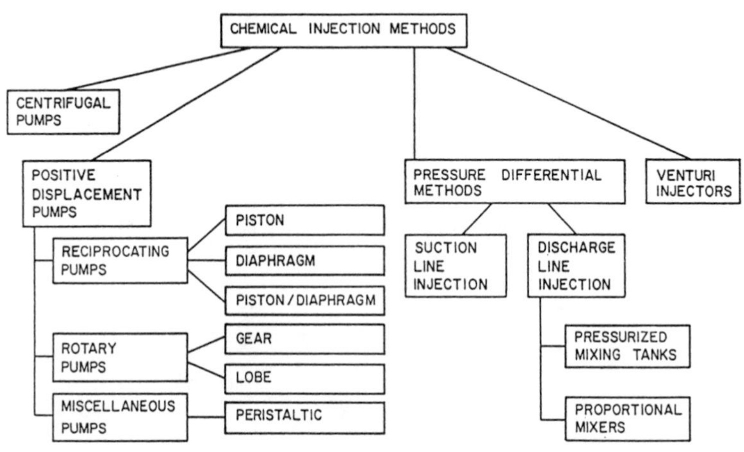

Classification of chemical injection methods for irrigation systems.

Adapted from D. Z. Haman, A. G. Smajstrla, and F. S. Zazueta. Chemical Injection Methods for Irrigation. Fla. Coop. Ext. Serv. Circ. 864 (1990).

COMPARISON OF VARIOUS CHEMICAL INJECTION METHODS

Injector	Advantages	Disadvantages
	Centrifugal Pumps	
Centrifugal pump injector	Low cost. Can be adjusted while running.	Calibration depends on system pressure. Cannot accurately control low injection rates.
	Positive Displacement Pumps	
Piston pumps	High precision. Linear calibration. Very high pressure. Calibration independent of pressure.	High cost. May need to stop to adjust calibration. Chemical flow not continuous.
Diaphragm pumps	Adjust calibration while injecting. High chemical resistance.	Non-linear calibration. Calibration depends on system pressure. Medium to high cost. Chemical flow not continuous.
Piston/diaphragm	High precision. Linear calibration. High chemical resistance. Very high pressure. Calibration independent of pressure.	High cost. May need to stop to adjust calibration.
Rotary Pumps		
Gear pumps Lobe pumps	Injection rate can be adjusted when running.	Fluid pumped cannot be abrasive. Injection rate is dependent on system pressure. Continuity of chemical flow depends on number of lobes in a lobe pump.

COMPARISON OF VARIOUS CHEMICAL INJECTION METHODS—Continued

Injector	Advantages	Disadvantages
Miscellaneous		
Peristaltic pumps	High chemical resistance. Major adjustment can be done by changing tubing size. Injection rate can be adjusted when running.	Short tubing life expectancy. Injection rate dependent on system pressure. Low to medium injection pressure.
	Pressure Differential Methods	
Suction line injection	Very low cost. Injection can be adjusted while running.	Permitted only for surface water source and injection of fertilizer. Injection rate depends on main pump operation.
Discharge Line Injection		
Pressurized mixing tanks	Low to medium cost. Easy operation. Total chemical volume controlled.	Variable chemical concentration. Cannot be calibrated accurately for constant injection rate.
Proportional mixers	Low to medium cost. Calibrate while operating. Injection rates accurately controlled.	Pressure differential required. Volume to be injected is limited by the size of the injector. Frequent refills required.

	Venturi Injectors	
Venturi injector	Low cost. Water powered. Simple to use. Calibrate while operating. No moving parts.	Pressure drop created in the system. Calibration depends on chemical level in the tank.
	Combination Methods	
Proportional mixers/venturi	Greater precision than proportional mixer or venturi alone.	Higher cost than proportional mixer or venturi alone.

Adapted from D. Haman, A. Smajstrla, and F. Zazueta. Chemical Injection Methods for Irrigation. Fla. Coop. Ext. Serv. Circ. 864 (1990).

SINGLE ANTISYPHON DEVICE ASSEMBLY

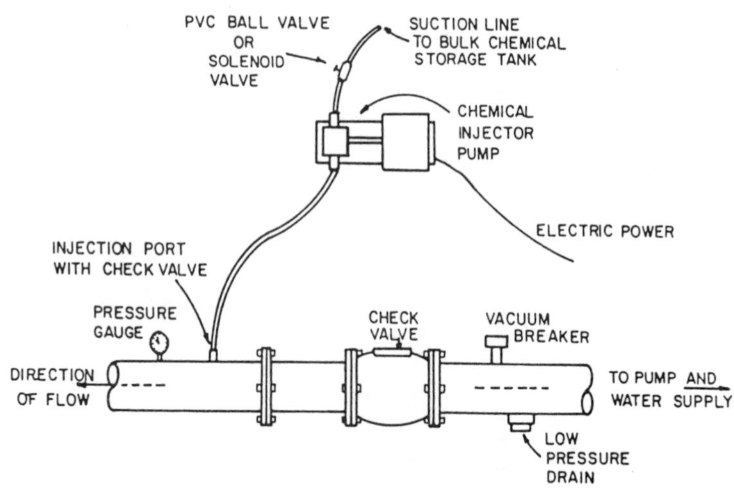

DOUBLE ANTISYPHON DEVICE ASSEMBLY

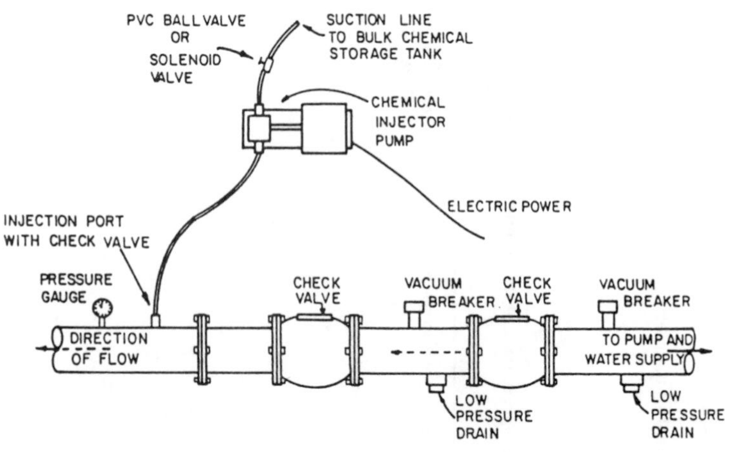

Adapted from A. G. Smajstrla, D. S. Harrison, W. J. Becker, F. S. Zazueta, and D. Z. Haman. Backflow Prevention Requirements for Florida Irrigation Systems. Fla. Coop. Ext. Serv. Bul. 217 (1985).

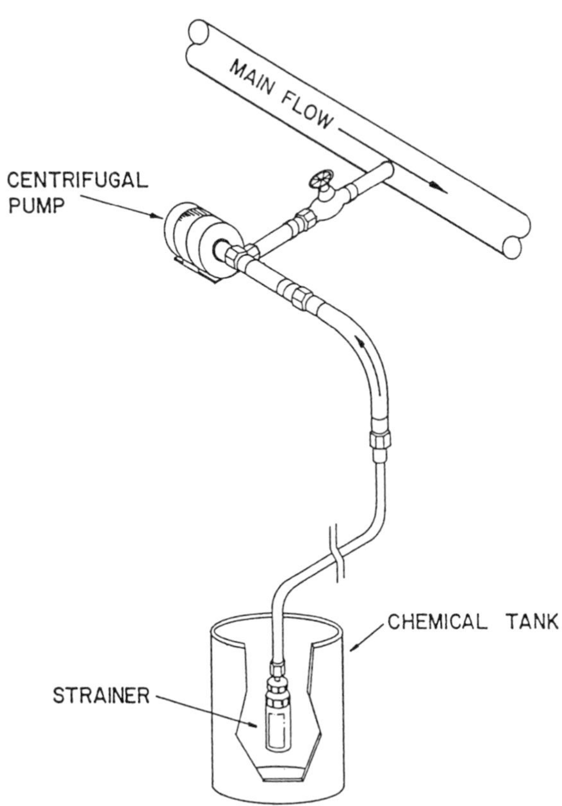

Centrifugal pump chemical injector.

Adapted from D. Z. Haman, A. G. Smajstrla, and F. S. Zazueta. Chemical Injection Methods for Irrigation. Fla. Coop. Ext. Serv. Circ. 864 (1990).

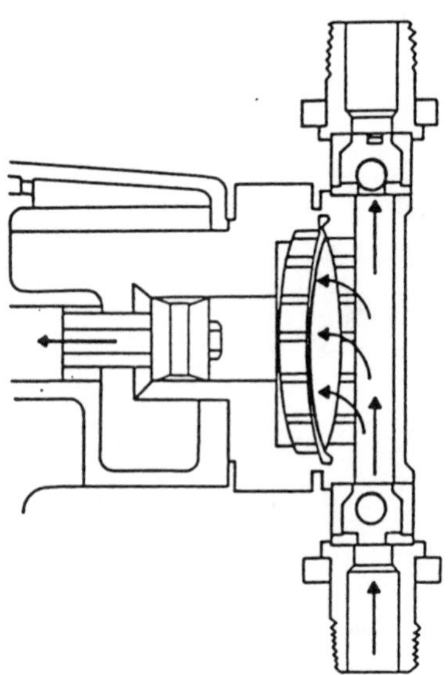

Diaphragm pump - suction stroke.

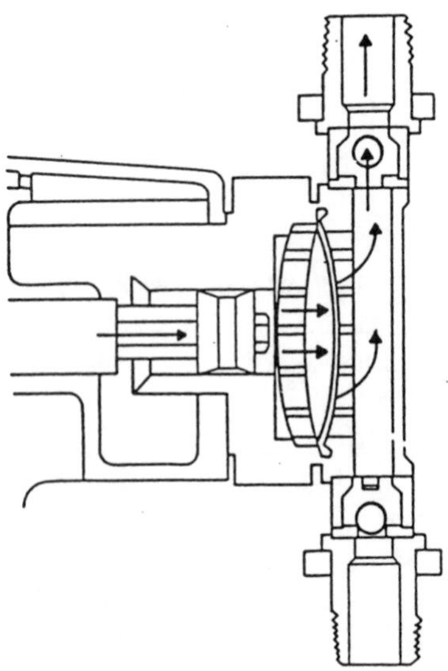

Diaphragm pump - discharge stroke.

Adapted from D. Z. Haman, A. G. Smajstrla, and F. S. Zazueta. Chemical Injection Methods for Irrigation. Fla. Coop. Ext. Serv. Circ. 864 (1990).

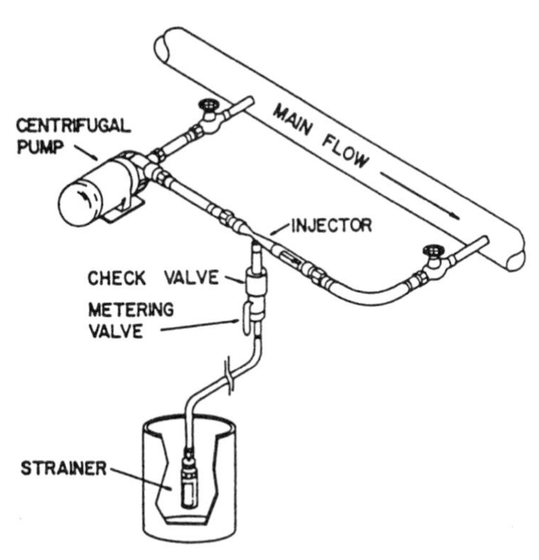

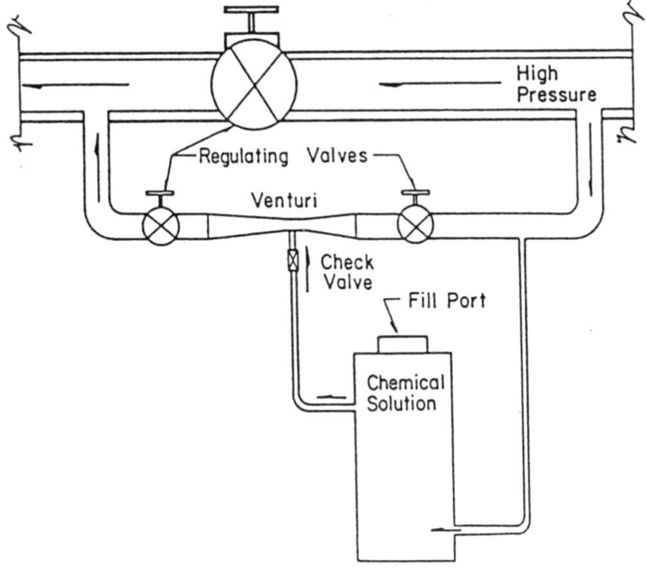

Adapted from D. Z. Haman, A. G. Smajstrla, and F. S. Zazueta. Chemical Injection Methods for Irrigation. Fla. Coop. Ext. Serv. Circ. 864 (1990).

WATER QUALITY GUIDELINES FOR IRRIGATION[1]

Type of Problem	Degree of Problem		
	None	Increasing	Severe
Salinity			
EC (dS/m) or	Less than 0.75	0.75–3.0	More than 3.0
TDS (mg/liter)	Less than 480	480–1920	More than 1920
Permeability			
Low EC (dS/m) or	More than 0.5	0.5–0	—
Low TDS (mg/liter)	More than 320	320–0	—
SAR	Less than 6.0	6.0–9.0	More than 9.0
Toxicity of Specific Ions to Sensitive Crops			
ROOT ABSORPTION			
Sodium (evaluated by SAR)	SAR less than 3	3–9	More than 9

Chloride			
meq/liter	Less than 2	2–10	More than 10.0
mg/liter	Less than 70	70–345	More than 345
Boron (mg/liter)	1.0	1.0–2.0	2.0–10.0
RELATED TO FOLIAR ABSORPTION (SPRINKLER IRRIGATED)			
Sodium			
meq/liter	Less than 3.0	More than 3	—
mg/liter	Less than 70	70	—
Chloride			
meq/liter	Less than 3.0	More than 3	—
mg/liter	Less than 100	100	—
MISCELLANEOUS			
NH_4 and NO_3-N (mg/liter)	Less than 5	5–30	More than 30
HCO_3			
meq/liter	Less than 1.0	1.5–8.5	More than 8.5
mg/liter	Less than 40	40–520	More than 520
pH	Normal range: 6.5–8.3	More than 8.3	—

Adapted from D. S. Farnham, R. F. Hasek, and J. L. Paul, Water Quality, University of California Division of Agricultural Science Leaflet 2995 (1985).

[1] Interpretation is related to type of problem and its severity, but is modified by circumstances of soil, crop, and locality.

MAXIMUM CONCENTRATIONS OF TRACE ELEMENTS IN IRRIGATION WATERS

Element	For Waters Used Continuously on All Soils (mg/liter)	For Use Up to 20 Years on Fine-Textured Soils of pH 6.0–8.5 (mg/liter)
Aluminum	5.0	20.0
Arsenic	0.10	2.0
Beryllium	0.10	0.50
Boron	0.75	2.0–10.0
Cadmium	0.01	0.05
Chromium	0.10	1.0
Cobalt	0.05	5.0
Copper	0.20	5.0
Fluoride	1.0	15.0
Iron	5.0	20.0
Lead	5.0	10.0
Lithium	2.5	2.5
Manganese	0.20	10.0
Molybdenum	0.01	0.05 [1]
Nickel	0.20	2.0
Selenium	0.02	0.02
Vanadium	0.10	1.0
Zinc	2.00	10.0

Adapted from D. S. Farnham, R. F. Hasek, and J. L. Paul, Water Quality, University of California Division of Agricultural Science Leaflet 2995 (1985).

[1] Only for acid, fine-textured soils or acid soils with relatively high iron oxide contents.

YIELD LOSS EXPECTED OWING TO SALINITY OF IRRIGATION WATER

Crop	Electrical Conductivity of Water (mmho/cm or dS/m) for Following % Yield Loss:			
	0	10	25	50
Bean	0.7	1.0	1.5	2.4
Carrot	0.7	1.1	1.9	3.1
Strawberry	0.7	0.9	1.2	1.7
Onion	0.8	1.2	1.8	2.9
Radish	0.8	1.3	2.1	3.4
Lettuce	0.9	1.4	2.1	3.4
Pepper	1.0	1.5	2.2	3.4
Sweet potato	1.0	1.6	2.5	4.0
Sweet corn	1.1	1.7	2.5	3.9
Potato	1.1	1.7	2.5	3.9
Cabbage	1.2	1.9	2.9	4.6
Spinach	1.3	2.2	3.5	5.7
Muskmelon	1.5	2.4	3.8	6.1
Cucumber	1.7	2.2	2.9	4.2
Tomato	1.7	2.3	3.4	5.0
Broccoli	1.9	2.6	3.7	5.5
Beet	2.7	3.4	4.5	6.4

Adapted from R. S. Ayers, *Journal of the Irrigation and Drainage Division* 103:135–154 (1977).

RELATIVE TOLERANCE OF VEGETABLE CROPS TO BORON IN IRRIGATION WATERS [1]

10–15 ppm Boron	4–6 ppm Boron	2–4 ppm Boron	1–2 ppm Boron	0.5–1 ppm Boron
Asparagus	Beet	Artichoke	Broccoli	Bean
	Parsley	Cabbage	Carrot	Garlic
	Tomato	Cauliflower	Cucumber	Lima bean
		Celery	Pea	Onion
		Corn	Pepper	
		Lettuce	Potato	
		Muskmelon	Radish	
		Turnip		

Adapted from E. V. Mass, Salt Tolerance of Plants, *Applied Agricultural Research* 1(1):12–26 (1986).

[1] Maximum concentrations of boron in soil water without yield reduction.

PART 6

VEGETABLE PESTS AND PROBLEMS

Plant damage by pollutants depends on meteorological factors leading to air stagnation, the presence of a pollution source, and the susceptibility of the plants.

Among the pollutants that affect vegetable crops are sulfur dioxide (SO_2), ozone (O_3), peroxyacetyl nitrate (PAN), chlorine (Cl_2), and ammonia (NH_3).

Sulfur Dioxide: SO_2 causes acute and chronic plant injury. Acute injury is characterized by dead tissue between the veins or on leaf margins. The dead tissue may be bleached, ivory, tan, orange, red, reddish-brown, or brown, depending on the plant species, time of year, and weather. Chronic injury is marked by brownish-red, turgid, or bleached white areas on the leaf blade. Young leaves rarely display damage, whereas fully expanded leaves are very sensitive.

Ozone: Common symptoms of O_3 injury are very small irregularly shaped spots that are dark brown to black (stipplelike) or light tan to white (flecklike) on the upper leaf surface. Very young and old leaves are normally resistant to ozone. Recently matured leaves are most susceptible. Injury is usually more pronounced at the leaf tip and along the margins. With severe damage, symptoms may extend to the lower leaf surface.

Peroxyacetyl Nitrate: Typically, PAN affects the underleaf surface of newly matured leaves and causes bronzing, glazing, or silvering on the lower surface of sensitive leaf areas.

The leaf apex of broad-leaved plants becomes sensitive to PAN approximately 5 days after leaf emergence. About four leaves on a shoot are sensitive at any one time. PAN toxicity is specific for tissue in a particular stage of development. Only with successive exposure to PAN will the entire leaf develop injury. Injury may consist of bronzing or glazing with little or no tissue collapse on the upper leaf surface. Pale green to white stipplelike areas may appear on upper and lower leaf surfaces. Complete tissue collapse in a diffuse band across the leaf is helpful in identifying PAN injury.

Chlorine: Injury from chlorine is usually of an acute type and is similar in pattern to sulfur dioxide injury. Foliar necrosis and bleaching are common. Necrosis is marginal in some species but scattered in others either between or along veins. Lettuce plants exhibit necrotic injury on the margins of outer leaves, which often extends in solid areas toward the center and base of the leaf. Inner leaves remain unmarked.

Ammonia: Field injury from NH_3 has been primarily due to accidental spillage.

Slight amounts of the gas produce color changes in the pigments of vegetable skin. The dry outer scales of red onion may become greenish or black, whereas scales of yellow or brown onion may turn dark brown.

Hydrocloric Acid Gas: HCl causes an acid-type burn. The usual acute response is a bleaching of tissue. Leaves of lettuce, endive, and escarole exhibit a tipburn that progresses toward the center of the leaf and soon dries out. Tomato plants develop interveinal bronzing.

Adapted from Commercial Vegetable Production Recommendations, Maryland Agricultural Extension Service EB-236 (1986).

REACTION OF VEGETABLE CROPS TO AIR POLLUANTS

Vegetable crops may be injured following exposure to high concentrations of various atmospheric pollutants. Prolonged exposure to lower concentrations may also result in plant damage.

Injury appears progressively as leaf chlorosis (yellowing), necrosis (death), and perhaps restricted growth and yields. On occasion, plants may be killed, but usually not until they have suffered persistent injury.

Symptoms of air pollution damage vary with the individual crops and plant age, specific pollutant, concentration, duration of exposure, and environmental conditions.

RELATIVE SENSITIVITY OF VEGETABLE CROPS TO AIR POLLUTANTS

Pollutant	Sensitive	Intermediate	Tolerant
Ozone	Bean	Carrot	Beet
	Broccoli	Endive	Cucumber
	Onion	Parsley	Lettuce
	Potato	Parsnip	
	Radish	Turnip	
	Spinach		
	Sweet corn		
	Tomato		
Sulfur dioxide	Bean	Cabbage	Cucumber
	Beet	Pea	Onion
	Broccoli	Tomato	Sweet corn
	Brussels sprouts		
	Carrot		
	Endive		
	Lettuce		
	Okra		
	Pepper		
	Pumpkin		
	Radish		
	Rhubarb		
	Spinach		
	Squash		
	Sweet potato		
	Swiss chard		
	Turnip		
Fluoride	Sweet corn		Asparagus
			Squash
			Tomato
Nitrogen dioxide	Lettuce		Asparagus
			Bean
PAN	Bean	Carrot	Broccoli
	Beet		Cabbage
	Celery		Cauliflower
	Endive		Cucumber
	Lettuce		Onion

RELATIVE SENSITIVITY OF VEGETABLE CROPS TO AIR POLLUTANTS—Continued

Pollutant	Sensitive	Intermediate	Tolerant
PAN (*Continued*)	Mustard Pepper Spinach Sweet corn Swiss chard Tomato		Radish Squash
Ethylene	Bean Cucumber Pea Sothern pea Sweet potato Tomato	Carrot Squash	Beet Cabbage Endive Onion Radish
2,4-D	Tomato	Potato	Bean Cabbage Eggplant Rhubarb
Chlorine	Mustard Onion Radish Sweet corn	Bean Cucumber Southern pea Squash Tomato	Eggplant Pepper
Ammonia	Mustard	Tomato	
Mercury vapor	Bean	Tomato	
Hydrogen sulfide	Cucumber Radish Tomato	Pepper	Mustard

Adapted from J. S. Jacobson and A. C. Hill (eds.), *Recognition of Air Pollution Injury to Vegetation*, Air Pollution Control Association, Pittsburgh, PA (1970); M. Treshow, *Environment and Plant Response*, McGraw-Hill, New York (1970); and R. G. Pearson et al., Air Pollution and Horticultural Crops, Ontario Ministry of Agriculture and Food AGDEX 200/691 (1973).

Integrated Pest Management (IPM) attempts to make the most efficient use of the strategies available to control pest populations by taking action to prevent problems, suppress damage levels and use chemical pesticides only where needed. Rather than seeking to eradicate all pests entirely, IPM strives to prevent their development or to suppress their population numbers below levels that would be economically damaging.

Integrated means that a broad, interdisciplinary approach is taken using scientific principles of crop protection in order to fuse into a single system a variety of methods and tactics.

Pest includes insects, mites, nematodes, plant pathogens, weeds, and vertebrates that adversely affect crop quality and yield.

Management refers to the attempt to control pest populations in a planned, systematic way by keeping their numbers or damage within acceptable levels.

Effective IPM consists of four basic principles:

Exclusion seeks to prevent pests from entering the field in the first place.

Suppression refers to the attempt to suppress pests below the level at which they would be economically damaging.

Eradication strives to eliminate entirely certain pests.

Plant resistance stresses the effort to develop healthy, vigorous strains that will be resistant to certain pests.

In order to carry out these four basic principles, the following steps are often taken:

1. *The identification of key pests and beneficial organisms* is a necessary first step.
2. *Preventive cultural practices* are selected to minimize pest population development.
3. *Pest populations must be monitored* by trained "scouts" who routinely sample fields.
4. *A prediction of loss and risks* involved is made by setting an economic threshold. Pests are controlled only when the pest population threatens acceptable levels of quality and yield. The level at which the pest population or its damage endangers quality and yield is often called the economic threshold. The economic threshold is set by predicting potential loss and risks at a given population density.
5. *An action decision must be made.* In some cases pesticide application will be necessary to reduce the crop threat, whereas in other cases, a decision will be made to wait and rely on closer monitoring.
6. *Evaluation and follow-up* must occur throughout all stages in order to make corrections, assess levels of success, and project future possibilities for improvement.

To be effective, IPM must make use of the following tools:

1. *Pesticides.* Some pesticides are applied preventively, for example, herbicides, fungicides, and nematicides. In an effective IPM program, pesticides are applied on a prescription basis tailored to the particular pest, and chosen so as to have minimum impact on people and the environment. They are applied only when a pest population has been diagnosed as large enough to threaten acceptable levels of yield and quality and no other economic control measure is available.
2. *Resistant crop varieties* are bred and selected when available in order to protect against key pests.
3. *Natural enemies* are used to regulate the pest population whenever possible.
4. *Pheromone* (sex lure) traps are used to lure and destroy male insects, thus helping monitoring procedures.
5. *Preventive measures* such as soil fumigation for nematodes and assurance of good soil fertility help to provide a healthy, vigorous plant.
6. *Avoidance* of peak pest populations can be brought about by a change in planting times or pest-controlling crop rotation.
7. *Improved application* is achieved by keeping equipment up-to-date and in excellent shape.
8. *Other assorted cultural practices* such as flooding, row spacing, and plant spacing can influence pest populations.

Adapted from K. Hoeller (ed.), IPM, An Integrated Pest Management Primer, Florida Cooperative Extension Service IPM-1 (1978).

Soil solarization is a nonchemical control method that is particularly effective in areas that have high temperatures and long days for the required 4–6 weeks. In the northern hemisphere, this generally means that solarization is done during the summer months in preparation for a fall crop or for a crop in the following spring.

Soil solarization captures radiant heat energy from the sun, thereby causing physical, chemical, and biological changes in the soil. Transparent polyethylene plastic placed on moist soil during the hot summer months increases soil temperatures to levels lethal to many soil-borne plant pathogens, weed seeds, and seedlings (including parasitic seed plants), nematodes, and some soil-residing mites. Soil solarization also improves plant nutrition by increasing the availability of nitrogen and other essential nutrients.

Time of Year

Highest soil temperatures are obtained when the days are long, air temperatures are high, the sky is clear, and there is no wind.

Plastic Color

Clear polyethylene should be used, not black plastic. Transparent plastic results in greater transmission of solar energy to the soil. Polyethylene should be UV stabilized so the tarp does not degrade during the solarization period.

Plastic Thickness

Polyethylene 1 mil thick is the most efficient and economical for soil heating. However, it is easier to rip or puncture and is less able to withstand high winds than thicker plastic. Users in windy areas may prefer to use plastic 1½ to 2 mils thick. Thick transparent plastic (4–6 mils) reflects more solar energy than does thinner plastic (1–2 mils) and results in slightly lower temperatures.

Preparation of the Soil

It is important that the area to be treated is level and free of weeds, plants, debris, and large clods that would raise the plastic off the ground. Maximum soil heating occurs when the plastic is close to the soil; therefore, air pockets caused by large clods or deep furrows should be avoided. Soil should be tilled as deep as possible and have moisture at field capacity.

Partial vs. Complete Soil Coverage

Polyethylene tarps may be applied in strips (a minimum of 2–3 ft wide) over the planting bed or as continuous sheeting glued, heat-fused, or held in place by soil. In some cases, strip coverage may be more practical and economical than full soil coverage, because less plastic is needed and plastic connection costs are avoided.

Soil Moisture

Soil must be moist (field capacity) for maximum effect because moisture not only makes organisms more sensitive to heat, but it also conducts heat faster and deeper into the soil.

Duration of Soil Coverage

Killing of pathogens and pests is related to time and temperature exposure. The longer the soil is heated, the deeper the control. Although some pest organisms are killed within days, 4–6 weeks of treatment in full sun during the summer is usually best. The upper limit for temperature is about 115°F for vascular plants, 130°F for nematodes, 140°F for fungi, and 160 to 212°F for bacteria.

Adapted from G. S. Pullman, J. E. DeVay, C. L. Elmore, and W. H. Hart, Soil Solarization, California Cooperative Extension Leaflet 21377 (1984), and from D. O. Chellemi, Soil Solarization for Management of Soilborne Pests. Florida Cooperative Extension Fact Sheet PPP51 (1995).

PRECAUTIONS IN THE USE OF PESTICIDES

All chemicals are potentially hazardous and should be used carefully. Follow exactly the directions, precautions, and limitations given on the container label. Store all chemicals in a safe place where children, pets, and livestock cannot reach them. Do not reuse pesticide containers. Avoid inhaling fumes and dust from pesticides. Avoid spilling chemicals; if they are accidently spilled, remove contaminated clothing and thoroughly wash the skin with soap and water immediately.

Observe the following rules:

1. Avoid drift from the application area to adjacent areas occupied by humans or livestock or to bodies of water.
2. Wear goggles, an approved respirator, and neoprene gloves when loading or mixing pesticides. Aerial applicators should be loaded by a ground crew.
3. Pour chemicals at a level well below the face to avoid splashing or spilling onto the face or eyes.
4. Have plenty of soap and water on hand to wash contaminated skin in the event of spilling.
5. Change clothing and bathe after the job is completed.
6. Know the insecticide, the symptoms of overexposure to it, and a physician who can be called quickly. In case symptoms appear (contracted pupils, blurred vision, nausea, severe headache, dizziness), stop operations at once and contact a physician.

The worker protection standard (WPS) is a set of regulations issued by the U.S. Environmental Protection Agency designed to protect agricultural workers and pesticide handlers from exposure to pesticides. The WPS applies to all agricultural employers whose employees are involved in the production of agricultural plants on a farm, forest, nursery, or greenhouse. The employers include owners or managers of farms, forests, nurseries, or greenhouses as well as commercial (custom) applicators and crop advisors who provide services for the production of agricultural plants on these sites. The WPS requires that specific protections be provided to workers and pesticide handlers to prevent pesticide exposure. The agricultural employer is responsible for providing those protections to employees.

Information at a Central Location

An information display at a central location must be provided and contain:

1. An approved EPA safety poster showing how to keep pesticides from a person's body and how to clean up any contact with a pesticide.
2. Name, address, and telephone number of the nearest emergency medical facility.
3. Information about each pesticide application, including description of treated area, product name, EPA registration number of product, active ingredient of pesticide, time and date of application, and the restricted entry interval (REI) for the pesticide.

Pesticide Safety Training

Employers must provide pesticide safety training for pesticide handlers and agricultural workers unless the handler or worker is a certified pesticide applicator. Workers must receive training within 5 days of beginning work.

Decontamination Areas Must Provide:

1. Water for washing and eye flushing
2. Soap
3. Single-use towels
4. Water for whole-body wash (pesticide handler sites only)
5. Clean coveralls (pesticide handler sites only)

Restricted Entry Interval

Pesticides have restricted entry intervals, a period after a pesticide application during which employers must keep everyone, except appropriately trained and equipped handlers, out of areas being treated with pesticides. Employers must orally inform all of their agricultural workers who will be within a quarter mile of a treated area. For certain pesticides, treated fields must also be posted with a WPS poster.

Personal Protective Equipment

Personal protective equipment (PPE) must be provided by the employer to all pesticide handlers.

1. All PPE must be clean, in operating condition, used correctly, inspected each day before use, and repaired or replaced as needed.
2. Respirators must fit correctly and filters or canisters replaced at recommended intervals.
3. Handlers must be warned about symptoms of heat illness when wearing PPE.
4. Handlers must be provided clean, pesticide-free areas to store PPE.
5. Contaminated PPE must not be worn or taken home and must be cleaned separate from other laundry.
6. Employers are responsible for providing clean PPE for each day.
7. Coveralls contaminated with undiluted Danger or Warning category pesticide must be discarded.

Adapted from O. N. Nesheim and T. W. Dean. The Worker Protection Standard. In: D. N. Maynard and G. J. Hochmuth (eds.). Vegetable Production Guide for Florida. Florida Coop. Ext. Serv. Circ. SP-170 (1996).

Agricultural Employer: Any person who:

- *employs or contracts for the services of agricultural workers* (including themselves and members of their families) for any type of compensation to perform tasks relating to the production of agricultural plants;
- *owns or operates an agricultural establishment* that uses such workers;
- *employs pesticide handlers* (including members of their family) for any type of compensation, or
- *is self-employed as a pesticide handler.*

Agricultural Establishment: Any farm, greenhouse, nursery, or forest that produces agricultural plants.

Agricultural Establishment Owner: Any person who owns, leases or rents an agricultural establishment covered by the Worker Protection Standard (WPS).

Agricultural Worker: Any person employed by an agricultural employer to do tasks such as harvesting, weeding, or watering related to the production of agricultural plants on a farm, forest, nursery, or greenhouse. By definition, "agricultural workers" do *not* apply pesticides or handle pesticide containers or equipment. Any employee can be an "agricultural worker" while performing one task and a "pesticide handler" while performing a different task.

Immediate Family: The spouse, children, stepchildren, foster children, parents, stepparents, foster parents, brothers and sisters of an agricultural employer.

Personal Protective Equipment (PPE): Clothing and equipment, such as goggles, gloves, boots, aprons, coveralls and respirators, that provide protection from exposure to pesticides.

Pesticide Handler: Any person employed by an agricultural establishment to mix, load, transfer or apply pesticides; or do other tasks that bring them into direct contact with pesticides.

Restricted Entry Interval (REI): The time immediately after a pesticide application when entry into the treated area is limited. Lengths of restricted entry intervals range between 4 and 72 hours. The exact amount of time is product-specific and is indicated on the pesticide label.

Adapted from O. N. Nesheim and T. W. Dean. The Worker Protection Standard. In: D. N. Maynard and G. J. Hochmuth (eds.). Vegetable Production Guide for Florida. Florida Coop. Ext. Serv. Circ. SP-170 (1996).

PESTICIDE HAZARDS TO HONEYBEES

Honeybees and other bees are necessary for pollination of vegetables in the gourd family—cucumber, muskmelon and other melons, pumpkin, squash, and watermelon. Bees and other pollinating insects are necessary for all the insect-pollinated vegetables grown for seed production. Some pesticides are extremely toxic to bees and other pollinating insects, so certain precautions are necessary to avoid injury to them.

Recommendations for Vegetable Growers and Pesticide Applicators

1. Participate actively in areawide integrated crop management programs.
2. Follow pesticide label directions and recommendations.
3. Apply hazardous chemicals in late afternoon, night, or early morning (generally 6 P.M. to 7 A.M.) when honeybees are not actively foraging. Evening applications are generally somewhat safer than morning applications.
4. Use pesticides that are relatively nonhazardous to bees whenever this is consistent with other pest-management strategies. Choose the least hazardous pesticide formulations or tank mixes.
5. Become familiar with bee foraging behavior and types of pesticide applications that are hazardous to bees.
6. Know the location of all apiaries in the vicinity of fields to be sprayed.
7. Avoid drift, overspray, and dumping of toxic materials in noncultivated areas.
8. Survey pest populations and be aware of current treatment thresholds in order to avoid unnecessary pesticide use.
9. Determine if bees are foraging in target area so protective measures can be taken.

The danger in handling pesticides does not depend exclusively on toxicity values. Hazard is a function of both toxicity and the amount and type of exposure. Some chemicals are very hazardous from dermal (skin) exposure as well as oral (ingestion). Although inhalation values are not given, this type of exposure is similar to ingestion. A compound may be highly toxic but present little hazard to the applicator if the precautions are followed carefully.

Toxicity values are expressed as acute oral LD_{50} in terms of milligrams of the substance per kilogram (mg/kg) of test animal body weight required to kill 50 percent of the population. The acute dermal LD_{50} is also expressed in mg/kg. These acute values are for a single exposure and not for repeated exposures such as may occur in the field. Rats are used to obtain the oral LD_{50}, and the test animals used to obtain the dermal values are usually rabbits.

Categories of Toxicity[1]

		LD_{50} Value (mg/kg)	
Categories	Signal Word	Oral	Dermal
I	Danger–Poison	0–50	0–200
II	Warning	50–500	200–2,000
III	Caution	500–5,000	2,000–20,000
IV	None[2]	5,000	20,000

[1] EPA accepted categories.
[2] No signal word required based on acute toxicity; however, products in this category usually display "Caution."

PESTICIDE FORMULATIONS

Several formulations of many pesticides are available commercially. Some are emulsifiable concentrates, flowables, wettable powders, dusts, and granules. After each pesticide recommendation in this publication, one of these formulations is suggested; however, unless stated to the contrary, equivalent rates of another formulation or concentration of that pesticide can be used.

In most cases, Cooperative Extension suggests that sprays rather than dusts be applied to control pests of vegetables. This is because sprays have produced better control and resulted in less drift.

The following table gives available formulations, concentrations, and acute toxicity of most pesticides commonly used.

TOXICITY OF CHEMICALS [1]

			LD_{50} Values (mg/kg) [5]			Toxicity [7]		
Name [2]	Type [3]	Use Class [4]	Oral	Dermal	Reentry [6] (Hours)	Bird	Fish	Bee
acephate, Orthene, Payload	I	G	tech 980	>10,250	24	M	N	H
Adios, carbaryl	I	G	tech 283	>2,000	12	S	N	H
Agree, *Bacillus thuringiensis aizawai + kurstaki*	I	G	See Footnote 8		12	N	N	N
Agri-Mycin-17, streptomycin	B	G	9,000	—	12	—	—	—
Agri-Strep, streptomycin	B	G	9,000	—	12	—	—	—
Agrox D-L Plus	F,I	G	—	—	12	H	H	—
Agrox 2-Way	F,I	G	—	—	12	H	—	—
alachlor, Micro-Tech, Partner	H	R-12	1,800	—	12	S	H	N
Alanap L, naptalam	H	G	8,200	—	24	—	N	N

Alcide, sodium chlorite	F	G	—	—	12	N	N	N
Aldicarb, Temik	A,I,N	R-8	tech 1	20	48	H	H	H
Aliette, fosetyl-Al	F	G	tech 5,000	>2,000	12,24	—	—	—
Align, azadirachtin	I	G	>5,000	>2,000	12	—	—	—
Ambush, permethrin	I	R-12	tech 430–4,000	>4,000	24	—	H	H
Ammo, cypermethrin	I	G	250	>2,000	12,24	N	H	H
Apron, metalaxyl	F	G	tech 669	>3,100	12	—	N	N
Asana XL, esfenvalerate	I	R-12	458	>2,000	12	—	H	H
Atrazine, atrazine	H	G	tech 1,780	7,500	12	S	S	N
azadirachtin, Align	I	G	>5,000	>2,000	12	—	—	—
azinphos-methyl, Guthion	I	R-1,2,3 8,10,12	tech 5–20	220	48	M	H	H
Bacillus thuringiensis	I	G	See Footnote 8		12	N	N	N
Banvel, dicamba	H	G	2,629	>2,000	24	—	—	—
Basagran, bentazon	H	G	2,063	>6,050	12	S	N	N
Basicop, fixed copper[10]	F	G	472	—	24	—	—	—
Bayleton, triadimefon	F	G	tech >1,000	>2,000	12	—	N	N
Benlate, benomyl	F	G	>10,000	>10,000	24	—	S	N
benomyl, Benlate	F	G	>10,000	>10,000	24	—	S	N
bensulide, Prefar	H	G	tech 271–1,470	—	12	—	H	—
bentazon, Basagran	H	G	2,063	>6,050	12	S	N	N
bifenthrin, Capture	I	G	375	>2,000	24	M	H	—
Biobit, *Bacillus thuringiensis kurstaki*	I	G	See Footnote 8		12	N	N	N
Bladex, cyanazine	H	R-13	288	>2,000	12	—	S	N
Botran, dicloran	F	G	tech >5,000	—	12	S	—	N
*Bravo 720, chlorothalonil	F	G	>10,000	>10,000	24	—	H	—
*Bravo C/M, chlorothalonil/ maneb	F	G	>10,000	>10,000	48	—	H	—

TOXICITY OF CHEMICALS [1]—Continued

Name [2]	Type [3]	Use Class [4]	LD_{50} Values (mg/kg) [5]		Reentry [6] (Hours)	Toxicity [7]		
			Oral	Dermal		Bird	Fish	Bee
Brominal, bromoxynil	H	G	tech 260	>2,000	12	H	H	H
bromoxynil, Brominal	H	G	tech 260	>2,000	12	H	H	H
Busan, metam-sodium	N	G	1,891	>3,074	48	—	H	N
butylate, Sutan +	H	G	tech 3,500–5,431	>4,640	12	S	H	N
*captan	F	G	9,000	—	96	S	H	N
Capture, bifenthrin	I	G	375	>2,000	24	M	H	—
*carbaryl, Sevin, Adios	I	G	500	850	12,24	S	N	H
carbofuran, Furadan	I,N	R-3	8	>3,000	48	H	M	N
CDAA, Randox	H	G	750	—	12	—	—	—
Champ, fixed copper [10]	F	G	1,000	—	12	—	—	—
Champion, fixed copper [10]	F	G	2,000	—	12	—	—	—
chlorine, Clorox (bleach)	F	G	—	—	12	N	N	N
Chloro IPC, chlorpropham	H	G	3,800	—	12	—	N	N
chloroneb	F	G	>5,000	>5,000	12	N	—	—
*chloropicrin, Telone C-17	F,N	R-3,10	250	—	72	—	H	N
*chlorothalonil, Bravo 720, Bravo C/M, Reach, Terranil	F	G	>10,000	>10,000	24,48	—	H	—
chlorpropham, Chloro IPC, Sprout Nip	H	G	3,800	—	12,48	—	N	N
*chlorpyrifos, Lorsban	I	R(NJ),G	92–276	2,000	12,24	M	H	H

clomazone, Command	H	G	1,369	>2,000	12,24	—	—	—
Clorox (bleach), chlorine	F	G	—	—	12	N	N	N
Command, clomazone	H	G	tech 2,077	>2,000	12,24	—	—	—
Condor, *Bacillus thuringiensis kurstaki*	I	G	See Footnote 8		12	N	N	N
COPPER-COUNT-N, fixed copper [10]	F	G	—	—	12	—	—	—
copper, fixed [10]	F	G	—	—	12,24,48	—	—	—
Counter, terbufos	I	R-1,2	tech 4.5	1.1	48	—	H	N
cryolite, Kryocide, Prokil	I	G	>5,000	—	12	N	N	N
Curbit 3E, ethalfluralin	H	G	>10,000	>10,000	24	—	—	—
Cutlass, *Bacillus thuringiensis kurstaki*	I	G	See Footnote 8		12	N	N	N
cyanazine, Bladex	H	R-13	288	>2,000	24	—	S	N
*cycloate, Ro-Neet	H	G	3,160–4,640	—	12	—	M	N
Cygon, dimethoate	I	R(NJ),G	tech 235	>400	24	H	H	H
Cymbush, cypermethrin	I	G	250	2,000	48	N	H	H
cypermethrin, Ammo Cymbush	I	G	250	2,000	12,24,48	N	H	H
cyromazine, Trigard	IGR	R,G	3,387	>3,100	12	S	H	H
Cythion, malathion	I	G	tech 5,500	>2,000	12	M	H	H
*Dacthal, DCPA	H	G	>10,000	>2,000	12	S	—	—
*dalapon, Dowpon M	H	G	9,330	—	24	S	N	N
DCP, dichloropropene	N	R(NJ),G	300	333	72	—	—	—
*DCPA, Dacthal	H	G	>10,000	>2,000	12	S	—	—
Deadline, metaldehyde	I	G	630	—	12,24	H	N	N
Des-i-Cate, endothall	H	D	51	—	48	H	—	H
Devrinol, napropamide	H	G	>4,640	—	12,48	—	—	—

TOXICITY OF CHEMICALS [1]—Continued

Name [2]	Type [3]	Use Class [4]	LD_{50} Values (mg/kg) [5]		Reentry [6] (Hours)	Toxicity [7]		
			Oral	Dermal		Bird	Fish	Bee
diazinon	I	R-11	tech 300–400	3,600	12,24	H	H	H
*Dibrom, naled	I	G	191	1,100	48	M	H	H
dicamba, Banvel	H	G	2,629	>2,000	24	—	—	—
dichloropropene, Telone II	N	R(NJ),G	300	333	72	—	—	—
dicloran, Botran	F	G	tech >5,000	—	12	S	—	N
dicofol, Kelthane, Kelthane MF	A	G	820–960	1,000 1,230	12,24	M	H	H
*dimethoate, Cygon	I	R(NJ),G	tech 235	>400	24	H	H	H
DiPel, *Bacillus thuringiensis kurstaki*	I	G	See Footnote 8		12	N	N	N
diquat	H	G	215–235	400	24	—	—	N
Di-Syston, disulfoton	I	R-2,3	tech 4	10	48	H	M	H
disulfoton, Di-Syston	I	R-2,3	tech 4	10	48	H	M	H
Dithane M-45, mancozeb	F	G	11,200	15,000	24	—	H	N
diuron, Karmex	H	G	tech >5,000	>5,000	24	—	—	N
dodine	F	G	1,000	>6,000	48	—	H	H
Dowpon M, dalapon	H	G	9,330	—	12	S	N	N
Dual, metolachlor	H	G	tech 2,780	>10,000	12,24	S	M	N
Du-Ter, triphenyltin hydroxide	F	R-7	156	1,600	48	—	—	—
*Dyfonate, fonophos	I	R-2	8–17.5	25	24,48	H	H	H

endosulfan, Thiodan, Phaser	I	R(NJ),G	tech 160	>500	48	H	H	N
endothall, Des-i-Cate	H	D	51	—	48	H	—	H
Eptam, EPTC	H	G	tech 1,630	—	12	—	H	H
EPTC, Eptam	H	G	tech 1,630	—	12	—	H	H
esfenvalerate, Asana XL	I	R-12	458	>2,000	12	—	H	H
ethalfluralin, Curbit 3E	H	G	>10,000	>10,000	24	—	—	—
ethephon, Ethrel	PGR	G	4,229	—	24,48	—	—	N
ethoprop, Mocap	N	R-2	6.2	2.4	24,48	H	H	H
Ethrel, ethephon	PGR	G	4,229	—	24,48	—	—	N
fenamiphos, Nemacur	N	R-2	tech 3	200	48	H	H	N
fenbutatin-oxide, Vendex	A	G	2,631	>2,000	48	—	—	—
fixed copper[10]	F	G	—	—	12,24,48	—	—	—
*fluazifop-P-butyl, Fusilade DX	H	G	3,328	—	12	—	—	—
Foil BFC, *Bacillus thuringiensis tenebrionis*	I	G	See Footnote 8		12	N	N	N
*fonophos, Dyfonate	I	R-2	8–17.5	25	24,48	H	H	H
Formula 40,2,4-D (acid)	H	R(NJ),G	375	—	48	M	N	H
fosetyl-Al, Aliette	F	G	5,000	>2,000	12,24	—	—	—
Furadan, carbofuran	I,N	R-3	8	>3,000	48	H	M	N
Fury, zeta-cypermethrin	I	R-10,12	—	—	24	—	H	H
Fusarex, TCNB	GR	G	—	—	—	—	—	—
*Fusilade DX, fluazifop-P-butyl	H	G	2,712	>2,420	12	—	—	—
glyphosate, Roundup	H	G	4,300	7,940	24	—	N	N
Goal, oxyfluorfen	H	G	tech >5,000	>10,000	24	—	H	N
Gramoxone Extra, paraquat	H	R-1,8	150	—	48	M	N	N
Guthion, azinphos-methyl	I	R-1,2,3,8, 10,12	tech 10	200	48	M	H	H

TOXICITY OF CHEMICALS [1]—Continued

Name [2]	Type [3]	Use Class [4]	LD_{50} Values (mg/kg) [5]		Reentry [6] (Hours)	Toxicity [7]		
			Oral	Dermal		Bird	Fish	Bee
imazethapyr, Pursuit	H	G	>5,000	>2,000	12,24	—	—	—
Imidan, phosmet	I	R(NJ),G	tech 147–316	>4,640	24	S	H	H
insecticidal soap, M-Pede	I	G	16,900	—	12	N	N	N
*iprodione, Rovral	F	G	>4,400	>2,000	12	—	S	N
Javelin, *Bacillus thuringiensis kurstaki*	I	G	See Footnote 8		12	N	N	N
Karmex, diuron	H	G	tech >5,000	>5,000	24	N	N	N
Kelthane, Kelthane MF, dicofol	A	G	570–595	>5,000	12,24	M	H	N
Kerb, pronamide	H	R-5	tech 8,350	>3,160	12	—	—	—
Kocide, fixed copper [10]	F	G	1,000	—	12,48	M	H	N
Kryocide, cryolite	I	G	>5,000	—	12	N	N	N
Lannate, methomyl	I	R-8,10	17	5,880	48	H	H	H
Larvin, thiodicarb	I	G	66	>2,000	12	H	H	M
Lentagran, pyridate	H	G	2,000	3,400	12	—	H	N
Lexone, metribuzin	H	R-14	tech 2,000	20,000	12	—	N	N
lindane	I	R-5	88–125	1,000	12,24	M	M	N
linuron, Lorox	H	G	tech 4,000	—	24	—	S	N
Lorox, linuron	H	G	tech 4,000	—	24	—	S	N
*Lorsban, chlorpyrifos	I	R(NJ),G	92–276	2,000	12,24	M	H	H
malathion, Cythion	I	G	tech 5,500	>2,000	12	M	H	H

mancozeb, Manzate 200, Dithane M-45, Manex II, Penncozeb	F	G	11,200	15,000	12,24	—	H	N
maneb, Manex	F	G	tech 7,990	>5,000	12	—	H	N
Manex, maneb	F	G	tech 7,990	>5,000	12	—	H	N
Manex II, mancozeb	F	G	11,200	>15,000	12	—	H	N
*Manzate 200, mancozeb	F	G	11,200	>15,000	24	—	H	N
*Marlate, methoxychlor	I	G	6,000	—	12	S	N	M
*Mertect, thiabendazole	F	G	3,100	—	12	—	S	N
metalaxyl, Apron, Ridomil, Ridomil MZ	F	G	tech 669	>3,100	12	—	N	N
metaldehyde, Deadline	I	G	630	—	12,24	H	N	N
metam-sodium, Busan, Vapam	N	G	1,700–1,800	—	48	—	H	N
*Metasystox-R, oxydementon-methyl	I	R(NJ),G	tech 50	150	24	—	H	H
methamidophos, Monitor	I	R-2,11	tech 20	130	48	H	M	H
methomyl, Lannate	I	R-8,10	17	5,880	48	H	H	H
*methoxychlor, Marlate	I	G	6,000	—	12	S	N	M
*methyl bromide	F,H,N	R-8	See Footnote 9		48	—	—	N
*methyl parathion	I	R-2,8,10,11	6	50	48	H	H	H
*methyl parathion (encapsulated), Penncap-M	I	R-2,8,10,11	>600	>5,400	48	H	H	H
metiram, Polyram	F	G	tech >6,810	>2,000	12	—	M	N
metolachlor, Dual	H	G	tech 2,780	10,000	12,24	S	M	N
metribuzin, Sencor, Lexone	H	R-14	tech 1,100–2,300	>20,000	12	—	M	N
Micro-Tech, alachlor	H	R-12	930–1,350	—	12	S	M	N

TOXICITY OF CHEMICALS [1]—Continued

Name [2]	Type [3]	Use Class [4]	LD_{50} Values (mg/kg) [5]		Reentry [6] (Hours)	Toxicity [7]		
			Oral	Dermal		Bird	Fish	Bee
Mocap, ethoprop	N	R-2	61.5	2.4	24,48	H	H	H
Monitor, methamidophos	I	R-2,11	tech 20	130	48	H	M	H
M-Pede, insecticidal soap	I	G	16,900	—	12	N	N	N
M-Trak, *Bacillus thuringiensis tenebrionis* encapsulated delta endotoxin	I	G	See Footnote 8		12	N	N	N
MVP, *Bacillus thuringiensis kurstaki* encapsulated delta endotoxin	I	G	See Footnote 8		12	N	N	N
naled, Dibrom	I	G	191	1,100	48	M	H	H
napropamide, Devrinol	H	G	>4,640	—	12,48	—	—	—
naptalam, Alanap L	H	G	1,770	—	24	—	N	N
Nemacur, fenamiphos	N	R-2	tech 3	200	48	H	H	N
norflurazon, Solicam	H	G	>8,000	>20,000	12	N	M	N
Novodor, *Bacillus thuringiensis tenebrionis*	I	G	See Footnote 8		12	N	N	N
Noxfire, rotenone	I	G	132–1,500	—	24	S	H	N
Orthene, acephate	I	G	tech 980	>10,250	24	M	N	H
oryzaliln, Surflan	H	G	>10,000	—	12	—	—	—
oxamyl, Vydate L	I,N	R	37	2,960	48	H	H	H

*oxydemeton-methyl, Metasystox-R	I	R(NJ),G	tech 50	150	24	—	H	H
oxyfluorfen, Goal	H	G	tech >5,000	>10,000	24	—	H	N
paraquat, Gramoxone Extra	H	R-1,8	150	—	48	M	N	N
Partner, alachlor	H	R-12	930–1,350	—	12	S	M	N
Payload, acephate	I	G	tech 980	>10,250	24	M	N	H
PBO (piperonyl butoxide)	I	G	>7,500	—	12	N	N	N
PCNB, Terraclor	F	G	tech 1,700–5000	2,000–4,000	12,24	S	—	—
pebulate, Tillam	H	G	tech 921–1,900	>4,640	12	—	M	S
pendimethalin, Prowl	H	G	1,250	>5,000	12,24	—	—	—
*Penncap-M, methyl parathion (encapsulated)	I	R-2,8,10,11	>600	>5,400	48	H	H	H
Penncozeb, mancozeb	F	G	11,200	>15,000	12	—	N	N
permethrin, Ambush, Pounce	I	R-12	tech >4,000	>4,000	12,24	N	H	H
Phaser, endosulfan	I	R(NJ),G	tech 160	>500	48	H	H	N
*phenmedipham, Spin-aid	H	G	>8,000	>4,000	24	—	—	—
*phorate, Thimet	I	R-2,10,11	tech 2–4	20–30	48	H	H	H
phosmet, Imidan	I	R(NJ),G	tech 147–316	>4,640	24	S	H	H
piperonyl butoxide (PBO)	I	G	>7,500	—	12	N	N	N
Poast, sethoxydim	H	G	3,200–3,500	>5,000	12,24	S	M	S
Polyram, metiram	F	G	tech >6,810	>2,000	12	—	M	N
Pounce, permethrin	I	R-12	tech 430–4,000	>4,000	12,24	N	H	H
Prefar, bensulide	H	G	tech 271–1,470	—	12	—	H	—
Prokil, cryolite	I	G	>5,000	—	12	N	N	N
pronamide, Kerb	H	R-5	tech 8,350	5,620	12	—	—	—
*propiconazole, Tilt	F	G	1,517	>4,000	24	—	N	—
Prowl, pendimethalin	H	G	3,956	2,200	12,24	—	—	—
Proxol, trichlorfon	I	R(NJ),G	tech 150–400	>2,100	24	H	H	M

Name [2]	Type [3]	Use Class [4]	LD_{50} Values (mg/kg) [5]		Reentry [6] (Hours)	Toxicity [7]		
			Oral	Dermal		Bird	Fish	Bee
Pursuit, imazethapyr	H	G	>5,000	>2,000	12,24	—	—	—
pyrethrum	I	G	1,500	>1,800	12	N	H	M
pyridate, Lentagran	H	G	2,000	3,400	12	—	H	N
Randox, CDAA	H	G	750	—	12	—	—	—
Reach, chlorothalonil	F	G	>10,000	>10,000	48	—	H	—
Ridomil/Bravo	F	G	tech 669	>3,100	48	—	N	N
Ridomil/Copper	F	G	tech 669	>3,100	48	—	M	N
Ridomil MZ, metalaxyl	F	G	tech 669	>3,100	24	—	N	N
Ridomil, metalaxyl	F	G	tech 669	>3,100	12	—	N	N
*Ro-Neet, cycloate	H	G	tech 2,000–4,100	—	12	—	M	N
Ronilan, vinclozolin	F	G	tech >10,000	—	12	—	S	N
Rotacide, rotenone	I	G	132–1,500	—	24	S	H	N
*rotenone, Rotenox, Rotacide, Noxfire	I	G	132–1,500	—	12,24,48	S	H	N
Rotenox, rotenone	I	G	132–1,500	—	48	S	H	N
Roundup, glyphosate	H	G	5,000	>5,000	24	N	N	N
*Rovral, iprodione	F	G	>4,400	>2,000	12	—	S	N
*Sencor, metribuzin	H	R-14	tech 2,000	>20,000	12	—	M	N
sethoxydim, Poast	H	G	2,676–3,125	>5,000	12,24	S	M	S
Sevin, carbaryl	I	G	tech 283	>2,000	12,24	S	N	H

*Sinbar, terbacil	H	G	5,000–7,500	—	12	—	—	—
sodium chlorite, Alcide	F	G	—	—	12	N	N	N
Solicam, noflurazon	H	G	>8,000	20,000	12	N	M	N
*Spin-aid, phenmedipham	H	G	>8,000	>4,000	24	—	—	—
Sprout Nip, chlorpropham	H	G	3,800	—	12	—	N	N
streptomycin, Agri-Mycin-17, Agri-Strep	B	G	9,000	—	12	—	—	—
sulfur	A,F,I	G	>5,000	>5,000	12,24,48	N	N	N
Super Cu, fixed copper[10]	F	G	—	—	12	—	—	—
Super Tin, triphenyltin hydroxide	F	R-7	156	1,600	24	—	—	—
Surflan, oryzalin	H	G	>10,000	—	12	—	—	—
Sutan+, butylate	H	G	tech 3,500–5,431	>4,640	12	S	S	N
TCNB, Fusarex	GR	G	—	—	—	—	—	—
Tedion, tetradifon	I	G	>10,000	>10,000	12	—	—	—
Telone C-17, chloropicrin	F,N	R-3,10	250	—	72	—	H	N
Telone II, dichloropropene	N	R(NJ),G	300	333	72	—	—	—
Temik, aldicarb	A,I,N	R-8	tech 1	20	48	H	H	H
Tenn-Cop, fixed copper[10]	F	G	—	—	24	—	—	—
*terbacil, Sinbar	H	G	5,000–7,500	—	12	—	—	—
terbufos, Counter	I	R-1,2	tech 4.5	1.1	48	—	H	N
Terraclor, PCNB	F	G	tech 1,700–5,000	2,000–4,000	12,24	S	—	—
*Terranil, chlorothalonil	F	G	>10,000	>10,000	24	—	H	—
*Terr-O-Gas 67, methyl bromide	F,H,N	R-8	See Footnote 9		48	—	—	N
tetradifon, Tedion	I	G	>10,000	>10,000	12	—	—	—
*thiabendazole, Mertect	F	G	3,100	—	12	—	S	N

TOXICITY OF CHEMICALS[1]—Continued

Name[2]	Type[3]	Use Class[4]	LD_{50} Values (mg/kg)[5]		Reentry[6] (Hours)	Toxicity[7]		
			Oral	Dermal		Bird	Fish	Bee
*Thimet, phorate	I	R-2,10,11	tech 2–4	20–30	48	H	H	H
Thiodan, endosulfan	I	R(NJ),G	tech 160	>500	48	H	H	N
thiodicarb, Larvin	I	G	66	>2,000	12	H	H	M
thiophanate-methyl, Topsin M	F	G	7,500	—	12	—	S	N
thiram, Thylate	F	G	tech 1,000	>5,000	12	S	H	N
Thylate, thiram	F	G	tech 1,000	>5,000	12	S	H	N
Tillam, pebulate	H	G	tech 921–1,900	>4,640	12	—	M	S
*Tilt, propiconazole	F	G	1,517	>4,000	24	—	H	—
Top Cop with Sulfur, fixed copper[10]	F	G	—	—	12	—	—	—
Top Cop Tri-Basic, fixed copper[10]	F	G	300	—	12	—	—	—
Topsin M, thiophanate-methyl	F	G	7,500	—	12	—	S	N
Treflan, trifluralin	H	G	>10,000	—	12,24	N	M	N
triadimefon, Bayleton	F	G	tech >1,000	>2,000	12	—	N	N
Tri-Basic Copper Sulfate, fixed copper[10]	F	G	472	—	24	—	—	—
trichlorfon, Proxol	I	R(NJ),G	tech 150–400	>2,100	24	H	H	M
trifluralin, Treflan, Trilin	H	G	>10,000	—	12,24	N	M	N
Trigard, cyromazine	IGR	R,G	3,387	3,100	12	S	H	H

Trilin, trifluralin	H	G	>10,000	—	12,24	N	M	N
triphenyltin hyroxide, Du-Ter, Super Tin	F	R-7	156–345	1,600	24,48	—	—	—
2,4-D (acid)	H	R(NJ),G	375	—	12,24	M	N	H
Vapam, metam-sodium	N	G	1,891	>3,074	48	—	H	N
Vendex, fenbutatin-oxide	A	G	2,631	>2,000	48	—	—	—
vinclozolin, Ronilan	F	G	tech 10,000	—	12	—	S	N
Vydate L, oxamyl	I,N	R	37	2,960	48	H	H	H
XenTari, *Bacillus thuringiensis aizawai*	I	G	See Footnote 8		12	N	N	N
zeta-cypermethrin, Fury	I	R-10,12	—	—	24	—	H	H

From E. Kee, R. P. Mulrooney, D. Caron, and J. Whalen in cooperation with University of Maryland, Pennsylvania State University, State University of New Jersey, and Virginia Polytechnic Institute and State University. Commercial Vegetable Production–Delaware, Del. Coop. Ext. Serv. Bul. 137 (1995).

— = Data not available.

* = Material covered under the Superfund Amendments and Reauthorization Act of 1986 (SARA) for storage notification.

[1] The Occupational Safety and Health Administration (OSHA) now requires growers to keep on file Material Safety Data (MSD) sheets for certain chemicals used during normal spray programs. These MSD sheets should be obtained from either your local pesticide dealer or directly from the chemical manufacturer. Some labels carry technical assistance phone numbers that you can call for further information. Call this number to request an MSD sheet from the manufacturer.

[2] Names: Trade names begin with capital letters; common names with small.

[3] Type: A = acaricide, B = bactericide, F = fungicide, H = herbicide, I = insecticide, IGR= insect growth regulator, N = nematicide, and PGR = plant growth regulator.

[4] Use Class: R = restricted use and G = general use. Chemicals are designated as general or restricted use as determined by state or federal agencies. Restricted use may not apply to all formulations or all uses of a formulation. Check the label to be sure. The designation (NJ) refers to a compound that is classified as restricted use in New Jersey. The number(s) after the R designation refer to the following reasons for being classified as a federal restricted-use product:

1. acute oral toxicity
2. acute dermal toxicity
3. acute inhalation toxicity
4. corrosive to eyes
5. potential to cause tumors
6. potential to cause genetic mutations
7. potential to cause adverse reproductive effects
8. accident history
9. exposure hazard to workers
10. potential effects on wildlife
11. potential effects on birds
12. potential effects on fish and/or other aquatic species
13. potential for groundwater contamination
14. lack of data

[5] LD_{50} = milligrams of substance per kilogram of body weight of the test animal. > = higher than the figure listed. Formulations: LD_{50} values given are for formulated material as you would purchase it; for example, 50WP, 4E, etc., unless otherwise noted. Source: 1994 Farm Chemicals Handbook; information is listed as supplied by manufacturer.

[6] Reentry: The EPA Worker Protection Standard now requires minimum 12-hour reentry times for all Category III (CAUTION) pesticides, 24-hour minimum reentry times for all Category II (WARNING) pesticides, and 48-hour minimum reentry times for all Category I (DANGER) pesticides. In New Jersey, the NJDEP Pesticide Control Program has designed 48-hour reentry times for some pesticides that the EPA has assigned 12- or 24-hour reentry times. Chemicals with multiple designations are based on product and/or formulation differences.

[7] N = nontoxic, S = slightly toxic, M = moderately toxic, and H = highly toxic.

[8] Toxicity of *Bacillus thuringiensis* is listed as harmless to humans, animals, and useful insects. *Bacillus thuringiensis* is listed under several commercially available trade names such as Agree, Biobit, Condor, Cutlass, DiPel, Foil BFC, Javelin, M-Trak, MVP, Novodor, and XenTari. *Bacillus thuringiensis* materials are marketed as several different subspecies such as *aizawai*, *kurstaki*, and *tenebrionis*. Different *Bacillus thuringiensis* subspecies may have different insect control properties. Please check labels for pest insects controlled before use.

[9] Acute vapor toxicity, 200 ppm, extremely hazardous by vapor inhalation. Liquid can cause eye and skin burns.

[10] Fixed coppers are listed under several commercially available trade names. Examples are: Basicop, Champ, Champion, COPPER-COUNT-N, Kocide, Super Cu, Tenn-Cop, Top Cop with Sulfur, Top Cop Tri-Basic, and Tri-Basic Copper Sulfate.

Pesticides sprayed onto soil or crops may be subject to movement or drift away from the target due mostly to wind. Drift may lead to risks to nearby people and wildlife, damage to nontarget plants, and pollution of surface water or groundwater.

Factors That Affect Drift

1. *Droplet size.* Smaller droplets can drift longer distances. Droplet size can be managed by selecting the proper nozzle type and size, adjusting the spray pressure, and by increasing the viscosity of the spray mixture.
2. *Equipment adjustments.* Routine calibration of spraying equipment and general maintenance should be practiced. Equipment can be fitted with hoods or shields to reduce drift away from the sprayed area.
3. *Weather conditions.* Spray applicators must be aware of wind speed and direction, relative humidity, temperature, and atmospheric stability at time of spraying.

Spraying Checklist to Minimize Drift

1. Do not spray on windy days (>12 mph).
2. Avoid spraying on extremely hot and dry days.
3. Use minimum required pressure.
4. Select correct nozzle size and spray pattern.
5. Keep the boom as close as possible to target.
6. Install hoods or shields on spray boom.
7. Leave unsprayed border of 50 to 100 feet near water supplies, wetlands, neighbors, and non-target crops.
8. Spray when wind direction is favorable for keeping drift off of non-target areas.

To calculate approximately the acreage of a crop in the field, multiply the length of the field by the number of rows or beds. Divide by the factor for spacing of beds.

Examples: Field 726 ft long with 75 rows 48 in. apart.

$$\frac{726 \times 75}{10890} = 5 \text{ acres}$$

Field 500 ft long with 150 beds on 40-in. centers.

$$\frac{500 \times 150}{13068} = 5.74 \text{ acres}$$

Row or Bed Spacing (in.)	Factor
12	43,560
18	29,040
24	21,780
30	17,424
36	14,520
40	13,068
42	12,445
48	10,890
60	8,712
72	7,260
84	6,223

DISTANCE TRAVELED AT VARIOUS TRACTOR SPEEDS

mph	ft/min	mph	ft/min
1.0	88	3.1	273
1.1	97	3.2	282
1.2	106	3.3	291
1.3	114	3.4	299
1.4	123	3.5	308
1.5	132	3.6	317
1.6	141	3.7	325
1.7	150	3.8	334
1.8	158	3.9	343
1.9	167	4.0	352
2.0	176	4.1	361
2.1	185	4.2	370
2.2	194	4.3	378
2.3	202	4.4	387
2.4	211	4.5	396
2.5	220	4.6	405
2.6	229	4.7	414
2.7	237	4.8	422
2.8	246	4.9	431
2.9	255	5.0	440
3.0	264		

CALCULATIONS OF SPEED OF EQUIPMENT AND AREA WORKED

To review the actual performance of a tractor determine the number of seconds required to travel a certain distance. Then use the formula

$$\text{Speed (mph)} = \frac{\text{distance traveled (ft)} \times 0.682}{\text{time to cover distance (secs)}}$$

or the formula

$$\text{Speed (mph)} = \frac{\text{distance traveled (ft)}}{\text{time to cover distance (secs)} \times 1.47}$$

Another method is to walk beside the machine counting the number of normal paces (2.93 ft) covered in 20 secs. Point off one place. Result equals tractor speed (mph).

CALCULATIONS OF SPEED OF EQUIPMENT AND AREA WORKED—Continued

Example: 15 paces/20 secs = 1.5 mph.

The working width of an implement multiplied by mph equals the number of acres covered in 10 hr. This includes an allowance of 17.5% for turning at the ends of the field. By moving the decimal point one place, which is equivalent to dividing by 10, the result is the acreage covered in 1 hr.

Example: A sprayer with a 20-ft boom is operating at 3.5 mph. So
20 × 3.5 = 70 acres/10 hr or 7 acres/hr.

APPROXIMATE TIME REQUIRED TO WORK AN ACRE [1]

Rate (mph):	1	2	3	4	5	10
Rate (ft/min):	88	176	264	352	440	880
Effective Working Width of Equipment (in.)	Approximate Time Required (min/acre)					
18	440	220	147	110	88	44
24	330	165	110	83	66	33
36	220	110	73	55	44	22
40	198	99	66	50	40	20
42	189	95	63	47	38	19
48	165	83	55	41	33	17
60	132	66	44	33	26	13
72	110	55	37	28	22	11
80	99	50	33	25	20	10
84	94	47	31	24	19	9
96	83	42	28	21	17	8
108	73	37	24	19	15	7
120	66	33	22	17	13	6
240	33	17	11	8	7	3
360	22	11	7	6	4	2

[1] These figures have been calculated on the basis of 75% field efficiency to allow for turning and other lost time.

Ground Application

Boom-Type Sprayers: High-pressure, high-volume sprayers have been used for row-crop pest control for many years. Now a trend exists toward the use of sprayers that utilize lower volumes and pressures.

Airblast-Type Sprayers: Airblast sprayers are used in the vegetable industry to control insects and diseases. Correct operation of an airblast sprayer is more critical than for a boom-type sprayer.

Do not operate an airblast sprayer under high wind conditions. Wind speed below 5 mph is preferable unless it becomes necessary to apply the pesticide for timely control measures, but drift and nearby crops must be considered.

Do not overextend the coverage of the machine. Considerable visible mist from the machine moves into the atmosphere and does not deposit on the plant. If in doubt, use black plastic indicator sheets in the rows to determine deposit and coverage before a pest problem appears as evidence.

Use correct gallonage and pressures to obtain proper droplet size to ensure uniform coverage across the effective swath width.

Adjust the vanes and nozzles on the sprayer unit to give best coverage. Vane adjustment must occur in the field, depending on terrain, wind, and crop.

Cross drives in the field allow the material to be blown down the rows instead of across them and help to give better coverage in some crops, such as tomato.

Air-boom Sprayers: These sprayers combine the airblast spray with the boom spray delivery characteristics. Air-boom sprayers are becoming popular with vegetable producers in an effort to achieve high levels of spray coverage with minimal quantity of pesticide.

Electrostatic Sprayers: These sprayers create an electrical field through which the spray droplet moves. Charged spray droplets are deposited more effectively onto plant surfaces and less drift results.

Aerial Application

Spraying should occur when wind is not excessive—less than 6 mph. A slight crosswind during spraying is advantageous in equalizing the distribution of the spray within the swath and between swaths.

Proper nozzle angle and arrangements along the boom are critical and necessary to obtain proper distribution at ground level. Use black plastic indicator sheets in the rows to determine deposit and coverage patterns. Cover a swath no wider than is reasonable for the aircraft and boom being used.

Fields of irregular shape or topography and ones bounded by woods, power lines, or other flight hazards should not be sprayed by aircraft.

Width of Boom: The boom coverage is equal to the number of nozzles multiplied by the space between two nozzles.

Ground Speed (mph): Careful control of ground speed is very important for accurate spray application. Select a gear and throttle setting to maintain constant speed. A speed of 2–3 mph is desirable. From a "running start," mark off the beginning and ending of a 30-sec run. The distance traveled in this 30-sec period divided by 44 will equal the speed in miles per hour.

Sprayer Discharge (gpm): Run the sprayer at a certain pressure, and catch the discharge from each nozzle for a known length of time. Collect all the discharge and measure the total volume. Divide this volume by the time in minutes to determine discharge in gallons per minute.

Before Calibrating:

1. Thoroughly clean all nozzles, screens, etc., to ensure proper operation.
2. Check to be sure that all nozzles are the same.
3. Check the spray patterns of all nozzles for uniformity. Check the volume of delivery by placing similar containers under each nozzle. Replace nozzles that do not have uniform patterns or do not fill containers at the same rate.
4. Select an operating speed. Note the tachometer reading or mark the throttle setting. When spraying, be sure to use the same speed as used for calibrating.
5. Select an operating pressure. Adjust to desired pressure (psi) while pump is operating at normal speed and water is actually flowing through the nozzles. This pressure should be the same during calibration and field spraying.

Calibration (Jar Method): Either a special calibration jar or a home-made one can be used. If you buy one, carefully follow the manufacturer's instructions.

Make accurate speed and pressure readings and jar measurements. Make several checks.

Any 1-qt or larger container, such as a jar or measuring cup, if calibrated in fluid ounces, can easily be used in the following manner:

1. Measure a course on the same type of surface (sod, plowed, etc.) and same type of terrain (hilly, level, etc.) as that to be sprayed, according to nozzle spacing as follows:

Nozzle spacing (in.)	16	20	24	28	32	36	40
Course length (ft)	255	204	170	146	127	113	102

2. Time the seconds it takes the sprayer to cover the measured distance at the desired speed.
3. With the sprayer standing still, operate at selected pressure and pump speed. Catch the water from several nozzles for the number of seconds measured in Step 2.
4. Determine the average output per nozzle in ounces. The ounces per nozzle equal the gallons per acre applied for one nozzle per spacing.

Calibration (Boom or Airblast Sprayer):

1. Fill sprayer with water.
2. Spray a measured area (width of area covered × distance traveled) at constant speed and pressure selected from manufacturer's information.
3. Measure amount of water necessary to refill tank (gallons used).
4. Multiply gallons used by 43,560 and divide by the number of square feet in area sprayed. This gives gallons per acre.

$$\text{Gal/acre} = \frac{\text{gal used} \times 43{,}560}{\text{area sprayed (sq ft)}}$$

5. Add correct amount of spray material to tank to give the recommended rate per acre.

EXAMPLE

Assume: 10 gal of water used to spray an area 660 ft long and 20 ft wide
Tank size: 100 gal
Spray material: 2 lb (actual)/acre

Calculation:

$$\frac{\text{Gal used} \times 43{,}560}{\text{area sprayed (sq ft)}} = \frac{10 \times 43{,}560}{660 \times 20} = 33 \text{ gal/acre}$$

$$\frac{\text{Tank capacity}}{\text{gal/acre}} \quad \frac{100 \text{ (tank size)}}{33} = 3.03 \text{ acres sprayed per tank}$$

3.03×2 (lb/acre) $=$ 6.06 lb material per tank

If 80% material is used:

$$\frac{6.06}{0.8} = 7.57 \text{ lb material needed per tank to give 2 lb/acre rate}$$

Adapted from Commercial Vegetable Production Recommendations, Maryland Agricultural Extension Service EB-236 (1994).

CALIBRATION OF GRANULAR APPLICATORS

Sales of granular fertilizer, herbicides, insecticides, etc., for application through granular application equipment have been on the increase.

Application rates of granular application equipment are affected by several factors: gate openings or settings, ground speed of the applicator, shape and size of granular material, and roughness of the ground.

Broadcast Application:

1. From the label, determine the application rate.
2. From the operator's manual, set dial or feed gate to apply desired rate.
3. On a level surface, fill hopper to a given level and mark this level.
4. Measure test area—length of run will depend on size of equipment. It need not be one long run but can be multiple runs at shorter distances.
5. Apply material to measured area, operating at the speed applicator will travel during application.
6. Weigh amount of material required to refill hopper to the marked level.
7. Determine application rate:

$$\text{Area covered} = \frac{\text{number of runs} \times \text{length of run} \times \text{width of application}}{43{,}560}$$

$$\text{Application rate} = \frac{\text{amount applied (pounds to refill hopper)}}{\text{area covered}}$$

Note. Width of application is width of the spreader for drop or gravity spreaders. For spinner applicators, it is the working width (distance between runs). Check operator's manual for recommendations, generally one-half to three-fourths of overall width spread.

EXAMPLE

Assume: 50 lb/acre rate
Test run: 200 ft
Four runs made
Application width: 12 ft
11.5 lb to refill hopper

Calculation:

$$\text{Area covered} = \frac{4 \times 200 \times 12}{43{,}560} = 0.22 \text{ acre}$$

$$\text{Application rate} = \frac{11.5}{0.22} = 52.27 \text{ lb}$$

8. If application rate is not correct, adjust feed gate opening and recheck.

Band Application:

1. From the label, determine application rate.
2. From the operator's manual, determine applicator setting and adjust accordingly.
3. Fill hopper half full.
4. Operate applicator until all units are feeding.
5. Stop applicator; remove feed tubes at hopper.
6. Attach paper or plastic bag over hopper openings.
7. Operate applicator over measured distance at the speed equipment will be operated.
8. Weigh and record amount delivered from each hopper. (Compare to check that all hoppers deliver the same amount.)

9. Calculate application rate:

$$\text{Area covered in bands} = \frac{\text{length of run} \times \text{band width} \times \text{number of bands}}{43{,}560}$$

Application rate:

$$\text{Amount applied in bands} = \frac{\text{total amount collected}}{\text{area covered in bands}}$$

Changing from broadcast to band application:

$$\frac{\text{Band width in inches}}{\text{row spacing in inches}} \times \text{broadcast rate per acre} = \text{amount needed per acre}$$

Adapted from Commercial Vegetable Production Recommendations, Maryland Agricultural Extension Service EB-236 (1994).

CALIBRATION OF AERIAL SPRAY EQUIPMENT

Calibration:

$$\text{Acres covered} = \frac{\text{length of swath (miles)} \times \text{width (ft)}}{8.25}$$

$$\text{Acres/min} = \frac{2 \times \text{swath width} \times \text{mph}}{1000}$$

$$\text{GPM} = \frac{2 \times \text{swath width} \times \text{mph} \times \text{gal/acre}}{1000}$$

Adapted from O. C. Turnquist et al., Weed, Insect, and Disease Control Guide for Commercial Vegetable Growers, Minnesota Agricultural Extension Service Special Report 5 (1978).

Select a convenient distance that multiplied by the width covered by the duster, both expressed in feet, equals a convenient fraction of an acre. With the hopper filled to a marked level, operate the duster at this distance. Take a known weight of dust in a bag or other container and refill hopper to the marked level. Weigh the dust remaining in the container. The difference is the quantity of dust applied to the fraction of an acre covered.

Example:

Distance duster is operated × width covered by duster = area dusted

$$= 108.9 \text{ ft} \times 10 \text{ ft} = 1089 \text{ sq ft} \ \frac{1089 \text{ sq ft}}{43{,}560} = \frac{1}{40} \text{ acre}$$

If it takes 1 lb of dust to refill the hopper, the rate of application is 40 lb/acre.

Pesticide containers give directions usually in terms of pounds or gallons of material in 100 gal of water. The following tables make easy the conversion for smaller quantities of spray solution.

Solid Equivalent Table

100 gal	25 gal	5 gal	1 gal
4 oz	1 oz	$^3/_{16}$ oz	$^1/_2$ oz
8 oz	2 oz	$^3/_8$ oz	1 tsp
1 lb	4 oz	$^7/_8$ oz	2 tsp
2 lb	8 oz	$1^3/_4$ oz	4 tsp
3 lb	12 oz	$2^3/_8$ oz	2 tbsp
4 lb	1 lb	$3^1/_4$ oz	2 tbsp + 2 tsp

Liquid Equivalent Table

100 gal	25 gal	5 gal	1 gal
1 gal	1 qt	$6^1/_2$ oz	$1^1/_4$ oz
2 qt	1 pt	$3^1/_4$ oz	$^5/_8$ oz
1 qt	$^1/_2$ pt	$1^9/_{16}$ oz	$^5/_{16}$ oz
$1^1/_2$ pt	6 oz	$1^1/_4$ oz	$^1/_4$ oz
1 pt	4 oz	$^7/_8$ oz	$^3/_{16}$ oz
8 oz	2 oz	$^7/_{16}$ oz	$^1/_2$ tsp
4 oz	1 oz	$^1/_4$ oz	$^1/_4$ tsp

Dilution of Liquid Pesticides to Various Concentrations

Dilution	1 gal	3 gal	5 gal
1:100	2 tbsp + 2 tsp	$^1/_2$ cup	$^3/_4$ cup + 5 tsp
1:200	4 tsp	$^1/_4$ cup	$6^1/_2$ tbsp
1:800	1 tsp	1 tbsp	1 tbsp + 2 tsp
1:1000	$^3/_4$ tsp	$2^1/_2$ tsp	1 tbsp + 1 tsp

PESTICIDE DILUTION CHART

Amount of formulation necessary to obtain various amounts of active ingredients:

Insecticide Formulation	Amount of formulation (at left) needed to obtain the following amounts of active ingredients			
	¼ lb	½ lb	¾ lb	1 lb
1% dust	25	50	75	100
2% dust	12½	25	37½	50
5% dust	5	10	15	20
10% dust	2½	5	7½	10
15% wettable powder	1⅔ lb	3⅓ lb	5 lb	6⅔ lb
25% wettable powder	1 lb	2 lb	3 lb	4 lb
40% wettable powder	⅝ lb	1¼ lb	1⅞ lb	2½ lb
50% wettable powder	½ lb	1 lb	1½ lb	2 lb
75% soluble/wettable	⅓ lb	⅔ lb	1 lb	1⅓ lb
23 to 25% liquid concentrate (2 lbs active ingredient per gallon)	1 pt	1 qt	3 pt	2 qt
42 to 46% liquid concentrate (4 lbs active ingredient per gallon)	½ pt	1 pt	1½ pt	1 qt
60 to 65% liquid concentrate (6 lbs active ingredient per gallon)	⅓ pt	⅔ pt	1 pt	1⅓ pt
72 to 78% liquid concentrate (8 lbs active ingredient per gallon)	¼ pt	½ pt	¾ pt	1 pt

Adapted from D. N. Maynard and G. J. Hochmuth (eds.). Vegetable Production Guide for Florida. Florida Coop. Ext. Serv. Circ. SP170 (1996).

PESTICIDE APPLICATION RATES FOR SMALL PLANTINGS

Distance Between Rows (ft)	Amount (gal/ acre)	Amount (per 100 ft of row)	Length of Row Covered (ft/gal)
1	75	22 oz	581
	100	30 oz	435
	125	1 qt, 5 oz	348
	150	1 qt, 12 oz	290
	175	1 qt, 20 oz	249
	200	1 qt, 27 oz	218
2	75	1 qt, 12 oz	290
	100	1 qt, 27 oz	218
	125	2 qt, 10 oz	174
	150	2 qt, 24 oz	145
	175	3 qt, 7 oz	124
	200	3 qt, 21 oz	109
3	75	2 qt, 2 oz	194
	100	2 qt, 24 oz	145
	125	3 qt, 14 oz	116
	150	4 qt, 4 oz	97
	175	4 qt, 26 oz	83
	200	5 qt, 16 oz	73

GUIDELINES FOR EFFECTIVE PEST CONTROL

Often failure to control a pest is blamed on the pesticide when frequently the cause lies elsewhere. Some common reasons for failure follow:

1. Delaying applications until pests are already well established.
2. Making applications with insufficient gallonage or clogged or poorly arranged nozzles.
3. Selecting the wrong pesticide.

The following points are suggested for more effective pest control:

1. *Inspect field regularly.* Frequent examinations (at least twice per week) help determine the proper timing of the next pesticide application.

2. *Control insects and mites according to economic thresholds or schedule.* Economic thresholds assist in determining whether pesticide applications or other management actions are needed to avoid economic loss from pest damage. Thresholds for insect pests are generally expressed as a numerical count of a given life stage or as a damage level based on certain sampling techniques. They are intended to reflect the population size that will cause economic damage and thus would warrant the cost of treatment. Guidelines for other pests are usually based on the field history, crop development, variety, weather conditions, and other factors.

   Rather than using economic thresholds, many pest problems can be predicted to occur at approximately the same time year after year. One application before buildup often eliminates the need for several applications later in the season. Often less toxic and safer-to-handle chemicals are effective when pests are small in size and population.

   Weather conditions. Spray only when wind velocity is less than 10 mph. Dust only when it is perfectly calm. Do not spray when sensitive plants are wilted during the heat of the day. If possible, make applications when ideal weather conditions prevail.

   Biological insecticides are ineffective in cool weather. Some pyrethroid insecticides (permethrin) do not perform well when field temperatures reach 85°F and above. Best control results with these insecticides are achieved when the temperature is in the 70s or low 80s (evening or early morning).

   Sprinkler irrigation washes pesticide deposits from foliage. Wait at least 48 hr after pesticide application before sprinkler irrigating. More frequent pesticide applications may be needed during and after periods of heavy rainfall.

3. *Strive for adequate coverage of plants.* The principal reason aphids, mites, cabbage loopers, and diseases are serious pests is that they occur beneath leaves, where they are protected from spray deposit or dust particles. Improved control can be achieved by adding and arranging nozzles so that the application is directed toward the plants from the sides as well as from the tops. In some cases, nozzles should be arranged so that the application is directed beneath the leaves. As the season progresses, plant size increases, as does the need for increased spray gallonage to ensure adequate coverage. Applying sprays with sufficient spray volume and pressure is important. Sprays from high-volume, high-pressure rigs (airblast) should be applied at 40–100 gal/acre at approximately 400 psi pressure. Sprays from low-volume, low-pressure rigs (boom type) should be applied at 50–100 gal/acre at approximately 100–300 psi pressure.

4. *Select the proper pesticide.* Know the pests to be controlled and choose the recommended pesticide and rate of application.

   For certain pests that are extremely difficult to control or are resistant, it may be important to alternate labeled insecticides, especially with different classes of insecticides; for example, alternate a pyrethroid insecticide with either a carbamate or an organophosphate insecticide.
5. *Pesticide compatibility.* To determine if two pesticides are compatible, using the following "jar test" before you tank mix pesticides or pesticides and fluid fertilizers:
   a. Add 1 pint of water or fertilizer solution to a clean quart jar. Then add the pesticide to the water or fertilizer solution in the same proportion as used in the field.
   b. To a second clean quart jar, add 1 pint of water or fertilizer solution. Then add ½ teaspoon of an adjuvant to keep the mixture emulsified. Finally, add the pesticide to the water–adjuvant or fertilizer–adjuvant in the same proportion as to be used in the field.
   c. Close both jars tightly and mix thoroughly by inverting 10 times. Inspect the mixtures immediately and again after standing for 30 min. If the mix in either jar remains uniform for 30 min, the combination can be used. If either mixture separates but readily remixes, constant agitation is required. If nondispersible oil, sludge, or clumps of solids form, do not use the mixture.
6. *Calibrate application equipment.* Periodic calibration of sprayers, dusters, and granule distributors is necessary to ensure accurate delivery rates of pesticides per acre. See pages 302–307.
7. *Select correct sprayer tips.* The selection of proper sprayer tips for use with various pesticides is very important. Flat fan-spray tips are designed for preemergence and postemergence application of herbicides. They can also be used with insecticides, fertilizers, and other pesticides. Flat fan-spray tips produce a tapered-edge spray pattern for uniform coverage where patterns overlap. Some flat fan-spray tips (SP) are designed to operate at low pressure (15–40 psi) and are usually used for preemergence herbicide applications. These lower pressures result in large spray particles than those from standard flat tips operating at higher pressures (30–60 psi). Spray nozzles with even flat-spray tips (often designated E) are designed for band spraying where uniform distribution is desired over a zone 8–14 in. wide; they are generally used for herbicides.

   Flood-type nozzle tips are generally used for complete fertilizer, liquid nitrogen, and so on, and sometimes for spraying herbicides onto the soil surface prior to incorporation. They are less suited for spraying postemergence herbicides or for applying fungicides or insecticides to plant foliage. Coverage of the target is often less uniform and complete when flood-type nozzles are used, compared with the coverage obtained with other types of nozzles. Space flood-type nozzles a maximum of 20 in. apart, rather than the standard 40-in spacing for better coverage. This will result in an overlapping spray pattern. Spray at the maximum pressure recommended for the nozzle.

Wide-spray angle tips with full or hollow cone patterns are usually used for fungicides and insecticides. They are used at higher water volume and spray pressures than are commonly recommended for herbicide application with flat fan or flood-type nozzle tips.

8. *pH and pesticides.* Unsatisfactory results with some pesticides may be related to the pH of the mixing water. Some materials carry a label cautioning the user against mixing the pesticide with alkaline materials because they undergo a chemical reaction known as "alkaline hydrolysis." This reaction occurs when the pesticide is mixed in water with a pH greater than 7.

   Many manufacturers provide information on the rate at which their product hydrolyzes. The rate is expressed as "half-life," meaning the time it takes for 50% hydrolysis or breakdown to occur.

   Check the pH of the water. If acidification is necessary, there are several commercial nutrient buffer materials available on the market.

Adapted from Commercial Vegetable Production Recommendations, Maryland Agricultural Extension Service EB-236 (1994).

Adjuvants are chemicals that, when added to a liquid spray, make it mix, wet, spread, stick, or penetrate better. Water is almost a universal diluent for pesticide sprays. However, water is not compatible with oily pesticides, and an *emulsifier* may be needed in order to obtain good mixing. Furthermore, water from sprays often remains as large droplets on leaf surfaces. A *wetting agent* lowers the interfacial tension between the spray droplet and the leaf surface and thus moistens the leaf. *Spreaders* are closely related to wetters and help to build a deposit on the leaf and improve weatherability. *Stickers* cause pesticides to adhere to the sprayed surface and are often called spray-stickers. They are oily and serve to increase the amounts of suspended solids held on the leaves or fruits by holding the particles in a resinlike film. *Extenders* form a sticky, elastic film that holds the pesticide on the leaves and thus reduces the rate of loss caused by sunlight and rainfall.

There are a number of adjuvants on the market. Read the label not only for dosages, but also for crop uses and compatibilities, because some adjuvants must not be used with certain pesticides. Although many formulations of pesticides contain adequate adjuvants, some do require additions on certain crops, especially cabbage, cauliflower, onion, and pepper.

Spray adjuvants for use with herbicides often serve a function distinctly different from that of adjuvants used with insecticides and fungicides. For example, adjuvants such as oils used with atrazine greatly improve penetration of the chemical into crop and weed leaves, rather than just give more uniform coverage. Do not use any adjuvant with herbicides unless there are specific recommendations for its use. Plant damage or even crop residues can result from using an adjuvant that is not recommended.

Adapted from Cornell Recommendations for Commercial Vegetable Production, New York Cooperative Extension Service (1986).

VEGETABLE SEED TREATMENTS

Various vegetable seed treatments prevent early infection by seedborne diseases, protect the seed from infection by soil microorganisms, and guard against a poor crop stand or crop failure caused by attacks on seeds by soil insects. Commercial seed is often supplied with the appropriate treatment.

Two general categories of vegetable seed treatments are used. Eradication treatments kill disease-causing agents on or within the seed, whereas protective treatments are applied to the surface of the seed to protect against seed decay, damping-off, and soil insects. Hot-water treatment is the principal means of eradication, and chemical treatments usually serve as protectants. Follow time–temperature directions precisely for hot-water treatment and label directions for chemical treatment. When insecticides are used, seeds should also be treated with a fungicide.

Hot-Water Treatment

To treat seeds with hot water, fill cheesecloth bags half full, wet seed and bag with warm water, and treat at exact time and temperature while stirring to maintain a uniform temperature. Use an accurate thermometer.

HOT-WATER TREATMENT OF SEEDS

Seed	Temperature (°F)	Time (min)	Diseases Controlled
Broccoli, cauliflower, collards, kale, kohlrabi, turnip	122	20	Alternaria, blackleg, black rot
Brussels sprouts, cabbage	122	25	Alternaria, blackleg, black rot
Celery	118	30	Early blight, late blight
Eggplant	122	30	Phomopsis blight, anthracnose
Pepper	122	25	Bacterial spot, rhizoctonia
Tomato	122	25	Bacterial canker, bacterial spot, bacterial speck
	132	30	Anthracnose

Chemical Seed Treatments

The most frequently used fungicides for vegetable seeds are thiram and captan applied as a dust or slurry. Large-seeded vegetables may require treatment with a labeled insecticide as well as a fungicide. Always follow label directions when pesticides are used.

Certain bacterial diseases on the seed surface can be controlled by other chemical treatments:

1. *Tomato Bacterial Canker.* Soak seeds in 1.05% sodium hypochlorite solution for 20–40 min or 5% hydrochloric acid for 5–10 hr, rinse, and dry.
2. *Tomato Bacterial Spot.* Soak seeds in 1.3% sodium hypochlorite for 1 min, rinse, and dry.
3. *Pepper Bacterial Spot.* Soak seeds in 1.3% sodium hypochlorite for 1 min, rinse, and dry. DO NOT USE CHEMICALLY TREATED SEED FOR FOOD OR FEED.

Adapted from Indiana Vegetable Production Guide for Commercial Growers, Cooperative Extension Service ID-56 (1985–86) and A. F. Sherf and A. A. MacNab, *Vegetable Diseases and Their Control*, Wiley, New York (1986).

Nematodes are unsegmented round worms that range in size from microscopic to many inches long. Some nematodes, usually those that are microscopic or barely visible without magnification, attack vegetable crops and cause maladies, restrict yields, or in severe cases, lead to total crop failure.

A large number of various nematodes are known to infest the roots and aboveground plant parts of vegetable crops. Their common names are usually descriptive of the affected plant part and the resulting injury.

Common Name	Scientific Name
Awl nematode	*Dolichodorus* spp.
Bud and leaf nematode	*Aphelenchoides* spp.
Cyst nematode	*Heterodera* spp.
Dagger nematode	*Xiphinema* spp.
Lance nematode	*Hopolaimus* spp.
Root-lesion nematode	*Pratylenchus* spp.
Root-knot nematode	*Meloidogyne* spp.
Spiral nematode	*Helicotylenchus* spp. and *Scutellonema* spp.
Sting nematode	*Belonolaimus* spp.
Stubby-root nematode	*Trichodorus* spp.
Stunt nematode	*Tylenchorhynchus* spp.

Nematodes are the most troublesome in areas with mild winters where soils are not subject to freezing and thawing. Management practices and chemical control are both required to keep nematode numbers low enough to permit normal plant growth where populations are not kept in check naturally by severe winters.

The first and most obvious control for nematodes is avoiding their introduction into uninfected fields or areas. This may be done by quarantine over large geographical areas or by means of good sanitation in smaller areas.

Once nematodes have been introduced into a field, several management practices will help to control them: rotating with crops that a particular species of nematode does not attack, frequent disking during hot weather, and alternating flooding and drying cycles.

If soil management practices are not possible or are ineffective, chemicals may have to be used to control nematodes (nematicides). Some fumigants are effective against soil-borne disease, insects, and weed seeds—these are termed multipurpose soil fumigants. Growers should select a chemical for use against the primary problem to be controlled and use it according to label directions.

PLANT PARASITIC NEMATODES KNOWN TO BE OF ECONOMIC IMPORTANCE TO VEGETABLES

Nematode	Bean and Peas	Carrot	Celery	Crucifers	Cucurbits	Leaf Crops	Okra	Onion	Potato	Sweet Corn	Sweet Potato	Tomato	Pepper	Eggplant
Root knot	X	X	X	X	X	X	X	X	X		X	X	X	X
Sting	X	X	X	X	X	X	X	X	X	X		X	X	X
Stubby root	X		X	X		X		X	X	X		X	X	X
Root lesion										X				
Cyst				X										
Awl	X		X							X				
Stunt										X				
Lance										X				
Spiral														
Ring														
Dagger														
Bud and leaf														
Reniform	X										X			

From J. Noling. Nematode Control. In: D. N. Maynard and G. J. Hochmuth (eds.). Vegetable Production Guide for Florida. Fla. Coop. Ext. Serv. Circ. SP-170 (1996).

CHEMICALS FOR CONTROL OF NEMATODES AND OTHER SOIL PESTS[1]

Nematicide	Effectiveness[2] Against				Comments
	Nematodes	Soil Insects	Soil Fungi	Weed Seeds	
aldicarb	+	+	−	−	Apply to moist soil before planting or at emergence
carbofuran	+	+	−	−	Apply before planting
chloropicrin	+	+	+	+	Keep soil moist and covered with polyethylene for at least 2 days. Aerate for 2 weeks before planting
1,3-D	+	−	−	−	Apply as preplant soil fumigants
ethoprop	+	+	−	−	Mix thoroughly with soil
metham	+	+	+	+	Improve effectiveness with a water seal
methyl bromide	+	+	+	+	Apply preplanting as a soil fumigant
oxamyl	+	+	−	−	Apply before, at, or after planting
terbufos	+	+	−	−	Apply at planting

[1] Follow label directions for use and observe the precautions listed.
[2] + denotes effective, − denotes not effective.

	Acute LD_{50} Levels (mg/kg)		
Nematicide	Oral	Dermal	Vapor
aldicarb	1	5	—
carbofuran	11	10,200	—
chloropicrin	250	—	—
1,3-D	250–500	—	500
ethoprop	61	2.4	—
metham	1,700–1,800	—	—
methyl bromide	—	—	200
oxamyl	5.4	2,960	—
terbufos	4–9	1	—

Adapted from Farm Chemicals Handbook, Meister Publishing Co., Willoughby, OH (1996).
Refer to Toxicity of Pesticides (page 281) for definitions.

Diseases of vegetable crops are caused by fungi, bacteria, viruses, and mycoplasms. For a disease to occur, organisms must be transported to a susceptible host plant. This may be done by infected seeds or plant material, contaminated soil, wind, water, animals (including humans), or insects. Suitable environmental conditions must be present for the organism to infect and thrive on the crop plant.

Effective disease control requires knowledge of the disease life cycle, time of likely infection, agent of distribution, plant part affected, and the symptoms produced by the disease.

Crop Rotation: Root-infecting diseases are the usual targets of crop rotation, although rotation can help reduce innocula of leaf- and stem-infecting organisms. Land availability and costs are making rotation challenging, but a well-planned rotation program is still a very important part of an effective disease control program.

Site Selection: Consider using fields that are free of volunteer crops and perimeter weeds that may harbor disease organisms. If aerial applications of fungicides are to be used, try to select fields that are geometrically adapted to aerial spraying (long and wide), are away from homes, and have no bordering trees or power lines.

Deep Plowing: Use tillage equipment such as plows to completely bury plant debris to fully decompose plant material and kill disease organisms.

Weed Control: Certain weeds, particularly ones botanically related to the crop, may harbor disease agents that could move to the crop, especially viruses. Also, weeds within the crop could harbor diseases and by their physical presence could interfere with deposition of fungicides on the crop. Crop volunteer plants should be carefully controlled in any nearby fallow fields.

Resistant Varieties: Where possible growers should choose varieties that carry genetic resistance to disease. Varieties with disease resistance will require less pesticide application.

Seed Protection: Seeds can be treated with fungicides to offer some degree of protection of the young seedling against disease attack. Seeds planted in warm soil will germinate fast and possibly outgrow disease development.

Healthy Transplants: Growers should always purchase or grow disease-free transplants. Growers should contract with good transplant growers and should inspect their transplants before having them shipped to the farm. Paying a little extra to a reputable transplant producer is good insurance.

Be Observant in the Field: The fields should be periodically checked for disease development by walking the field and inspecting the plants up close, not from behind the windshield. Have any suspicious situations diagnosed by a competent disease diagnosis laboratory.

Foliar Fungicides: Plant disease outbreaks sometimes can be prevented or minimized by timely use of fungicides. For some diseases, it is essential to have a preventative protectant fungicide program in place. For successful fungicide control, growers should consider proper chemical selection, use well-calibrated sprayers, use correct application rate, and follow all safety recommendations for spray application.

DISEASE CONTROL FOR VEGETABLES

When using fungicides, read the label and carefully follow the instructions. Do not exceed maximum rates given, observe the interval between application and harvest, and apply only to those crops for which use has been approved. Make a record of the product used, trade name, concentration of the fungicide, dilution, rate applied per acre, and dates of application. Follow local recommendations for efficacy and read the directions on the label for proper use.

Crop	Disease	Description	Control
Asparagus	Fusarium root rot	Damping-off of seedlings. Yellowing, stunting, or wilting of the growing stalks; vascular bundle discoloration. Crown death gives fields a spotty appearance	Use diseasefree crowns. Select fields where asparagus has not grown for 8 years. Preplanting fungicide crown dip
	Rust	Reddish or black pustules on stems and foliage	Cut and burn diseased tops. Use resistant varieties. Use approved fungicides
Bean	Anthracnose	Brown or black sunken spots with pink centers on pods, dark red or black cankers on stems and leaf veins	Use diseasefree seed and rotate crops every 2 years. Plow stubble. Do not cultivate when plants are wet. Use approved fungicides
	Bacterial blight	Large, dry, brown spots on leaves, often encircled by yellow border; water-soaked spots on pods; reddish cankers on stems. Plants may be girdled	Use diseasefree seed. Do not cultivate when plants are wet. Use 3-year rotation. Use approved fungicides
	Mosaic	Mottled (light and dark green) and curled leaves; stunting, reduced yields	Use mosaic-resistant varieties. Control weeds in areas adjacent to field. Control aphid carrier with insecticides

DISEASE CONTROL FOR VEGETABLES—Continued

Crop	Disease	Description	Control
Bean (*Continued*)	Powdery mildew	Faint, slightly discolored spots appear first on leaves, later on stems and pods, from which white powdery spots develop and may cover the entire plant	Use approved fungicides
	Rust	Red to black pustules on leaves; leaves yellow and drop	Use approved fungicides
	Seed rot	Seed or seedling decay, which results in poor stands. Occurs most commonly in cold, wet soils	Crop rotation. Treat seed with approved fungicides
	White mold	Water-soaked spots on plants. White, cottony masses on pods	Use approved fungicides
Beet	Cercospora	Numerous light tan to brown spots with reddish to dark brown borders on leaves	Long rotation. Use approved fungicides
	Damping-off	Seed decay in soil; young seedlings collapse and die	Avoid wet soils, rotate crops. Treat seed with approved fungicides
	Downy mildew	Lighter than normal leaf spots on upper surface and white mildew areas on lower side. Roots, leaves, flowers, and seed balls distorted on stecklings	Use approved fungicides
Broccoli, Brussels sprouts, cabbage, cauliflower,	Alternaria leaf spot	Damping-off of seedlings. Small, circular yellow areas that enlarge in concentric circles, and become black and sooty	Use approved fungicides
	Black leg	Sunken areas on stem near ground line resulting in girdling; gray spots	Use hot-water-treated seed and long rotation. Sanitation

kale, kohlrabi		speckled with black dots on leaves and stems	
	Black rot	Yellowing and browning of the foliage; blackened veins; stems show blackened ring when cross-sectioned	Use hot-water-treated seed and long rotation. Do not work wet fields. Sanitation
	Club root	Yellow leaves or green leaves that wilt on hot days; large, irregular swellings or "clubs" on roots	Start plants in new, steamed or fumigated plant beds. Adjust soil pH to 7.2 with hydrated lime before planting. Use approved fungicides
	Downy mildew	Begins as slight yellowing on upper side of leaves; white mildew on lower side; spots enlarge until plant dies	Use approved fungicides
	Fusarium yellows	Yellowish-green leaves; stunted plants; lower leaves drop	Use yellows-resistant varieties
Carrot	Alternaria leaf blight	Small, brown to black, irregular spots with yellow margins may enlarge to infect the entire top	Use approved fungicides
	Cercospera leaf blight	Small, necrotic spots that may enlarge and infect the entire top	Use approved fungicides
	Yellows	Purpling of tops; yellowed young leaves at center of crown followed by bushiness due to excessive petiole formation. Roots become woody and form numerous adventitious roots	Control leafhopper carrier with insecticides
Celery	Aster yellows	Yellowed leaves; stunting; tissues brittle and bitter in taste	Use resistant varieties. Control leafhopper carrier with insecticides. Control weeds in adjacent areas

DISEASE CONTROL FOR VEGETABLES—Continued

Crop	Disease	Description	Control
Celery (*Continued*)	Bacterial blight	Bright-yellow leaf spots, center turns brown and a yellow halo appears with enlargement	Seedbed sanitation. Copper compounds
	Early blight	Dead, ash gray, velvety areas on leaves	Use approved fungicides
	Late blight	Yellow spots on old leaves and stalks that turn dark gray speckled with black dots	Use approved fungicides
	Mosaic	Dwarfed plants with narrow, gray, or mottled leaves	Control weeds in adjacent areas. Control aphid carrier with insecticides
	Pink rot	Water-soaked spots; white- to pink-colored cottony growth at base of stalk leads to rotting	Crop rotation. Flooding for 4–8 weeks. Use approved fungicides
Cucumber (*See* Vine crops)			
Eggplant	Anthracnose	Sunken, tan fruit lesions	Use diseasefree seed. Use approved fungicides
	Phomopsis blight	Young plants blacken and die; older plants have brown spots on leaves and fruit covered with brownish-black pustules	Use resistant varieties. Use approved fungicides
	Verticillium wilt	Slow wilting; browning between leaf veins; stunting	Fumigate soil with methyl bromide or 1,3-D. Use verticillium-tolerant varieties. Use long rotation
Endive, escarole, lettuce	Aster yellows	Center leaves bleached, dwarfed, curled or twisted. Heads do not form; young plants particularly affected	Control leafhopper carrier with insecticides

	Big vein	Leaves with light green, enlarged veins developing into yellow, crinkled leaves; stunting; delayed maturity	Avoid cold, wet soils. Use tolerant varieties. Crop rotation
	Bottom rot	Damage begins at base of plants; blades of leaves rot first, then the midrib but the main stem is hardly affected	Avoid wet, poorly drained areas. Plant on raised beds. Practice 3-year rotation. Use approved fungicides
	Downy mildew	Light green spots on upperside of leaves; lesions enlarge and white mycelium appears on opposite side of spots; browning and dwarfing of plant	Use approved fungicides
	Drop	Wilting of outer leaves; watery decay on stems and old leaves	Crop rotation. Deep plowing. Raised beds. Use approved fungicides
	Mosaic	Mottling (yellow and green), ruffling, or distortion of leaves; plants have unthrifty appearance	Use virusfree MTO seed. Plant away from old lettuce beds. Control weeds. Control aphid carrier with insecticide
	Tipburn	Edges of tender leaves brown and die; may interfere with growth; most severe on head lettuce	Use tolerant varieties. Prevent stress by providing good growing conditions
Lima bean	Downy mildew	Purpling and distortion of leaf veins; white downy mold on pods; blackened beans	Use resistant varieties and diseasefree seed. Use approved fungicides
Muskmelon (*See* Vine crops)			
Okra	Southern blight	Mass of pinkish fungus bodies around base of plant; sudden loss of leaves	Crop rotation. Deep plowing of plant stubble
	Verticillium wilt	Stunting; chlorosis; shedding of leaves	Crop rotation. Avoid planting where disease previously present
Onion	Blight (blast)	Papery spots on leaves; browning and death of upper portion of leaves; delayed maturity	Use approved fungicides

DISEASE CONTROL FOR VEGETABLES—Continued

Crop	Disease	Description	Control
Onion (*Continued*)	Downy mildew	Begins as pale-green spot near tip of leaf; purple mold found when moisture present; infected leaves olive-green to black	Use approved fungicides
	Neck rot	Soft, brownish tissue around neck; scales around neck are dry, and black sclerotia may form. Essentially a dry rot if soft rot bacteria not present	Undercut, and windrow plants until inside neck tissues are dry before storage. Cure at 93–95°F for 5 days
	Pink rot	Plants are affected from seedling stage onward throughout life cycle. Affected roots turn pink, shrivel, and die	Avoid infected soils. Use tolerant varieties
	Purple blotch	Small, white sunken lesions with purple centers enlarge to girdle leaf or seed stem. Leaves and stems fall over 3–4 weeks after infection in severe cases. Bulb rot at and after harvest	Use approved fungicides
	Smut	Black spots on leaves; cracks develop on side of spot revealing black, sooty powder within	Crop rotation. Use approved fungicides
Parsnip	Canker	Brown discoloration near shoulder or crown of root	Ridge soil over shoulders
	Leaf blight	Leaves and petioles turn yellow and then brown. Entire plant may be killed	Practice 2-year rotation, use well-drained soil with pH 7.0
Pea	Powdery mildew	White, powdery mold on leaves, stems, and pods. Mildewed areas become brown and necrotic	Use diseasefree seed and resistant varieties. Use approved fungicides

	Root rot	Rotted and yellowish-brown or black stems (below ground) and roots; outer layers of root slough off leaving a central core	Early planting and 3-year rotation. Do not double crop with bean. Seed treatment
	Virus	Several viruses affect pea causing mottling, distortion of leaves, rosetting, chlorosis, or necrosis	Use resistant varieties. Control aphid carrier with insecticides
	Wilt	Yellowing leaves; dwarfing, browning of xylem; wilting	Early planting and 3-year rotation. Use resistant varieties
Pepper	Anthracnose	Dark, round spots with black specks on fruits	Use approved fungicides
	Bacterial leaf spot	Yellowish-green spots on young leaves; raised, brown spots on undersides of older leaves; brown, cracked, rough spots on fruit; old leaves turn yellow	Use diseasefree seed, hot-water-treated seed. Use approved bactericides. Use resistant varieties
	Mosaic	Mottled (yellowed and green) and curled leaves; fruits yellow or show green ring spots; stunted; reduced yields	Use resistant varieties. Control insect carriers (particularly aphids) and weed hosts. Stylet oil
Potato	Early blight	Dark brown spots on leaves; foliage injured; reduced yields	Bury all cull potatoes. Use approved fungicides
	Late blight	Dark, then necrotic area on leaves and stem; infected tubers rot in storage. Disease is favored by moist conditions	Bury cull piles. Use approved fungicides
	Rhizoctonia	Necrotic spots, girdling and death of sprouts before or shortly after emergence. Brown to black raised spots on mature tubers	Avoid deep planting to encourage early emergence. Use diseasefree seed. Use approved fungicides
	Scab	Rough, scabby, raised or pitted lesions on tubers	Crop rotation. Use resistant varieties. Keep soil pH about 5.3

DISEASE CONTROL FOR VEGETABLES—Continued

Crop	Disease	Description	Control
Potato (*Continued*)	Virus	A large number of viruses infect potato causing leaf mottling, distortion, and dwarfing. Some viruses cause irregularly shaped or necrotic area in tubers	Use certified seed. Control aphid and leafhopper carriers with insecticides
Radish	Downy mildew	Internal discoloration of root crown tissue. Outer surface may become dark and rough at the soil line	Select clean, well-drained soils. Use approved fungicides
	Fusarium wilt	Young plants yellow and die rapidly in warm weather. Stunting, unilateral leaf yellowing; vascular discoloration of fleshy roots	Use tolerant varieties. Avoid infected soil
Rhubarb	Crown rot	Wilting of leaf blades; browning at base of leaf stalk leading to decay	Plant in well-drained soil
	Leaf spot	Tiny, greenish-yellow spots (resembling mosaic) on upper side of leaf, eventually browning and forming a white spot surrounded by a red band; these spots may drop out to give a shot-hole appearance	Use approved fungicides
Rutabaga, turnip	Alternaria	Small, circular, yellow areas that enlarge in concentric circles and become a black sooty color. Roots may become infested in storage	Use hot-water-treated seed. Use approved fungicides

	Anthracnose	Small, water-soaked spots on all above ground parts, which become light colored and may drop out. Small, sunken, dry spots on turnip roots, which are subject to secondary decay	Use approved fungicides
	Club root	Tumorlike swellings on taproot. Main root may be distorted. Diseased roots decay prematurely	Avoid soil previously infected with club root. Adjust acid soil to pH 7.3 by liming
	Downy mildew	Small, purplish, irregular spots on leaves, stems, and seedpods, which produce fluffy white growth. Desiccation of roots in storage	Use approved fungicides
	Mosaic virus	Stunted plants having ruffled leaves. Infected roots store poorly	Destroy volunteer plants. Control aphid carrier with insecticides
Southern pea	Fusarium wilt	Yellowed leaves; wilted plants; interior of stems lemon yellow	Avoid infected soil
Spinach	Blight (CMV)	Yellowed and curled leaves; stunted plants; reduced yields	Use tolerant varieties. Control aphid carrier with insecticides
	Downy mildew	Yellow spots on upper surface of leaves; downy or violet-gray mold on undersides	Use resistant varieties. Use approved fungicides
Squash (*See* Vine crops)			
Strawberry	Anthracnose	Spotting and girdling of stolens and petioles, crown rot, fruit rot, and a black leaf spot; occurs in southeastern United States	Use diseasefree plants and resistant varieties. Use approved fungicides
	Gray mold	Rot on green or ripe fruit, beginning at calyx or contact with infected fruit; affected area supports white or gray mycelium	Use less susceptible varieties. Use approved fungicides

DISEASE CONTROL FOR VEGETABLES—Continued

Crop	Disease	Description	Control
Strawberry (*Continued*)	Leaf scorch	Numerous irregular, purplish blotches with brown centers; entire leaves dry up and appear scorched	Use diseasefree plants and resistant varieties. Renew perennial plantings frequently. Use approved fungicides
	Leaf spot	Indefinite-shaped spots with brown, gray, or white centers and purple borders	Use diseasefree plants and resistant varieties. Use approved fungicides
	Powdery mildew	Characteristic white mycelium on leaves, flower, and fruit	Use resistant varieties. Use approved fungicides
	Red stele	Stunted plants having roots with red stele that is seen when root is cut lengthwise	Improve drainage and avoid compaction of soil. Use diseasefree plants and resistant varieties
	Verticillium	Marginal and interveinal necrosis of outer leaves, inner leaves remain green	Preplant soil fumigation. Use resistant varieties
Sweet corn	Bacterial blight	Dwarfing; premature tassels die; yellow bacterial slime oozes from wet stalks; stem dries and dies	Use resistant varieties. Control corn flea beetle with insecticides
	Leaf blight	Canoe-shaped spots on leaves	Use resistant varieties. Use approved fungicides
	Maize dwarf mosaic	Stunting; mottling of new leaves in whorl and poor ear fill at the base	Use tolerant varieties. Plant tolerant varieties around susceptible ones. Control aphid carrier with insecticides
	Seed rot	Seed decays in soils	Use seed treated with approved fungicides

	Smut	Large, smooth, whitish galls, or outgrowths on ears, tassels, and nodes; covering dries and breaks open to release black, powdery, or greasy spores	Use tolerant varieties. Control corn borers with insecticides
Sweet potato	Black rot	Black depressions on sweet potato; black cankers on underground stem parts	Select diseasefree potato seed. Rotate crops and planting beds. Use vine cuttings rather than slips
	Internal cork	Dark brown to black, hard, corky lesions in flesh developing in storage at high temperature. Yellow spots with purple borders on new growth of leaves	Select diseasefree seed potatoes
	Pox	Plants dwarfed; only one or two vines produced; leaves thin and pale green; soil rot pits on roots	Use diseasefree stock and clean planting beds. Sulfur to lower soil pH to 5.2
	Scurf	Brown to black discoloration of root; uniform rusting of root surface	Rotation of crops and beds. Use diseasefree stock. Use vine cuttings rather than slips
	Stem rot	Yellowing between veins; vines wilt; stems darken inside and may split	Select diseasefree seed potatoes. Rotate fields and plant beds
Tomato	Anthracnose	Begins with circular, sunken spots on fruit; as spots enlarge, center becomes dark and fruit rots	Use approved fungicides
	Bacterial canker	Wilting; rolling, and browning of leaves; pith may discolor or disappear; fruit displays bird's-eye spots	Use hot-water-treated seed. Avoid planting in infected fields for 3 years
	Bacterial spot	Young lesions on fruit appear as dark, raised spots; older lesions blacken and appear sunken with brown centers; leaves brown and dry	Use hot-water-treated seed. Use approved bactericides

DISEASE CONTROL FOR VEGETABLES—Continued

Crop	Disease	Description	Control
Tomato (*Continued*)	Early blight	Dark brown spots on leaves; brown cankers on stems; girdling; dark, leathery, decayed areas at stem end of fruit	Use approved fungicides
	Late blight	Dark, water-soaked spots on leaves; white fungus on undersides of leaves; withering of leaves; water-soaked spots on fruit turn brown. Disease is favored by moist conditions	Use approved fungicides
	Fusarium wilt	Yellowing and wilting of lower, older leaves; disease affects whole plant eventually	Use resistant varieties
	Gray leaf spot	Symptoms appear first in seedlings. Small brown to black spots on leaves, which enlarge and have shiny gray centers. The centers may drop out to give shotgun appearance. Oldest leaves affected first	Use resistant varieties. Use approved fungicides
	Leaf mold	Chlorotic spots on upper side of oldest leaves appear in humid weather. Underside of leaf spot may have green mold. Spots may merge until entire leaf is affected. Disease advances to younger leaves	Use resistant varieties. Staking and pruning to provide air movement. Use approved fungicides

	Mosaic	Mottling (yellow and green) and roughening of leaves; dwarfing; reduced yields; russeting of fruit	Avoid contact by smokers. Control aphid carrier with insecticides. Stylet oil
	Verticillium wilt	Differs from fusarium wilt by appearance of disease on all branches at the same time; yellow areas on leaves become brown; midday wilting; dropping of leaves beginning at bottom	Use resistant varieties
Vine crops; cucumber, muskmelon, pumpkin, squash, watermelon	Alternaria leaf spot	Circular spots showing concentric rings as they enlarge, appear first on oldest leaves	Field sanitation. Use diseasefree seed. Use approved fungicides
	Angular leaf spot	Irregular, angular, water-soaked spots on leaves which later turn gray and die. Dead tissue may tear away leaving holes. Nearly circular fruit spots, which become white	Use tolerant varieties. Use approved bactericides
	Anthracnose	Reddish-black spots on leaves; elongated tan cankers on stems; fruits have sunken spots with flesh-colored ooze in center, later turning black	Use tolerant varieties. Use approved fungicides
	Bacterial wilt	Vines wilt and die; stem sap produces strings; no yellowing occurs	Control striped cucumber beetles with insecticides. Remove wilting plants from field
	Black rot (squash and pumpkin only)	Water-soaked areas appear on rinds of fruit in storage. Brown or black infected tissue rapidly invades entire plant	Use diseasefree seed. Crop rotation. Cure fruit for storage at 85°F for 2 weeks, store at 50–55°F. Use approved fungicides

DISEASE CONTROL FOR VEGETABLES—Continued

Crop	Disease	Description	Control
Vine crops (*Continued*)	Downy mildew	Angular, yellow spots on older leaves; purple fungus on undersides of leaves when moisture present; leaves wither, die; fruit may be dwarfed with poor flavor	Use tolerant varieties. Use approved fungicides
	Fusarium wilt	Stunting and yellowing of vine; water-soaked streak on one side of vine turning yellow eventually cracks and oozes sap	Use resistant varieties. Avoid infected soils
	Gummy stem blight	Lesions may occur on stems, leaves, and fruit from which a gummy exudate may ooze	Use diseasefree seed. Rotate crops. Use approved fungicides
	Mosaic	Mottling (yellow and green) and curling of leaves; mottled and warty fruit; reduced yields; burning and dwarfing of entire plant	Control striped cucumber beetle and aphid with insecticides. Use resistant varieties. Destroy surrounding perennial weeds
	Powdery mildew	White, powdery growth on upper leaf surface and petioles; wilting of foliage	Use tolerant varieties. Use approved fungicides
	Scab	Water-soaked spots on leaves turning white; sunken cavity on fruit later covered by grayish-olive fungus; fruit destroyed by soft rot	Use resistant varieties. Use approved fungicides

When using insecticides, read the label and carefully follow the instructions. Do not exceed maximum rates given; observe the interval between application and harvest, and apply only to crops for which use is approved. Make a record of the product used, trade name, formulation, dilution, rate applied per acre, and dates of application. Read and follow all label precautions to protect the applicator and workers from insecticide injury, and environment from contamination. Follow local recommendations for efficacy and read the label for proper use.

Crop	Insect	Description
Artichoke	Aphid	Small, green, pink, or black soft-body insects that rapidly reproduce to large populations. Damage results from sucking plant sap; indirectly from virus transmission to crop plants
	Plume moth	Small wormlike larvae blemish bracts and may destroy the base of the bract
Asparagus	Beetle and 12-spotted beetle	Metallic blue or black beetles (¼ in.) with yellowish wing markings and reddish, narrow head. Larvae are humpbacked, slate gray. Both feed on shoots and foliage
	Cutworm	Dull-colored moths lay eggs in the soil producing dark-colored smooth worms, 1–2 in. long, which characteristically curl up when disturbed. May feed belowground, or aboveground at night
Bean	Aphid	*See* Artichoke
	Corn earworm	Gray-brown moth (1½ in.) with dark wing tips deposits eggs, especially on fresh corn silk. Brown, green, or pink larvae (2 in.) feed on silk, kernels, and foliage
	Leafhopper	Green wedge-shaped, soft bodies (⅛ in.). When present in large numbers, sucking of plant sap causes plant distortion or burned appearance. Secondary damage results from transmission of yellows disease

Crop	Insect	Description
Bean (*Continued*)	Mexican bean beetle	Copper-colored beetle (¼ in.) with 16 black spots on its back. Orange to yellow spiny larva (⅓ in.) Beetle and larvae feeding on leaf undersides cause a lacework appearance
	Seed corn maggot	Grayish-brown flies (1/5 in.) deposit eggs in the soil near plants. Cream-colored, wedge-shaped maggots (¼ in.) tunnel into seeds, potato seed pieces, and sprouts
	Spider mite	Reddish, yellow, or greenish, tiny, eight-legged spiders that suck plant sap from leaf undersides causing distortion. Fine webs may be visible when mites are present in large numbers. Mites are not true insects
	Spotted-cucumber beetle	Yellowish, elongated beetle (¼ in.) with 11 or 12 black spots on its back. Leaf-feeding may destroy young plants when present in large numbers. Transmits bacterial wilt of curcurbits
	Striped-cucumber beetle	Yellow (1/5 in.) with three black stripes on its back; feeds on leaves. White larvae (⅓ in.) feed on roots and stems. Transmits bacterial wilt of curcurbits
	Tarnish plant bug	Brownish, flattened, oval bugs (¼ in.) with a clear triangular marking at the rear. Bugs damage plants by sucking plant sap
Beet	Aphid	*See* Artichoke
	Flea beetle	Small (1/6 in.) variable-colored, usually dark beetles, often present in large numbers in the early part of the growing season. Feeding results in numerous small holes, giving a shotgun appearance. Indirect damage results from diseases transmitted

Crop	Insect	Description
Beet (*Continued*)	Leaf miner	Tiny, black and yellow adults. Yellowish-white maggotlike larvae tunnel within leaves and cause white or translucent, irregularly damaged areas
	Webworm	Yellow to green worm (1¼ in.) with a black stripe and numerous black spots on its back
Broccoli, Brussels sprouts, cabbage, cauliflower, kale, kohlrabi	Aphid	*See* Artichoke
	Flea beetle	*See* Beet
	Harlequin cabbage bug	Black, shield-shaped bug (⅜ in.) with red or yellow markings
	Cabbage maggot	Housefly-like adult lays eggs in the soil at the base of plants. Yellowish, legless maggot (¼–⅓ in.) tunnels into roots and lower stem
	Worms Cabbage looper	A brownish moth (1½ in.) that lays eggs on upper leaf surfaces. Resulting worms (1½ in.) are green with thin white lines. Easily identified by their looping movement
	Diamondback moth	Small, slender, gray or brown moths. The folded wings of male moths show three diamond markings. Small (⅓ in.) larvae with distinctive V at rear, wiggle when disturbed
	Imported cabbage worm	White butterflies with black wing spots lay eggs on undersides of leaves. Resulting worms (1¼ in.) are sleek, velvety, green
Carrot	Leafhopper	*See* Bean
	Rust fly	Shiny, dark fly with a yellow head; lays eggs in the soil at the base of plants. Yellowish-white, legless maggot tunnel into roots
Celery	Aphid	*See* Artichoke
	Leaf miner	Adults are small, shiny, black flies with a bright yellow spot on upper thorax. Eggs are laid within the leaf. Larvae mine between upper and lower leaf surfaces

Crop	Insect	Description
Celery (*Continued*)	Spider mite	*See* Bean
	Tarnished plant bug	*See* Bean
	Loopers and worms	*See* Broccoli, etc.
Cucumber (*See* Vine crops)		
Eggplant	Aphid	*See* Artichoke
	Colorado potato beetle	Oval beetle (3/8 in.) with 10 yellow and 10 black stripes lays yellow eggs on undersides of leaves. Brick-red, humpbacked larvae (1/2 in.) have black spots. Beetles and larvae are destructive leaf feeders
	Flea beetle	*See* Beet
	Leaf miner	*See* Celery
	Spider mite	*See* Bean
Endive, escarole, lettuce	Aphid	*See* Artichoke
	Flea beetle	*See* Beet
	Leafhopper	*See* Bean
	Leaf miner	*See* Beet
	Looper	*See* Broccoli
Muskmelon (*See* Vine crops)		
Mustard greens	Aphid	*See* Artichoke
	Worms	*See* Broccoli, etc.
Okra	Aphid	*See* Artichoke
	Green stinkbug	Large, flattened, shield-shaped, bright green bugs; various-sized nymphs with reddish markings
Onion	Maggot	Slender, gray flies (1/4 in.) lay eggs in soil. Small (1/3 in.) maggots bore into stems and bulbs
	Thrips	Yellow or brown winged or wingless tiny (1/25 in.) Damages plant by sucking plant sap causing white areas or brown leaf tips
Parsnip	Carrot rust fly	*See* Carrot
Pea	Aphid	*See* Artichoke
	Seed maggot	Housefly-like gray adults lay eggs that develop into maggots (1/4 in.) with sharply pointed heads

Crop	Insect	Description
Pea (*Continued*)	Weevil	Brown-colored adults marked by white, black, or gray (1/5 in.) lay eggs on young pods. Larvae are small and whitish with a brown head and mouth. Adults feed on blossoms. May infect seed before harvest and remain in hibernation during storage
Pepper	Aphid	*See* Artichoke
	Corn borer	*See* Sweet corn
	Flea beetle	*See* Beet
	Leaf miner	*See* Beet
	Maggot	Housefly-sized adults have yellow stripes on body and brown stripes on wings. Larvae are typical maggots with pointed heads
	Weevil	Black-colored, gray or yellow marked, snout beetle, with the snout about one-half the length of the body. Grayish-white larvae are legless and have a pale brown head. Both adults and larvae feed on buds and pods; adults also feed on foliage
Potato	Aphid	*See* Artichoke
	Colorado potato beetle	*See* Eggplant
	Cutworm	*See* Asparagus
	Flea beetle	*See* Beet
	Leafhopper	*See* Bean
	Leaf miner	*See* Beet
	Tuberworm	Small, narrow-winged, grayish-brown moths (½ in.) lay eggs on foliage and exposed tubers in evening. Purplish or green caterpillars (¾ in.) with brown heads burrow into exposed tubers in the field or in storage
	Wireworm	Adults are dark-colored, elongated beetles (click beetles). Yellowish, tough-bodied, segmented larvae feed on roots and tunnel through fleshy roots and tubers

Crop	Insect	Description
Radish	Maggot	*See* Broccoli, etc.
Rhubarb	Curculio	Yellow-dusted snout beetle that damages plants by puncturing stems
Rutabaga,	Flea beetle	*See* Beet
turnip	Maggot	*See* Broccoli, etc.
Squash (*See* Vine crops)		
Southern pea	Curculio	Black, humpbacked snout beetle. Eats small holes in pods and peas. Larvae are white with yellowish head and no legs
	Leafhopper	*See* Bean
	Leaf miner	*See* Beet
Spinach	Aphid	*See* Artichoke
	Leaf miner	*See* Beet
Strawberry	Aphid	*See* Artichoke
	Mites	Several mite species attack strawberry *See* Bean
	Tarnished plant bug	*See* Bean
	Thrips	*See* Onion
	Weevils	Several weevil species attack strawberry
	Worms	Several worm species attack strawberry
Sweet corn	Armyworms	Moths (1½ in.) with dark gray front wings and light-colored hind wings lay eggs on leaf undersides. Tan, green, or black worms (1¼ in.) feed on plant leaves and corn ears
	Earworm	*See* Bean
	European corn borer	Pale, yellowish moths (1 in.) with dark bands lay eggs on undersides of leaves. Caterpillars hatch, feed on leaves briefly, and tunnel into stalk and to the ear
	Flea beetle	*See* Beet

Crop	Insect	Description
Sweet corn (*Continued*)	Japanese beetle	Shiny, metallic green with coppery-brown wing covers, oval beetles (½ in.). Severe leaf feeding results in a lacework appearance. Larvae are grubs that feed on grass roots
	Seed-corn maggot	*See* Bean
	Stalk borer	Grayish moths (1 in.) lay eggs on weeds. Small, white, brown-striped caterpillars hatch and tunnel into weed and crop stalks. Most damage is usually at edges of fields
Sweet potato	Flea beetle	*See* Beet
	Weevil	Blue-black and red adult (¼ in.) feeds on leaves and stems, grublike larva tunnels into roots in the field and storage
	Wireworm	*See* Potato
Tomato	Aphid	*See* Artichoke
	Colorado potato beetle	*See* Eggplant
	Corn earworm (tomato fruitworm)	*See* Bean
	Flea beetle	*See* Beet
	Fruit fly	Small, dark-colored flies usually associated with overripe or decaying vegetables
	Hornworm	Large (4–5 in.) moths lay eggs that develop into large (3–4 in.) green fleshy worms with prominent white lines on sides and a distinct horn at the rear. Voracious leaf feeders
	Leaf miner	*See* Beet
	Pinworm	Tiny yellow, gray, or green, purple-spotted, brown-headed caterpillars cause small fruit lesions, mostly near calyx. Presence detected by large white blotches near folded leaves
	Mite	*See* Bean

Crop	Insect	Description
Tomato (*Continued*)	Stink bug	*See* Okra
	White fly	Small, white flies that move when disturbed
Vine crops: cucumber, muskmelon, pumpkin squash, watermelon	Aphid	*See* Artichoke
	Cucumber beetle (spotted or striped)	*See* Bean
	Leafhopper	*See* Bean
	Leaf miner	*See* Beet
	Mite	*See* Bean
	Pickleworm	White moths (1 in.), later become greenish with black spots, with brown heads and brown-tipped wings with white centers, and a conspicuous brush at the tip of the body, lay eggs on foliage. Brown-headed, white, later becoming greenish with black spots. Larvae (¾ in.) feed on blossoms, leaves, and fruit
	Squash bug	Brownish, flat stinkbug (⅝ in.). Nymphs (⅜ in.) are gray to green. Plant damage is due to sucking of plant sap
	Squash vine borer	Black, metallic moth (1½ in.) with transparent hind wings and abdomen ringed with red and black; lays eggs at the base of the plant. White caterpillars bore into the stem and tunnel throughout

Effective insect management requires accurate identification, and a thorough knowledge of the insect's habits and life cycle.

Aphid
Winged adult (*l.*), Wingless adult (*r.*)
(1.6–2.4 mm long)

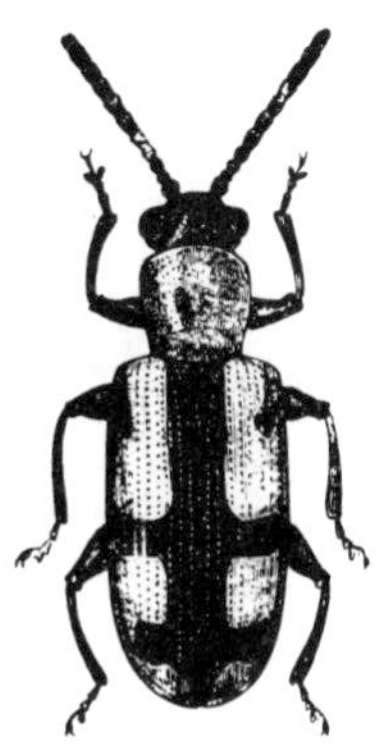

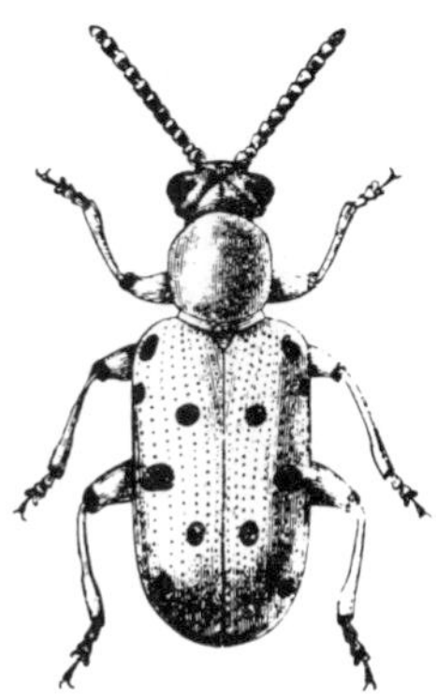

Asparagus beetle
Common (*l.*), Spotted (*r.*)
(6.0–9.5 mm long)

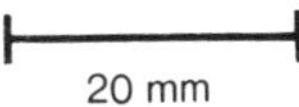

20 mm

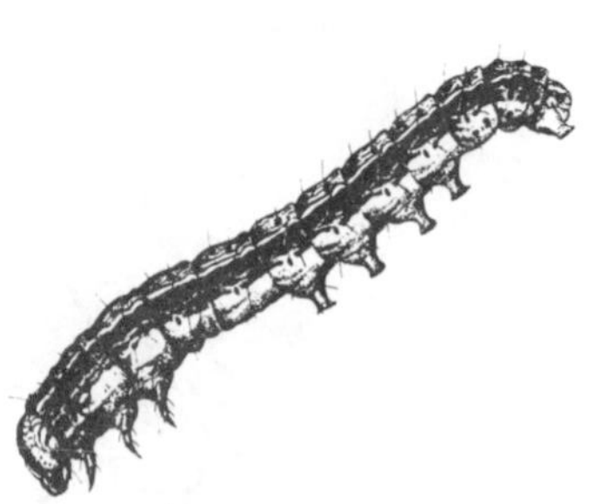

Armyworm
(30–40 mm long)

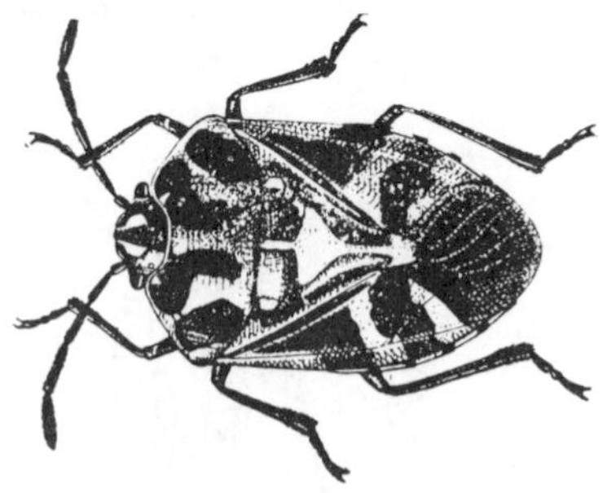

Cabbage harlequin bug
(7–10 mm long)

Cabbage looper
(30 mm long)

Cabbage maggot
(6 mm long)

Cabbage worm
(32 mm long)

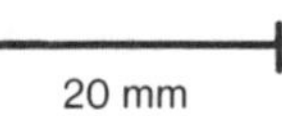

Carrot rust fly larva
(9 mm long)

Colorado potato beetle
Adult (*l.*) Larva (*r.*)
(9–14 mm long) (10 mm long)

Corn borer
(25 mm long)

Corn seed maggot
(5–7 mm long)

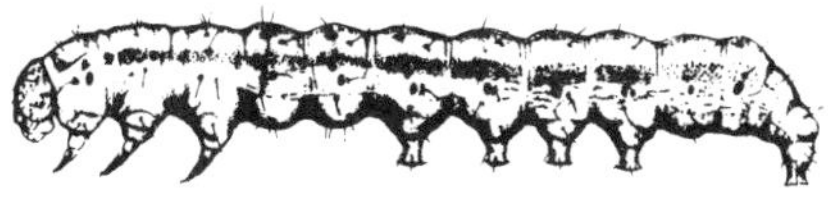

Corn earworm
(44 mm long)

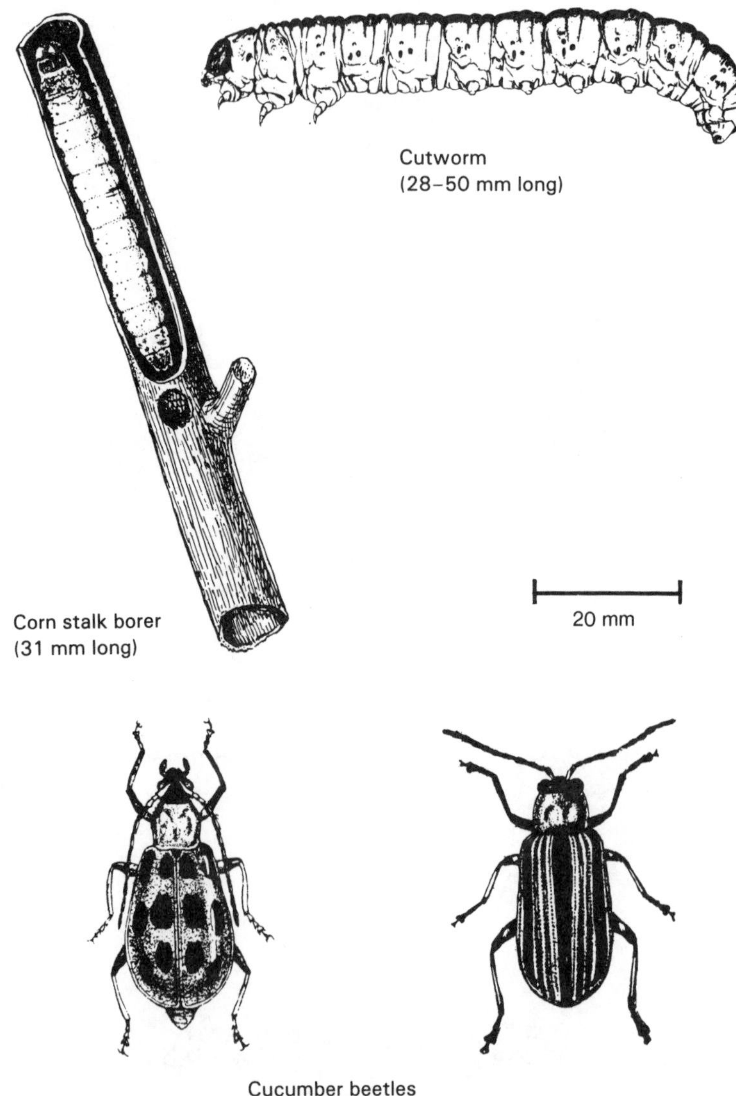

Cutworm
(28–50 mm long)

Corn stalk borer
(31 mm long)

Cucumber beetles
Spotted (*l.*) Striped (*r.*)
(6 mm long) (5 mm long)

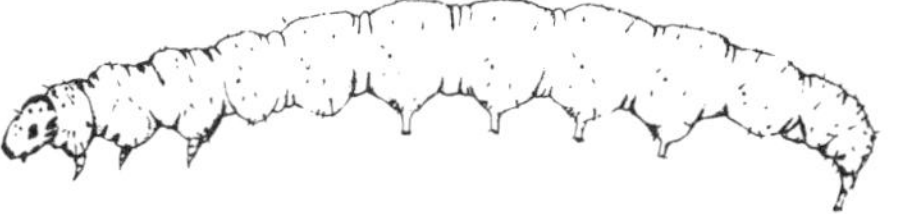

Diamondback moth larva
(7 mm long)

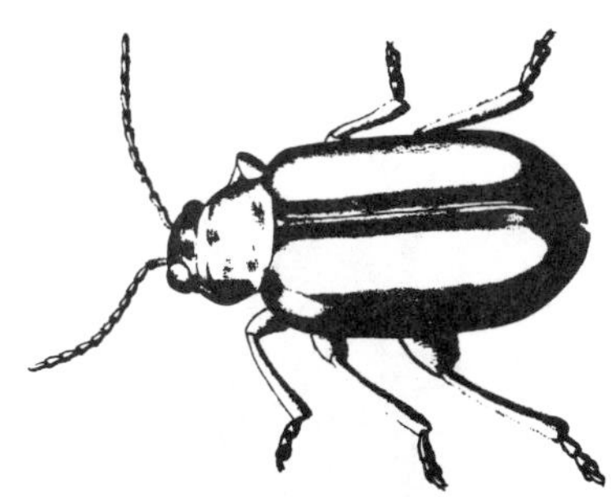

Flea beetle
(2.5 mm long)

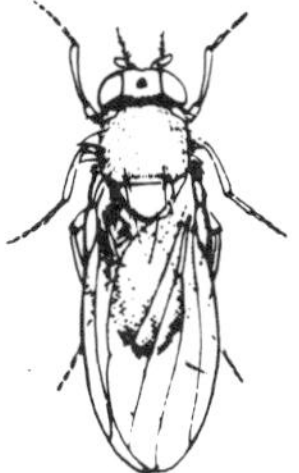

Fruit fly
(3 mm long)

Hornworm
(75–85 mm long)

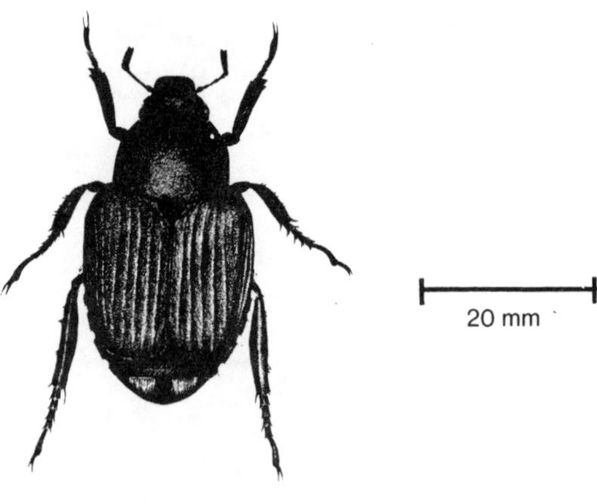

Japanese beetle
(13 mm long)

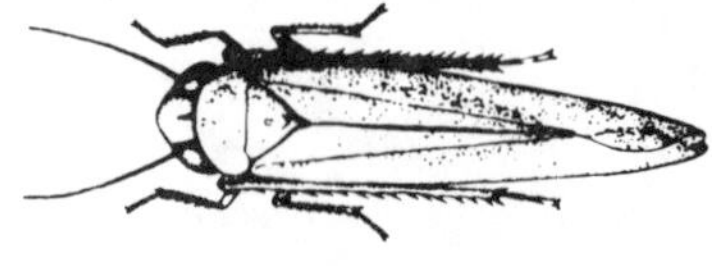

Leafhopper
(3 mm long)

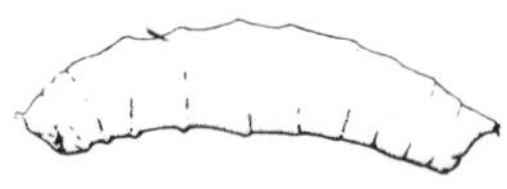

Leaf miner
(3 mm long)

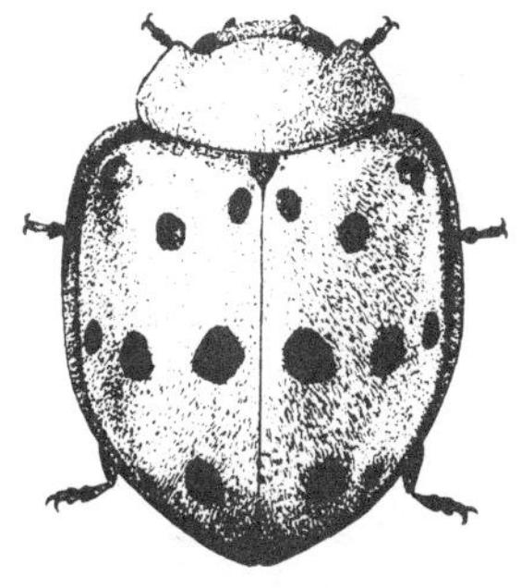
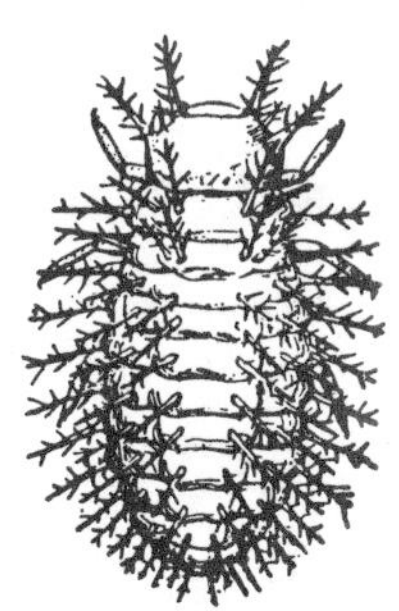

Mexican bean beetle
Adult (*l.*) Larva (*r.*)
(6–8.5 mm long) (8.5 mm long)

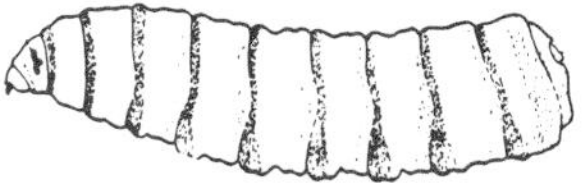

Pepper maggot
(10–12 mm long)

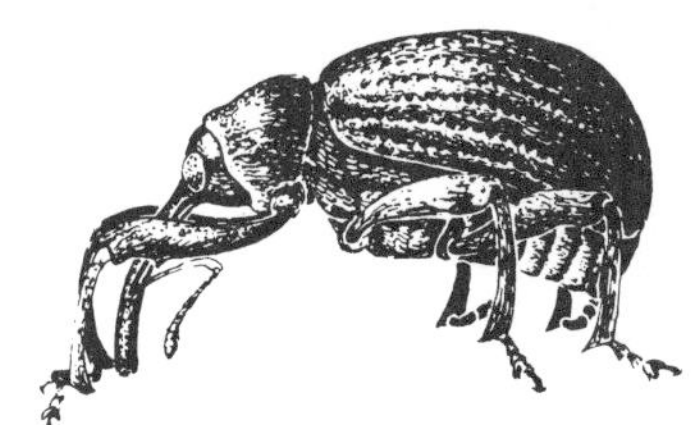
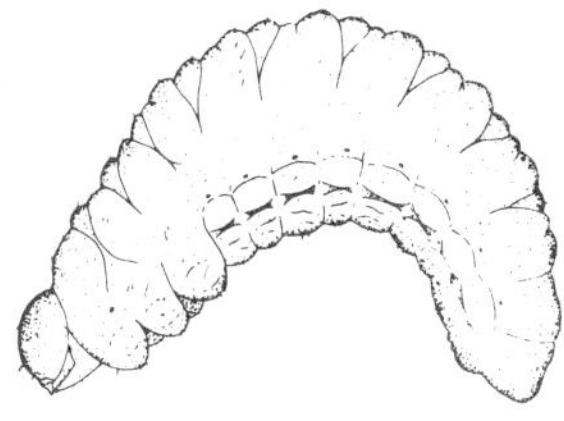

Pepper weevil
Adult (*l.*) Larva (*r.*)
(3 mm long) (6 mm long)

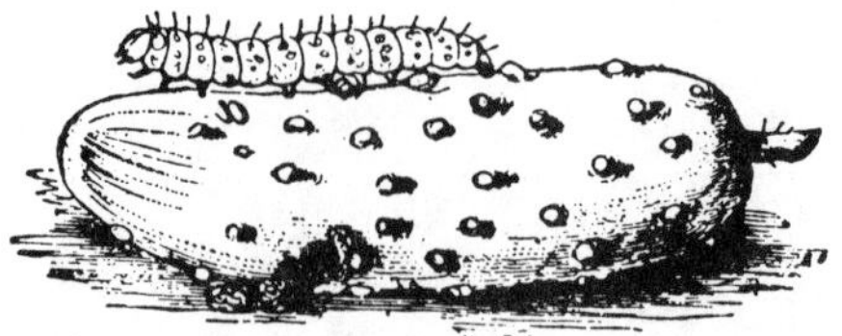

Pickleworm
(25–30 mm long)

Pinworm
(0.8 mm long)

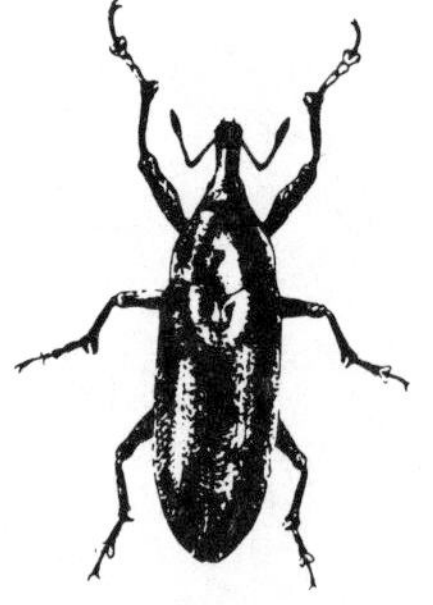

Rhubarb curculio
(12 mm long)

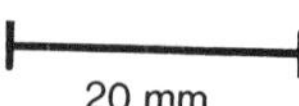

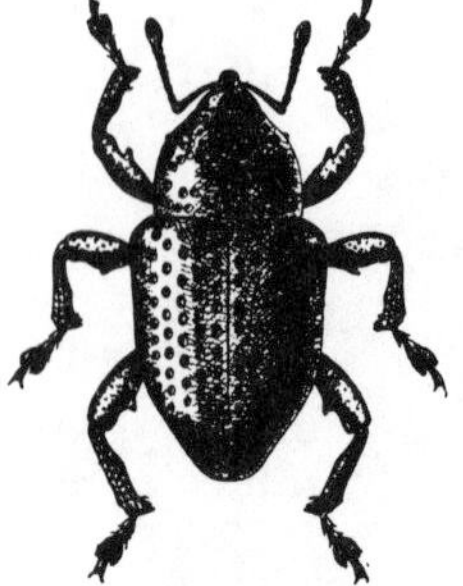

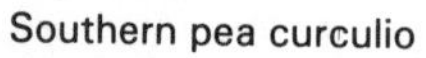

Southern pea curculio
Adult (*l.*) (6–7 mm long)
Larva (*r.*) (6–7 mm long)

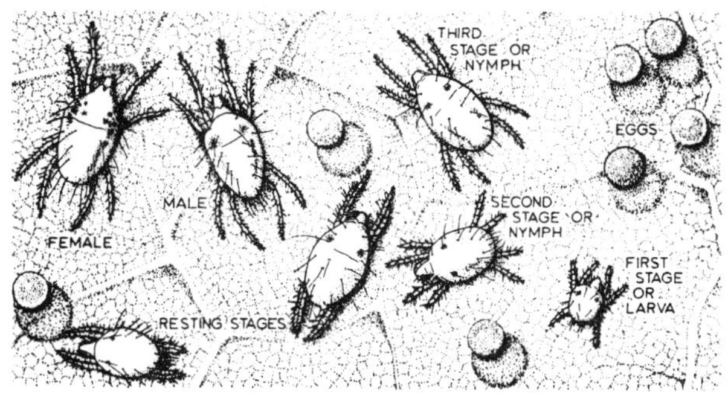

Spider mite
(0.3–0.5 mm long)

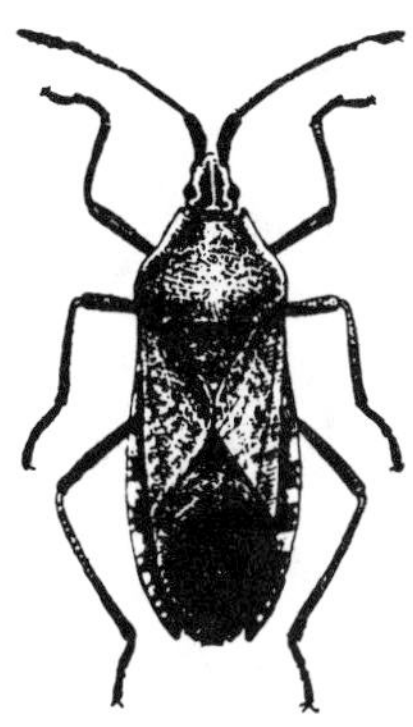

Squash bug
(16 mm long)

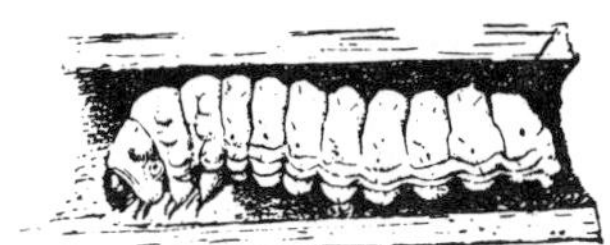

Squash vine borer
(25 mm long)

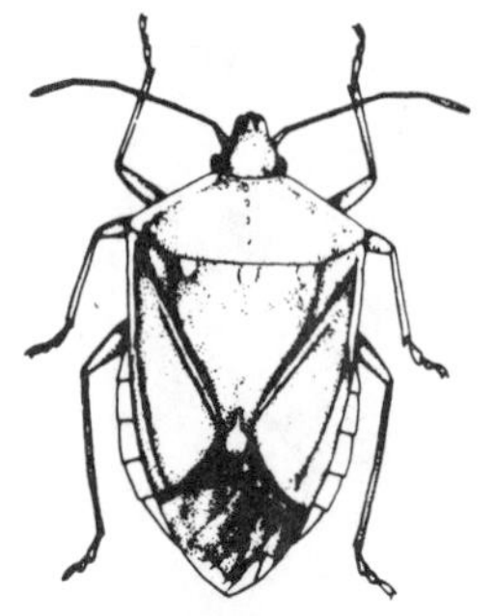

Stinkbug
(14–19 mm long)

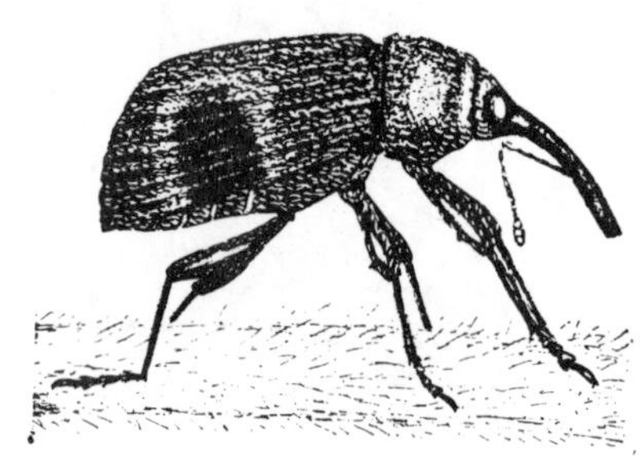

Strawberry bud weevil
(3 mm long)

20 mm

Strawberry root weevil
Adult (*l.*) (5–10 mm long)
Larva (*r.*) (10 mm long)

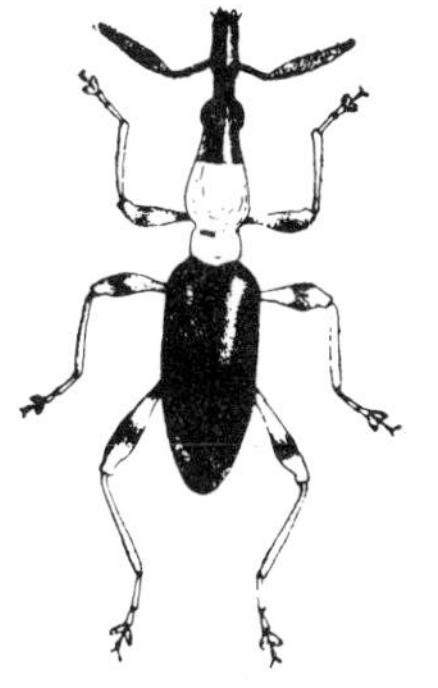

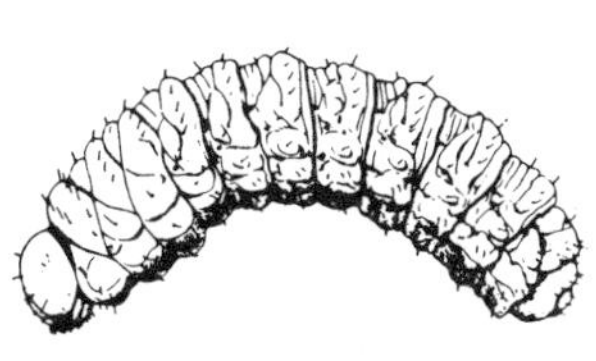

Sweet potato weevil
Adult (*l.*) (6 mm long)
Larva (*r.*) (9 mm long)

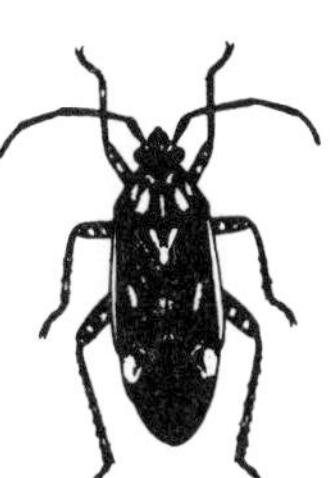

Tarnished plant bug
(6.4 mm long)

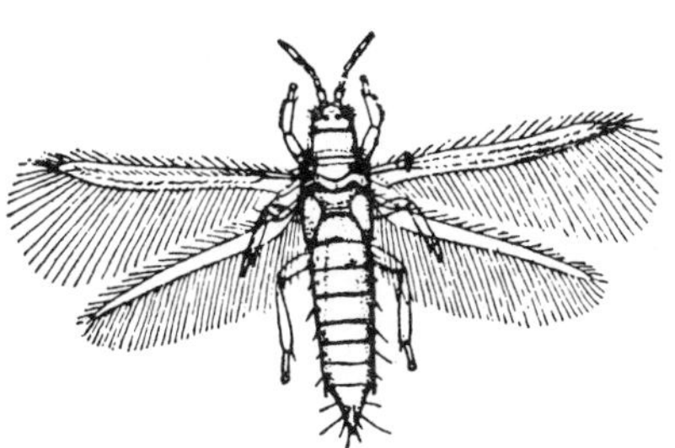

Thrips
(2 mm long)

Tuberworm
(13–19 mm long)

Webworm
(13–15 mm long)

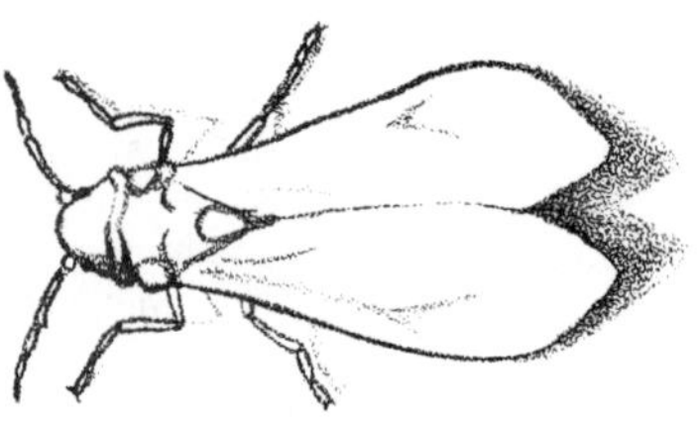

Whitefly
(1.5 mm long)

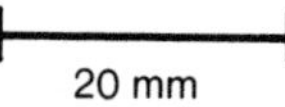

Wireworm
(21–25 mm long)

Adapted from K. A. Sorenson and J. R. Baker (eds.), Insects and related pests of vegetables, North Carolina Agricultural Extension Service AG-295 (1983) and reprinted with permission from R. H. Davidson and W. F. Lyon, *Insect Pests of Farm, Garden, and Orchard*, 8th ed., Wiley, New York (1987).

1. *Deer*

   Repellants. May be effective for low-density deer populations. Apply before damage is expected, when no precipitation is expected, and when temperatures are between 40 and 80°F.

   Fencing. Woven wire fences are the most effective and should be 8 to 10 feet tall. Electric fences may act as a deterrent. Some growers have success with a 5- or 6-foot high-tensile electric fence even though deer might be able to jump fences this tall.

2. *Raccoons.* Many states have laws controlling the manner in which these pests can be removed. Usually trapping is the only means of ridding a field of raccoons. Crops can be protected with a double-strand electric fence with wires at 5 and 10 inches above the ground.

3. *Birds*

   Exclusion. Bird-proof netting can be used to protect vegetables of high value.

   Sound devices. Some success has been reported with recorded distress calls. Other sound devices such as propane guns might be effective for short periods. Use of these devices should be random and with a range of sound frequency and intervals.

   Visual devices. Eye-spot balloons have been used with some success against grackles, blue jays, crows, and starlings and might be the control method of choice for urban farms. Reflective tape has been used with variable success and is very labor intensive to install.

4. *Mice*

   Habitat control. Remove any possible hiding or nesting sites near the field. Sometimes mice will nest underneath polyethylene mulch not applied tightly to the ground and in thick windbreaks.

   Traps and baits. Strategically placed traps and bait stations can be used to reduce mice populations.

   Transplanting. For some particularly attractive crops, such as curcurbits, the seed is a favorite mouse food and the seed is often removed from the ground soon after planting. One option to reduce stand losses would be transplanting instead of direct-seeding.

PART 7

WEED CONTROL

HERBICIDES

EQUIPMENT AND APPLICATION

WEED-CONTROL PRACTICES

EFFECTIVENESS AND LONGEVITY OF HERBICIDES

Weeds reduce yield and quality of vegetables through direct competition for light, moisture, and nutrients as well as by interference with harvest operations.

Early season competition is most critical and a major emphasis on control should be made during this period. Common amaranth reduces yields of lettuce, watermelon, and muskmelon at least 20% if allowed to compete with these crops for only the first 3 weeks of growth. Weeds can be controlled, but this requires good management practices in all phases of production. Because there are many kinds of weeds, with much variation in growth habit, they obviously cannot be managed by a single method.

The incorporation of several of the following management practices into vegetable production practices increases the effectiveness for controlling weeds.

Crop Competition

An often overlooked tool in reducing weed competition is to establish a good crop stand, in which plants emerge and rapidly shade the ground. The plant that emerges first and grows the most rapidly is the plant that will have the competitive advantage. Utilization of good production management practices such as fertility, well-adapted varieties, proper water control (irrigation and drainage), and establishment of adequate plant populations is very helpful in reducing weed competition. Everything possible should be done to ensure that vegetables, not weeds, have the competitive advantage.

Crop Rotation

If the same crop is planted in the same field year after year, there usually will be some weed or weeds favored by the cultural practices and herbicides used on that crop.

By rotating to other crops, the cultural practices and herbicide program are changed. This often reduces the population of specific weeds which were tolerant in the previous cropping rotation. Care should be taken, however, in not replanting vegetables back into soil treated with a non-registered herbicide. Crop injury as well as vegetables containing illegal residues may result. Check the labels for plant back limitations before application and planting rotational crops.

Mechanical Control

Mechanical control includes field preparation by plowing or discing, cultivation, mowing, hoeing, and hand pulling of weeds. Mechanical control practices are among the oldest of weed management techniques.

Weed control is a primary reason for preparing land for crops planted in rows. Seedbed preparation by plowing or discing exposes many weed seeds to variations in light, temperature, and moisture. For some weeds, this process breaks weed-seed dormancy, leading to early season control with herbicides or additional cultivation.

Cultivate only deep enough in the row to achieve weed control; deep cultivation may prune roots, bring weed seeds to the surface, and disturb the soil previously treated with a herbicide. Follow the same precautions between rows.

When weeds can be controlled without cultivation, there is no advantage to cultivating. In fact, there may be disadvantages, such as drying out the soil surface, bringing weed seeds to the surface, and disturbing the root system of the crop.

Mulching

The use of polyethylene mulch increases yield and earliness of vegetables. The proper injection of fumigants under the mulch will control nematodes, soil insects, soil-borne diseases, and weed seeds. Mulches act as a barrier to the growth of many weeds. Nutsedge, however, is one weed that can and will grow through the mulch.

Prevention

Preventing weeds from infesting or reinfesting a field should always be considered. Weed seed may enter a field in a number of ways. It may be distributed by wind, water, machinery, in cover crop seed, and other ways. Fence rows and ditch banks are often neglected when controlling weeds in the crop. Seed produced in these areas may move into the field. Weeds in these areas can also harbor insects and diseases (especially viruses) that may move onto the crop.

It is also important to clean equipment before entering fields or when moving from a field with a high weed infestation to a relatively clean field. Nutsedge tubers especially are moved easily on discs, cultivators, and other equipment.

Herbicides

Properly selected herbicides are effective tools for weed control. Herbicides may be classified several ways, depending on how they are applied and their mode of action in or on the plant. Generally, herbicides are either soil applied or foliage applied. They may be selective or non-selective, and they may be either contact or translocated through the plant. For example, paraquat is a foliage-applied, contact, non-selective herbicide, whereas atrazine usually is described as a soil-applied, translocated, selective herbicide.

Foliage-applied herbicides may be applied to leaves, stems, and shoots of plants. Herbicides that kill only those parts of the plants which the spray touches are contact herbicides. Those herbicides that are taken into the plant and moved throughout the plant are translocated herbicides. Paraquat is a contact herbicide, whereas glyphosate (Roundup) or Sethoxydim (Poast) are translocated herbicides.

For foliage-applied herbicides to be effective, they must enter the plant. Good coverage is very important. Most foliage-applied herbicides require either the addition of a specified surfactant or a specified formulation to be used for best control.

Soil-applied herbicides are either applied to the surface or incorporated. Surface-applied herbicides require rainfall or irrigation shortly after application for best results. Lack of moisture often results in poor weed control.

Incorporated herbicides are not dependent on rainfall or irrigation and have generally given more consistent and wider-spectrum control. They do, however, require more time and equipment for incorporation.

Herbicides which specify incorporation into the soil improve the contact of the herbicide with the weed seed and/or minimize the loss of the herbicide by volatilization or photodecomposition. Some herbicides, if not incorporated, may be lost from the soil surface.

Although most soil-applied herbicides must be moved into the soil to be effective, the depth of incorporation into the soil can be used to achieve selectivity. For example, if a crop seed is planted 2 inches deep in the soil and the herbicide is incorporated by irrigation only in the top 1 inch where most of the problem weed seeds are found, the crop roots will not come in contact with the herbicide. If too much irrigation or rain moves the herbicide down into the crop seed zone or if the herbicide is incorporated mechanically too deep, crop injury may result.

Adapted from W. M. Stall. Weed Management. In: D. N. Maynard and G. J. Hochmuth (eds.). Commercial Vegetable Production Guide for Florida. Fla. Coop. Ext. Serv. SP-170 (1996).

WEED CONTROL WITH HERBICIDES

Chemical weed control minimizes labor and is effective if used with care. The following precautions should be observed:

1. Do not use a herbicide unless the label states that it is registered for that particular crop. Be sure to use as directed by the manufacturer.
2. Use herbicides so that no excessive residues remain on the harvested product, which may otherwise be confiscated. Residue tolerances are established by the Environmental Protection Agency.
3. Note that some herbicides will kill only certain weeds.
4. Make certain that the soil is sufficiently moist for effective action of preemergence sprays. Do not expect good results in dry soil.
5. Keep in mind that postemergence herbicides are most effective when conditions favor rapid weed germination and growth.
6. Avoid using too much herbicide. Overdoses can injure the vegetable crop. Few crops, if any, are entirely resistant.
7. Use less herbicide on light sandy soils than on heavy clay soils. Muck soils reqire somewhat greater rates than do heavy mineral soils.
8. When using wettable powders, be certain the liquid in the tank is agitated constantly as spraying proceeds.
9. Use a boom and nozzle arrangement that will fan out the material close to the ground in order to avoid drift.
10. Thoroughly clean spray tank after use.

CLEANING SPRAYERS AFTER USE WITH HERBICIDES

Sprayers must be kept clean to avoid injury to the crop on which they are to be used for applying insecticides or fungicides, as well as to prevent possible deterioration of the sprayers after use of certain materials.

1. Rinse all parts of sprayer with water before and after any special cleaning operation is undertaken.
2. If in doubt about the effectiveness of water alone to clean tank, pump, boom, hoses, and nozzles of the herbicide, use a cleaner. In some cases, it is desirable to use activated carbon to reduce contamination.
3. Fill tank with water. Use one of the following materials for each 100 gal of water: 5 lb of paint cleaner (trisodium phosphate), 1 gal of household ammonia, or 5 lb of sal soda.
4. If hot water is used, let the solution stand in the tank for 18 hr. If cold water is used, leave it for 36 hr. Pump solution through sprayer.
5. Rinse tank and parts several times with clear water.
6. If copper has been used in the sprayer before a weed control operation is to be performed, put 1 gal of vinegar in 100 gal of water and let the solution stay in the sprayer for 2 hr. Drain the solution and rinse thoroughly. Copper will interfere with the effectiveness of some herbicides.

DETERMINING RATES OF APPLICATION OF WEED-CONTROL MATERIALS

Commercially available herbicide formulations differ in their content of the active ingredient. The label will indicate the amount of the active ingredient (lb/gal). By referring to this amount in the table, it is possible to determine how much of the formulation you need in order to supply the recommended amount of the active ingredient per acre. For calibration of herbicide application equipment see pages 302–306.

HERBICIDE DILUTION TABLE: QUANTITY OF LIQUID CONCENTRATES TO USE TO GIVE DESIRED DOSAGE OF ACTIVE CHEMICAL

Active Ingredient Needed (lb/acre):	0.125	0.25	0.50	1	2	3	4
Active Ingredient Content of Liquid Concentrate (lb/gal)	Liquid Concentrate to Use (pint/acre)						
1	1.0	2.0	4.0	8.0	16.0	24.0	32.0
1½	0.67	1.3	2.6	5.3	10.6	16.0	21.3
2	0.50	1.0	2.0	4.0	8.0	12.0	16.0
3	0.34	0.67	1.3	2.7	5.3	8.0	10.7
4	0.25	0.50	1.0	2.0	4.0	6.0	8.0
5	0.20	0.40	0.80	1.6	3.2	4.8	6.4
6	0.17	0.34	0.67	1.3	2.6	4.0	5.3
7	0.14	0.30	0.60	1.1	2.3	3.4	4.6
8	0.125	0.25	0.50	1.0	2.0	3.0	4.0
9	0.11	0.22	0.45	0.9	1.8	2.7	3.6
10	0.10	0.20	0.40	0.8	1.6	2.4	3.2

Adapted from Spraying Systems Co., Catalog 36, Wheaton, IL (1978).

State recommendations for herbicides vary, because the effect of herbicides is influenced by growing area, soil type, temperature, and soil moisture. Growers should consult local authorities for specific recommendations. The Environmental Protection Agency has established residue tolerances for those herbicides that may leave injurious residues in or on a harvested vegetable and has approved certain materials, rates, and methods of application. Laws regarding vegetation and herbicides are constantly changing. Growers and commercial applicators should not use a chemical on a crop for which the compound is not registered. Herbicides should be used exactly as stated on the label, regardless of information presented here. Growers are advised to give special attention to any plant-back restrictions.

ESTIMATED EFFECTIVENESS OF HERBICIDES ON SELECTED BROADLEAF WEEDS IN VEGETABLES GROWN IN SOUTHERN UNITED STATES

Herbicide	Amaranthus	Cocklebur	Evening Primrose	Eclipta Alba	Florida Beggerweed	Florida Pursley	Parthenium	Lambsquarter	Purslane	Morningglories	Nightshade	Ragweed	Sicklepod	Southernside
Preplant Incorporated														
Command	F–G	P–F	G	—	—	G	—	G–E	E	P	—	F–G	P	—
Dacthal	F–G	P	F–G	—	F	F	—	G	G	P	F	—	P	F
Devrinol	F–G	P	G	P	P	G–E	P	G–E	G	P	P	—	P	—
Dual	G	P	G–E	G	F–G	G–E	—	F–G	G	P	F–G	F	P	G
Eptam	G	P	G	G	P	G–E	—	G	G	F	P–F	F	F	G
Prefar	F	P	F	P	P	E	—	F–G	F	P	P	P	P	P
Pursuit	G–E	—	E	E	E	F	—	E	E	G–E	G–E	G	P	G
Sencor/Lexone	E	G	E	G	G–E	G	G	E	G	G–E	P	G	G	G
Sutan+	G–E	P	G–E	G	P	G–E	—	G	G	F–G	—	F	F–G	G
Treflan	G–E	P	G	F–G	P	E	P	G–E	E	P	P	P	P	P

ESTIMATED EFFECTIVENESS OF HERBICIDES ON SELECTED BROADLEAF WEEDS IN VEGETABLES GROWN IN SOUTHERN UNITED STATES—Continued

Herbicide	Amaranthus	Cocklebur	Evening Primrose	Eclipta Alba	Florida Beggerweed	Florida Pursley	Parthenium	Lambsquarter	Purslane	Morningglories	Nightshade	Ragweed	Sicklepod	Southernside
Preemergence														
Alanap	G–E	F	G	G	F	G	—	E	G	F	F	F	P	G
Atrazine	E	G–E	E	G–E	G–E	E	E	E	E	G	G	E	F–G	G–E
Caparol	G–E	—	—	—	—	F–G	—	F–G	G–E	—	F–G	F–G	—	—
Command	F–G	P	G	—	—	G	—	G	E	P	—	F	P	—
Curbit	G	P	G	—	P	E	P	G–E	E	P	P	P	P	P
Dacthal	F–G	P	F–G	—	F	F	—	G	G	P	F	—	P	F
Devrinol	F	P	G	P	P	G	P	G	G	P	P	—	P	—
Dual	G	F	G	G	F	G	—	F	G	P	F	F	P	G
Goal	E	E	E	E	G	G	G	E	E	G	G	G	F	G
Kerb	F–G	—	G	—	—	G	—	E	G–E	F–G	G	—	—	—
Lorox	G	F	E	—	G	E	—	E	E	F	—	G	—	F
Prowl	G–E	P	G	—	P	G	P	E	G	P	P	P	P	—
Pursuit	G–E	G–E	E	E	P	F	—	G–E	G–E	G–E	G–E	G	P	G
Sencor/Lexone	G	F	E	F–G	G	G	G	E	G	F	P–F	G	G	G

Postemergence

Atrazine	G–E	F	E	G	P	G–E	F–G	G	F–G	G	F	F	F–G	
Basagran	G	G	G	G	P	F	—	—	G	F–G	F–G	G	P	G
Byctril	G	E	E	E	E	G–E	—	G	G–E	G	G	G	—	G
Diquat	E	G	E	E	G–E	G	E	E	G	F–G	G	G	G	G
Enquik	E	G	E	E	E	G	G	F–G	G	F	G	G	G	G
Fusilade 2000	N	N	N	N	N	N	N	N	N	N	N	N	N	N
Gramoxone	E	G	E	E	G–E	G	P	E	G	F–G	F	G	G	G
Lorox	E	G	—	—	G	G	—	E	E	F–G	—	G	G	G
Poast	N	N	N	N	N	N	N	N	N	N	N	N	N	N
Pursuit	E	G	G	G	—	F	—	F–G	P–F	G	G	G	P	—
Sencor/Lexone	E	G	G	F	G	G	P	G	F–G	P	P	F–G	F	F

Adapted from W. M. Stall. Weed Management. pp. 84–85. In D. N. Maynard and G. J. Hochmuth (eds.). Vegetable Production Guide for Florida. Florida Coop. Ext. Serv. SP170 (1995).

E = 90–100%, N = no control, G = 80–90%, — = no data, F = 60–80%, P = below 60%.

ESTIMATED EFFECTIVENESS OF HERBICIDES ON SELECTED BROADLEAF WEEDS IN VEGETABLES GROWN IN SOUTHERN UNITED STATES—Continued

	Grasses							Sedges		
Herbicide	Barnyardgress	Bermudagrass	Broadleaf Signalgrass	Crabgrass	Goosegrass	Panicums (Fall & Texas)	Sprangletop	Purple Nutsedge	Yellow Nutsedge	Annual Sedges
Preplant Incorporated										
Command	E	G–E	E	E	E	G–E	—	P	P	P
Dacthal	G	G	F	G	G	F	—	P	P	P
Devrinol	E	E	E	E	E	G–E	—	P	F	F
Dual	G	G–E	E	E	E	G	G	P–F	G	G–E
Eptam	E	E	G	E	E	G–E	—	G–E	G	E
Prefar	G	G	G	G	G–E	F–G	—	P	P	P
Pursuit	F	P	F	F	F	P–F	P	F–G	G	E
Sencor/Lexone	G	F–G	G	G–E	G–E	F–G	—	P	P	P
Sutan+	E	E	G–E	E	E	G	—	G	G–E	E
Treflan	E	G	G–E	E	E	G	—	P	P	P

Preemergence										
Alanap	P	P	F	F	P	P	—	P	P	P
Atrazine	F	P	F–G	F	F	P	P	P	P	P
Caparol	F–G	F–G	F–G	G	F–G	F	—	P	P	P
Command	E	E	E	E	E	E	—	P	P	P
Curbit	E	G–E	E	E	E	G–E	G	P	P	P
Dacthal	F–G	F–G	F	G	G	F	—	P	P	P
Devrinol	E	E	E	E	E	G–E	—	P–F	F	F–G
Dual	E	E	E	E	E	G–E	G	P–F	F–G	E
Goal	F	P	F	F	F	P	—	P	F	G
Kerb	G–E	P	G	G–E	G–E	F–G	—	P	P	P
Lorox	F–G	—	G	G	G	F–G	—	F	F	F
Prowl	E	E	E	E	E	G–E	E	P	P	P
Pursuit	F	P	F	F	F	P–F	P	G	G–E	E
Sencor/Lexone	F–G	F	G	G	G–E	P	P	P	P	P
Postemergence										
Atrazine	F–G	F	F	F	F	F	F	P	P	P
Basagran	P	P	P	P	P	P	P	P–F	F–G	G–E
Buctril	P	P	P	P	P	P	P	P	P	P
*Diquat	E–G	G	E	G–E	G–E	G	G	F–G	F–G	G
Enquik	P–F	P–F	P–F	P–F	P–F	P–F	—	F	F	F
Fusilade	E	E	E	E	E	E	E	P	P	P

ESTIMATED EFFECTIVENESS OF HERBICIDES ON SELECTED GRASSES AND SEDGES IN VEGETABLES GROWN IN SOUTHERN UNITED STATES—Continued

Herbicide	Grasses							Sedges		
	Barnyardgress	Bermudagrass	Broadleaf Signalgrass	Crabgrass	Goosegrass	Panicums (Fall & Texas)	Sprangletop	Purple Nutsedge	Yellow Nutsedge	Annual Sedges
Postemergence (Continued)										
*Gramoxone	E	E	E	E	E	E	E	F–G	F–G	G
Lorox	G	F–G	G	G	G	G	G	F	F	F–G
Poast	E	G–E	E	E	E	E	E	P	P	P
Pursuit	F	P	P–F	P–F	F	P–F	P	G–E	G–E	G–E
Sencor/Lexone	F	P	P	F	F	P	P	P	P	P

Adapted from W. M. Stall. Weed Management. pp. 85–86. In D. N. Maynard and G. J. Hochmuth (eds.). Vegetable Production Guide for Florida. Florida Coop. Ext. Serv. SP170 (1995).

E = 90–100%, N = no control, G = 80–90%, — = no data, F = 60–80%, P = below 60%.
*Initial burndown with sedges and other perennial weed can be complete, but regrowth occurs.

ESTIMATED EFFECTIVENESS OF HERBICIDES ON SOME WEEDS IN VEGETABLES GROWN IN NORTHERN UNITED STATES

Herbicide	Barnyardgrass	Crabgrass, Large	Fall Panicum	Foxtail sp.	Goosegrass	Johnsongrass (Seedlings)	Yellow Nutsedge	Carpetweed	Cocklebur, Common	Cranesbill	Galinsoga, Hairy	Jimsonweed	Lambsquarters, Common	Morningglory sp.	Shepherds-purse	Pigweed sp.	Purslane, Common	Ragweed, Common	Smartweed, Pennsylvania	Night shade, Eastern Black	Velvetleaf
Preplant Incorporated																					
Command	G	G	G	G	G	G	N	N	N/F	—	F	G	G	P	F	N/P	G	F	G	—	G
Devrinol	G	G	G	G	G	G	N/P	G	N	—	F/P	N	F/G	N	—	F/G	G	P/F	P	N	N
Eptam	G	G	G	G	G	G	G	G	P	G	N	P	F	F	—	G	G	P	P	F/G	F/G
Prefar	G	G	G	G	F/G	G	N	N	N	N	N	N	F/G	N	P/F	F	F	N	N	N	N
Ro-Neet	G	G	G	G	G	—	N/P	G	N	G	N	N	F	—	G	G	G	N	—	—	F
Sutan+	G	G	G	G	G	G	F/G	—	N	—	N	N	P	F	—	G	P	P	P	F	F
Tillam	G	F	F	G	F	—	F	—	N	—	N	N	P	—	—	G	P/F	N	—	F/G	—
Treflan	G	G	G	G	G	G	N	G	N	—	N	N	F/G	P/F	N	F	G	N	P/F	P	N

ESTIMATED EFFECTIVENESS OF HERBICIDES ON SOME WEEDS IN VEGETABLES GROWN IN NORTHERN UNITED STATES—Continued

Herbicide	Barnyardgrass	Crabgrass, Large	Fall Panicum	Foxtail sp.	Goosegrass	Johnsongrass (Seedlings)	Yellow Nutsedge	Carpetweed	Cocklebur, Common	Cranesbill	Galinsoga, Hairy	Jimsonweed	Lambsquarters, Common	Morningglory sp.	Shepherds-purse	Pigweed sp.	Purslane, Common	Ragweed, Common	Smartweed, Pennsylvania	Night shade, Eastern Black	Velvetleaf
Preemergence or Preplant Incorporated																					
Alanap	P	P/F	P	F	P/F	—	N	F	P	N	F	F	G	F	N	F/G	F/G	F	P	P	F
Atrazine	F	P/F	P	F	—	P	P/F	G	F/G	—	G	G	G	G	G	G	G	G	G	G	F
Bladex	P	P	F	P	—	—	P	G	F	—	G	P	G	F	G	P	G	F	—	G	P
Dual	G	G	G	G	G	G	F/G	F	N	—	G	N	P	N	—	G	F/G	N	P	G	P
Micro-Tech/Partner	G	F/G	G	G	G	G	F	G	N	—	G	P	P/F	N	G	G	G	N	P	G	P
Prowl	G	G	G	G	—	G	N	G	N	—	N	N	F/G	P	N	F/G	F/G	N	F	P	G
Pursuit	P/F	P/F	P/F	P/F	P/F	—	N	G	F	—	P	F	G	F	F	G	G	P	G	F	G
Sencor/Lexone	F	F	F	F	F	—	N	G	F	—	G	F/G	G	F/P	—	F/G	F	G	G	P	G
Preemergence																					
Curbit	F	G	G	—	G	—	N	G	N	—	N	N	P/F	P	—	F	F/G	N	P	P	P
Dacthal	F/G	G	F/G	G	F/G	—	N	P	N	P	N	P	G	N	P	F/G	G	N	N	N	N

Goal	P	P	P	P	P	P	P	G	P	—	G	F	G	F	G	G	G	F	G	G	F
Karmex	G	F/G	G	G	F/G	N	N	G	—	—	G	G	G	G	G	G	G	G	G	G	G
Kerb	G	G	G	G	G	—	N	G	N	—	P	N	G	—	—	G	G	P	—	—	P
Lorox	F	P/F	P	F	P/F	—	N	G	P	—	G	P/F	G	P	F	G	G	F	G	G	P
Sinbar	F	F	—	F	F	—	P	G	—	G	G	G	G	G	G	P	G	G	G	G	G
Solicam	G	G	G	G	—	F	F	—	—	—	—	F	F	P	—	G	G	G	—	—	F
Postemergence																					
Atrazine	F	F	F	F	F	—	G	—	F	—	G	G	G	G	G	G	G	G	G	G	F/G
Banvel	N	N	N	N	N	N	P	G	G	G	G	G	G	G	G	G	G	G	G	G	G
Basagran	N	N	N	N	N	N	F	N	G	—	F	G	F	P	—	F	F/G	G	G	P	G
Fusilade DX	G	F/G	G	G	G	G	N	N	N	N	N	N	N	N	N	N	N	N	N	N	N
Goal	P	P	P	P	P	P	N	F/G	—	—	F	—	F	—	G	G	G	F	—	—	—
Gramoxone Extra[1]	F/G	F/G	F/G	G	F/G	—	G	G	G	—	G	G	F/G	F/G	—	G	F/G	G	—	—	—
Lentagran	P	P	P	P	P	P	—	—	G	—	G	G	G	F	P	G	G	P	—	—	F
Lorox	F	F	F	F	F	F	F	G	P/F	—	F/G	P/F	G	—	G	G	G	G	G	F/G	G
Poast	G	G	G	G	G	G	N	N	N	N	N	N	N	N	N	N	N	N	N	N	N
Pursuit	F/G	F/G	F/G	F/G	P	F/G	—	G	F	—	G	F	G	F	P/F	G	G	P/F	—	—	G
Roundtrip[1]	G	G	G	G	G	G	F	G	G	G	G	G	G	F	G	G	G	F	G	G	G
Sencor/Lexone	F	F	F	F	F	—	—	G	—	—	G	G	G	P	G	G	G	G	F	P	P/F
Spin-aid	P	P	P	P	P	P	P	—	P	—	G	G	F	G	G	P/F	G	F/G	—	—	N
2,4D	N	N	N	N	N	N	P	G	F/G	G	P	F	F/G	G	G	G	G	G	F	G	G

Adapted from Ed Kee, et al. 1995 Commercial Vegetable Production in Delaware. Del. Coop. Ext. Serv. Bul. 137 (1995).

[1] Nonselective.

Herbicide performance is affected by weather, soil type, herbicide rate, weed pressure, and other factors. These ratings indicate ONLY relative effectiveness in tests conducted by the University of Delaware, University of Maryland System, The Pennsylvania State University, Rutgers, The State University of New Jersey, and Virginia Polytechnic Institute and State University. Actual performance may be better or worse than indicated in this chart. G = good, F = fair, P = poor, N = no control, — = insufficient data.

PART 8
HARVESTING AND STORAGE

APPROXIMATE TIME FROM PLANTING TO MARKET MATURITY UNDER OPTIMUM GROWING CONDITIONS

Vegetable	Time to Market Maturity[1] (days)		
	Early Variety	Late Variety	Common Variety
Bean, broad	—	—	120
Bean, bush	48	60	—
Bean, pole	62	68	—
Bean, lima, bush	65	78	—
Bean, lima, pole	78	88	—
Beet	56	70	—
Broccoli[2]	55	78	—
Broccoli raab	60	70	—
Brussels sprouts[2]	90	100	—
Cabbage	62	120	—
Cardoon	—	—	120
Carrot	50	95	—
Cauliflower[2]	50	125	—
Celeriac	—	—	110
Celery[2]	90	125	—
Chard, Swiss	50	60	—
Chervil	—	—	60
Chicory	65	150	—
Chinese cabbage	70	80	—
Chive	—	—	90
Collards	70	85	—
Corn, sweet	64	95	—
Corn salad	—	—	60
Cress	—	—	45
Cucumber, pickling	48	58	—
Cucumber, slicing	62	72	—
Dandelion	—	—	85
Eggplant[2]	50	80	—
Endive	85	100	—
Florence fennel	—	—	100
Kale	—	—	55
Kohlrabi	50	60	—
Leek	—	—	150
Lettuce, butterhead	55	70	—
Lettuce, cos	70	75	—
Lettuce, head	70	85	—
Lettuce, leaf	40	50	—

APPROXIMATE TIME FROM PLANTING TO MARKET MATURITY UNDER OPTIMUM GROWING CONDITIONS—Continued

Vegetable	Time to Market Maturity[1] (days)		
	Early Variety	Late Variety	Common Variety
Melon, casaba	—	—	110
Melon, honeydew	—	—	110
Melon, Persian	—	—	110
Muskmelon	85	95	—
Mustard	35	55	—
New Zealand spinach	—	—	70
Okra	50	60	—
Onion, dry	90	150	—
Onion, green	45	60	—
Parsley	70	80	—
Parsley root	—	—	90
Parsnip	—	—	120
Pea	56	75	—
Pea, edible-podded	60	70	—
Pepper, hot[2]	65	80	—
Pepper, sweet[2]	65	80	—
Potato	90	120	—
Pumpkin	100	120	—
Radish	22	30	—
Radish, winter	50	60	—
Roselle	—	—	175
Rutabaga	—	—	90
Salsify	—	—	150
Scolymus	—	—	150
Scorzonera	—	—	150
Sorrel	—	—	60
Southern pea	65	85	—
Spinach	37	45	—
Squash, summer	40	50	—
Squash, winter	85	110	—
Sweet potato	120	150	—
Tomato[2]	60	90	—
Turnip	40	75	—
Watercress	—	—	180
Watermelon	75	95	—

[1] Maturity may vary depending on season, latitude, production practices, and other factors.
[2] Time from transplanting. See page 51.

APPROXIMATE TIME FROM POLLINATION TO MARKET MATURITY UNDER WARM GROWING CONDITIONS

Vegetable	Time to Market Maturity (days)
Bean	7–10
Corn,[1] market	18–23
Corn,[1] processing	21–27
Cucumber, pickling (¾–1⅛ in. in diameter)	4–5
Cucumber, slicing	15–18
Eggplant (⅔ maximum size)	25–40
Muskmelon	42–46
Okra	4–6
Pepper, green stage (about maximum size)	45–55
Pepper, red stage	60–70
Pumpkin, Connecticut Field	80–90
Pumpkin, Dickinson	90–110
Pumpkin, Small Sugar	65–75
Squash, summer, Crookneck	6–7[2]
Squash, summer, Early Prolific Straightneck	5–6[2]
Squash, summer, Scallop	4–5[2]
Squash, summer, Zucchini	3–4[2]
Squash, winter, Banana	70–80
Squash, winter, Boston Marrow	60–70
Squash, winter, Buttercup	60–70
Squash, winter, Butternut	60–70
Squash, winter, Golden Delicious	60–70
Squash, winter, Hubbard	80–90
Squash, winter, Table Queen or Acorn	55–60
Strawberry	25–42
Tomato, mature green stage	35–45
Tomato, red ripe stage	45–60
Watermelon	42–45

[1] Days from 50% silking.
[2] For a weight of ¼–½ lb.

The prediction of crop yields before the harvest aids in the scheduling of harvests of various fields for total yields, as well as harvest to obtain highest yields of a particular grade or stage of maturity. To estimate yields, follow these steps:

1. Select and measure a typical 10-ft section of a row. If the field is variable or large, you may want to select several 10-ft sections.
2. Harvest the crop from the measured section or sections.
3. Weigh the entire sample for total yields or grade the sample and weigh the graded sample for yield of a particular grade.
4. If you have harvested more than one 10-ft section, divide the yield by the number of sections harvested.
5. Multiply the sample weight by the conversion factor in the table for your row spacing. The value obtained will equal hundredweight (cwt) per acre.

Conversion Factors for Estimating Yields

Row Spacing (in.)	Multiply Sample Weight (lb) by Conversion Factor to Obtain cwt/acre
12	43.6
15	34.8
18	29.0
20	26.1
21	24.9
24	21.8
30	17.4
36	14.5
40	13.1
42	12.4
48	10.9

Example 1: A 10-ft sample of carrots planted in 12-in. rows yields 9 lb of No. 1 carrots.

$$9 \times 43.6 = 392.4 \text{ cwt/acre}$$

Example 2: The average yield of three 10-ft samples of No. 1 potatoes planted in 36-in. rows is 26 lb.

$$26 \times 14.5 = 377 \text{ cwt/acre}$$

YIELDS OF VEGETABLE CROPS

Vegetable	Approximate Average Yield in the United States (cwt/acre)	Good Yield (cwt/acre)
Artichoke	115	160
Asparagus	30	45
Bean, fresh market	50	100
Bean, processing	75	120
Bean, lima, processing	25	40
Beet, fresh market	140	200
Beet, processing	310	400
Broccoli	105	140
Brussels sprouts	160	200
Cabbage, fresh market	315	450
Cabbage, processing	575	800
Carrot, topped	300	800
Cauliflower	120	170
Celeriac	—	200
Celery	600	750
Chard, Swiss	—	150
Chinese cabbage, napa	—	400
Chinese cabbage, bok-choy	—	300
Collards	—	200
Corn, fresh market	90	200
Corn, processing	130	200
Cucumber, fresh market	175	300
Cucumber, processing	110	320
Eggplant	245	350
Endive, escarole	135	200
Garlic	165	200
Horseradish	—	80
Lettuce, head	325	400
Lettuce, leaf	205	325
Lettuce, Romaine	270	350
Melon, Persian	130	160
Melon, honeydew	170	250
Muskmelon	175	200
Okra	—	150
Onion	385	650
Pea, fresh market	40	60
Pea, processing (shelled)	30	45
Pepper, bell	230	330

Vegetable	Approximate Average Yield in the United States (cwt/acre)	Good Yield (cwt/acre)
Pepper, chili (dried)	40	60
Pepper, pimiento	—	100
Potato	315	400
Pumpkin	—	400
Radish	—	75
Rhubarb	—	200
Rutabaga	—	400
Snowpea	—	80
Southern pea	—	35
Spinach, fresh market	125	200
Spinach, processing	160	220
Squash, summer	—	300
Squash, winter	—	400
Sweet potato	145	300
Strawberry	290	550
Tomato, fresh market	280	410
Tomato, processing	650	900
Tomato, cherry	—	600
Turnip	—	400
Watermelon	180	420

STATUS OF HAND VS. MECHANICAL HARVEST OF VEGETABLES

Acreage Hand Harvested (%)	Vegetable			
76–100	Artichoke	Asparagus	Broccoli[1]	Cabbage
	Cauliflower	Celery	Cucumber[1]	Lettuce
	Green onion	Collards	Cress	Dandelion
	Eggplant	Endive	Escarole	Fennel
	Kale	Kohlrabi	Mushroom[1]	Okra
	Pepper	Rapini	Rhubarb[1]	Romaine
	Sorrel	Squash	Watercress	Cassava
	Celeriac	Ginger	Parsley root	Parsnip
	Rutabaga	Salsify	Turnip	Taro[1]
	Jerusalem artichoke			
51–75	Sweet potato	Mustard greens	Parsley	Swiss chard
	Turnip greens			
26–50	Dry onion	Pumpkin[1]	Tomato[1]	
0–25	Beet [1]	Carrot	Potato[1]	Lima bean[1]
	Snap bean[1]	Sweet corn[1]	Spinach[1]	Horseradish[1]
	Pea[1]	Garlic	Brussels sprouts[1]	Malanga
	Boniato	Radish		

Adapted from A. A. Kader (ed.). Postharvest Technology of Horticultural Crops. University of California, Division of Agriculture and Natural Resources Publication 3311 (1992).

[1] More than 50% of the crop is processed.

GENERAL COOLING METHODS FOR VEGETABLES

Method[1]	Vegetable	Comments
Room cooling	All vegetables	Too slow for many perishable commodities. Cooling rates vary extensively within loads, pallets, and containers
Forced-air cooling (pressure cooling)	Strawberry, fruit-type vegetables, tubers, cauliflower	Much faster than room cooling; cooling rates very uniform if properly used. Container venting and stacking requirements are critical to effective cooling
Hydrocooling	Stems, leafy vegetables, some fruit-type vegetables	Very fast cooling; uniform cooling in bulk if properly used, but may vary extensively in packed shipping containers; daily cleaning and sanitation measures essential; product must tolerate wetting; water-tolerant shipping containers may be needed
Package-icing	Roots, stems, some flower-type vegetables, green onion, Brussels sprouts	Fast cooling; limited to commodities that can tolerate water–ice contact; water-tolerant shipping containers are essential
Vacuum cooling	Leafy vegetables; some stem and flower-type vegetables	Commodities must have a favorable surface-to-mass ratio for effective cooling. Causes about 1% weight loss for each 6°C cooled. A procedure that adds water during cooling prevents this weight loss but equipment is more expensive, and water-tolerant shipping containers are needed

GENERAL COOLING METHODS FOR VEGETABLES—Continued

Method[1]	Vegetable	Comments
Transit Cooling:		
Mechanical refrigeration	All vegetables	
Top-icing and channel-icing	Some roots, stems, leafy vegetables, muskmelon	Cooling in most available equipment is too slow and variable; generally not effective. Slow and irregular, top-ice weight reduces net pay load; water-tolerant shipping containers needed

Adapted from A. A. Kader (ed.) Postharvest Technology of Horticultural Crops. University of California, Division of Agriculture and Natural Resources Publication 3311 (1992).

[1] For these methods to be effective, the product must be cooled continuously until reaching the consumer.

SPECIFIC COOLING METHODS FOR VEGETABLES

Vegetable	Size of Operation		Remarks
	Large	Small	
Leafy Vegetables			
Cabbage	VC, FA	FA	
Iceberg lettuce	VC	FA	
Kale, collards	VC, R, WV	FA	
Leaf lettuces, spinach, endive, escarole, Chinese cabbage, bok choy, romaine	VC, FA, WV, HC	FA	
Root Vegetables			
with tops	HC, PI, FA	HC, FA	Carrots can be VC
topped	HC, PI	HC, PI, FA	
Irish potato, sweet potato	R w/evap coolers, HC	R	With evap coolers, facilities should be adapted to curing
Stem and Flower Vegetables			
Artichoke	HC, PI	FA, PI	
Asparagus	HC	HC	

SPECIFIC COOLING METHODS FOR VEGETABLES—Continued

Vegetable	Size of Operation		Remarks
	Large	Small	
Broccoli, brussels sprouts	HC, FA, PI	FA, PI	
Cauliflower	FA, VC	FA	
Celery, rhubarb	HC, WV, VC	HC, FA	
Green onion, leek	PI, HC	PI	
Mushroom	FA, VC	FA	
Pod Vegetables			
Bean	HC, FA	FA	
Pea	FA, PI, VC	FA, PI	
Bulb Vegetables			
Dry onion	R	R, FA	Should be adapted to curing
Garlic	R		
Fruit-type Vegetables			

Cucumber, eggplant	R, FA, FA-EC	FA, FA-EC	Fruit-type vegetables are chilling sensitive but at varying temperatures. See pages 408–409
Melons			
cantaloupe, muskmelon, honeydew, casaba	HC, FA, PI	FA, FA-EC	
crenshaw	FA, R	FA, FA-EC	
watermelon	FA, HC	FA, FA-EC	
Pepper	R, FA, FA-EC, VC	FA, FA-EC	
Summer squash, okra	R, FA, FA-EC	FA, FA-EC	
Sweet corn	HC, VC, PI	HC, FA, PI	
Tomatillo	R, FA, FA-EC	FA, FA-EC	
Tomato	R, FA, FA-EC		
Winter squash	R	R	
Fresh Herbs			
not packaged	HC, FA	FA, R	Can be easily damaged by water beating in HC
packaged	FA	FA, R	
Cactus			
leaves (nopalitos)	R	FA	
fruit (tunas or prickly pears)	R	FA	

Adapted from A. A. Kader (ed.). Postharvest Technology of Horticultural Crops. University of California, Division of Agriculture and Natural Resources Publication 3311 (1992).

R = Room Cooling; FA = Forced-Air Cooling; HC = Hydrocooling; VC = Vacuum Cooling; WV = Water Spray Vacuum Cooling; FA-EC = Forced-Air Evaporative Cooling; PI = Package Icing.

HALF-COOLING TIMES[1] FOR SOME VEGETABLES

Vegetable	Coolant	Conditions during Cooling	Half-cooling Time
Artichoke	Water	Single buds, size 36	8 min
		In crate, uncovered	12 min
Asparagus	Water	Single spear	1.1 min
		In lidded pyramid crate	2.2 min
Broccoli	Water	Single head	2.1 min
		In crate with liner, three-quarters filled with water, four layers deep	2.2 min
		In crate without liners, four layers deep	3.1 min
Brussels sprouts	Water	Single sprout	4.4 min
		In carton, 9. deep, filled with water	4.8 min
Cabbage	Water	Single head	1.1 hr
		In carton, two layers, lid open, filled with water	1.3 hr
Carrot	Water	Single root, 1½ in. diameter	3.2 min
		In 50-lb mesh bag, lying flat	4.4 min
Cauliflower	Water	Single head, trimmed	7.2 min
	Air-forced	In single-layer cartons; head film wrapped	1.5 hr
Celery	Water	Single stalk	5.8 min
		In "Sturdy" crate, lidded on edge, paper liner	9.1 min
	Air-forced	In wirebound crates, air movement side to side	35 min
		In ⅔-size cartons	60 min
Muskmelon	Water	Single fruit, size 36 or 27	15 min
	Air	In crate, tunnel cooler, airflow unknown	1.3 hr
Pea	Water	Single pod	1.9 min
		In bushel basket, lid off	2.8 min

Vegetable	Coolant	Conditions during Cooling	Half-cooling Time
Potato	Water	Single tuber or stacked 9 in. deep	11 min
Radish, bunched	Water	Single bunch	1.1 min
		In crate, 9 in. deep	1.9 min
		In carton, 9 in. deep, filled with water	1.4 min
Radish, topped	Water	Stack, 9 in. deep	2.2 min
Sweet corn	Water	Single ear, in husk	20 min
		In wirebound crates, five ears deep	28 min
Tomato	Water	Single fruit	10 min
		Stack 5 fruit (10 in.) deep	11 min
	Air	Forced air, pressure difference 0.1 in., water cartons	47 min

Reprinted with permission from A. L. Ryall and W. J. Lipton, *Handling Transportation and Storage of Fruits and Vegetables*, Vol. 1, 2nd ed., AVI Publishing Co., Westport, CT (1979).

[1] Half-cooling time is the interval during which the initial temperature difference between product and coolant is halved. For example, if muskmelons are at 92°F and water is at 32°F, a difference of 60°, the time required to cool the melons by 30° is the half-cooling time.

OPTIMUM CONDITIONS FOR CURING ROOT, TUBER, AND BULB VEGETABLES PRIOR TO STORAGE

Vegetable	Temperature (°F)	Relative Humidity (%)	Duration of Curing (days)
Cassava	86–104	90–95	2–5
Onion and garlic	86–113	60–75	4–7
Potato	59–68	85–90	5–10
Sweet potato	85–90	85–90	4–7
Yam	90–104	90–100	1–4

Adapted from A. A. Kader (ed.). Postharvest Technology of Horticultural Crops. University of California, Division of Agriculture and Natural Resources Publication 3311 (1992).

EFFECT OF TEMPERATURE ON THE RATE OF DETERIORATION OF A VEGETABLE NOT SENSITIVE TO CHILLING INJURY

Temperature (°F)	Temperature (°C)	Assumed Q_{10}[1]	Relative Rate of Deterioration	Relative Shelf Life	Loss Per Day (%)
32	0		1.0	100	1
50	10	3.0	3.0	33	3
68	20	2.5	7.5	13	8
86	30	2.0	15.0	7	14
104	40	1.5	22.5	4	25

Adapted from A. A. Kader (ed.). Postharvest Technology of Horticultural Crops. University of California, Division of Agriculture and Natural Resources Publication 3311 (1992).

[1] $$Q_{10} = \frac{\text{Rate of deterioration at T + 10°C}}{\text{Rate of deterioration at T}}$$

MOISTURE LOSS FROM VEGETABLES

High	Medium	Low
Broccoli	Artichoke	Eggplant
Chard	Asparagus	Garlic
Green onion	Bean, snap	Ginger
Kohlrabi	Beet [1]	Melons
Leafy greens	Brussels sprouts	Onion
Mushroom	Cabbage	Potato
Muskmelon	Carrot [1]	Pumpkin
Oriental vegetables	Cassava [2]	Winter squash
Parsley	Cauliflower	
Strawberry	Celeriac [1]	
	Celery	
	Sweet corn [3]	
	Cucumber [2]	
	Endive	
	Escarole	
	Leek	
	Lettuce	
	Okra	
	Parsnip [1]	
	Pea	
	Pepper	
	Radish [1]	
	Rutabaga [1,2]	
	Sweet potato	
	Summer squash	
	Tomato [2]	
	Yam	

Adapted from B. M. McGregor, Tropical Products Transport Handbook, USDA Agricultural Handbook 668 (1987).

[1] Root crops with tops have a high rate of moisture loss.

[2] Waxing reduces the rate of moisture loss.

[3] Husk removal reduces water loss.

RELATIVE PERISHABILITY AND POTENTIAL STORAGE LIFE OF FRESH VEGETABLES IN AIR AT NEAR OPTIMUM STORAGE TEMPERATURE AND RELATIVE HUMIDITY

Potential Storage Life (weeks)			
<2	2–4	4–8	8–16
Asparagus	Artichoke	Beet	Garlic
Bean sprouts	Green bean	Carrot	Onion
Broccoli	Brussels sprouts	Potato (immature)	Potato (mature)
Cauliflower	Cabbage	Radish	Pumpkin
Green onion	Cassava (waxed)		Winter squash
Leaf lettuce	Celery		Sweet potato
Mushroom	Eggplant		Taro
Muskmelon	Head lettuce		Yam
Pea	Mixed melons		
Spinach	Pepino		
Sweet corn	Okra		
Tomato (ripe)	Pepper		
	Summer squash		
	Tomato (partially ripe)		

Adapted from A. A. Kader (ed.). Postharvest Technology of Horticultural Crops. University of California, Division of Agriculture and Natural Resources Publication 3311 (1992).

RECOMMENDED TEMPERATURE AND RELATIVE HUMIDITY CONDITIONS AND APPROXIMATE STORAGE LIFE OF FRESH VEGETABLES

Vegetable	Storage Conditions: Temperature (°F)	Storage Conditions: Relative Humidity (%)	Storage Life
Amaranth	32–36	95–100	10–14 days
Anise	32–36	90–95	2–3 weeks
Artichoke, globe	32	95–100	2–3 weeks
Artichoke, Jerusalem	31–32	90–95	4–5 months
Asparagus	32–35	95–100	2–3 weeks
Bean, lima	37–41	95	5–7 days
Bean, snap	40–45	95	10–14 days
Bean, sprouts	32	95–100	7–9 days
Beet, bunched	32	98–100	10–14 days
Beet, topped	32	98–100	4–6 months
Bitter melon	53–55	85–90	2–3 weeks
Bok choy	32	95–100	3 weeks
Boniato	55–60	85–90	4–5 months
Broccoli	32	95–100	10–14 days
Brussels sprouts	32	95–100	3–5 weeks
Cabbage, early	32	98–100	3–6 weeks
Cabbage, late	32	98–100	5–6 months
Cabbage, Chinese	32	95–100	2–3 months
Cactus, leaves	36–40	90–95	3 weeks
Cactus, pear	36–40	90–95	3 weeks
Calabaza	50–55	50–70	2–3 months
Carrot, bunched	32	95–100	2 weeks
Carrot, mature	32	98–100	7–9 months
Carrot, immature	32	98–100	4–6 weeks
Cassava (waxed)	32–41	85–90	1–2 months
Cauliflower	32	95–98	3–4 weeks
Celeriac	32	97–99	6–8 months
Celery	32	98–100	2–3 months
Chard	32	95–100	10–14 days
Chayote	45	85–90	4–6 weeks
Chicory, witloof	32	95–100	2–4 weeks
Chinese broccoli	32	95–100	10–14 days
Chinese long bean	40–45	90–95	7–10 days
Collards	32	95–100	10–14 days

RECOMMENDED TEMPERATURE AND RELATIVE HUMIDITY CONDITIONS AND APPROXIMATE STORAGE LIFE OF FRESH VEGETABLES—Continued

Vegetable	Storage Conditions		Storage Life
	Temperature (°F)	Relative Humidity (%)	
Cucumber	50–55	95	10–14 days
Daikon	32–34	95–100	4 months
Eggplant	46–54	90–95	1 week
Endive, escarole	32	95–100	2–3 weeks
Garlic	32	65–70	6–7 months
Ginger	55	65	6 months
Greens	32	95–100	10–14 days
Haricot vert	40–45	95	7–10 days
Horseradish	30–32	98–100	10–12 months
Japanese eggplant	46–54	90–95	1 week
Jicama	55–65	65–70	1–2 months
Kale	32	95–100	2–3 weeks
Kohlrabi	32	98–100	2–3 months
Leek	32	95–100	2–3 months
Lettuce	32	98–100	2–3 weeks
Lo bok	32–35	95–100	2–4 months
Malanga	45	70–80	3 months
Melon			
Casaba	50	90–95	3 weeks
Crenshaw	45	90–95	2 weeks
Honeydew	45	90–95	3 weeks
Muskmelon, ¾ slip	36–41	95	15 days
Muskmelon, full slip	32–36	95	5–14 days
Persian	45	90–95	2 weeks
Watermelon	50–60	90	2–3 weeks
Mushroom	32	95	3–4 days
Okra	45–50	90–95	7–10 days
Onion, dry	32	65–70	1–8 months
Onion, green	32	95–100	3–4 weeks
Parsley	32	95–100	8–10 weeks
Parsnip	32	98–100	4–6 months

RECOMMENDED TEMPERATURE AND RELATIVE HUMIDITY CONDITIONS AND APPROXIMATE STORAGE LIFE OF FRESH VEGETABLES—Continued

Vegetable	Storage Conditions		Storage Life
	Temperature (°F)	Relative Humidity (%)	
Pea, English	32	95–98	1–2 weeks
Pea, southern	40–41	95	6–8 days
Pepino	40	85–90	1 months
Pepper, chili (dry)	32–50	60–70	6 months
Pepper, sweet	45–55	90–95	2–3 weeks
Potato, early	—[1]	90–95	—[1]
Potato, late	—[2]	90–95	5–10 months
Pumpkin	50–55	50–70	2–3 months
Radicchio	31–32	90	2–3 months
Radish, spring	32	95–100	3–4 weeks
Radish, winter	32	95–100	2–4 months
Rhubarb	32	95–100	2–4 weeks
Rutabaga	32	98–100	4–6 months
Salisfy	32	95–98	2–4 months
Scorzonera	32–34	95–98	6 months
Snowpea	32–34	90–95	1–2 weeks
Spinach	32	95–100	10–14 days
Squash, summer	41–50	95	1–2 weeks
Squash, winter	50	50–70	—[4]
Strawberry	32	90–95	5–7 days
Sweet corn, shrunken 2	32	90–95	10–14 days
Sweet corn, sugary	32	95–98	5–8 days
Sweet potato	55–60[3]	85–90	4–7 months
Tamarillo	37–40	85–95	10 weeks
Tomatillo	55–60	85–90	3 weeks
Taro	45–50	85–90	4–5 months
Tomato, mature green	55–70	90–95	1–3 weeks
Tomato, firm ripe	46–50	90–95	4–7 days
Turnip	32	95	4–5 months
Turnip greens	32	95–100	10–14 days
Water chestnut	32–36	98–100	1–2 months
Watercress	32	95–100	2–3 weeks
Yam	61	70–80	6–7 months

RECOMMENDED TEMPERATURE AND RELATIVE HUMIDITY CONDITIONS AND APPROXIMATE STORAGE LIFE OF FRESH VEGETABLES—Continued

Adapted from R. E. Hardenburg, A. E. Watada, and C. Y. Wang, The Commercial Storage of Fruits, Vegetables, and Florist and Nursery Stocks, USDA Agriculture Handbook 66 (1986), and B. M. McGregor, Tropical Products Transport Handbook, USDA Agriculture Handbook 658 (1987).

[1] Winter, spring, or summer-harvested potatoes are usually not stored. However, they can be held 4–5 months at 40°F if cured 4 or more days at 60–70°F before storage. Potatoes for chips should be held at 70°F or conditioned for best chip quality.

[2] Fall-harvested potatoes should be cured at 50–60°F and high relative humdiity for 10–14 days. Storage temperatures for table stock or seed should be lowered gradually to 38–40°F. Potatoes intended for processing should be stored at 50–55°F; those stored at lower temperatures or with a high reducing sugar content should be conditioned at 70°F for 1–4 weeks, or until cooking tests are satisfactory.

[3] Sweet potatoes should be cured immediately after harvest by holding at 85°F and 90–95% relative humidity for 4–7 days.

[4] Winter squash varieties differ in storage life.

POSTHARVEST HANDLING OF FRESH CULINARY HERBS

Herb	Storage Conditions		Relative Ethylene Sensitivity
	Temperature (°F)	Relative Humdiity (%)	
Basil	40–42	95–98	Slightly sensitive
Marjoram	33–35	95–98	Sensitive
Mint	33–35	95–98	Sensitive
Oregano	33–35	95–98	Slightly sensitive
Parsley	33–35	95–98	Sensitive
Rosemary	33–35	95–98	Insensitive
Sage	33–35	95–98	Insensitive
Savory	33–35	95–98	Slightly sensitive
Thyme	33–35	95–98	Slightly sensitive

Adapted from D. Joyce and M. Reid, Postharvest Handling of Fresh Culinary Herbs, University of Massachusetts Cooperative Extension Service, *The Herb, Spice, and Medicinal Plant Digest* 4(2):1–2, 5–7 (1986).

RESPIRATION RATES AND Q_{10} VALUES OF SPRIGS OF SELECTED FIELD-GROWN CULINARY HERBS

	Respiration Rates[1] (mg/kg/hr of CO_2)			Q_{10} Value	
	Temperature (°F)			Temperature (°F)	
Herb	32	50	68	32–50	50–68
Basil	18	37	98	2.0	2.6
Chervil	6	42	94	7.1	2.2
Chives	11	58	300	5.3	5.2
Dill	11	54	180	4.9	3.4
Epazote	16	83	110	5.2	1.3
Mache	6	44	77	7.3	1.8
Marjoram	14	36	—	2.7	—
Mint	10	40	140	4.0	3.5
Mitsuba	6	24	55	4.4	2.3
Oregano	11	53	98	4.8	1.8
Parsley	11	56	123	5.1	2.2
Sage	18	54	87	3.0	1.6
Shiso	12	25	52	2.1	2.1
Tarragon	20	54	130	2.6	2.5
Thyme	19	43	113	2.3	2.6
Mean	13	47	118	3.6	2.5

Adapted from M. I. Cantwell and M. S. Reid, University of California, Davis. Unpublished.

[1] Respiration rates after three days.

RESPIRATION RATES OF VEGETABLES AT VARIOUS TEMPERATURES [1]

Vegetable	Respiration Rate (mg/kg/hr of CO_2)					
	32°F	40–41°F	50°F	59–60°F	68–70°F	77–80°F
Artichoke, globe	15–45	26–60	55–98	76–145	135–233	145–300
Asparagus	27–80	55–136	90–304	160–327	275–500	500–600
Bean, lima	10–30	20–36	—	100–125	133–179	—
Bean, snap	20	35	58	93	130	193
Beet, topped	5–7	9–10	12–14	17–23	—	—
Beet, with tops	11	14	22	25	40	—
Broccoli	19–21	32–37	75–87	161–186	278–320	—
Brussels sprouts	10–30	22–48	63–84	64–136	86–190	—
Cabbage	4–6	9–12	17–19	20–32	28–49	49–63
Carrot, topped	10–20	13–26	20–42	26–54	46–95	—
Carrot, with tops	18–35	25–51	33–62	55–106	87–121	—
Cauliflower	16–19	19–22	32–36	43–49	75–86	84–140
Celery	5–7	9–11	24	30–37	64	—
Celeriac	7	15	25	39	50	—
Cucumber	—	—	23–29	24–33	14–48	19–55
Endive	45	52	73	100	133	200
Garlic	4–14	9–33	9–10	14–29	13–25	—
Kale	16–27	34–47	72–84	120–155	186–265	—
Kohlrabi	10	16	31	49	—	—
Leek	10–20	20–29	50–70	75–117	110	107–119

Lettuce, head	6–17	13–20	21–40	32–35	51–60	73–91
Lettuce, leaf	19–27	24–35	32–46	51–74	82–119	120–173
Lettuce, romaine	—	18–23	31–40	39–50	60–77	95–121
Melon						
Honeydew	—	3–5	7–9	12–16	20–27	26–35
Muskmelon	5–6	9–10	14–16	34–39	45–65	62–71
Watermelon	—	3–4	6–9	—	17–25	—
Mushroom	28–44	71	100	—	264–316	—
Onion, dry	3	3–4	7–8	10–11	14–19	27–29
Onion, green	10–32	17–39	36–62	66–115	79–178	98–210
Okra	—	53–59	86–95	138–153	248–274	328–362
Parsley	30–40	53–76	85–164	144–184	196–225	291–324
Parsnip	8–15	9–18	20–26	32–46	—	—
Pea	30–47	55–76	68–117	179–202	245–361	343–377
Pea, shelled	47–75	79–97	—	—	349–556	—
Pepper, sweet	—	10	14	23	44	55
Potato, immature	—	12	14–21	14–31	18–45	—
Potato, mature	—	3–9	7–10	6–12	8–16	—
Radish, topped	3–9	6–13	15–16	22–42	44–58	60–89
Radish, with tops	14–17	19–21	31–36	70–78	124–136	158–193
Rhubarb	9–13	11–18	25	31–48	40–57	—
Rutabaga	2–6	5–10	15	11–28	41	—
Spinach	19–22	35–58	82–138	134–223	172–287	—
Squash, butternut	—	—	—	—	—	66–121
Squash, summer	12–13	14–19	34–36	75–90	85–97	—
Strawberry	12–18	16–23	49–95	71–92	102–196	169–211
Sweet corn, in husk	30–51	43–83	104–120	151–175	268–311	282–435
Sweet potato, uncured	—	—	—	29	—	54–73
Sweet potato, cured	—	—	14	20–24	—	—

RESPIRATION RATES OF VEGETABLES AT VARIOUS TEMPERATURES[1]—Continued

Vegetable	Respiration Rate (mg/kg/hr of CO_2)					
	32°F	40–41°F	50°F	59–60°F	68–70°F	77–80°F
Tomato, mature green	—	5–8	12–18	16–28	28–41	35–51
Tomato, ripening	—	—	13–16	24–29	24–44	30–52
Turnip, topped	6–9	10	13–19	21–24	24–25	—
Watercress	15–26	44–49	91–121	136–205	302–348	348–438

Adapted from R. E. Hardenburg, A. E. Watada, and C. Y. Wang, The Commercial Storage of Fruits, Vegetables, and Florist and Nursery Stocks, USDA Agriculture Handbook 66 (1986).

[1] Some data are included for low temperatures which may cause injury to chilling-sensitive vegetables; these low temperatures are potentially dangerous and should be avoided for these vegetables.

GENERATION OF HEAT BY VEGETABLES AT VARIOUS TEMPERATURES

Vegetable	Heat Generated (1000 Btu/ton/day)					
	32°F	40–41°F	50°F	59–60°F	68–70°F	77–80°F
Artichoke, globe	3.3–9.9	5.7–13.2	12.1–21.6	16.7–31.9	29.7–51.3	31.9–66.0
Asparagus	5.9–17.6	12.1–29.9	19.8–66.9	35.2–71.9	60.5–110.0	110.0–132.0
Bean, lima	2.2–6.6	4.4–7.9	—	22.0–27.5	29.3–39.4	—
Bean, snap	4.4	7.7	12.8	20.5	28.6	37.2
Beet, topped	1.0–1.4	1.7–2.2	2.3–2.7	3.3–5.1	—	—
Beet, with tops	2.4	3.1	4.8	5.5	8.8	—
Broccoli	4.2–4.6	7.0–8.1	16.5–19.1	35.4–40.9	61.2–70.4	—
Brussels sprouts	2.2–6.6	4.8–10.6	13.9–18.5	14.1–29.9	18.9–41.8	—
Cabbage	0.9–1.3	2.0–2.6	3.7–4.2	4.4–7.0	6.2–10.8	10.8–13.9
Carrot, topped	2.2–4.4	2.9–5.7	4.4–9.2	5.7–11.9	10.1–20.9	—
Carrot, with tops	4.0–7.7	5.5–11.2	7.3–13.6	12.1–23.3	19.1–26.6	—
Cauliflower	3.5–4.2	4.2–4.8	7.0–7.9	9.5–10.8	16.5–18.9	18.5–30.8
Celery	1.1–1.5	2.0–2.4	5.3	6.6–8.1	14.1	—
Celeriac	1.5	3.3	5.5	8.6	11.0	—
Cucumber	—	—	5.1–6.4	5.3–7.3	3.1–10.6	4.2–12.1
Endive	9.9	11.4	16.1	22.0	29.3	44.0
Garlic	0.9–3.1	2.0–7.3	2.0–2.2	3.1–6.4	3.9–5.5	—
Kale	3.5–5.9	7.5–10.3	15.8–18.5	26.4–34.1	40.9–58.3	—
Kohlrabi	2.2	3.5	6.8	10.8	—	—
Leek	2.2–4.4	4.4–6.4	11.0–15.4	16.5–25.7	24.2	23.5–26.2

GENERATION OF HEAT BY VEGETABLES AT VARIOUS TEMPERATURES—Continued

Vegetable	Heat Generated (1000 Btu/ton/day)					
	32°F	40–41°F	50°F	59–60°F	68–70°F	77–80°F
Lettuce, head	1.3–3.7	2.9–4.4	4.6–8.8	7.0–7.7	11.2–13.2	16.1–20.0
Lettuce, leaf	4.2–5.9	5.3–7.7	57.0–10.1	11.2–16.3	18.0–26.2	26.4–38.1
Lettuce, romaine	—	4.0–5.1	6.8–8.8	8.6–11.0	13.2–16.9	20.9–26.6
Melon						
Honeydew	—	0.7–1.1	1.5–2.0	2.6–3.5	4.4–5.9	5.7–7.7
Muskmelon	1.1–1.3	2.0–2.2	3.1–3.5	7.5–8.6	9.9–14.3	13.6–15.6
Watermelon	—	0.7–0.9	1.3–2.0	—	3.7–5.5	—
Mushroom	6.7–9.7	15.6	22.0	—	58.1–69.5	—
Onion, dry	0.7	0.7–0.9	1.5–1.8	2.2–2.4	3.1–4.2	5.9–6.4
Onion, green	2.2–7.0	3.7–8.6	7.9–13.6	14.5–25.3	17.4–39.2	21.6–46.2
Okra	—	11.7–13.0	18.9–20.9	30.4–33.7	54.6–60.3	72.2–79.6
Parsley	6.6–8.8	11.7–36.1	18.7–36.1	31.7–40.1	43.1–49.5	64.0–71.3
Parsnip	1.8–3.3	2.0–4.0	4.4–5.7	7.0–10.1	—	—
Pea	6.6–10.3	12.1–16.7	15.0–25.7	39.4–44.4	53.9–79.4	75.5–82.9
Pea, shelled	10.3–16.5	17.4–21.3	—	—	76.8–122.3	—
Pepper, sweet	—	2.2	3.1	5.1	9.7	12.1
Potato, immature	—	2.6	3.1–4.6	3.1–6.8	4.0–9.9	—
Potato, mature	—	0.7–2.0	1.5–2.2	1.3–2.6	1.8–3.5	—
Radish, topped	0.7–2.0	1.3–2.9	3.3–3.5	4.8–9.2	9.7–12.8	13.2–19.6
Radish, with tops	3.1–3.7	4.2–4.6	6.8–7.9	15.4–17.2	27.3–29.9	34.8–42.5
Rhubarb	2.0–2.9	2.4–4.0	5.5	6.8–10.6	8.8–12.5	—

Rutabaga	0.4–1.3	1.1–2.2	3.3	2.4–6.2	9.0	—
Spinach	4.2–4.8	7.7–12.8	18.0–30.4	29.5–49.1	37.8–63.1	—
Squash, butternut	—	—	—	—	—	14.5–26.6
Squash, summer	2.6–2.9	3.1–4.2	7.5–7.9	16.5–19.8	18.7–21.3	—
Strawberry	2.6–4.0	3.5–5.1	10.8–20.9	15.6–20.2	22.4–43.1	37.2–46.4
Sweet corn, in husk	6.6–11.2	9.5–18.3	22.9–26.4	33.2–38.5	59.0–68.4	62.0–95.7
Sweet potato, uncured	—	—	—	6.4	—	11.9–16.1
Sweet potato, cured	—	—	3.1	4.4–5.3	—	—
Tomato, mature green	—	1.1–1.8	2.6–4.0	3.5–6.2	6.2–9.0	7.7–11.2
Tomato, ripening	—	—	2.9–3.5	5.3–6.4	5.3–9.7	6.6–11.4
Turnip, topped	1.3–2.0	2.2	2.9–4.2	4.6–5.3	5.3–5.5	—
Watercress	3.3–5.7	9.7–10.8	20.0–26.6	29.9–45.1	66.4–76.6	76.6–96.4

Adapted from R. E. Hardenburg, A. E. Watada, and C. Y. Wang, *The Commercial Storage of Fruits, Vegetables, and Florist and Nursery Stocks*, USDA Agriculture Handbook 66 (1986).

RECOMMENDED CONTROLLED ATMOSPHERE OR MODIFIED ATMOSPHERE CONDITIONS DURING TRANSPORT AND/OR STORAGE OF SELECTED VEGETABLES

Vegetable	Temperature[1] (°F)	Controlled Atmosphere[2] (%)		Potential for Benefit	Remarks[3]
		O_2	CO_2		
Artichoke	32–41	2–3	2–3	Good	No commercial use
Asparagus	32–41	air	5–10	Excellent	Limited commercial use
Bean, snap	41–50	2–3	4–7	Fair	Potential for use by processors
Beet	32–41	None		None	98–100% RH is best
Broccoli	32–41	1–2	5–10	Excellent	Limited commercial use
Brussels sprouts	32–41	1–2	5–7	Good	No commercial use
Cabbage	32–41	2–3	3–6	Excellent	Some commercial use for long-term storage of certain varieties
Carrot	32–41	None		None	98–100% RH is best
Cauliflower	32–41	2–3	2–5	Fair	No commercial use
Celery	32–41	1–4	0–5	Good	Limited commercial use in mixed loads with lettuce
Corn, sweet	32–41	2–4	5–10	Good	Limited commercial use
Cucumber	46–54	3–5	0	Fair	No commercial use
Honeydew melons	50–54	3–5	0	Fair	No commercial use

Muskmelon	37–45	3–5	10–15	Good	Limited commercial use
Leek	32–41	1–2	3–5	Good	No commercial use
Lettuce	32–41	1–3	0	Good	Some commercial use with 2–3% CO_2 added
Mushroom	32–41	air	10–15	Fair	Limited commercial use
Okra	46–54	3–5	0	Fair	No commercial use; 5–10% CO_2 is beneficial at 41–46°F
Onion, dry	32–41	1–2	0–5	Good	No commercial use; 75% RH
Onion, green	32–41	1–2	10–20	Fair	Limited commercial use
Pepper, bell	46–54	3–5	0	Fair	Limited commercial use
Pepper, chili	46–54	3–5	0	Fair	No commercial use; 10–15% CO_2 is beneficial at 41–46°F
Potato	39–54	None		None	No commercial use
Radish	32–41	None		None	98–100% RH is best
Spinach	32–41	air	10–20	Good	No commercial use
Tomato					
mature-green	54–68	3–5	0–3	Good	Limited commercial use
partially ripe	46–54	3–5	0–5	Good	Limited commercial use

Adapted from A. A. Kader (ed.). Postharvest Technology of Horticultural Crops. University of California, Division of Agriculture and Natural Resources Publication 3311 (1992).

[1] Usual and/or recommended range. A relative humidity of 90% to 98% is recommended unless otherwise indicated under "Remarks."

[2] Best CA combination may vary among varieties and according to storage temperature and duration.

[3] Comments about use refer to domestic marketing only; many of these commodities are shipped under MA for export marketing.

SUSCEPTIBILITY OF VEGETABLES TO CHILLING INJURY [1]

Vegetable	Approximate Lowest Safe Temperature (°F)	Appearance When Stored Between 32°F and Safe Temperature
Asparagus	32–36	Dull, gray-green, and limp tips
Bean, lima	34–40	Rusty-brown specks, spots, or areas
Bean, snap	45	Pitting and russeting
Cucumber	45	Pitting, water-soaked spots, decay
Eggplant	45	Surface scald, alternaria rot, blackening of seeds
Jicama	55–65	Surface decay, discoloration
Melon		
Casaba	45–50	Pitting, surface decay, failure to ripen
Crenshaw	45–50	Pitting, surface decay, failure to ripen
Honeydew	45–50	Reddish-tan discoloration, pitting, surface decay, failure to ripen
Muskmelon	36–41	Pitting, surface decay
Persian	45–50	Pitting, surface decay, failure to ripen
Watermelon	40	Pitting, objectionable flavor
Okra	45	Discoloration, water-soaked areas, pitting, decay
Pepper, sweet	45	Sheet pitting, alternaria rot on fruit and calyx, darkening of seed
Potato	38	Mahogany browning (Chippewa and Sebago), sweetening

Pumpkin and hard-shell squash	50	Decay, especially alternaria rot
Sweet potato	55	Decay, pitting, hadcore when cooked
Tamarillo	37–40	Surface pitting, discoloration
Tomato, ripe	45–50	Watersoaking and softening, decay
Tomato, mature green	55	Poor color when ripe, alternaria rot

Adapted from R. E. Hardenburg, A. E. Watada, and C. Y. Wang, The Commercial Storage of Fruits, Vegetables, and Florist and Nursery Stock, USDA Agriculture Handbook 66 (1986).

[1] Severity of injury is related to temperature and time.

VEGETABLES CLASSIFIED ACCORDING TO CHILLING INJURY SUSCEPTIBILITY

Not Susceptible to Chilling Injury	Susceptible to Chilling Injury
Artichoke	Snap bean
Asparagus	Cassava
Lima bean	Cucumber
Beet	Eggplant
Broccoli	Ginger
Brussels sprouts	Jicama
Cabbage	Muskmelon
Carrot	Okra
Cauliflower	Pepper
Celery	Pepino
Sweet corn	Prickly pear
Endive	Pumpkin
Garlic	Squash
Lettuce	Sweet potato
Mushroom	Tamarillo
Onion	Taro
Parsley	Tomato
Parsnip	Watermelon
Pea	Yam
Radish	
Spinach	
Strawberry	
Turnip	

Adapted from A. A. Kader (ed.). Postharvest Technology of Horticultural Crops. University of California, Division of Agriculture and Natural Resources Publication 3311 (1992).

RELATIVE SUSCEPTIBILITY OF VEGETABLES TO CHILLING INJURY

Most Susceptible	Moderately Susceptible	Least Susceptible
Asparagus	Broccoli	Beet
Bean, snap	Cabbage, new	Brussels sprouts
Cucumber	Carrot, topped	Cabbage, old and savoy
Eggplant	Cauliflower	Kale
Jicama	Celery	Kohlrabi
Lettuce	Onion, dry	Parsnip
Okra	Parsley	Rutabaga
Pepper, sweet	Pea	Salsify
Potato	Radish, topped	Turnip, topped
Squash, summer	Spinach	
Strawberry	Squash, winter	
Sweet potato		
Tomato		

Adapted from R. E. Hardenburg, A. E. Watada, and C. Y. Wang, The Commercial Storage of Fruits, Vegetables, and Florist and Nursery Stocks, USDA, Agriculture Handbook 66 (1986).

SYMPTOMS OF FREEZING INJURY ON SOME VEGETABLES

Vegetable	Symptoms
Artichoke	Epidermis becomes detached and forms whitish to light-tan blisters. When blisters are broken, underlying tissue turns brown
Asparagus	Tip becomes limp and dark, the rest of the spear is water-soaked. Thawed spears become mushy
Beet	External and internal water-soaking and sometimes blackening of conducting tissue
Broccoli	The youngest florets in the center of the curd are most sensitive to freezing injury. They turn brown and give strong off-odors upon thawing
Cabbage	Leaves become water-soaked, translucent, and limp upon thawing; separated epidermis
Carrot	A blistered appearance; jagged lengthwise cracks. Interior becomes water-soaked and darkened upon thawing
Cauliflower	Curds turn brown and have a strong off-door when cooked
Celery	Leaves and petioles appear wilted and water-soaked upon thawing. Petioles freeze more readily than leaves
Garlic	Thawed cloves appear water-soaked, grayish-yellow
Lettuce	Blistering, dead cells of the separated epidermis on outer leaves become tan; increased susceptibility to physical damage and decay
Onion	Thawed bulbs are soft, grayish-yellow, and water-soaked in cross section; often limited to individual scales
Pepper, bell	Dead, water-soaked tissue in part of or all pericarp surface; pitting, shriveling, and decay follow thawing
Potato	Freezing injury may not be externally evident, but shows as gray or bluish-gray patches beneath the skin. Thawed tubers become soft and watery
Radish	Thawed tissues appear translucent; roots soften and shrivel
Sweet potato	A yellowish-brown discoloration of the vascular ring, and a yellowish-green water-soaked appearance of other tissues. Roots soften and become very susceptible to decay
Tomato	Water-soaked and soft upon thawing. In partially frozen fruits, the margin between healthy and dead tissue is distinct, especially in green fruits
Turnip	Small water-soaked spots or pitting on the surface. Injured tissues appear tan or gray and give off an objectionable odor

Adapted from A. A. Kader, J. M. Lyons, and L. L. Morris, Postharvest Responses of Vegetables to Preharvest Field Temperature, *HortScience* 9:523–527 (1974).

SOME POSTHARVEST PHYSIOLOGICAL DISORDERS OF VEGETABLES, ATTRIBUTABLE DIRECTLY OR INDIRECTLY TO PREHARVEST FIELD TEMPERATURES

Vegetable	Disorder	Symptoms and Development
Asparagus	Feathering	Bracts of the spears are partly spread as a result of high temperature
Brussels sprouts	Black leaf speck	Becomes visible after storage for 1–2 weeks at low temperature. Has been attributed in part to cauliflower mosaic virus infection in the field, which is influenced by temperature and other environmental factors
	Tip burn	Leaf margins turn light tan to dark brown
Garlic	Waxy breakdown	Enhanced by high temperature during growth; slightly sunken, light-yellow areas in fleshy cloves, then the entire clove becomes amber, slightly translucent, and waxy but still firm
Lettuce	Tip burn	Light-tan to dark-brown margins of leaves. Has been attributed to several causes, including field temperature; it can lead to soft rot development during postharvest handling
	Rib dis-coloration	More common in lettuce grown when day temperatures exceed 81°F or when night temperatures are between 55 and 64°F than in lettuce grown during cooler periods
	Russet spotting	Small tan, brown, or olive spots randomly distributed over the affected leaf; a postharvest disorder of lettuce induced by ethylene. Lettuce is more susceptible to russet spotting when harvested after high field temperatures (above 86°F) for 2 days or more during the 10 days before harvest
	Rusty-brown discolor-ation	Rusty-brown discoloration has been related to internal rib necrosis associated with lettuce mosaic virus infection, which is influenced by field temperature and other environmental factors

SOME POSTHARVEST PHYSIOLOGICAL DISORDERS OF VEGETABLES, ATTRIBUTABLE DIRECTLY OR INDIRECTLY TO PREHARVEST FIELD TEMPERATURES—Continued

Vegetable	Disorder	Symptoms and Development
Muskmelon	Vein tract browning	Discoloration of unnetted longitudinal stripes; related partly to high temperature and virus diseases
Onion	Translucent scale	Grayish water-soaked appearance of the outer two or three fleshy scales of the bulb; translucency makes venation very distinct. In severe cases, the entire bulb softens and off-odors may develop
Potato	Blackheart	May occur in the field during excessively hot weather in waterlogged soils. Internal symptom is dark-gray to purplish or black discoloration usually in the center of the tuber
Radish	Pithiness	Textured white spots or streaks in cross section, large air spaces near the center, tough and dry roots. Results from high temperature

Adapted from A. A. Kader, J. M. Lyons, and L. L. Morris, Postharvest Responses of Vegetables to Preharvest Field Temperature, *HortScience* 9:523–527 (1974).

SYMPTOMS OF SOLAR INJURY ON SOME VEGETABLES

Vegetable	Symptoms
Bean, snap	Very small brown or reddish spots on one side of the pod coalesce and become water-soaked and slightly shrunken
Cabbage	Blistering of some outer leaves which leads to a bleached papery appearance. Desiccated leaves are susceptible to decay
Cauliflower	Discoloration of curds from yellow to brown to black (solar browning)
Lettuce	Papery areas on leaves, especially the cap leaf, develop during clear weather when air temperatures are higher than 77°F; affected areas become focus for decay
Honeydew melon	White to gray area at or near the top, may be slightly wrinkled, undesirable flavor or brown blotch, when is tan to brown discolored areas caused by death of epidermal cells due to excessive ultraviolet radiation
Muskmelon	Sunburn: dry, sunken, and white to light tan areas. In milder sunburn, ground color is green or spotty brown
Onion and garlic	Sunburn: dry scales are wrinkled and this may extend to one or two fleshy scales, injured area may be bleached depending on the color of the bulb
Pepper, bell	Dry and papery areas, yellowing and sometimes wilting
Potato	Sunscald: water and blistered areas on the tuber surface. Injured areas become sunken and leathery and subsurface tissue raidly turns dark-brown to black when exposed to air
Tomato	Sunburn (solar yellowing): affected areas on the fruit become whitish, translucent, thin walled, a netted appearance may develop. Mild solar injury might not be noticeable at harvest, but becomes more appearent after harvest as uneven ripening

Adapted from A. A. Kader, J. M. Lyons, and L. L. Morris, Postharvest Responses of Vegetables to Preharvest Field Temperature, *HortScience* 9:523–527 (1974).

CLASSIFICATION OF HORTICULTURAL COMMODITIES ACCORDING TO ETHYLENE PRODUCTION RATES

Very Low	Low	Moderate	High	Very High
Artichoke	Blueberry	Banana	Apple	Cherimoya
Asparagus	Cranberry	Fig	Apricot	Mamey sapote
Cauliflower	Cucumber	Guava	Avocado	Passion fruit
Cherry	Eggplant	Honeydew melon	Feijoa	Sugar apple
Citrus	Okra	Mango	Kiwi fruit (ripe)	
Grape	Olive	Plantain	Muskmelon	
Jujube	Pepper	Tomato	Nectarine	
Leafy vegetables	Persimmon		Papaya	
Most cut flowers	Pineapple		Peach	
Potato	Pumpkin		Pear	
Root vegetables	Raspberry		Plum	
Strawberry	Tamarillo			
	Watermelon			

Adapted from A. A. Kader (ed.). Postharvest Technology of Horticultural Crops. University of California, Division of Agriculture and Natural Resources Publication 3311 (1992).

COMPATIBILITY OF FRESH PRODUCE IN MIXED LOADS UNDER VARIOUS RECOMMENDED TRANSIT CONDITIONS

Shipper or receivers of fresh fruits and vegetables frequently prefer to handle shipments that consist of more than one commodity. In mixed loads, it is important to combine only those commodities that are compatible in their requirements for temperature, modified atmosphere, relative humidity, protection from odors, and protection from physiologically active gases such as ethylene.

RECOMMENDED TRANSIT CONDITIONS FOR COMPATIBLE GROUPS

Temp.: 55–60°F; Relative humidity: 85–95%. Ice: No contact with commodity	Temp.: 36–41°F; Relative humidity: 90–95%. Ice: Contact muskmelon only	Temp.: 40–45°F; Relative humidity: about 95%. Ice: No contact with commodity	Temp.: 40–55°F; Relative humidity: 85–90%. Ice: No contact with commodity
Avocado	Cranberry	Snap bean	Cucumber
Banana	Lemon	Lychee	Eggplant
Grapefruit (AZ and CA, FL before Jan. 1)	Muskmelon	Okra	Ginger (not with eggplant)
Guava	Orange	Pepper, green (not with bean)	Grapefruit (FL after Jan. 1 and TX)
Mango	Tangerine	Pepper, red	Lime
Casaba melon		Summer squash	Potato
Crenshaw melon		Tomato, pink	Pumpkin
Honeydew melon		Watermelon	Watermelon
Persian melon			Winter squash
Olive			

RECOMMENDED TRANSIT CONDITIONS FOR COMPATIBLE GROUPS—Continued

Temp.: 55–60°F; Relative humidity: 85–95%. Ice: No contact with commodity	Temp.: 36–41°F; Relative humidity: 90–95%. Ice: Contact muskmelon only	Temp.: 40–45°F; Relative humidity: about 95%. Ice: No contact with commodity	Temp.: 40–55°F; Relative humidity: 85–90%. Ice: No contact with commodity
Papaya Pineapple (not with avocado) Tomato, green Tomato, pink Watermelon			
Temp.: 32–34°F; Relative humidity: 95–100%. Ice: No contact with asparagus, fig, grape, mushroom	Temp.: 32–34°F Relative humidity: 95–100%. Ice: Contact acceptable with all commodities	Temp.: 55–65°F; Relative humidity: 85–90%. Ice: No contact with any commodity	Temp.: 32–34°F; Relative humidity: 65–75%. Ice: No contact with any commodity
Artichoke Asparagus Beet Carrot Endive, escarole	Broccoli Brussels sprouts Cabbage Cauliflower Celeriac	Ginger Sweet potato	Garlic Onion, dry

Fig	Celery
Grape	Horseradish
Greens	Kohlrabi
Leek (not with fig or grape)	Onion, green (not with rhubarb, fig, or grape; probably not with mushroom or sweet corn)
Lettuce	Radish
Mushroom	Rutabaga
Parsley	Turnip
Parsnip	
Pea	
Rhubarb	
Salsify	
Spinach	
Sweet corn	
Watercress	

Adapted from W. J. Lipton, Compatibility of Fruits and Vegetables During Transport in Mixed Loads, USDA, ARS, Marketing Research Report 1070 (1977).

VEGETABLE QUALITY

Quality is defined as *any of the features that make something what it is* or *the degree of excellence or superiority.* The word *quality* is used in various ways in reference to fresh fruits and vegetables such as *market* quality, *edible* quality, *dessert* quality, *shipping* quality, *table* quality, *nutritional* quality, *internal* quality, and *appearance* quality.

Quality of fresh vegetables is a combination of characteristics, attributes, and properties that give the vegetables value to humans for food and enjoyment. Producers are concerned that their commodities have good appearance and few visual defects, but for them a useful variety must score high on yield, disease resistance, ease of harvest, and shipping quality. To receivers and market distributors, appearance quality is most important; they are also keenly interested in firmness and long storage life. Consumers consider good-quality vegetables to be those that look good, are firm, and offer good flavor and nutritive value. Although consumers buy on the basis of appearance and feel, their satisfaction and repeat purchases depend on good edible quality.

QUALITY COMPONENTS OF FRESH VEGETABLES

Main Factors	Components
Appearance (visual)	*Size:* dimensions, weight, volume *Shape and form:* diameter/depth ratio, smoothness, compactness, uniformity *Color:* uniformity, intensity *Gloss:* nature of surface wax *Defects,* external and internal: morphological, physical and mechanical, physiological, pathological, entomological
Texture (feel)	Firmness, hardness, softness Crispness Succulence, juiciness Mealiness, grittiness Toughness, fibrousness
Flavor (taste and smell)	Sweetness Sourness (acidity) Astringency Bitterness Aroma (volatile compounds) Off-flavors and off-orders

QUALITY COMPONENTS OF FRESH VEGETABLES—Continued

Main Factors	Components
Nutritive value	Carbohydrates (including dietary fiber) Proteins Lipids Vitamins Minerals
Safety	Naturally occurring toxicants Contaminants (chemical residues, heavy metals) Mycotoxins Microbial contamination

Adapted from A. A. Kader (ed.) Postharvest Technology of Horticultural Crops. University of California, Division of Agriculture and Natural Resources Publication 3311 (1992).

U.S. STANDARDS FOR FRESH VEGETABLES

Grade standards issued by the U.S. Department of Agriculture are currently in effect for most vegetables for fresh market and for processing. Some standards have been unchanged since they became effective, whereas others have been revised quite recently.

A publication—U.S. Standards and Inspection Instructions for Fresh Fruits and Vegetables and Other Special Products—lists the crops for which standards have been established and their effective date. This publication can be obtained free of charge from Fresh Products Branch, AMS, FV; U.S. Department of Agriculture, Room 2056, South Building, Washington, DC 20250.

QUALITY FACTORS FOR FRESH VEGETABLES IN THE U.S. STANDARDS FOR GRADES

Vegetable	Date When Issued	Quality Factors
Anise, sweet	1973	Firmness, tenderness, trimming, blanching, and freedom from decay and damage caused by growth cracks, pithy branches, wilting, freezing, seedstems, insects, and mechanical means
Artichoke	1969	Stem length, shape, overmaturity, uniformity of size, compactness, and freedom from decay and defects
Asparagus	1966	Freshness (turgidity), trimming, straightness, freedom from damage and decay, diameter of stalks, percent green color
Bean, lima	1938	Uniformity, maturity, freshness, shape, and freedom from damage (defect) and decay
Bean, snap	1936	Uniformity, size, maturity, freshness (firmness), and freedom from defect and decay
Beet, bunched or topped	1955	Root shape, trimming of rootlets, firmness (turgidity), smoothness, cleanness, minimum size (diameter), and freedom from defect
Beet, greens	1959	Freshness, cleanness, tenderness, and freedom from decay, other kinds of leaves, discoloration, insects, mechanical injury, and freezing injury
Broccoli	1943	Color, maturity, stalk diameter and length, compactness, base cut, and freedom from defects and decay
Brussels sprouts	1954	Color, maturity (firmness), no seedstems, size (diameter and length), and freedom from defect and decay
Cabbage	1945	Uniformity, solidity (maturity or firmness), no seedstems, trimming, color, and freedom from defect and decay

Cantaloupe	1968	Soluble solids (>9 percent), uniformity of size, shape, ground color and netting; maturity and turgidity; and freedom from "wet slip," sunscald, and other defects
Carrot, bunched	1954	Shape, color, cleanness, smoothness, freedom from defect, freshness, length of tops, and root diameter
Carrot, topped	1965	Uniformity, turgidity, color, shape, size, cleanness, smoothness, and freedom from defect (growth cracks, pithiness, woodiness, internal discoloration)
Carrots with short trimmed tops	1954	Roots; firmness, color, smoothness, and freedom from defect (sunburn, pithiness, woodiness, internal discoloration, and insect and mechanical injuries) and decay; leaves: (cut to <4 inches) freedom from yellowing or other discoloration, disease, insects, and seedstems
Cauliflower	1968	Curd cleanness, compactness, white color, size (diameter), freshness and trimming of jacket leaves, and freedom from defect and decay
Celery	1959	Stalk form, compactness, color, trimming, length of stalk and midribs, width and thickness of midribs, no seedstems, and freedom from defect and decay
Collard greens or Broccoli greens	1953	Freshness, tenderness, cleanness, and freedom from seedstems, discoloration, freezing injury, insects, and diseases
Corn, sweet	1992	Uniformity of color and size, freshness, milky kernels, cob length, freedom from defect, coverage with fresh husks
Cucumber	1958	Color, shape, turgidity, maturity, size (diameter and length), and freedom from defect and decay
Cucumber, greenhouse	1985	Freshness, shape, firmness, color, size (length of 11 inches or longer), and freedom from decay, cuts, bruises, scars, insect injury and other defects
Dandelion greens	1955	Freshness, cleanness, tenderness, and freedom from damage caused by seed stems, discoloration, freezing, diseases, insects, and mechanical injury

QUALITY FACTORS FOR FRESH VEGETABLES IN THE U.S. STANDARDS FOR GRADES—Continued

Vegetable	Date When Issued	Quality Factors
Eggplant	1953	Color, turgidity, shape, size, and freedom from defect and decay
Endive, Escarole, or Chicory	1964	Freshness, trimming, color (blanching), no seedstems, and freedom from defect and decay
Garlic	1944	Maturity, curing, compactness, well-filled cloves, bulb size, and freedom from defect
Honeydew and Honey Ball melons	1967	Maturity, firmness, shape, and freedom from decay and defect (sunburn, bruising, hail spots, and mechanical injuries)
Horseradish roots	1936	Uniformity of shape and size, firmness, smoothness, and freedom from hollow heart, other defects, and decay
Kale	1934	Uniformity of growth and color, trimming, freshness, and freedom from defect and decay
Lettuce, crisp-head	1975	Turgidity, color, maturity (firmness), trimming (number of wrapper leaves), and freedom from tip burn, other physiological disorders, mechanical damage, seedstems, other defects, and decay
Lettuce, greenhouse leaf	1964	Well-developed, well-trimmed, and freedom from coarse stems, bleached or discolored leaves, wilting, freezing, insects, and decay
Lettuce, romaine	1960	Freshness, trimming, and freedom from decay and damage caused by seedstems, broken, bruised, or discolored leeaves, tipburn, and wilting
Mushroom	1966	Maturity, shape, trimming, size, and freedom from open veils, disease, spots, insect injury, and decay

Mustard greens and Turnip greens	1953	Freshness, tenderness, cleanness, and freedom from damage caused by seedstems, discoloration, freezing, disease, insects, or mechanical means; roots (if attached): firmness and freedom from damage
Okra	1928	Freshness, uniformity of shape and color, and freedom from defect and decay
Onion, dry		
Creole	1943	Maturity, firmness, shape, size (diameter), and freedom from decay, wet sunscald, bottlenecks, sprouting, and other defects
Bermuda-Granex-Grano	1985	
Other varieties	1971	
Onion, green	1947	Turgidity, color, form, cleanness, bulb trimming, no seedstems, and freedom from defect and decay
Onion sets	1940	Maturity, firmness, size, and freedom from decay and damage caused by tops, sprouting, freezing, mold, moisture, dirt, disease, insects, or mechanical means
Parsley	1930	Freshness, green color, and freedom from defects, seedstems, and decay
Parsnip	1945	Turgidity, trimming, cleanness, smoothness, shape, freedom from defects and decay, and size (diameter)
Pea, fresh	1942	Maturity, size, shape, freshness, and freedom from defects and decay
Pea, Southern (cowpea)	1956	Maturity, pod shape, and freedom from discoloration and other defects
Pepper, sweet	1963	Maturity, color, shape, size, and freedom from defects (sunscald, freezing injury, hail, scars, insects, mechanical damage) and decay
Potato	1972	Uniformity, maturity, firmness, cleanness, shape, size, and freedom from sprouts, blackheart, greening, and other defects
Radish	1968	Tenderness, cleanness, smoothness, shape, size, and freedom from pithiness and other defects. Bunched radishes have tops which are fresh and free from damage

QUALITY FACTORS FOR FRESH VEGETABLES IN THE U.S. STANDARDS FOR GRADES—Continued

Vegetable	Date When Issued	Quality Factors
Rhubarb	1966	Color, freshness, straightness, trimming, cleanness, stalk diameter and length, and freedom from defect
Shallot, bunched	1946	Firmness, form, tenderness, trimming, cleanness, and freedom from decay and damage caused by seedstems, disease, insects, mechanical and other means; tops: freshness, green color, and no mechanical damage
Spinach bunches	1987	Freshness, cleanness, trimming, and freedom from decay and damage caused by coarse stalks or seedstems, discoloration, insects, and mechanical means
Spinach leaves	1946	Color, turgidity, cleanness, trimming, and freedom from seedstems, coarse stalks, and other defects
Squash, summer	1984	Immaturity, tenderness, shape, firmness, and freedom from decay, cuts, bruises, scars, and other defects
Squash, winter and Pumpkin	1983	Maturity, firmness, freedom from discoloration, cracking, dry rot, insect damage, and other defects; uniformity of size
Strawberry	1965	Maturity ($>½$ or $>¾$ of surface showing red or pink color, depending on grade), firmness, attached calyx, size, and freedom from defect and decay
Sweet potato	1963	Firmness, smoothness, cleanness, shape, size, and freedom from mechanical damage, growth cracks, internal breakdown, insect damage, other defects, and decay

Tomato	1976	Maturity and ripeness (color chart), firmness, shape, size, and freedom from defect (puffiness, freezing injury, sunscald, scars, catfaces, growth cracks, insect injury, and other defects) and decay
Tomato, greenhouse	1966	Maturity, firmness, shape, size, and freedom from decay, sunscald, freezing injury, bruises, cuts, shriveling, puffiness, catfaces, growth cracks, scars, disease, and insect
Turnip or Rutabaga	1955	Uniformity of root color, size, and shape, trimming, freshness, and freedom from defects (cuts, growth cracks, pithiness, woodiness, water core, dry rot)
Watermelon	1978	Maturity and ripeness (optional internal quality criteria: soluble solids content = >10 percent very good, >8 percent good), shape, uniformity of size (weight), and freedom from anthracnose, decay, sunscald, and whiteheart

Adapted from A. A. Kader (ed.). Postharvest Technology of Horticultural Crops. University of California, Division of Agriculture and Natural Resources Publication 3311 (1992).

QUALITY FACTORS FOR PROCESSING VEGETABLES IN THE U.S. STANDARDS FOR GRADES

Vegetable	Date When Issued	Quality Factors
Asparagus, green	1972	Freshness, shape, green color, size (spear length), and freedom from defect (freezing damage, dirt, disease, insect injury, and mechanical injuries) and decay
Bean, shelled lima	1953	Tenderness green color, and freedom from decay and from injury caused by discoloration, shriveling, sunscald, freezing, heating, disease, insects, or other means
Bean, snap	1985	Freshness, tenderness, shape, size, and freedom from decay and from damage caused by scars, rust, disease, insects, bruises, punctures, broken ends, or other means
Beet	1945	Firmness, tenderness, shape, size, and freedom from soft rot, cull material, growth cracks, internal discoloration, white zoning, rodent damage, disease, insects, and mechanical injury
Broccoli	1959	Freshness, tenderness, green color, compactness, trimming, and freedom from decay and damage caused by discoloration, freezing, pithiness, scars, dirt, or mechanical means
Cabbage	1944	Firmness, trimming, and freedom from soft rot, seedstems, and from damage caused by bursting, discoloration, freezing, disease, birds, insects, or mechanical or other means
Carrot	1984	Firmness, color, shape, size (root length), smoothness, not woody, and freedom from soft rot, cull material, and from damage caused by growth cracks, sunburn, green core, pithy core, water core, internal discoloration, disease, or mechanical means

Cauliflower	1959	Freshness, compactness, color, and freedom from jacket leaves, stalks, and other cull material, decay, and damage caused by discoloration, bruising, fuzziness, enlarged bracts, dirt, freezing, hail, or mechanical means
Corn, sweet	1962	Maturity, freshness, and freedom from damage by freezing, insects, birds, disease, cross-pollination, or fermentation
Cucumber, pickling	1936	Color, shape, freshness, firmness, maturity, and freedom from decay and from damage caused by dirt, freezing, sunburn, disease, insects, or mechanical or other means
Mushroom	1964	Freshness, firmness, shape, and freedom from decay, disease spots, and insects, and from damage caused by insects, bruising, discoloration, or feathering
Okra	1965	Freshness, tenderness, color, shape, and freedom from decay and insects, and from damage caused by scars, bruises, cuts, punctures, discoloration, dirt or other means
Onion	1944	Maturity, firmness, and freedom from decay, sprouts, bottlenecks, scallions, seedstems, sunscald, roots, insects, and mechanical injury
Pea, fresh shelled for canning/freezing	1946	Tenderness, succulence, color, and freedom from decay, scald, rust, shriveling, heating, disease, and insects
Pea, southern	1965	Pods: maturity, freshness, and freedom from decay; seeds: freedom from scars, insects, decay, discoloration, splits, cracked skin, and other defects
Pepper, sweet	1948	Firmness, color, shape, and freedom from decay, insects, and damage by any means that results in 5 to 20 percent trimming (by weight) depending on grade

QUALITY FACTORS FOR PROCESSING VEGETABLES IN THE U.S. STANDARDS FOR GRADES—Continued

Vegetable	Date When Issued	Quality Factors
Potato	1983	Shape, smoothness, freedom from decay and defect (freezing injury, blackheart, sprouts), size, specific gravity, glucose content, and fry color
Potato for chipping	1978	Firmness, cleanness, shape, freedom from defect (freezing, blackheart, decay, insect injury, and mechanical injury), size; optional tests for specific gravity and fry color are included
Spinach	1956	Freshness, freedom from decay, grass weeds, and other foreign material, and freedom from damage caused by seedstems, discoloration, coarse stalks, insects, dirt, or mechanical means
Sweet potato for canning/freezing	1959	Firmness, shape, color, size, and freedom from decay and defect (freezing injury, scald, cork, internal discoloration, bruises, cuts, growths cracks, pithiness, stringiness, and insect injury)
Sweet potato for dicing/pulping	1951	Firmness, shape size, and freedom from decay and defect (scald, freezing injury, cork, internal discoloration, pithiness, growth cracks, insect damage, and stringiness)
Tomato	1983	Firmness, ripeness (color as determined by a photoelectric instrument), and freedom from insect damage, freezing, mechanical damage, decay, growth cracks, sunscald, gray wall, and blossom-end rot
Tomato, green	1950	Firmness, color (green), and freedom from decay and defect (growth cracks, scars, catfaces, sunscald, disease, insects, or mechanical damage)

Tomato, Italian type for canning	1957	Firmness, color uniformity, and freedom from decay and defect (growth cracks, sunscald, freezing, disease, insects, or mechanical injury)

Adapted from A. A. Kader (ed.). Postharvest Technology of Horticultural Crops. University of California, Division of Agriculture and Natural Resources Publication 3311 (1992).

EC REGIME
THE COMMON ORGANIZATION OF THE MARKET FOR HORTICULTURE

The main features of the Common Organization of the market provide for the removal of barriers to intra-Community trade and the application of rules for fair competition; the adoption of common quality standards in internal and external trade; the application of the Common Customs Tariff (CCT) to trade with third countries together with the liberalization of import arrangements and a reference price system for sensitive products; compensation for the withdrawal of produce; special aids in the citrus sector; and export subsidies. Full details can be obtained from MAFF, Horticulture Division, Room 517 Ergon House, c/o Nobel House, 17 Smith Square, London SW1P 3JR. Tel: 071 238 6497.

Common Quality Standards

Quality standards are in operation for a wide range of fresh horticultural produce. Their main objectives are to keep products of unsatsifactory quality off the market, to guide production to meet consumer requirements and to facilitate trade under fair conditions. The standards apply at all stages of distribution including imports and exports.

Commodities Subject to Quality Standards

The vegetables subject to quality standards are:

Artichoke
Asparagus
Bean
Brussels sprouts
Cabbage
Carrot
Cauliflower
Celery
Chicory
Cucumber
Eggplant
Endive
Garlic
Leek
Lettuce
Onion
Pea
Pepper
Spinach
Strawberry
Summer squash
Tomato

STORAGE SPROUT INHIBITORS

Sprout inhibitors are most effective when used in conjunction with good storage; their use cannot substitute for poor storage or poor storage management. However, storage temperatures may be somewhat higher when sprout inhibitors are used than when they are not. Follow label directions.

Vegetable	Material	Application
Potato (do not use on seed potatoes)	Maleic hydrazide	When most tubers are 1½ to 2 in. in diameter. Vines must remain green for several weeks after application
	Chlorprophan (CIPC)	In storage, 2–3 weeks after harvest as an aerosol treatment. Do not store seed potatoes in a treated storage.
		During washing, as an emulsifiable concentrate added to wash water to prevent sprouting during marketing
Onion	Maleic hydrazide	Apply when 50% of the tops are down, the bulbs are mature, the necks soft, and 5–8 leaves are still green

SHIPPING CONTAINERS FOR FRESH VEGETABLES

Vegetable		Container[1]	Approximate Net Weight (lb)[2]
Alfalfa sprouts		Cartons or flats	5
		Film bags	5
		Film bags	1
Amaranth		Carton or crate	20
Anise		15½-in. wirebound crate	40–50
		Carton and crate packed, 1½ to 2½ dozen	25
		Crate	60–70
Artichoke		Carton by count or loose pack	23
Asparagus		Pyramid cartons or crates	30
		Cartons or crates, bunched	28
		Lugs or cartons, loose	25
		Cartons, 16 1½-lb bunches	24–25
		Lugs or cartons, loose	21
		Pyramid carton or crate, ½	20
		Carton, bunched	20
		Pyramid carton or crate, ½	15–17
		Carton	14
		Carton, ½	12
		Carton or crate, ⅓	12–13
		Carton or crate	11
Bean		Wirebound crate or hamper, bushel	26–31
		Carton or crate	25–30
	Green	Carton	20–22
		Carton	15
	Yellow	Wirebound crate or hamper	30
	Sprouts	Carton or film bag	10
		Carton	6
		Film bag	5
Beet	Bunched	Wirebound crate or carton, 12 bunches	45
		Carton or crate, 24 bunches	38
	Topped	Mesh sack	50
		Sack	25
		Carton or crate, 12 bunches	20
Bitter melon		Crate	40
Boniato		Crate or sack	50
Broccoli		Carton or crate, 14–18 bunches	23
		Carton, crown cut	20
Brussels sprouts		Carton, loose	25
		Flat or carton, 16 12-ounce bags or cups	10

Vegetable	Container[1]	Approximate Net Weight (lb)[2]
Cabbage	Bulk bin	2,000
	Bulk bin	1,000
	Flat crate	50–60
	Carton or sack	50
	Crate, 1¾ bushel	50
	Carton	45
	Carton or sack	40
Savoy	Crate, 1¾ bushel	40
Cactus leaves	Carton or crate	10
	Carton or crate	20
Cactus pear	Carton, 45, 50, 60, or 70 count	18
Calabaza	Sack	50
Carrot	Carton or sack, loose or 10 5-lb bags	50
	Sack, 48 1-lb, 24 2-lb, or 16 3-lb bags	48
	Sack, loose	25
	Carton, 24 1-lb bags	24
	Carton, 20 12-oz bags	15
Bunched	Crates, 24 bunches	26
Baby	Carton, 20 1-lb bags	20
	Carton, 20 12-oz bags	15
	Carton, 24 1-lb bags	24
Cassava	Carton, crate, or sack	50
	Various containers	40
	Various containers	30
	Various containers	20
	Various containers	10
Cauliflower	Long Island wirebound crate	60
	Catskill carton	50
	Carton, 12 or 16 heads	25–30
Celery	Carton or crate	50–60
Hearts	Carton, 12, 18, or 24 film bags	28
Chayote	Carton, 24–30 count	20
Chinese broccoli	Carton or crate	35–40
	Crate or lug	25
Chinese cabbage		
Bok choy	Western Growers Association Crate	70
	Crate	60
	Carton or crate	50
	Carton or crate	40
	Carton or crate	35

Vegetable	Container[1]	Approximate Net Weight (lb)[2]
Chinese cabbage		
Bok choy		
(*Continued*)	Carton or crate	30
Napa	Western Growers Association crate	70
	Celery crate	50
	Carton	50
	Crate, 1.3 bushel	45
	Carton	45
	Crate, 1$^{1}/_{9}$ bushel	40
	Carton	30
Chinese long bean	Crate	35–40
Chive	Flat of 12 pots	10
Corn, sweet	Carton or crate	50
	Carton, crate, or sack	42
	Sack	37
Cucumber	Carton or crate, bushel or $^{1}/_{9}$ bushel	55
	Carton, 48 count	30
	Carton or crate, $^{5}/_{9}$ bushel	28
	Carton, 36–42 count	24
	Carton, 24 count	22
Greenhouse	Carton, film wrapped	16
	Carton or flat, film wrapped	12
Daikon	Carton or crate	50
	Carton or crate	45
	Carton or crate, 1$^{1}/_{9}$ bushel	40
	Carton	20
	Carton	10
	Carton	5
Eggplant	Carton, crate, or basket, bushel or 1$^{1}/_{9}$ bushel	33
	Carton, crate, or lug	26–28
	Carton	25
	L.A. lug or carton, 18–24 count	22
	Lug, ½ and $^{5}/_{9}$ bushel	17
Chinese	Lug	26
	Carton	25
	Carton or crate, ½ and $^{5}/_{9}$ bushel	15
Italian	Lug	26
	Carton or crate, ½ and $^{5}/_{9}$ bushel	15

Vegetable	Container[1]	Approximate Net Weight (lb) [2]
Eggplant (*Continued*)		
Japanese	Carton or crate, ½ and 5/9 bushel	15
	Carton	11
	Carton, 1 1/9 bushel	33
Endive/Escarole	Carton, 24 count	34
	Celery crate, 24 count	30–40
	Wirebound crate, 1 1/9 bushel	25–28
Belgian	Carton	10
Garlic	Carton	5
	Carton	10
	Carton	15
	Carton	22
	Carton	30
Ginger	Carton	30
	Carton	20
	Carton or film bag	5
Greens	Crate, 1 2/5 and 1 3/5 bushel	30–35
	Baskets, crates, or cartons, bushel	20–25
	Crates or cartons, 12–24 bunches	—
Haricot vert	Tray	11
Horseradish	Sack	50–60
Jerusalem artichoke	Carton	10
Jicama	Crate, 1 1/9 bushel	45
	Carton or crate	20
	Carton	10
Kohlrabi	Carton, 12, 18, 24 bunches of 3–5	Count
Leek	Carton, 12 bunches	30
	Carton, 24 bunches	24–30
	Carton or crate, 4/5 bushel	20
	Carton, 10 1-lb bags	10
Lettuce		
Iceberg	Carton, 18, 24, or 30 count	50
	Carton	30
	Carton	20
	Crate, 1 1/9 bushel	22
Boston	Carton or crate, 24 count	20
	Carton or crate	10
	Basket or carton, 12 quart	5

Vegetable	Container[1]	Approximate Net Weight (lb)[2]
Lettuce (*Continued*)		
Bibb	Flat carton or crate	10
	Basket or carton, 12 quart	5
	Basket, greenhouse	5
Leaf	Carton or crate, 24 count	25
	Crate, 4/5 bushel	20
	Crate, 1 1/9 bushel	14
	Basket or carton, 24 count	10
Red leaf	Carton	3
	Carton	2
Romaine	Carton, 24 count	40
	Carton	40
	Carton, 1⅓ bushel	28
	Carton or crate, 1 1/9 bushel	22
	Carton, 24 count	22
Processed	Bulk bin	1,000
	Carton, chopped, cored	30
	Carton, chopped	20
Lo bok	Carton, crate, lug	25
	Carton, crate	40
Long bean	Carton	40
	Crate	30
	Carton	10
	Carton	5
Malanga	Carton, crate, or sack	50
	Crate, 1 1/9 bushel	45
	Carton or crate	40
	Carton	10
Melon		
Honeydew	Flat crate	35
	⅔ carton	30
	Carton	30
Mixed	Flat crate	35
	Carton, various counts	30
Muskmelon	Bin	1,000
	Jumbo crate	80
	Cartons or crates, 1¾ bushel	60
	⅔ cartons or crates	54
	½ wirebound crate	45–50

Vegetable	Container[1]	Approximate Net Weight (lb) [2]
Melon		
Muskmelon		
(Continued)	½ carton or crate	40
	Carton or crate, 1¹/₉ bushel	40
	Basket, bushel	40
Winter	Crate	70
	Carton, crate, or sack	50
	Various containers	50
	Various containers	40
	Various containers	30
	Various containers	20
	Various containers	10
Mushroom	Carton, 12 1-lb trays	12
	Carton	10
	Carton, 16 8-oz or 8 1-lb trays	8
	Carton, 12 8-oz trays	6
	Basket, 4 quart	3
Okra	Basket, crate, or hamper, bushel	30
	Hamper, ¾ bushel	23
	Basket, crate, or lug, ½ and ⁵/₉ bushel	15
Onion		
Bulb	Carton, sack, or crate	50
	Master container, 10 5-lb bags	50
	Master container, 16 3-lb bags or 24 2-lb bags	48
	Master container, 15 3-lb bags	45
	Master container, 20 2-lb bags	40
	Carton	40
	Master container, 12 3-lb bags	36
	Master container, 16 2-lb bags	32
	Sack or carton	25
	Master container, 12 2-lb sacks	24
	Sack	10
Green	Carton, bunches bulb type	28
	Carton or crate, 24 bunches bulb type	20
	Carton, 48 bunches	13
	Carton, 36 bunches	11
Parsley	Carton or crate, 1¹/₉ bushel bunched	21
	Carton, crate, or basket, bunched	11
Parsnip	Carton or crate, ½ bushel	25

Vegetable	Container[1]	Approximate Net Weight (lb) [2]
Parsnip	Film sack	20
(*Continued*)	Carton, 12 1-lb film bags	12
Pea		
Green	Basket, crate, or hamper, 1 or 1$\frac{1}{9}$ bushel	30
Snow	Carton	10
Southern	Hamper, bushel	25
Pepino	Tray pack	10
Pepper	Carton, 1¼ bushel	35
	Carton or crate	30
	Carton or crate, 1 and 1$\frac{1}{9}$ bushel	28
	Carton	25
	Carton, ½ bushel	14–15
	Flat carton	11
Potato	Sack	100
	Carton or sack	50
	Master container, 5 10-lb or 10 5-lb bags	50
Pumpkin	Bin	1,000
	Carton, crate, or sack	50
	Carton or crate, ½ bushel	25
Radicchio	Carton, 16 count	7
Radish		
Topped	Sack or bag, loose	40
	Bag	25
	Carton, 14 1-lb bags	14
	Basket or carton, 30 6-ounce bags	12
Bunched	Carton or crate, 24 or 48	35
	Carton or lug, $\frac{4}{5}$ bushel	30
	Carton or crate, 24	20
	Carton or crate, 24	15
Sprouts	Various containers	50
	Carton or crate, 1$\frac{1}{9}$ bushel	40
	Various containers	30
	Various containers	25
	Carton	20
	Carton	10
	Various containers	8
	Carton	5
	Various containers	4
Rhubarb	Carton or lug	20
	Carton	15

Vegetable	Container[1]	Approximate Net Weight (lb) [2]
Rhubarb		
(*Continued*)	Carton	10
Salsify	Carton, 5 4-lb film bags	20
Scorzonera	Carton, 4 5-lb film bags	20
Shallot	Bag	5
	Carton, 16 quarts	32
Snowpea	Carton, crate	10
	Carton, crate	20
Spinach	Carton or crate, 1⅖ bushel	32
	Crate or basket, bushel	25
	Carton, 24 12-ounce bags	20
	Carton, 12 10-ounce bags	8
Squash		
Summer	Carton or crate, 1 and 1⅑ bushel	42
	Carton or crate	35
	Carton or crate, ¾ bushel	30
	Carton or lug	26
	Basket, carton, or crate, ½ or 5/9 bushel	21
	Basket or carton, 8 quart	10
Winter	Carton or crate, 1⅑ bushel	50
	Carton or crate	40
	Carton or crate	35
Strawberry	Flat, 12 1-pint baskets	12
	Flat, 6 1-quart baskets	12
	Crate, 8 1-lb or 4 2-lb clamshells	9
	Clamshell, 4 × 12 count stem	4
Sweet potato	Carton or crate	40
	Box	20
	Box	10
Taro	Carton, crate, or sack	50
	Carton	10
Tomatillo	Carton	10
Tomato	Carton, ½ or 4/7 bushel	28
	Carton	25
	Carton or flat	20
Cherry	Flat, 12 1-pint basket	15
	Carton, 9 250-gram cups	5
Green	Carton	25
Greenhouse	Flat, 1 layer	15
Plum	Carton	25

Vegetable	Container[1]	Approximate Net Weight (lb)[2]
Turnip	Basket or sack, bushel	50
	Carton, bunched	40
	Basket, carton, crate, or bag, ½ bushel	25
	Carton, 12 bunches	20
Watercress	Carton, 24 bunches	8
	Carton, bunched	4
Watermelon	Bulk	45,000
	Bin	1,050
	Cwt	100
	Carton	85
	Carton	35
Winged bean	Carton, crate, ½ bushel	N.A.
Witloof chicory	Carton, crate, 48–56 count	10
Yam	Carton	25
	Carton	50

Adapted from THE PACKER Sourcebook, Vance Publishing Corp., 10901 W. 84th Terr., Lenexa, KS 66214-1632 (1995), reprinted by permission from The Packer. The Packer does not review or endorse products, services, or opinions; and B. M. McGregor, Tropical Products Transport Handbook, USDA Agriculture Handbook 658 (1987).

[1] Other containers are being developed and used in the marketplace. The requirements of each market should be determined.

[2] Actual weights larger and smaller than those shown may be found. The midpoint of the range should be used if a single value is desired.

OUTSIDE DIMENSIONS OF MODULAR SHIPPING CONTAINERS

Container No.	Length	Width	Depth	Inside Volume (ft^3)
1A	60 cm ×	40 cm ×	10 cm (3.9 in)	0.73
1B	60 cm ×	40 cm ×	20 cm (7.9 in)	1.54
1C	60 cm ×	40 cm ×	30 cm (11.8 in)	2.35
	23.6 in ×	15.7 in		
2A	50 cm ×	40 cm ×	10 cm	0.61
2B	50 cm ×	40 cm ×	20 cm	1.30
2C	50 cm ×	40 cm ×	30 cm	1.95
	19.7 in ×	15.7 in		
3A	50 cm ×	30 cm ×	10 cm	0.45
3B	50 cm ×	30 cm ×	20 cm	0.95
3C	30 cm ×	30 cm ×	30 cm	1.28
	19.7 in ×	11.8 in		
4A	40 cm ×	30 cm ×	10 cm	0.36
4B	40 cm ×	30 cm ×	20 cm	0.76
4C	40 cm ×	30 cm ×	30 cm	1.16
	15.7 in ×	11.8 in		

COMMON SHIPPING PLATFORMS FOR VEGETABLES

			Hardwood Slip Sheet			Wood		Wood, One Way	
Slip Sheet 48 × 40	Pallet[1] 48 × 40	Disposable 48 × 40	48 × 36	42 × 35	40 × 40	39 × 39	37½ × 39	36 × 39	35 × 42
				(inches)					
Asparagus	Belgian endive	Cabbage	Honeydew melon	Cucumber	Pepper	Cucumber	Strawberry	Bean	Muskmelon
Sweet corn	Broccoli	Cauliflower		Eggplant	Tomato	Melons		Eggplant	
Onion	Cabbage	Celery		Muskmelon		Strawberry		Squash	
Potato	Cauliflower	Lettuce		Pepper		Tomato		Tomato	
	Celery	Melons		Tomato					
	Sweet corn	Onion							
	Cucumber	Pepper							
	Lettuce	Tomato							
	Melons								
	Mushrooms								
	Onion								
	Pepper								
	Potato								
	Sweet potato								
	Spinach								
	Sprouts								
	Tomato								
	Watermelon								

Adapted from THE PACKER Sourcebook, Vance Publishing, 10901 W. 84th Terr., Lenexa, KS 66214-1631 (1995). Reprinted by permission from The Packer. The Packer does not review or endorse products, services, or opinions.

[1] In North America, the 48- × 40-inch pallet is becoming standard.

Most carriers check their transport equipment before presenting it to the shipper for loading. The condition of the equipment is critical to maintaining the quality of the products. Therefore, the shipper also should check the equipment to ensure it is in good working order and meets the needs of the product. Carriers provide guidance on checking and operating the refrigeration systems.

All transportation equipment should be checked for:

- cleanliness—the load compartment should be regularly steam-cleaned.
- damage—walls, floors, doors, ceilings should be in good condition.
- temperature control—refrigerated units should be recently calibrated and supply continuous air circulation for uniform product temperatures

Shippers should insist on clean equipment. A load of products can be ruined by:

- odors from previous shipments.
- toxic chemical residues.
- insects nesting in the equipment.
- decaying remains of agricultural products.
- debris blocking drain openings or air circulation along the floor.

Shipper should insist on well-maintained equipment and check for the following:

- damage to walls, ceilings, or floors which can let in the outside heat, cold moisture, dirt, and insects.
- operation and condition of doors, ventilation openings, and seals.
- provisions for load locking and bracing.

For refrigerated trailers and van containers, the following additional checks are important:

- with the doors closed, have someone inside the cargo area check for light—the door gaskets must seal. A smoke generator also can be used to detect leaks.
- the refrigeration unit should cycle from high to low speed when the desired temperature is reached and then back to high speed.
- determine the location of the sensing element which controls the discharge air temperature. If it measures return air temperature, the thermostat may have to be set higher to avoid chilling injury or freezing injury of the products.

- a solid return air bulkhead should be installed at the front of the trailer.
- a heating device should be available for transportation in areas with extreme cold weather.
- equipment with a top air delivery system must have a fabric air chute or metal ceiling duct in good condition.

Adapted from B. M. McGregor. Tropical Products Handbook. USDA Agr. Handbook 668 (1987).

CHARACTERISTICS OF DIRECT MARKETING ALTERNATIVES FOR FRESH VEGETABLES

Grower Characteristics	Pick-Your-Own	Roadside Market	Farmer's Market
Harvesting cost	Customer assumes the cost	Usual cost	Usual cost
Transportation cost	Customer assumes the cost	Usually very minimal for produce	Depends on grower's distance to market
Selling cost	Field attendant is needed. Harvesting instructions should be provided. Advertising	Checkout attendant is needed. Advertising	Checkout attendant is needed
Grower liability	Liable for accidents. Absorbs damages to property and crop	Liable for accidents at market	Owner of market is responsible
Market investment	Containers. Locational signs. Available parking	Building or stand. Available parking. Containers	Usually parking or building space is rented. Containers
Volume of produce desired	Enough for customer traffic demands	Enough to visibly attract customers to stop. Variety is helpful	Enough to justify transportation and other costs
Prices received for produce	Often lower than other alternatives because transportation and harvesting cost is assumed by the customer. Producer sets the price	Producer sets the price given perceived demand competitive conditions	Producer sets the price. There may be competition from other sellers

CHARACTERISTICS OF DIRECT MARKETING ALTERNATIVES FOR FRESH VEGETABLES—Continued

Grower Characteristics	Pick-Your-Own	Roadside Market	Farmer's Market
Quality	Can sell whatever the customers will pick	Can classify produce and sell more than one grade	Ability to sell may depend on the competing qualities available from other growers
Other	Balance between number of pickers and amount needing to be harvested sometimes is difficult to achieve	Sometimes other items besides produce are sold to supplement income. Produce spoilage can be minimized if adequate cooling facilities are used	Sometimes other items besides produce are sold to supplement income. Bulk sales are sometimes recommended

Adapted from Cucurbit Production and Pest Management, Oklahoma Cooperative Extension Circular E-853 (1986).

CHARACTERISTICS OF SOME WHOLESALE MARKETING ALTERNATIVES FOR FRESH VEGETABLES

Grower Consideration	Terminal Market	Cooperative and Private Packing Facilities	Peddling to Grocer or Restaurant	Wholesale/Broker
Harvesting cost	Usual cost	Sometimes harvesting equipment is provided	Usual cost	Usual cost
Transportation cost	Depends on distance to market	Sometimes transportation is provided	Depends on distance traveled	Depends on prior arrangements for delivery or pick up
Prices received for produce	Grower is usually the price taker	Prices received by growers depend on market prices, costs, and revenues	Buyer and grower may compromise on price or grower fixes price	Grower is usually the price taker
Required volume	Usually large quantities are needed	Depends on the products to be sold	Depends on the size of outlets and route	Usually large quantities are needed
Market investment	Truck or some transportation arrangements. Specialized containers are required	Relatively low on a per unit basis	Truck. Containers	Depends on arrangements. Usually minimal costs to grower. Specialized containers are required

CHARACTERISTICS OF SOME WHOLESALE MARKETING ALTERNATIVES FOR FRESH VEGETABLES—Continued

Grower Consideration	Terminal Market	Cooperative and Private Packing Facilities	Peddling to Grocer or Restaurant	Wholesale/Broker
Quality	Must meet buyer's standards or U.S. grades	Must meet buyer's standards or U.S. grades	High quality is needed	Must meet standards or U.S. grades so that produce can be handled in bulk
Other	Good source of market information. Can move very large quantities at one time. Many buyers are located at terminal markets	May provide technical assistance to growers. Firms help in planning of growing and selling. Equipment may be shared by growers	Long-term outlet for consistent quality. Good price for quality produce. Difficult to enter market and develop customers	Good wholesaler/broker can sell produce quickly at good prices. A long-term buyer/seller relationship is desirable. Broker does not necessarily take title of produce

Adapted from Cucurbit Production and Pest Management, Oklahoma Cooperative Extension Circular E-853 (1986).

PART 9

SEED PRODUCTION AND STORAGE

Seeds entering into interstate commerce must meet the requirements of the Federal Seed Act. Most state seed laws conform to federal standards. However, the laws of the individual states vary considerably with respect to the kinds and tolerances for noxious weeds. The noxious weed seed regulations and tolerances, if any, may be obtained from the State Seed Laboratory of any state.

Vegetable seed in packets or in larger containers shall be labeled in any form that is clearly legible with the following required information:

- *Kind, variety, and hybrid.* The name of the kind and variety and hybrid, if appropriate, must be on the label. Words or terms that create a misleading impression as to the history or characteristics of kind or variety shall not be used.
- *Name of shipper or consignee.* The full name and address of either the shipper or consignee shall appear on the label.
- *Germination.* Vegetable seeds in containers of 1 pound or less with germination equal to or more than the standards need not be labeled to show the percentage germination or date of test. Vegetable seeds in containers of more than 1 pound shall be labeled to show the percentage of germination, the month and year of test, and the percentage of hard seed, if any.
- *Lot number.* The lot number or other lot identification of vegetable seed in containers or more than 1 pound shall be shown on the label and shall be the same as that used in the records pertaining to the same lot of seed.
- *Seed treatment.* Any vegetable seed that has been treated shall be labeled in no smaller than 8-point type to indicate that the seed has been treated and to show the name of any substance used in such treatment.

Adapted from Federal Seed Act Regulations. USDA, AMS. Seed Regulating and Testing Branch, Beltsville, MD (1993).

REQUIREMENTS FOR VEGETABLE SEED GERMINATION TESTS

Seed	Substrata[1]	Temperature[2] (°F)	First Count (Days)	Final Count (Days)	Additional Directions: Specific Requirements	Additional Directions: Fresh and Dormant Seed
Artichoke	B,T	68–86	7	21		
Asparagus	B,T,S	68–86	7	21		
Asparagus bean	B,T,S	68–86	5	8[3]		
Bean:						
Garden	B,T,S,TC	68–86;77	none	8		Use 0.3–0.6% $Ca(NO_3)_2$ to moisten substratum for retesting if hypocotyl collar rot is observed in initial test
Lima	B,T,C,S	68–86	5	9[3]		
Runner	B,T,S	68–86	5	9[3]		
Beet	B,T,S	68–86	3	14	Presoak seeds in water for 2 hrs	
Broadbean	S,C	64	4	14[3]		Prechill at 50°F for 3 days
Broccoli	B,P,T	68–86	3	10		Prechill at 41° or 50°F for 3 days; KNO_3 and light

REQUIREMENTS FOR VEGETABLE SEED GERMINATION TESTS—Continued

Seed	Substrata[1]	Temperature[2] (°F)	First Count (Days)	Final Count (Days)	Additional Directions	
					Specific Requirements	Fresh and Dormant Seed
Brussels sprouts	B,P,T	68–86	3	10		Prechill at 41° or 50°F for 3 days; KNO_3 and light
Burdock, great	B,T	68–86	7	14		
Cabbage	B,P,T	68–86	3	10		Prechill at 41° or 50°F for 3 days; KNO_3 and light
Cabbage, Chinese	B,T	68–86	3	7		
Cabbage, tronchuda	B,P	68–86	3	10		Prechill at 41° or 50°F for 3 days; KNO_3 and light
Cardoon	B,T	68–86	7	21		
Carrot	B,T	68–86	6	14		
Cauliflower	B,P,T	68–86	3	10		Prechill at 41° or 50°F for 3 days; KNO_3 and light
Celeriac	P	59–77;68	10	21	Light; 750–1250 lux from cool-white fluorescent source	

Celery	P	59–77;68	10	21	Light; 750–1250 lux from cool-white fluorescent source	
Chard, Swiss	B,T,S	68–86	3	14	Presoak seed in water for 2 hrs	
Chicory	P,TS	68–86	5	14	Light; KNO_3 or soil; 750–1250 lux from cool-white fluorescent source	
Chives	B,T	68	6	14		
Citron	B,T	68–86	7	14	Soak seeds 6 hrs	Test at 86°F
Collards	B,P,T	68–86	3	10		Prechill at 41° or 50°F for 3 days; KNO_3 and light
Corn, sweet	B,T,S,TC	68–86;77	4	7		
Corn salad	B,T	59	7	28		Test at 50°F
Cowpea	B,T,S	68–86	5	8[3]		
Cress:						
Garden	B,P,T	59	4	10		Light
Upland	P,TB	68–86	4	7	Light; KNO_3	
Water	P	68–86	4	14	Light	
Cucumber	B,T,S	68–96	3	7	Keep substratum on dry side; remove excess moisture	
Dandelion	P,TB	68–86	7	21	Light, 750–1250 lux from cool-white fluorescent source	
Dill	B,T	68–86	7	21		
Eggplant	P,TB,RB,T	68–86	7	14		Light; KNO_3
Endive	P,TS	68–86	5	14	Light, KNO_3 or soil	Add 1/8 inch tap water at beginning of test and remove 24 hrs later

REQUIREMENTS FOR VEGETABLE SEED GERMINATION TESTS—Continued

Seed	Substrata[1]	Temperature[2] (°F)	First Count (Days)	Final Count (Days)	Additional Directions: Specific Requirements	Additional Directions: Fresh and Dormant Seed
Gherkin, West India	B,T,S	68–86	3	7		Test at 86°F
Kale	B,P,T	68–86	3	10		Prechill at 41° or 50°F for 3 days; KNO_3 and light
Kale, Chinese	B,P,T	68–86	3	10		Prechill at 41° or 50°F for 3 days; KNO_3 and light
Kale, Siberian	B,P,T	68–86;68	3	7		
Kohlrabi	B,P,T	68–86	3	10		Prechill at 41° or 50°F for 3 days; KNO_3 and light
Leek	B,T	68	6	14		
Lettuce	P	68	None	7	Light	Prechill at 50°F for 3 days or test at 59°F
Melon	B,T,S	68–86	4	10	Keep substratum on dry side; remove excess moisture	
Mustard, India	P	68–86	3	7	Light	Prechill at 50°F for 7 days and test for 5 additional days;

Mustard, spinach	B,T	68–86	3	7		
Okra	B,T	68–86	4	14[3]		
Onion	B,T	68	6	10		
Alternate method	S	68	6	12		
Onion, Welsh	B,T	68	6	10		
Pak-choi	B,T	68–86	3	7		
Parsley	B,T,TS	68–86	11	28		
Parsnip	B,T,TS	68–86	6	28		
Pea	B,T,S	68	5	8[3]		
Pepper	TB,RB,T	68–86	6	14		Light and KNO_3
Pumpkin	B,T,S	68–86	4	7	Keep substratum on dry side; remove excess moisture	
Radish	B,T	68	4	6		
Rhubarb	TB,TS	68–86	7	21	Light	
Rutabaga	B,T	68–86	3	14		
Sage	B,T,S	68–86	5	14		
Salsify	B,T	59	5	10		Prechill at 50°F for 3 days
Savory, summer	B,T	68–86	5	21		
Sorrel	P,TB,TS	68–86	3	14	Light	Test at 59°F
Soybean	B,T,S,TC	68–86;77	5	8[3]		
Spinach	TB,T	59,50	7	21	Keep substratum on dry side; remove excess moisture	
Spinach, New Zealand	T	59,68	5	21	Soak fruits overnight (16 hrs), air dry 7 hrs; plant in very wet towels; do not rewater unless later counts exhibit drying out	On 21st day scrape fruits and test for 7 additional days

REQUIREMENTS FOR VEGETABLE SEED GERMINATION TESTS—Continued

					Additional Directions	
Seed	Substrata[1]	Temperature[2] (°F)	First Count (Days)	Final Count (Days)	Specific Requirements	Fresh and Dormant Seed
Alternate method	B,T	59	5	21	Remove pulp from basal end of fruit	
Squash	B,T,S	68–86	4	7	Keep substratum on dry side; remove excess moisture	
Tomato	B,P,RB,T	68–86	5	14		Light; KNO_3
Tomato, husk	P,TB	68–86	7	28	Light; KNO_3	
Turnip	B,T	68–86	3	7		
Watermelon	B,T,S	68–86;77	4	14	Keep substratum on dry side; remove excess moisture	Test at 86°F

Adapted from Federal Register, Vol. 59, No. 239, Wednesday, December 14, 1994. Rules and Regulations. 64512-64514. See original source for more details.

[1] B = between blotters
TB = top of blotters
T = paper toweling, used either as folded towel tests or as roll towel tests in horizontal or vertical position
S = sand or soil
TS = top of sand or soil
P = covered Petri dishes: with two layers of blotters; with one layer of absorbent cotton; with five layers of paper toweling; with three thicknesses of filter paper; or with sand or soil

C = creped cellulose paper wadding (0.3-inch thick Kimpak or equivalent) covered with a single thickness of blotter through which holes are punched for the seed that are pressed for about one-half their thickness into the paper wadding

TC = on top of creped cellulose paper without a blotter

RB = blotters with raised covers, prepared by folding up the edges of the blotter to form a good support for the upper fold which serves as a cover, preventing the top from making direct contact with the seeds

[2] Temperature. A single number indicates a constant temperature. Two numerals separated by a dash indicate an alternation of temperature; the test is to be held at the first temperature for approximately 16 hrs and at the second temperature for approximately 8 hrs per day.

[3] Hard seeds. Seeds which remain hard at the end of the prescribed test because they have not absorbed water, due to an impermeable seed coat, are to be counted as "hard seed." If at the end of the germination period provided for legume and okra there are still present swollen seeds or seeds of these kinds which have just started to germinate, all seeds or seedlings except the above-stated shall be removed and the test continued for 5 additional days and the normal seedlings included in the percentage of germination.

GERMINATION STANDARDS FOR VEGETABLE SEEDS IN INTERSTATE COMMERCE

Seed	%	Seed	%
Artichoke	60	Kale	75
Asparagus	70	Kale, Chinese	75
Bean, asparagus	75	Kale, Siberian	75
Bean, broad	75	Kohlrabi	75
Bean, garden	70	Leek	60
Bean, lima	70	Lettuce	80
Bean, runner	75	Muskmelon	75
Beet	65	Mustard, India	75
Broccoli	75	Mustard, spinach	75
Brussels sprouts	70	Mustard, vegetable	75
Burdock, great	60	Okra	50
Cabbage	75	Onion	70
Cabbage, tronchuda	75	Onion, Welsh	70
Cardoon	60	Pak-choi	75
Carrot	55	Parsley	60
Cauliflower	75	Parsnip	60
Celeriac	55	Pea	80
Celery	55	Pepper	55
Chard, Swiss	65	Pumpkin	75
Chicory	65	Radish	75
Chinese cabbage	75	Rhubarb	60
Chives	50	Rutabaga	75
Citron	65	Sage	60
Collards	80	Salsify	75
Corn, sweet	75	Savory, summer	55
Corn salad	70	Sorrel	65
Cowpea (southern pea)	75	Soybean	75
Cress, garden	75	Spinach	60
Cress, upland	60	Spinach, New Zealand	40
Cress, water	40	Squash	75
Cucumber	80	Tomato	75
Dandelion	60	Tomato, husk	50
Dill	60	Turnip	80
Eggplant	60	Watermelon	70
Endive	70		

Adapted from Federal Register, Vol. 59, No. 239, Wednesday, December 14, 1994. Rules and Regulation 64491.

VEGETABLE CROPS NEEDING EXPOSURE TO COOL WEATHER IN ORDER TO PRODUCE SEEDSTALKS

Generally, the biennial vegetables listed below should be partly developed before they are exposed to cold. Those that are too small may not be greatly affected by the cold; cabbage stems, for example, should be at least as large as a lead pencil in diameter. The average chilling temperature should be below 45°F, and the chilling should continue for 1–2 months. Cooler temperatures may shorten the period of exposure. In seed production it is important to obtain close to 100% of the plants developing seedstalks. Every effort should therefore be made to have them large enough to react to the cold stimulus.

Beet	Kohlrabi
Brussels sprouts	Leek
Cabbage	Onion
Carrot	Parsley
Celeriac	Parsnip
Celery	Radish, winter type
Chard, Swiss	Rutabaga
Collards	Salsify
Florence fennel	Turnip
Kale	

ISOLATION DISTANCES BETWEEN PLANTINGS OF VEGETABLES FOR OPEN-POLLINATED SEED PRODUCTION

Self-Pollinated Vegetables

Self-pollinated crops have little outcrossing. Consequently, the only isolation necessary is to have plantings spaced far enough apart to prevent mechanical mixture at planting or harvest. A tall-growing crop is often planted between different varieties.

Bean	Bean, lima	Chicory	Endive
Lettuce	Pea	Tomato	

Cross-Pollinated Vegetables

Cross-pollination of vegetables may occur by wind or insect activity. Therefore, plantings of different varieties of the same crop or different crops in the same family that will cross with each other must be isolated. Some general isolation guidelines are provided; however, the seed grower should follow the recommendations of the seed company for whom the seed is being grown.

Wind-Pollinated Vegetables	Distance (miles)
Beet	½ to 2
	5 from sugar beet or Swiss chard
Sweet corn	1
Spinach	¼ to 3
Swiss chard	¾ to 5
	5 for sugar beet or beet

Insect-Pollinated Vegetables	Distance (miles)
Asparagus	¼
Broccoli	½ to 3
Brussels sprouts	½ to 3
Cabbage	½ to 3
Cauliflower	½ to 3
Collards	¾ to 2
	5 from other cole crops
Kale	¾ to 2
	5 from other cole crops
Kohlrabi	½ to 3

ISOLATION DISTANCES BETWEEN PLANTINGS OF VEGETABLES FOR OPEN-POLLINATED SEED PRODUCTION—Continued

Insect-Pollinated Vegetables (*Continued*)	Distance (miles) (*Continued*)
Carrot	½ to 3
Celeriac	1
Celery	1
Chinese cabbage	1
Cucumber	1½ for varieties ¼ from other cucurbits
Eggplant	¼
Gherkin	¼
Melons	1½ to 2 for varieties ¼ from other cucurbits
Mustard	1
Onion	½
Parsley	½ to 1
Pepper	½
Pumpkin	1½ to 2 for varieties ¼ from other cucurbits
Radish	¼ to 2
Rutabaga	¼ to 2
Squash	1½ to 2 for varieties ¼ from other cucurbits
Turnip	¼ to 2

Adapted in part from Seed Production in the Pacific Northwest. Pacific Northwest Extension Publications (1985).

CONDITIONS FOR CLASSES OF CERTIFIED VEGETABLE SEED

Vegetable	Foundation				Registered				Certified			
	Land [1]	Isolation [2]	Field [3]	Seed [4]	Land [1]	Isolation [2]	Field [3]	Seed [4]	Land [1]	Isolation [2]	Field [3]	Seed [4]
Bean	1	0	2,000	0.05	1	0	1,000	0.1	1	0	500	0.2
Bean, broad	1	0	2,000	0.05	1	0	1,000	0.1	1	0	500	0.2
Bean, mung	1	0	1,000	0.1	1	0	500	0.2	1	0	200	0.5
Corn, sweet	—	—	—	—	—	—	—	—	0	660	—	0.5
Cowpea	1	0	2,000	0.1	1	0	1,000	0.2	1	0	500	0.5
Okra	1	1,320	0	0	1	1,320	2,500	0.5	1	825	1,250	1.0
Onion	1	5,280	200	0	1	2,640	200	0.5	1	1,320	200	1.0
Pepper	1	200	0	0	1	100	300	0.5	1	30	150	1.0
Tomato	1	200	0	0	1	100	300	0.5	1	30	150	1.0
Watermelon	1	2,640	0	0	1	2,640	0	0.5	1	1,320	500	1.0

Adapted from Federal Seed Act Regulations, USDA, AMS. Seed Regulatory and Testing Branch, Beltsville, MD (1993).

[1] Years that must elapse between destruction of a previous crop of the same kind.

[2] Distance in feet from any contaminating source, but sufficient to prevent mechanical mixture.

[3] Minimum number of plants in which one off-type plant is permitted.

[3] Maximum percentage of off-type seeds that are permitted in cleaned seed.

STECKLINGS FOR SEED PRODUCTION

Crop	Spacing Between Rows (in.)	Spacing Between Plants (in.)	Root Bed Seed Requirement (lb/acre)	Area (acres) To Be Set from 1 Acre of Seedbed
Beet	32–36	12–24	8–10	5–15
Carrot	30–36	8–12	6–8	8–20
Onion	36	Practically touching	4–6	2–5
Parsnip	36–48	12–24	3–4	10–20
Rutabaga and turnip	24–36	8–18	3–4	6–10

SEED-TO-SEED PRODUCTION

Whenever the seed-to-seed method is used for producing a commercial seed crop, it is important to use stock seed for very high quality. Roguing is difficult with root crops because there is less opportunity for selection than with stecklings.

	Spacing Between		
Vegetable	Rows (in.)	Plants in Row (in.)	Rate of Seeding (lb/acre)
Beet	20–36	1	7–20
Cabbage	20–36	10–12	2–3
Carrot	20–36	1	2–3
Chard, Swiss	36	12–18	6–8
Lettuce	20–36	4–6	1–2
Onion	20–36	1	4–6
Parsnip	36–46	8–12	3–4
Radish, summer and winter types	20–36	2–12	3–4
Rutabaga and turnip	20–36	1	3–4
Salsify	20–36	12	8–10

Vegetable	Average U.S. Yields, 1976–1977 (lb/acre)	Very Good Yield (lb/acre)
Asparagus	—	1000
Bean, snap	1510	2000
Bean, lima	1965	2500
Beet	1188	2000
Broccoli	444	800
Brussels sprouts	—	1000
Cabbage	693	1000
Carrot	611	1000
Cauliflower	397	500
Celeriac	—	1000
Celery	578	1000
Chard, Swiss	1351	2000
Chicory	—	600
Chinese cabbage	—	1000
Corn, sweet	1726	2500
Cucumber	427	700
Eggplant	132	200
Endive, curled or smooth	580	800
Florence fennel	—	2000
Kale	1034	1200
Kohlrabi	706	1000
Leek	450	600
Lettuce	356	600
Muskmelon	313	500
Mustard	1168	1500
New Zealand spinach	—	2000
Okra	1211	2000
Onion	318	800
Parsley	607	1200
Parsnip	698	1300
Pea	1694	2500
Pepper	127	200
Pumpkin	534	800
Radish	982	2000
Rutabaga	2000	2500
Salsify	300	1000
Southern pea	—	1500
Spinach	1560	2500

Vegetable	Average U.S. Yields, 1976–1977 (lb/acre)	Very Good Yield (lb/acre)
Squash, summer	640	1000
Squash, winter	404	800
Tomato	121	200
Turnip	1380	2000
Watermelon	251	400

U.S. yields adapted from Vegetable Crop Reporting Board ESCS, USDA (1978).

STORAGE OF VEGETABLE SEEDS

High moisture and temperature cause rapid deterioration in vegetable seeds. The longer seeds are held, the more important becomes the control of moisture and temperature conditions. Low moisture in the seeds means longer life, especially if they must be held at warm temperatures. Kinds of seeds vary in their response to humidity (page 468).

The moisture content of seeds can be lowered by drying them in moving air at 120°F. This may be injurious to seeds with an initial moisture content of 25–40%. With such seeds 110°F is preferred. It may require less than 1 hr to reduce the moisture content of small seeds or up to 3 hr for large seeds. This will depend on the depth of the layer of seeds, the volume of air, dryness of air, and original moisture content of seed. When seeds cannot be dried in this way, seal them in airtight containers over, but not touching, some calcium chloride. Use enough calcium chloride so that the moisture absorbed from the seeds will produce no visible change in the chemical. Dried silica gel can be used in place of the calcium chloride.

Bean and okra may develop hard seeds if their moisture content is lowered to 7% or below. White-seeded beans are likely to become hard if the moisture content is reduced to about 10%. Dark-colored beans can be dried to less than 10% moisture before they become hard. Hard seeds will not germinate satisfactorily.

The moisture content of seed will reach an equilibrium with the atmosphere after a period of time. This takes about 3 weeks for small seeds and 3–6 weeks for large seeds.

Storage temperatures near 32°F are not necessary. Between 40 and 50°F is quite satisfactory when the moisture content of the seed is low.

If the moisture content is reduced to 4–5% and the seeds put in sealed containers, a storage temperature of about 70°F will be satisfactory for more than 1 year.

EQUILIBRIUM MOISTURE CONTENTS OF VEGETABLE SEEDS AT VARIOUS RELATIVE HUMIDITIES AND APPROXIMATELY 77°F WET BASIS

	Relative Humidity (%)						
Vegetable	10	20	30	45	60	75	80
	Seed Moisture (%)						
Bean, lima	4.6	6.6	7.7	9.2	11.0	13.8	15.0
Bean, snap	3.0	4.8	6.8	9.4	12.0	15.0	16.0
Beet, garden	2.1	4.0	5.8	7.6	9.4	11.2	15.0
Broadbean	4.2	5.8	7.2	9.3	11.1	14.5	17.2
Cabbage	3.2	4.6	5.4	6.4	7.6	9.6	10.0
Cabbage, Chinese	2.4	3.4	4.6	6.3	7.8	9.4	—
Carrot	4.5	5.9	6.8	7.9	9.2	11.6	12.5
Celery	5.8	7.0	7.8	9.0	10.4	12.4	13.5
Corn, sweet	3.8	5.8	7.0	9.0	10.6	12.8	14.0
Cucumber	2.6	4.3	5.6	7.1	8.4	10.1	10.2
Eggplant	3.1	4.9	6.3	8.0	9.8	11.9	—
Lettuce	2.8	4.2	5.1	5.9	7.1	9.6	10.0
Mustard, leaf	1.8	3.2	4.6	6.3	7.8	9.4	—
Okra	3.8	7.2	8.3	10.0	11.2	13.1	14.5
Onion	4.6	6.8	8.0	9.5	11.2	13.4	13.6
Onion, Welsh	3.4	5.1	6.9	9.4	11.8	14.0	—
Parsnip	5.0	6.1	7.0	8.2	9.5	11.2	—
Pea	5.4	7.3	8.6	10.1	11.9	15.0	15.5
Pepper	2.8	4.5	6.0	7.8	9.2	11.0	12.0
Radish	2.6	3.8	5.1	6.8	8.3	10.2	—
Spinach	4.6	6.5	7.8	9.5	11.1	13.2	14.5
Squash, winter	3.0	4.3	5.6	7.4	9.0	10.8	—
Tomato	3.2	5.0	6.3	7.8	9.2	11.1	12.0
Turnip	2.6	4.0	5.1	6.3	7.4	9.0	10.0
Watermelon	3.0	4.8	6.1	7.6	8.8	10.4	11.0

Adapted from O. L. Justice and L. N. Bass, Principles and Practices of Seed Storage, USDA Agricultural Handbook 506 (1978).

ESTIMATED MAXIMUM SAFE SEED-MOISTURE CONTENTS FOR STORAGE FOR 1 YEAR AT DIFFERENT TEMPERATURES

	Temperature (°F)		
Vegetable	40–50	70	80
	Seed Moisture (%)		
Bean	15	11	8
Bean, lima	15	11	8
Beet	14	11	9
Cabbage	9	7	5
Carrot	13	9	7
Celery	13	9	7
Corn, sweet	14	10	8
Cucumber	11	9	8
Lettuce	10	7	5
Okra	14	12	10
Onion	11	8	6
Pea	15	13	9
Pepper	10	9	7
Spinach	13	11	9
Tomato	13	11	9
Turnip	10	8	6
Watermelon	10	8	7

Adapted from E. H. Toole, Storage of Vegetable Seeds, USDA Leaflet 220 (1958).

STORAGE OF VEGETABLE SEEDS IN HERMETICALLY SEALED CONTAINERS

The 5-month limitation on the date of test shall not apply when:

a. The seed was packaged within 9 months of harvest.
b. The container does not allow water vapor penetration through any wall or seal greater than 0.05 grams of water per 100 square inches of surface at 100°F with a relative humidity on one side of 90% and on the other side of 0%.
c. The container is conspicuously labeled in not less than 8-point type that the container is hermetically sealed, that the seed has been preconditioned as to moisture content, and the calendar month and year in which the germination test was completed; not to exceed 24 months.
d. The seed in the container does not exceed the percentage of moisture, on a wet weight basis, as listed below.

Vegetable	Moisture (%)	Vegetable	Moisture (%)
Bean, garden	7.0	Leek	6.5
Bean, lima	7.0	Lettuce	5.5
Beet	7.5	Muskmelon	6.0
Broccoli	5.0	Mustard, India	5.0
Brussels sprouts	5.0	Onion	6.5
Cabbage	5.0	Onion, Welsh	6.5
Carrot	7.0	Parsley	6.5
Cauliflower	5.0	Parsnip	6.0
Celeriac	7.0	Pea	7.0
Celery	7.0	Pepper	4.5
Chard, Swiss	7.5	Pumpkin	6.0
Chinese cabbage	5.0	Radish	5.0
Chive	6.5	Rutabaga	5.0
Collards	5.0	Spinach	8.0
Corn, sweet	8.0	Squash	6.0
Cucumber	6.0	Tomato	5.5
Eggplant	6.0	Turnip	5.0
Kale	5.0	Watermelon	6.5
Kohlrabi	5.0	All others	6.0

Adapted from Federal Register, Vol. 59, No. 239, Wednesday, December 14, 1994. Rules and Regulations 64492.

APPROXIMATE LIFE EXPECTANCY OF VEGETABLE SEEDS STORED UNDER FAVORABLE CONDITIONS

Vegetable	Years	Vegetable	Years
Asparagus	3	Kohlrabi	3
Bean	3	Leek	2
Beet	4	Lettuce	6
Broccoli	3	Martynia	2
Brussels sprouts	4	Muskmelon	5
Cabbage	4	Mustard	4
Cardoon	5	New Zealand spinach	3
Carrot	3	Okra	2
Cauliflower	4	Onion	1
Celeriac	3	Parsley	1
Celery	3	Parsnip	1
Chard, Swiss	4	Pea	3
Chervil	3	Pepper	2
Chicory	4	Pumpkin	4
Chinese cabbage	3	Radish	5
Ciboule	2	Roselle	3
Collards	5	Rutabaga	4
Corn, sweet	2	Salsify	1
Corn salad	5	Scorzonera	2
Cress, garden	5	Sea kale	1
Cress, water	5	Sorrel	4
Cucumber	5	Southern pea	3
Dandelion	2	Spinach	3
Eggplant	4	Squash	4
Endive	5	Tomato	4
Fennel	4	Turnip	4
Kale	4	Watermelon	4

Adapted from J. F. Harrington and P. A. Minges, Vegetable Seed Germination, University of California Agricultural Extension Leaflet, unnumbered (1954).

GERMINATION OF VEGETABLE SEEDS FOLLOWING LONG-TERM STORAGE

Vegetable/Variety	Age[1] (years)	Germination (%) 1963[2]	Germination (%) 1991[3]
Bean			
Wyoming Pinto	48	72	24[4]
Idaho Pinto	47	70	8[4]
Dwarf Green Pod	46	64	64[4]
Vermont Cranberry	45	78	52
Hidatsa	45	78	30[5]
Avg		72	36
Beet			
Extra Early Bassano	59	71	8[2]
Long Smooth Blood Turnip	56	62	18
Earlidark	53	63	14
Extra Early Red Turnip	49	85	36
Green Top Bunching	48	64	28
Early Flat Egyptian	47	94	78
Avg		73	30
Carrot			
Nantes Touchon Strain	46	63	24
Selected Long Orange Improved	46	70	22
Nancy	45	61	26
New Early Coreless	43	76	72
Wonderkugel	43	61	14
Avg		66	32
Corn			
Early Surprise	50	82	56
Marcross Northern	48	94	64
Lee (Resistant)	47	90	72
Earligold	46	92	84
Golden No. 10	45	90	70
Avg		90	69
Cucumber			
Danish Common	58	69	28[4]
Snake	58	70	28
Lange Kecskemeter	54	79	48
Marketer	46	73	62
National Pickling	45	87	62
Avg		76	46

GERMINATION OF VEGETABLE SEEDS FOLLOWING LONG-TERM STORAGE—Continued

Vegetable/Variety	Age[1] (years)	Germination (%) 1963[2]	Germination (%) 1991[3]
Eggplant			
Ebony King	56	69	4
Fort Myers Market	55	67	44
Blackee	50	62	12
Minnoval	48	92	80
Avg		72	35
Muskmelon			
Extra Early Sunrise	58	82	42
Perfection	56	75	28
Bush Jenny Lind	55	79	52
New Ideal	53	99	76
Early Sunrise	50	92[6]	74
Avg		85	54
Okra			
Extra Early Dwarf Green Pod	50	60[3]	34
Wyoming No. 9	48	99[3]	62
Wyoming No. 10	47	84[3]	72
Wyoming No. 5	45	96[3]	90[5]
Wyoming No. 4	45	82[3]	70[5]
Avg		84	66
Onion			
Valencia Sweet Spanish	52	76	20[5]
Early Yellow Sweet Spanish	49	66	32
Yellow Sweet Spanish	48	79	14
San Joaquin	47	94	20
Espanola	46	61	38
Avg		75	25
Pea			
Alaska	51	86[3]	94
Buxbom I	51	76[3]	82
Randolph Indian Var. 13, St. D.	51	64[3]	56
Radio	51	76[3]	45[2]
Pedigree Extra Early	48	90[3]	82
Extra Early D.S.C.	45	100[3]	92
Avg		82	75

GERMINATION OF VEGETABLE SEEDS FOLLOWING LONG-TERM STORAGE—Continued

Vegetable/Variety	Age[1] (years)	Germination (%) 1963[2]	1991[3]
Pepper			
Sweet (Thomsen's Own Select)	51	84	28
Early Market	49	70	2
Victory	45	76	10
World Beater No. 13	45	66	26
Avg		74	16
Spinach			
Blight Resistant Savoy	45	67	60[5]
Mt. Evergreen	45	66	14
Viking	43	83	40
Avg		72	38
Swiss Chard			
Burpee's Rhubarb	48	88[3]	70
Special Large White Ribbed	47	76[3]	66
Fordhook Giant	45	74[3]	70
Dark Green	45	88[3]	60
Avg		82	66
Tomato			
Marmon	60	87	82
Early Bird	59	96	40
Florida Special	58	92	76
Morse's Special Early	57	95	82
Beauty of Loraine	56	95	98
Avg		93	76
Watermelon			
Colorado Preserving Citron	58	82	32[4]
Arikara	57	76	20
Will' Sugar (28140.01)	57	88	24
New Winter	56	92	34
Will' Sugar (28142.01)	55	76	52[4]
Avg		83	32

Adapted from E. E. Roos and D. A. Davidson, Record Longevities of Vegetable Seeds in Storage, HortScience 27:393–396 (1992).

[1] Calculated from year seed was purchased to 1991.

[2] Germination test of 100 seeds unless noted.

[3] Germination test of 50 seeds unless noted.

[4] Germination test of 25 seeds.

[5] Germination test of 10 seeds.

[6] Germination tested in 1967.

Seed storage conditions from purchase to 1962 were in an office in Cheyenne, WY, from 1962 until 1977 storage conditions were 41°F and <40% RH, and after 1977 in sealed moisture-proof bags at 0°F.

PART 10

APPENDIX

SOURCES OF INFORMATION AND PUBLICATIONS ON VEGETABLES

Requests for information should be addressed to the Agricultural Extension Service or Agricultural Experiment Station in your state.

State	Post Office
Alabama	Auburn 36849
Alaska	Fairbanks 99775-0500
Arizona	Tucson 85721
Arkansas	Fayetteville 72701
California	Berkeley 94720
	Davis 95616
	Riverside 92521
Colorado	Fort Collins 80523
Connecticut	New Haven 06504
	Storrs 06269
Delaware	Newark 19717-1303
Florida	Gainesville 32611
Georgia	Athens 30602-7503
Hawaii	Honolulu 96822
Idaho	Moscow 83843
Illinois	Urbana 61801
Indiana	Lafayette 47907
Iowa	Ames 50011
Kansas	Manhattan 66506
Kentucky	Lexington 40546
Louisiana	Baton Rouge 70893
Maine	Orono 04469-0163
Maryland	College Park 20742
Massachusetts	Amherst 01003
Michigan	East Lansing 48824
Minnesota	St. Paul 55108
Mississippi	Mississippi State 39762
Missouri	Columbia 65211
Montana	Bozeman 59717
Nebraska	Lincoln 68583
Nevada	Reno 89557
New Hampshire	Durham 03824
New Jersey	New Brunswick 08903
New Mexico	Las Cruces 88003
New York	Geneva 14456
	Ithaca 14853

State	Post Office
North Carolina	Raleigh 27695
North Dakota	Fargo 58105
Ohio	Columbus 43210
	Wooster 44691-6900
Oklahoma	Stillwater 74078
Oregon	Corvallis 97331
Pennsylvania	University Park 16802
Puerto Rico	Mayaguez 00681-5000
Rhode Island	Kingston 02881
South Carolina	Clemson 29634
South Dakota	Brookings 57007
Tennessee	Knoxville 37901
Texas	College Station 77843
Utah	Logan 84322
Vermont	Burlington 05405
Virginia	Blacksburg 24061
Washington	Pullman 99164
West Virginia	Morgantown 26506
Wisconsin	Madison 53706
Wyoming	Laramie 82071-3354

A List of Available Publications can be obtained from the Office of Governmental and Public Affairs, U.S. Department of Agriculture, Washington, DC 20250. "For sale only" publications of the USDA can be obtained from the Superintendent of Documents, Government Printing Office, Washington, DC 20402.

Many state and USDA publications are available from County Extension Offices. This may be the easiest and quickest way of obtaining needed information on vegetables.

American Fruit Grower
37841 Euclid Ave.
Willoughby, OH 44094-5992

American Vegetable Grower
37841 Euclid Ave.
Willoughby, OH 44094-5992

Citrus and Vegetable Magazine
7402 N. 56th St., Suite 560
Tampa, FL 33617

Florida Grower & Rancher
1331 N. Mills Ave.
Orlando, FL 32803-2598

Great Lakes Vegetable Growers News
343 S. Union St.
Sparta, MI 49345

Greenhouse Grower
37841 Euclid Ave.
Willoughby, OH 44094-5992

The Grower
50 Doughty St.
London, England WCIN 2LP

The Grower
7950 College Blvd.
PO Box 2939
Shawnee Mission, KS 66201-9990

The Packer
7950 College Blvd.
PO Box 2939
Shawnee Mission, KS 66201

The Produce News
2185 Lemoine Ave.
Fort Lee, NJ 07024

Vegetable
The Magazine for the Western Vegetable Industry
1755 North Fine
Fresno, CA 93727

Western Grower and Shipper
PO Box 2130
Newport Beach, CA 92658

SOURCES OF VEGETABLE INFORMATION IN CANADA

For bulletins published in Canada write to Communication Branch, Agriculture Canada, Ottawa, Ontario, Canada K1A OC7, or to the Ministry of Agriculture in a particular province.

Province	Post Office
Alberta	Edmonton
British Columbia	Victoria
Manitoba	Winnipeg
New Brunswick	Fredericton
Newfoundland	St. Johns
Novia Scotia	Halifax
Ontario	Toronto
Prince Edward Island	Charlottetown
Quebec	Quebec
Saskatchewan	Regina

A

Abbott & Cobb, Inc.
PO Box 307
Feasterville, PA 19053-0307
Ph (800) 345-SEED
Fax (215) 245-9043

Abundant Life Seed Foundation
PO Box 772
Port Townsend, WA 98368
Ph (360) 385-5660

Agrisales, Inc.
PO Box 2060
Plant City, FL 33564-2060
Ph (813) 433-4088
Fax (813) 433-4526

Agri-Seed & Chemical Corp.
850 Dryden Rd.
Metamora, MI 48455

American Seed Corp.
58233 N. Gratiot Ave.
New Haven, MI 48048

American Sunmelon
4200 Perimeter Center Drive
Suite 200
Oklahoma City, OK 73116
Ph (405) 943-9327
Fax (405) 943-5461

American Takii, Inc.
301 Natividad Road
Salinas, CA 93906
Ph (408) 443-4901
Fax (408) 443-3976

Amsa Seed Co.
PO Box 5301
Modesto, CA 95352-5301

Arkansas Valley Seed Co.
4625 Colorado Blvd.
Denver, CO 80216

Asgrow Seed Co.
2605 E. Kilgore Rd.
Kalamazoo, MI 49002-1744
Ph (616) 384-5519
Fax (616) 384-5678

B

Bakker Brothers of Idaho, Inc.
PO Box 1964
Twin Falls, ID 83303-1964
Ph (203) 733-0015
Fax (203) 734-9842

Ball Seed Co.
622 Town Rd.
West Chicago, IL 60185-2698
Ph (800) 879-2255
Fax (800) 234-0370

Walter Baxter Seed Co.
PO Box 8175
Weslaco, TX 78596

Bejo Seeds
PO Box 859
Oceano, CA 93445

Bejo Zaden B.V.
Postbus 50
1749 ZH Warmenhuizen
Holland

Bojo's Garden Seeds
PO Box 1408
Caldwell, ID 83606

Bonanza Seeds International, Inc.
PO Box V
Gilroy, CA 95020

Booker Seeds, Ltd.
Boston Road
Sleaford, Lincs, NG34 7HA
England

Bountiful Gardens Seeds
19550 Walker Road
Willits, CA 95490
Ph (707) 459-6410

Brawley Seed Co.
PO Box 180
Mooreville, NC 28115

Breeders' Seed Ltd.
17 Summerwood Lane
Halsall Ormskirk
Lancs. L39 8RQ
England

Broersen Bros.
PO Box 4
Tuitjenhoorn
The Netherlands

Brotherton Seed Co., Inc.
PO Box 1136
Moses Lake, WA 98837

DT Brown & Co. Ltd.
Station Rd, Poulton le Fylde
Blackpool FY6 7HX
England

Bruinsma Seed Co.
PO Box 1463
High River, Alberta
Canada TOL 1BO

Bunch Seed, Inc.
4th & Texas Blvd.
Texarkana, TX 75501

Burgess Seed and Plant Co.
905 Four Seasons Rd.
Bloomington, IL 61701

Burpee Vegetables/Ball Seed Co.
622 Town Rd.
West Chicago, IL 60185-2698
Ph (800) 388-3449
Fax (708) 231-1383

W. Atlee Burpee & Co.
300 Park Ave.
Warminster, PA 18991
Ph (800) 999-8552
Fax (215) 674-8402

D. V. Burrell Seed Growers Co.
PO Box 150
Rocky Ford, CO 81067
Ph (719) 254-3318
Fax (719) 254-3319

C

California Asparagus Seed
2815 Anza Ave.
Davis, CA 95616
Ph (916) 753-2437
Fax (916) 753-1209

California Gardener's Seed Co.
904 Silver Spur Rd.
Suite 414
Rolling Hills Estates, CA 90274

California Valley Seed Co.
PO Box 1600
El Centro, CA 92243
Ph (619) 337-3120
Fax (619) 337-3132

Canners Seed Corporation
PO Box 18
Lewisville, ID 83431

Carolina Seeds
PO Box 2625
Boone, NC 28607
Ph (704) 297-7333
Fax (704) 297-3888

Central Valley Seeds, Inc.
8539 W. California
Fresno, CA 93706
Ph (209) 233-9076
Fax (209) 233-7859

Champion Seed Co.
529 Mercury Lane
Brea, CA 92621-4894
Ph (714) 529-0702
Fax (714) 990-1280

Chesmore Seed Co.
PO Box 8368
St. Joseph, MO 64508
Ph (816) 279-0865
Fax (816) 236-6134

Chon & Sons Oriental Produce
PO Box 251
Malaga, NJ 08328

Alf Christianson Seed Co.
PO Box 98
Mt. Vernon, WA 98273
Ph (206) 336-9727
Fax (206) 336-3191

Clause Semences
1 Avenue Lucien Clause
91221 Bretigny-Sur-Orge Cedex
France

Clause UK Ltd.
Countess Avenue, Stanly Green
Ind Est. Cheadle Hulme
Cheshire SK8 6QS
England

Clover Garden Products
200 Weakley Lane
Smyrna, TN 37167

Comstock, Ferre & Co.
263 Main St.
Wethersfield, CT 06109

The Cook's Garden
PO Box 65
Londonderry, VT 05148
Ph (802) 824-3400

Crites Moscow Growers, Inc.
PO Box 8912
Moscow, ID 83843
Ph (208) 882-5519

Crookham Co.
PO Box 520
Caldwell, ID 83606

Crop King Inc.
PO Box 310
Medina, OH 44258
Ph (216) 725-5656
Fax (216) 722-3958

D

Daehnfeldt, Inc.
PO Box 947
Albany, OR 97321
Ph (541) 928-5868
Fax (541) 928-5581

L. Daehnfeldt A/S
Faborgvej 248B
Postbus 185
DK 5100 Odense C
Denmark

DeGroot, Inc.
PO Box 575
Coloma, MI 49038

Deltapine
Box 155
Scott, MS 38772
Ph (601) 742-3351

Demonchaux Co.
827 N. Kansas St.
PO Box 8330
Topeka, KS 66608

DeRuiter Seeds, Inc.
PO Box 20228
Columbus, OH 43220
Ph (614) 459-1498
Fax (614) 442-1716

Dominion Seed House
Georgetown, Ontario
Canada L7G 4A2

E

Elsoms Seeds Ltd.
Spalding
Lincolnshire PE11 1QG
England

Enza Zaden
1188 Padre Dr.
Suite 150
Salinas, CA 93901
Ph (408) 751-0937
Fax (408) 751-6103

Epicure Seeds, Ltd.
PO Box 450
Brewster, NY 10509

Exotica Seed Co.
8033 Sunset Blvd.
Suite 125
West Hollywood, CA 90046

Express Seed Co.
300 Artino Dr.
Oberlin, OH 44074
Ph (216) 774-2259
Fax (216) 774-2728

F

Farmer Seed & Nursery Co.
Div. of Plantron, Inc.
Reservation Center
2207 East Oakland Ave.
Bloomington, IL 61701

Ferry-Morse Seed Co.
PO Box 4938
555 Codoni Ave.
Modesto, CA 95352-4938
Ph (209) 579-7333
Fax (203) 527-5312

Henry Field Seed & Nursery Co.
407 Sycamore St.
Shenandoah, IA 51602

Florida Seed Co., Inc.
4950 South Frontage Rd.
Lakeland, FL 33801
Ph (941) 686-6683
Fax (941) 686-5833

Fonseca Seed Company
PO Box 474
Isleton, CA 95641

Dean Foster Nurseries, Inc.
PO Box 127
Hartford, MI 49057

Fredonia Seed Co., Inc.
183 Main St.
Fredonia, NY 14063

Frontier Seed Co., Inc.
5537 W. Maryland Avenue
Glendale, AZ 85311
Ph (602) 934-3654
Fax (602) 937-1675

G

Genecorp Seeds
910 Duncan Ave.
San Juan Bautista, CA 95045
Ph (408) 623-0606
Fax (408) 623-0646

Germania Seed Co.
5952 N. Milwaukee Ave.
Chicago, IL 60646

Gleckler Seedsmen
Metamora, OH 43540
Ph (419) 644-2211

Global Seeds, Inc.
7530 Fairview Ave.
PO Box 1207
Hollister, CA 95024

Fred C. Gloeckner & Co., Inc.
15 East 26th St.
New York, NY 10010

Grace's Gardens
10 Bay St.
Westport, CT 06880

Green Barn Seed Co.
18855 Park Avenue
Deephaven, MN 55391
Ph (612) 476-0324

Greenleaf Seeds
PO Box 98
Conway, MA 01341
Ph (413) 628-4750

G. S. Grimes
PO Box 640
Concord, OH 44077-0640
Ph (800) 241-SEED

GSN Seed
PO Box 1530
El Centro, CA 92243
Ph (619) 337-3100
Fax (619) 337-3135

Gurney's Seed & Nursery Co.
110 Capital St.
Yankton, SD 57079

H

H and H Seed Co., Inc.
PO Box 1688
Yuma, AZ 85364

H and M Seed Inc.
635 S. Sanborn Place #9
Salinas, CA 93901

Harris Moran Seed Co.
PO Box 3091
Modesto, CA 95353
Ph (800) 320-4672
Fax (209) 544-0335

Harris Seeds
PO Box 22960
Rochester, NY 14692-2960
Ph (800) 544-7938
Fax (716) 442-9386

The Chas. C. Hart Seed Co.
PO Box 9169
Wethersfield, CT 06109

Hastings
PO Box 4274
Atlanta, GA 30302

Hazera Seed Ltd.
PO Box 1565
Haifa, Israel

Hirahara Seed
PO Box 5158
Salinas, CA 93901

Hollar and Company, Inc.
PO Box 106
Rocky Ford, CO 81067
Ph (719) 254-7411
Fax (719) 254-3539

Holmes Seed Co.
2125 46th St. N.W.
Canton, OH 44709
Ph (216) 492-0123

A. H. Hummert Seed Co.
2746-48 Chouteau Ave.
St. Louis, MO 63103

Hung Nong Seed Co.
867 Hopkins Rd.
Williamsville, NY 14221

Hydro-Gardens, Inc.
PO Box 9707
Colorado Springs, CO 80932

I

Illinois Foundation Seeds, Inc.
PO Box 722
Champaign, IL 61820

J

Jersey Asparagus Farms, Inc.
105 Porchtown Rd.
Pittsgrove, NJ 08318
Ph (609) 358-2548
Fax (609) 358-6127

Johnny's Selected Seeds
RD 1, Box 2580
Albion, ME 04910-9731
Ph (207) 437-9294
Fax (800) 437-4290

Jordan Seeds, Inc.
6400 Upper Aston Rd.
Woodbury, MN 55125
Ph (612) 738-3422
Fax (612) 731-7690

J. W. Jung Seed Co.
333 S. High St.
Randolph, WI 53957

K

Kees Broerson Seeds
Bogtmanweg 7
1747 HV Tuitjenhorn, Holland

Keithly-Williams Seeds
PO Box 177
Holtville, CA 92250
Ph (619) 356-5533
Fax (619) 356-2409

Kellog Seed Co.
PO Box 417
Crows Landing, CA 95313

Kilgore Seed Co.
1400 West First St.
Sanford, FL 32771

E W King & Co. Ltd.
Monks Farm, Coggeshall Road
Kelvedon, Essex C05 9PG
England

King Crown Quality Seeds
Grange Hill, Coggershall
Colchester, Essex C06 1RA
England

Kitazawa Seed Co.
1748 Laine Avenue
Santa Clara, CA 95051

Known-You Seed Co., Ltd.
26, Chung Cheng 2nd Road
Kaohsiung, Taiwan
Republic of China

KPR Sales, Inc.
PO Box 608
Wendell, ID 83355-0608

Kyowa Seed Co., Ltd.
15-13 Nanpeidai
Shibuya-ku
Tokyo, Japan

L

Laval Seeds, Inc.
3505 Boul St. Martin Quest
Laval, Quebec
Canada H7T 1A2

Leckler's, Inc.
13001 Telegraph Rd.
LaSalle, MI 48145

Orol Ledden & Sons
PO Box 7
Sewell, NJ 08080-0007
Ph (609) 468-1000
Fax (609) 464-0947

Leen de Mos
PO Box 54
2690AB's-Gravenzande, Holland

Leighton Seed Co., Inc.
PO Box 1982
731 S. Sanborn Road
Salinas, CA 93902
Ph (408) 422-2820
Fax (408) 422-2261

Le Jardin du Gourmet
PO Box 75N
St. Johnsbury Center, VT 05863
Ph (802) 748-1446

Letherman's Seed Co.
1221 E. Tuscarawas St.
Canton, OH 44707

Liberty Seed Co.
PO Box 806
New Philadelphia, OH 44663-0806
Ph (216) 364-1611
Fax (330) 364-6415

Liefgreen Seed Co.
PO Box 836
Glendale, AZ 85311
Ph (602) 937-1674
Fax (602) 937-1675

Livingstone Seed Co.
880 Kinnear Rd.
Columbus, OH 43216

Lockhart Seeds
PO Box 1361
Stockton, CA 95201
Ph (209) 466-4401
Fax (209) 466-9766

M

Market More Inc.
PO Box 445
Palmetto, FL 34220
Ph (941) 722-6512
Fax (941) 722-7711

Marutane Co., Ltd.
CPO Box 65
Kyoto 600, Japan

Earl May Seed & Nursery Co.
208 N. Elm St.
Shenandoah, IA 51603

Mesa Maize Co.
60936 Falcon Rd.
Olathe, CO 81425

McFayden Seed Co., Ltd.
PO Box 1600
Brandon, Manitoba
Canada, R7A 6A6

McKenzie, Steele, Briggs
PO Box 1060
Brandon, Manitoba
Canada R7A 6E1

Mellinger, Inc.
2310 W. South Range
North Lima, OH 44452

Meyer Seed Co.
600 S. Caroline St.
Baltimore, MD 21231

Midwest Seed Growers, Inc.
10559 Lackman Rd.
Lenexa, KS 66219
Ph (913) 894-0500
Fax (913) 894-0501

Mikado Seed Growers Co., Ltd.
1203 Hoshikuki, Chuo
Chiba City, 260 Japan

Henry F. Mitchell Co.
PO Box 160
King of Prussia, PA 19406

Mixon Seed Co., Inc.
PO Box 1652
Orangeburg, SC 29116
Ph (800) 922-1377
Fax (803) 534-5027

J. W. Moles & Son
Seed Merchants, Turkey Cock Lane
Stanway, Colchester, Essex CO3 5PO
England

Mushroompeople
PO Box 159
Inverness, CA 94937

Musser Seed Co.
PO Box 1406
Twin Falls, ID 83303

N

Nanto Seed Company
6-4, Minami-Yagimachi 2-Chome
Kashihara-Shi
Nara 634
Japan

Namdhari Seeds
Unit No. 107, 1st Floor
"Royal Comer", 1&2, Lalbagh Rd.
Bangalore-560 027
India

Native Seeds/SEARCH
2509 N. Campbell Ave.
#325
Tucson, AZ 85719
Ph (520) 327-9123

Nickerson Seeds
JNRC, Rothwell
Lincoln LN7 6DT
England

Nickerson-Zwaan B.V.
PO Box 119
2990AA Barendrecht
Netherlands

Nichol's Garden Nursery
1190 North Pacific Highway
Albany, OR 97321

Nicklow's Vegetables, Inc.
PO Box 457
Ashland, MA 01721-0457
Ph (800) 642-5569
Fax (508) 881-1707

Nourse Farms, Inc.
41 River Rd.
South Deerfield, MA 01373
Ph (413) 665-2658
Fax (413) 665-7888

NPI
417 Wakara Way
Salt Lake City, UT 84103

Nunhems Seed
PO Box 18
Lewisville, ID 83431
Ph (208) 754-8666
Fax (208) 754-8669

Nutting & Sons, Ltd.
Long Stanton
Cambridge CB4 5DU
England

O

J. E. Ohlsens Enke A/S
Roskildevej 325A
DK-2630 Taastrup
Denmark

L. L. Olds Seed Co.
PO Box 7790
Madison, WI 53707

Ontario Seed Co.
Box 144
Waterloo, Ontario
Canada N2J 3Z9

Oriental Vegetable Seeds
Evergreen Y. H. Enterprises
PO Box 17538
Anaheim, CA 92817

Ornamental Edibles
3622 Weedin Court
San Jose, CA 95132
Ph (408) 946-7333
Fax (408) 946-0181

Orsetti Seed Co., Inc.
2339-A Technology Parkway
Hollister, CA 95023
Ph (408) 636-4822
Fax (408) 636-4814

P

The Page Seed Co.
PO Box 158
Greene, NY 13778

Pan American Seed Co.
1017 W. Roosevelt Rd.
West Chicago, IL 60185
Ph (708) 231-1400
Fax (708) 231-1419

Paramount Seeds, Inc.
PO Box 1866
Palm City, FL 34990
Ph (407) 221-0653
Fax (407) 221-0102

Park Seed Co.
Cokesbury Rd.
Greenwood, SC 29647-0001
Ph (800) 845-3366

Penn State Seed Co.
Box 390, Rt. 309
Dallas, PA 18612

Pennington Seeds, Inc.
PO Box 13541
Columbia, SC 29201

Pepper Gal
PO Box 23006
Ft. Lauderdale, FL 33307
Ph (954) 537-5540
Fax (954) 566-2208

Pepper Research
980 S.E. 4th St.
Belle Glade, FL 33430
Ph (407) 736-4954
Fax (407) 732-3892

W. H. Perron & Co. Ltd.
P.P. 408
Laval, Quebec
Canada H75 2A6

Peter-Edward Seed Co., Inc.
302 S. Center St.
Eustis, FL 32726
Ph (800) 227-7687
Fax (904) 589-1413

Petoseed Co., Inc.
PO Box 4206
Saticoy, CA 93307-4206
Ph (805) 647-1188
Fax (805) 656-4818

Pinetree DeRuiter Seeds Ltd.
Lower Rd.
Effingham, Leatherhead
Surrey KT24 5JP
England

Pinetree Garden Seeds
New Glouster, ME 04260

Plant Genetics, Inc.
1930 Fifth St.
Davis, CA 95616

Porter and Son, Seedsmen
PO Box 104
Stephenville, TX 76401-0104

Precision Agricultural Products, Inc.
PO Box 496
Immokalee, FL 33934
Ph (941) 657-3691

Pybas Vegetable Seed Co.
301 N. Depot
Santa Maria, CA 93454
Ph (805) 922-4624
Fax (805) 928-0293

Q

Quali-Sel Seed
PO Box 4370
1143 Madison Lane
Salinas, CA 93912

Quantil Seeds Ltd.
Robinsons Farms, Cranes Lane
Lathom, Ormskirk L40 5UJ
England

R

Redwood City Seed Co.
PO Box 361
Redwood City, CA 94064

Reed's Seeds
3334 NYS Route 215
Cortland, NY 13045-9440
Ph (607) 753-9095
Fax (607) 753-9511

Rijk Zwaan
PO Box 40
2678 ZG DeLier
The Netherlands

Rio Colorado Seeds
4701 Gila Ridge Rd.
Yuma, AZ 85365
Ph (520) 344-4775

Ripley's Believe It or Not
10 Bay St.
Westport, CT 06880

Rispins Seeds, Inc.
PO Box 5
Lansing, IL 60438
Ph (708) 474-0241
Fax (708) 474-4127

Robson Corp.
1 Seneca Circle
Hall, NY 14463-0270
Ph (716) 526-6396
Fax (716) 526-5350

Rogers Seed Co.
PO Box 4188
Boise, ID 83711-4188
Ph (208) 322-7272
Fax (208) 378-6625

Royal Sluis
Postbus 22-1600
AA Enkhuizen
Holland

Royal Sluis Inc.
1293 Harkins Rd.
Salinas, CA 93901
Ph (408) 757-4191
Fax (408) 757-7405

Rupp Seeds, Inc.
Rt. 5, 17919 Co. Rd. B
Wauseon, OH 43567
Ph (419) 337-1841
Fax (419) 337-5491

S

Sakata Seed America, Inc.
18095 Serene Dr.
Morgan Hill, CA 95037
Ph (408) 778-7758
Fax (408) 778-7768

Sakata Florida
PO Box 1103
Lehigh, FL 33920-1103
Ph (941) 369-0032
Fax (941) 939-2715

Sakata Seed Corp.
Yokohama Minami No. 20
Yokohama, Japan 232

Samen Mauser America
PO Box 663
El Centro, FL 92244
Ph (619) 353-7779
Fax (619) 353-7736

Santa Clara
PO Box 468
Oxnard, CA 93032

Scattini Seeds
1061 Terven Ave.
Salinas, CA 93901

Seedcoat, Inc.
1081 Harkins Rd.
Salinas, CA 93901

Seedless Unlimited
RR2, Townline Rd.
Leamington, Ontario
Canada N8H 3V5

Seeds Blum
HC 33 Idaho City Stage
Boise, ID 83706
Ph (800) 742-1423
Fax (203) 338-5658

Seeds of Change
621 Old Santa Fe Trail, #10
Santa Fe, NM 87501
Ph (505) 438-8080
Fax (505) 438-7052

Seed Savers Exchange
3076 North Winn Rd.
Decorah, IA 52101
Ph (319) 382-5872

Seeds of Tomorrow
Route 2, Box 2145
Davis, CA 95616

Seedway, Inc.
1225 Zeager Rd.
Elizabethtown, PA 17022
Ph (800) 952-7333
Fax (800) 645-2574

Select Seed Co., Inc.
PO Box 175
Holtville, CA 92250

Seminole Stores, Inc.
PO Box 940
Ocala, FL 32678
Ph (904) 732-4143

Shamrock Seed Co.
3 Harris Place
Salinas, CA 93901
Ph (800) 351-4443
Fax (408) 771-1517

Sharpes International Seeds
Boston Road
Sleaford, Lincs, NG34 7HA
England

Shepherd's Garden Seeds
6116 Highway 9
Felton, CA 95018
Ph (408) 335-6910

R. H. Shumway's
PO Box 10
Graniteville, SC 29829
Ph (803) 663-9771

Siegers Seed Co.
8265 Felch Street
Zeeland, MI 49464-9503
Ph (800) 962-4999
Fax (616) 772-0333

S & M Farm Supply
PO Box 4319
Princeton, FL 33032
Ph (305) 258-0421

Snow Seed Co.
PO Box 294
Salinas, CA 93902
Ph (408) 758-9869
Fax (408) 757-4550

Southern Exposure Seed Exchange
PO Box 158
North Garden, VA 22959
Ph (804) 973-4703

Southern Seeds
PO Box 2091
Melbourne, FL 32902-2091
Ph (407) 727-3662
Fax (407) 728-8493

SPB Sales
PO Box 278
Nash, TX 75569

Steve Howe Seeds Ltd.
Fresh Fields, Long Hedges
Fishtoft, Boston
Lincs PE21 ORH
England

Stokes Seeds, Inc.
PO Box 548
Buffalo, NY 14240-0548
Ph (800) 263-7233
Fax (716) 695-9649

Sunrise Enterprises
PO Box 1960
Chesterfield, VA 23832
Ph (804) 796-5796
Fax (804) 796-6735

Sunseeds
18640 Sutter Blvd.
Morgan Hill, Ca 95037
Ph (408) 776-1111
Fax (408) 776-9397

WHW Symodson
Robinsons Farm
Cranes Lane, Lathom
Ormskirk L40 5UJ
England

T

Takii & Co., Ltd.
180 Umekoji Inokuma
Shimokyoku, Kyoto
Japan

Takii Europe B.V.
Hoofdweg 19
1424 PC De Kwakel
The Netherlands

Geo. Tait & Sons
PO Box 5545
PP Anex
Norfolk, VA 23516

Taylor Seed, Inc.
1441 Arizona Ave.
Yuma, AZ 85364
Ph (520) 782-9234
Fax (520) 782-0097

Terra Co.
4144 Highway 39 North
Plant City, FL 33565
Ph (813) 752-1177
Fax (813) 754-3840

Tezier Seeds
Rue Louis Saillant-B.P. 83
26800 Portes-les-Valence
France

Thompson & Morgan, Inc.
PO Box 1308
Jackson, NJ 08527-0308
Ph (908) 363-2225
Fax (908) 363-9356

Tokita Seed Co., Ltd.
Nakagawa
Omiya-Shi
Saitama-Ken
Japan 330

Tomato Grower's Supply Co.
PO Box 2237
Fort Myers, FL 33902
Ph (941) 768-1119

Topgreen Seed Co., Ltd.
PO Box 468
Kaohsiung, Taiwan

A. L. Tozer LTD
Pyports, Cogham
Surrey, KT11 3EH
England

Tsang and Ma
1306 Old Country Rd.
Belmont, CA 94002

Otis S. Twilley Seed Co., Inc.
PO Box 65
Trevose, PA 19053
Ph (215) 639-8800
Fax (215) 245-1949

U

The Urban Farmer, Inc.
PO Box 444
Convent Station, NJ 07961

V

Van den Berg Seeds BV
Grote Woerdlaan 1
2671 CK Naaldwijk
Holland

Vaughan's Seed Co.
5300 Katrine Ave.
Downers Grove, IL 60515
Ph (708) 969-6300
Fax (708) 969-6373

Vermont Bean Seed Co., Inc.
Garden Lane
Fair Haven, VT 05743

Vesey's Seeds Ltd.
PO Box 9000
Houlton, ME 04730-0829

Vilmorin Inc.
PO Box 707
Empire, CA 95319
Ph (209) 529-6000
Fax (209) 529-5848

Vilmorin Seed Co.
49250, Beaufort
En Vallee
La Menitre, France

Vreeken's Zaden
PO Box 182
3300 AD Dordrecht
The Netherlands

W

Weibull Tradgard AB
Box 510
26124 Landskrona
Sweden

Wetsel Seed Co., Inc.
961 N. Liberty Street
Harrisonburg, VA 22801

Whilhite Seed Co.
Box 23
Poolville, TX 76487
Ph (817) 599-5843
Fax (817) 599-5843

Wyatt-Quarles Seed Co.
PO Box 739
Garner, NC 27529

Y

Arthur Yates & Co. Pty. Ltd.
244-254 Horsley Road
Milperra, N.S.W. 2214
Australia

Samuel Yates, Ltd.
Withyfold Dr., Macclesfield
Cheshire SKI0 2BE
England

Dr. Yoo Farm
PO Box 290
College Park, MD 20740

Z

Zeraim Seed Growers Co., Ltd.
PO Box 103
Gedera 70700
Israel

Zwaan Seed Inc.
Box 397
Woodstown, NJ 08098-0397

Adapted from D. N. Maynard, Vegetable Seed Sources, Bradenton (University of Florida) GCREC Extension Report, BRA1996-1 (1996).

[1] This list is provided with the understanding that no discrimination is intended and no guarantee of reliability is implied.

U.S. UNITS OF MEASUREMENT

Length

1 foot	=	12 inches
1 yard	=	3 feet
1 yard	=	36 inches
1 rod	=	16.5 feet
1 mile	=	5280 feet

Area

1 acre	=	43,560 square feet
1 section	=	640 acres
1 section	=	1 square mile

Volume

1 liquid pint	=	16 liquid ounces
1 liquid quart	=	2 liquid pints
1 liquid quart	=	32 liquid ounces
1 gallon	=	8 liquid pints
1 gallon	=	4 liquid quarts
1 gallon	=	128 liquid ounces
1 peck	=	16 pints (dry)
1 peck	=	8 quarts (dry)
1 bushel	=	4 pecks
1 bushel	=	64 pints (dry)
1 bushel	=	32 quarts (dry)

Mass or Weight

1 pound	=	16 ounces
1 hundredweight	=	100 pounds
1 ton	=	20 hundredweight
1 ton	=	2000 pounds

CONVERSION FACTORS FOR U.S. UNITS

Multiply	By	To Obtain
	Length	
feet	12.	inches
feet	0.33333	yards
inches	0.08333	feet
inches	0.02778	yards
miles	5,280.	feet
miles	63,360.	inches
miles	1,760.	yards
rods	16.5	feet
yards	3.	feet
yards	36.	inches
yards	0.000568	miles
	Area	
acres	43,560.	square feet
acres	160.	square rods
acres	4,840.	square yards
square feet	144.	square inches
square feet	0.11111	square yards
square inches	0.00694	square feet
square miles	640.	acres
square miles	27,878,400.	square feet
square miles	3,097,600.	square yards
square yards	0.0002066	acres
square yards	9.	square feet
square yards	1,296.	square inches
	Volume	
bushels	2,150.42	cubic inches
bushels	4.	pecks
bushels	64.	pints
bushels	32.	quarts
cubic feet	1,728.	cubic inches
cubic feet	0.03704	cubic yards
cubic feet	7.4805	gallons
cubic feet	59.84	pints (liquid)
cubic feet	29.92	quarts (liquid)

Multiply	By	To Obtain
	Volume (Continued)	
cubic yards	27.	cubic feet
cubic yards	46,656.	cubic inches
cubic yards	202.	gallons
cubic yards	1,616.	pints (liquid)
cubic yards	807.9	quarts (liquid)
gallons	0.1337	cubic feet
gallons	231.	cubic inches
gallons	128.	ounces (liquid)
gallons	8.	pints (liquid)
gallons	4.	quarts (liquid)
gallons of water	8.3453	pounds of water
pecks	0.25	bushels
pecks	537.605	cubic inches
pecks	16.	pints (dry)
pecks	8.	quarts (dry)
pints (dry)	0.015625	bushels
pints (dry)	33.6003	cubic inches
pints (dry)	0.0625	pecks
pints (dry)	0.5	quarts (dry)
pints (liquid)	28.875	cubic inches
pints (liquid)	0.125	gallons
pints (liquid)	16.	ounces (liquid)
pints (liquid)	0.5	quarts (liquid)
quarts (dry)	0.03125	bushels
quarts (dry)	67.20	cubic inches
quarts (dry)	2.	pints (dry)
quarts (liquid)	57.75	cubic inches
quarts (liquid)	0.25	gallons
quarts (liquid)	32.	ounces (liquid)
quarts (liquid)	2.	pints (liquid)
	Mass or Weight	
ounces (dry)	0.0625	pounds
ounces (liquid)	1.805	cubic inches
ounces (liquid)	0.0078125	gallons
ounces (liquid)	0.0625	pints (liquid)
ounces (liquid)	0.03125	quarts (liquid)

Multiply	By	To Obtain
	Mass or Weight (Continued)	
pounds	16.	ounces
pounds	0.0005	tons
pounds of water	0.01602	cubic feet
pounds of water	27.68	cubic inches
pounds of water	0.1198	gallons
tons	32,000.	ounces
tons	20.	hundredweight
tons	2,000.	pounds
	Rate	
feet per minute	0.01667	feet per second
feet per minute	0.01136	miles per hour
miles per hour	88.	feet per minute
miles per hour	1.467	feet per minute

METRIC UNITS OF MEASUREMENT

Length

1 millimeter	=	1000 microns
1 centimeter	=	10 millimeters
1 meter	=	100 centimeters
1 meter	=	1000 millimeters
1 kilometer	=	1000 meters

Area

1 hectare	=	10,000 square meters

Volume

1 liter	=	1000 milliliters

Mass or Weight

1 gram	=	1000 milligrams
1 kilogram	=	1000 grams
1 quintal	=	100 kilograms
1 metric ton	=	1000 kilograms
1 metric ton	=	10 quintals

CONVERSION FACTORS FOR SI AND NON-SI UNITS

To Convert Column 1 into Column 2, Multiply by	Column 1 SI Unit	Column 2 non-SI Unit	To Convert Column 2 into Column 1 Multiply by
		Length	
0.621	kilometer, km (10^3 m)	mile, mi	1.609
1.094	meter, m	yard, yd	0.914
3.28	meter, m	foot, ft	0.304
1.0	micrometer, μm (10^{-6} m)	micron, μ	1.0
3.94×10^{-2}	millimeter, mm (10^{-3} m)	inch, in	25.4
10	nanometer, nm (10^{-9} m)	Angstrom, Å	0.1
		Area	
2.47	hectare, ha	acre	0.405
247	square kilometer, km^2 (10^3 m)^2	acre	4.05×10^{-3}
0.386	square kilometer, km^2 (10^3 m)^2	square mile, m^2	2.590
2.47×10^{-4}	square meter, m^2 (10^3 m)^2	acre	4.05×10^3
10.76	square meter, m^2 (10^3 m)^2	square foot, ft^2	9.29×10^{-2}
1.55×10^{-3}	square millimeter, m^2 (10^{-6} m)^2	square inch, in^2	645
		Volume	
6.10×10^4	cubic meter, m^3	cubic inch, in^3	1.64×10^{-5}
2.84×10^{-2}	liter, L (10^{-3} m^3)	bushel, bu	35.24

1.057	liter, L (10^{-3} m^3)	quart (liquid), qt	0.946
3.53×10^{-2}	liter, L (10^{-3} m^3)	cubic foot, ft^3	28.3
0.265	liter, L (10^{-3} m^3)	gallon	3.78
33.78	liter, L (10^{-2} m^3)	ounce (fluid), oz	2.96×10^{-2}
2.11	liter, L (10^{-3} m^3)	pint (fluid), pt	0.473
1.06	liter, L (10^{-3} m^3)	quart (liquid), qt	0.946
9.73×10^{-3}	$meter^3$, m^3	acre-inch	102.8
35.7	$meter^3$, m^3	cubic foot, ft^3	2.80×10^{-2}

Mass

2.20×10^{-3}	gram, g (10^{-3} kg)	pound, lb	454
3.52×10^{-2}	gram, g	ounce (advp), oz	28.4
2.205	kilogram, kg	pound, lb	0.454
10^{-2}	kilogram, kg	quintal (metric), q	10^{2}
1.10×10^{-3}	kilogram, kg	ton (2000 lb), ton	907
1.102	megagram, Mg (tonne)	ton (U.S.), ton	0.907

Yield and Rate

0.893	kilogram per hectare, kg ha^{-1}	pound per acre, lb $acre^{-1}$	1.12
7.77×10^{-2}	kilogram per cubic meter, kg m^{-3}	pound per bushel, lb bu^{-1}	12.87
1.49×10^{-2}	kilogram per hectare, kg ha^{-1}	bushel per acre, 60 lb	67.19
1.59×10^{-2}	kilogram per hectare, kg ha^{-1}	bushel per acre, 56 lb	62.71
1.86×10^{-2}	kilogram per hectare, kg ha^{-1}	bushel per acre, 48 lb	53.75
0.107	liter per hectare, L ha^{-1}	gallon per acre	9.35
893	megagram per hectare, Mg ha^{-1}	pound per acre, lb $acre^{-1}$	1.12×10^{-3}
0.4.46	megagram per hectare, Mg ha^{-1}	ton (2000 lb) per acre, ton $acre^{-1}$	2.24
2.10	meter per second, m s^{-1}	mile per hour	0.477

CONVERSION FACTORS FOR SI AND NON-SI UNITS—Continued

To Convert Column 1 into Column 2, Multiply by	Column 1 SI Unit	Column 2 non-SI Unit	To Convert Column 2 into Column 1 Multiply by
		Specific Surface	
10	square meter per kilogram, $m^2\ kg^{-1}$	square centimeter per gram, $cm^2\ g^{-1}$	0.1
10^3	square meter per kilogram, $m^2\ kg^{-1}$	square millimeter per gram, $mm^2\ g^{-1}$	10^{-3}
		Pressure	
9.90	megapascal, MPa (10^6 Pa)	atmosphere	0.101
10	megapascal, MPa (10^6 Pa)	bar	0.1
1.00	megagram per cubic meter, $Mg\ m^{-3}$	gram per cubic centimeter, $g\ cm^{-3}$	1.00
2.09×10^{-2}	pascal, Pa	pound per square foot, $lb\ ft^{-2}$	47.9
1.45×10^{-4}	pascal, Pa	pound per square inch, $lb\ in^{-2}$	6.90×10^3
		Temperature	
1.00 (°K − 273)	Kelvin, K	Celsius, °C	1.00 (°C + 273)
(9/5°C) + 32	Celsius, °C	Fahrenheit, °F	5/9 (°F − 32)

Energy, Work, Quantity of Heat

9.52×10^{-4}	joule, J	British thermal unit, Btu	1.05×10^{3}
0.239	joule, J	calorie, cal	4.19
10^{7}	joule, J	erg	10^{-7}
0.735	joule, J	foot-pound	1.36
2.387×10^{-5}	joule per square meter, J m^{-2}	calorie per square centimeter (langley)	4.19×10^{4}
10^{5}	newton, N	dyne	10^{-5}
1.43×10^{-3}	watt per square meter, W m^{-2}	calorie per square centimeter minute (irradiance), cal cm^{-2} min^{-1}	698

Transpiration and Photosynthesis

3.60×10^{-2}	milligram per square meter second, mg m^{-2} s^{-1}	gram per square decimeter hour, g dm^{-2} h^{-1}	27.8
5.56×10^{-3}	milligram (H_2O) per square meter second, mg m^{-2} s^{-1}	micromole (H_2O) per square centimeter second, μmol cm^{-2} s^{-1}	180
10^{-4}	milligram per square meter second, mg m^{-2} s^{-1}	milligram per square centimeter second, mg cm^{-2} s^{-1}	10^{4}
35.97	milligram per square meter second, mg m^{-2} s^{-1}	milligram per square decimeter hour, mg dm^{-2} h^{-1}	2.78×10^{-2}

CONVERSION FACTORS FOR SI AND NON-SI UNITS—Continued

To Convert Column 1 into Column 2, Multiply by	Column 1 SI Unit	Column 2 non-SI Unit	To Convert Column 2 into Column 1 Multiply by
		Angle	
5.73	radian, rad	degrees (angle), °	1.75×10^{-2}
		Electrical Conductivity	
10	siemen per meter, $S\ m^{-1}$	millimho per centimeter, mmho	0.1
		Water Measurement	
9.73×10^{-3}	cubic meter, m^3	acre-inches, acre-in	102.8
9.81×10^{-3}	cubic meter per hour, $m^3\ h^{-1}$	cubic feet per second, $ft^3\ s^{-1}$	101.9
4.40	cubic meter per hour, $m^3\ h^{-1}$	U.S. gallons per minute, gal min^{-1}	0.227
8.11	hectare-meters, ha-m	acre-feet, acre-ft	0.123
97.28	hectare-meters, ha-m	acre-inches, acre-in	1.03×10^{-2}
8.1×10^{-2}	hectare-centimeters, ha-cm	acre-feet, acre-ft	12.33

	Concentrations		
1	centimole per kilogram, cmol kg^{-1} (ion exchange capacity)	milliequivalents per 100 grams, meq 100 g^{-1}	1
0.1	gram per kilogram, g kg^{-1}	percent, %	10
1	megagram per cubic meter, Mg m^{-3}	gram per cubic centimeter, g cm^{-3}	1
1	milligram per kilogram, mg kg^{-1}	parts per million, ppm	1

CONVERSIONS FOR RATES OF APPLICATION

1 ton per acre = 20.8 grams per square foot
1 ton per acre = 1 pound per 21.78 square feet
1 ton per acre furrow slice (6-inch depth) = 1 gram per 1000 grams soil
1 gram per square foot = 96 pounds per acre
1 pound per acre = 0.0104 grams per square foot
1 pound per acre = 1.12 kilograms per hectare
100 pounds per acre = 0.2296 pounds per 100 square feet
grams per square foot × 96 = pounds per acre
kilograms per 48 square feet = tons per acre
pounds per square feet × 21.78 = tons per acre

Concentration

1 decisiemens per meter (dS/m) = 1 millimho per centimeter (mmho/cm)

1 decisiemens per meter (dS/m) = approximately 640 milligrams per liter salt

1 part per million (ppm) = 1/1,000,000

1 percent = 0.01 or 1/100

1 ppm × 10,000 = 1 percent

ppm × 0.00136 = tons per acre-foot of water

ppm = milligrams per liter

ppm = 17.12 × grains per gallon

grains per gallon = 0.0584 × ppm

ppm = 0.64 × micromhos per centimeter (in range of 100–5000 micromhos per centimeter)

ppm = 640 × millimhos per centimeter (in range of 0.1–5.0 millimhos per centimeter)

ppm = grams per cubic meter

mho = reciprocal ohm

millimho = 1000 micromhos

millimho = approximately 10 milliequivalents per liter (meq/liter)

milliequivalents per liter = equivalents per million

millimhos per centimeter = EC × 10^3 (EC × 1000) at 25°C (EC = electrical conductivity)

micromhos per centimeter = EC × 10^6 (EC × 1,000,000) at 25°C

millimhos per centimeter = 0.1 siemens per meter

millimhos per centimeter = (EC × 10^3) = decisiemens per meter (dS/m)

1000 micromhos per centimeter = approximately 700 ppm

1000 micromhos per centimeter = approximately 10 milliequivalents per liter

1000 micromhos per centimeter = 1 ton of salt per acre-foot of water

milliequivalents per liter = 0.01 × (EC × 10^6) (in range of 100–5000 micromhos per centimeter)

milliequivalents per liter = 10 × (EC × 10^3) (in range of 0.1–5.0 millimhos per centimeter)

Pressure and Head

1 atmosphere at sea level = 14.7 pounds per square inch

1 atmosphere at sea level = 29.9 inches of mercury

1 atmosphere at sea level = 33.9 feet of water

Pressure and Head—Continued

1 atmosphere = 0.101 megapascal (MPa)
1 bar = 0.10 megapascal (MPa)
1 foot of water = 0.8826 inch of mercury
1 foot of water = 0.4335 pound per square inch
1 inch of mercury = 1.133 feet of water
1 inch of mercury = 0.4912 pound per square inch
1 inch of water = 0.07355 inch of mercury
1 inch of water = 0.03613 pound per square inch
1 pound per square inch = 2.307 feet of water
1 pound per square inch = 2.036 inches of mercury
1 pound per square foot = 47.9 pascals

Weight and Volume (U.S. Measurements)

1 acre-foot of soil = about 4,000,000 pounds
1 acre-foot of water = 43,560 cubic feet
1 acre-foot of water = 12 acre-inches
1 acre-foot of water = about 2,722,500 pounds
1 acre-foot of water = 325,851 gallons
1 cubic-foot of water = 7.4805 gallons
1 cubic foot of water at 59°F = 62.37 pounds
1 acre-inch of water = 27,154 gallons
1 gallon of water at 59°F = 8.337 pounds
1 gallon of water = 0.1337 cubic foot or 231 cubic inches

Flow (U.S. Measurements)

1 cubic foot per second = 448.8 gallons per minute
1 cubic foot per second = about 1 acre-inch per hour
1 cubic foot per second = 23.80 acre-inches per hour
1 cubic foot per second = 3600 cubic feet per hour
1 cubic foot per second = about 7½ gallons per second
1 gallon per minute = 0.00223 cubic feet per second
1 gallon per minute = 0.053 acre-inch per 24 hours
1 gallon per minute = 1 acre-inch in 4½ hours
1000 gallons per minute = 1 acre-inch in 27 minutes

Flow (U.S. Measurements)—Continued

1 acre-inch per 24 hours = 18.86 gallons per minute
1 acre-foot per 24 hours = 226.3 gallons per minute
1 acre-foot per 24 hours = 0.3259 million gallons per 24 hours

U.S.—Metric Equivalents

1 cubic meter = 35.314 cubic feet
1 cubic meter = 1.308 cubic yards
1 cubic meter = 1000 liters
1 liter = 0.0353 cubic feet
1 liter = 0.2642 U.S. gallon
1 liter = 0.2201 British or Imperial gallon
1 cubic centimeter = 0.061 cubic inch
1 cubic foot = 0.0283 cubic meter
1 cubic foot = 28.32 liters
1 cubic foot = 7.48 U.S. gallons
1 cubic foot = 6.23 British gallons
1 cubic inch = 16.39 cubic centimeters
1 cubic yard = 0.7645 cubic meter
1 U.S. gallon = 3.7854 liters
1 U.S. gallon = 0.833 British gallon
1 British gallon = 1.201 U.S. gallons
1 British gallon = 4.5436 liters
1 acre-foot = 43,560 cubic feet
1 acre-foot = 1,233.5 cubic meters
1 acre-inch = 3,630 cubic feet
1 acre-inch = 102.8 cubic meters
1 cubic meter per second = 35.314 cubic feet per second
1 cubic meter per hour = 0.278 liter per second
1 cubic meter per hour = 4.403 U.S. gallons per minute
1 cubic meter per hour = 3.668 British gallons per minute
1 liter per second = 0.0353 cubic feet per second
1 liter per second = 15.852 U.S. gallons per minute
1 liter per second = 13.206 British gallons per minute
1 liter per second = 3.6 cubic meters per hour

U.S.—Metric Equivalents—Continued

1 cubic foot per second = 0.0283 cubic meter per second
1 cubic foot per second = 28.32 liters per second
1 cubic foot per second = 448.8 U.S. gallons per minute
1 cubic foot per second = 373.8 British gallons per minute
1 cubic foot per second = 1 acre-inch per hour (approximately)
1 cubic foot per second = 2 acre-feet per day (approximately)
1 U.S. gallon per minute = 0.06309 liter per second
1 British gallon per minute = 0.07573 liter per second

Power and Energy

1 horsepower = 550 foot-pounds per second
1 horsepower = 33,000 foot-pounds per minute
1 horsepower = 0.7457 kilowatts
1 horsepower = 745.7 watts
1 horsepower-hour = 0.7457 kilowatt-hour
1 kilowatt = 1.341 horsepower
1 kilowatt-hour = 1.341 horsepower-hours
1 acre-foot of water lifted 1 foot = 1.372 horsepower-hours of work
1 acre-foot of water lifted 1 foot = 1.025 kilowatt-hours of work

HEAT AND ENERGY EQUIVALENTS AND DEFINITIONS

1 joule = 0.239 calorie

1 joule = Nm (m^2 kg s^{-2})

temperature of maximum density of water = 3.98°C (about 39°F)

1 British thermal unit (Btu) = heat needed to change 1 pound of water at maximum density of 1°F

1 Btu = 1.05506 kilojoules (kJ)

1 Btu/lb = 2.326 k J/kg

1 Btu per minute = 0.02356 horsepower

1 Btu per minute = 0.01757 kilowatts

1 Btu per minute = 17.57 watts

1 horsepower = 42.44 Btu per minute

1 horsepower-hour = 2547 Btu

1 kilowatt-hour = 3415 Btu

1 kilowatt = 56.92 Btu per minute

1 pound of water at 32°F changed to solid ice requires removal of 144 Btu

1 pound of ice in melting takes up to 144 Btu

1 ton of ice in melting takes up to 288,000 Btu

INDEX